LIVING ABROAD IN
CHINA

STUART & BARBARA STROTHER

Welcome to the Middle Kingdom, as China calls itself. This is a land of ancient culture and modern progress, old ways and hip new styles, the proverbial yin and yang of contemporary Chinese life. This is a place where you'll see fields still plowed by oxen, although look a little closer and you'll see the farmer chatting on his mobile phone as he works. Executives in Armani suits dash between high-powered business meetings, yet spend their holidays with Nai Nai (grandma) at her village home where she keeps ducks, grows plum trees, and cooks spicy tofu in her kitchen wok over an open fire.

China is a challenging land that is changing unbelievably fast. The poor have next to nothing and the rich can have it all, yet both find their incomes rising every year. Futuristic skyscrapers tower over colorful old Buddhist temples, and bullet trains race past donkeys pulling their carts to market. China's growing economy is taking the world by storm and making the world notice this giant nation that seemed so backward just a few years ago. Governments are starting to worry about its growing power; educators are hailing Chinese as the language that most needs to be taught to prepare our kids for the truth of their global future. Individuals

lighting temple candles at the Red Mansion near Zhouzhuang

and businesses from every corner of the globe are coming here in an effort to ride the economic wave of growing prosperity.

Yet despite all their development and modernization, the Chinese are still an enigma to westerners. They wear dress shoes to go hiking and two-piece suits to do construction, but put on pajamas to go shopping. They open the windows on the coldest winter days. They'd rather eat chicken feet than boneless chicken breast. They tell jokes that seem to have no punch line. But it is just this sense of enigmatic mystery, this sense that this is a place so very different from anything you've ever known that makes people fall in love with China — and keeps them coming back for more.

When we were offered the opportunity to take jobs in China, we had a comfortable Midwestern American lifestyle: a house in the country with a split rail-fenced yard where our twin two-year-olds chased our fat black cat. But when we got that call, it didn't take much convincing to decide to trade the monotony of middle management for adventure in the Middle Kingdom.

Although we'd traveled in China on several occasions before, we were apprehensive about our move. We didn't know what our

A river cuts through terraced land in southern China.

© BARBARA STROTHER

apartment would look like, what the job would really be like, if we would love living there, or if we would be tempted to beat a hasty retreat. We were fond of our American amenities: central air-conditioning, long hot showers, Maytag washer and dryer, plush carpeted floors, minivan, and local Target store. Of all the modern conveniences we had come to rely on, how many would China be able to offer? And how would we get along without them? We didn't know if daily life in China would be as difficult to handle as we had always predicted, but we were willing to give it a try.

As we made our preparations for the big move, our excitement grew. The thrill of experiencing a new culture and the opportunity to expose our boys to foreign worlds gradually overtook our fears of the unknown. We put our house on the market, got passports for the kids, and watched the movie *Big Bird in China* until we could sing along by heart.

We arrived in Shanghai on the eve of the Chinese New Year. Thankfully our employer put us up in a decent modern apartment, but we didn't know how to operate all the appliance controls labeled in Chinese. In our effort to warm the place up on that chilly night, we had somehow turned all but one of the heating and

Great Wall of China

© PURESTOCKX.COM

cooling units to full-blast air-conditioning. The four of us ended up spending our first night huddled together on the kids' two beds in the only warm room in the apartment, watching exploding fireworks out the window until we all drifted off to sleep.

As we settled into our new life in China, we delightedly found that more often than not, life is actually easier in China. Without the hectic American do-all-you-can-do schedule, life slows down considerably. With this slower pace, we found we could make frequent forays beyond our city to discover the innumerable fascinating spots within China.

And travel we did. We've discovered picturesque spots that aren't listed in any travel guides. We've had dusty days in Kashgar chatting with locals over lamb kebabs, muggy days in Hangzhou sweating over cool watermelons and icy green-tea popsicles, and wintery days in Beijing laughing during snowball fights on the Great Wall.

Granted, life in China isn't all rosy. The language poses an especially difficult hurdle, like the time we didn't understand the salesclerk's warning about the bad ice cream until our son vomited in the taxi on the way home, or the time we ended up in the city of Ninghai when we had asked for bus tickets to Linhai.

enjoying a bowl of *shui jiao* (boiled dumplings) from a sidewalk lunch cart

Always getting the foreigner's markup in prices gets old quickly, as does constantly being stared at and talked about.

But in our opinion the rewards far outweigh the hardships, and nothing is as rewarding as the friendships. We'll never forget playing mahjong with coworkers until the wee hours of the morning. Or surprising and delighting old men at public parks when we ask to join in their *xiangqi* (Chinese chess) games. Or spending countless hours on the basketball court with Kevin Garnett, Scotty Pippen, and Vince Carter... not the real stars, of course, just the chosen English names of our basketball-crazed students.

It's from all these experiences that this book came about, and we hope that it will prepare you for what's in store and paint a vivid picture of what your life in China may look like. So go ahead, and begin your joyful exploration of the Middle Kingdom. We'll get you started, but most of all, this is your adventure to create. Enjoy it!

engraving a name on a Chinese chop

Contents

PRIME LIVING LOCATIONS **237**

RESOURCES **395**

INDEX 425

WELCOME TO CHINA

INTRODUCTION

Is China right for you? Life in China can be both richly rewarding and incredibly frustrating. To live here for an extended period of time takes an incredible amount of flexibility and fortitude. If you are adventurous, if you genuinely like engaging people of other cultures even when there is a language barrier, and if you can handle roughing it when you need to, then you may find your time in China to be one of the best times of your life. Living in China will give you an amazing opportunity to learn intimately its history, geography, and culture, as well as be a part of the exciting changes that are happening in China right now. The press and the experts are hailing the current time as the China Century, and this might just be a wave that you'll want to ride. On the other hand, if you get stressed when things don't go as planned or get angry when your expectations aren't met, it would be better just to enjoy China as a short-term travel destination. If you are a control freak who is particular about ordering your life just the way you like it, China is simply not for you. You'll have a rough time if you have special

needs (such as wheelchair access, allergies, or a strict diet), if you have no intention of learning any Chinese, or if you have high standards for cleanliness and service. Don't underestimate how much you may miss English books and magazines, your favorite foods, ice, drinkable tap water, western medicine, and above all, the simple ability to understand what's going on around you. One recent figure put the percentage of expats returning home early as high as 70 percent. These are people who come to China with grand expectations but leave disappointed and disillusioned.

Despite the difficulties, the good news is that you'll come away from your time in China enriched with the knowledge of a new culture and language, with amazing stories to tell and pictures to show. You can expect to have a lot of fun, a lot of laughs, and a lot of new friends, people you may never have met if you'd played it safe and stayed home. And in the end, you can hold your head that much higher, knowing you've taken on the very difficult task of living in a new culture. As with so many difficulties life throws our way, the greater the challenge, the greater the reward.

The Lay of the Land

China is close to the same size as the United States, and is laid out in much the same way. Both have a cold rugged northeast, a humid south that speaks with its own distinct sounds, a capital city close to the eastern seaboard, and an east coast lined with important cities. Both the western

tea bushes and terraced hills in Zhejiang Province

© RYAN SHAW

HOW DOES CHINA COMPARE TO THE UNITED STATES?

	United States of America	People's Republic of China
Land Mass	9.6 million sq. km.	9.3 million sq. km.
Arable land	20 percent	15 percent
Urbanization	80 percent	36 percent
Population	295 million	1,315 million
Ethnic mix	white 82 percent black 13 percent, Asian 4 percent	Han 92 percent others 8 percent
Median age	36.2 years	32.7 years
Life expectancy	77.7 years	72.6 years
Literacy	97 percent	91 percent
GDP	$11.8 trillion	$1.8 trillion
GDP per capita	$40,100	$1,368
Average work week	39 hours	44.6 hours
Unemployment rate	5.5 percent	9.8 percent in cities
Inflation	2.5 percent	4 percent
People in poverty	12 percent	10 percent
Infant mortality	6.5 deaths/ 1,000 live births	24 deaths/ 1,000 live births
Religion	Protestant 52 percent Catholic 24 percent Jewish 1 percent Muslim 1 percent	Buddhist 8 percent Muslim 2 percent Christian 4 percent (officially atheist)

Source: CIA World Fact Book

United States and western China have reputations as places for the independent-minded and the tough, places where you might ride your horse (or yak or motorcycle) to round up your herd. Both countries have important waterways along which key inland cities have sprung up.

The three most prominent economic areas are centered around the Bohai Sea to the north (Tianjin and therefore Beijing, Dalian, and farther out to Qingdao), the Yangtze River Delta to the east (Shanghai, Suzhou, Nanjing, and farther down to Hangzhou and Ningbo), and the Pearl River Delta in the south (Hong Kong, Shenzhen, Macau, Guangzhou, Zhuhai).

Northern China is marked by an ever-expanding desert, and northern cities struggle with sandstorms and dry, dusty conditions. Southern China, on the other hand, is a humid land of verdant greens and lush vegetation. Central China is graced with picturesque terraced hills of rice paddies and tea plantations. Eastern fields of neon yellow rape flowers contrast with the barren, lunar landscapes of the northwest. And in the southwest lie the piercing highlands of the Himalayas and the great Mt. Everest, the highest spot in the world. Though most people know the Himalayas have one foot in China, many don't realize just how hilly and mountainous the rest of the country can be, with mountains long considered sacred to the Taoists and Buddhists scattered throughout the land.

COUNTRY DIVISIONS

The People's Republic of China (PRC) is divided into 22 provinces, four independent municipalities (Beijing, Tianjin, Shanghai, Chongqing), five autonomous regions, and two Special Administrative Regions, or SARs (Hong Kong and Macau—although the central government is trying to work out an agreement with Taiwan to join this list). Within each province and autonomous region there is a capital city, and further governmental powers are given to each municipality and county. Cities are broken down into districts, and some neighborhoods within a district have their own additional governing body.

Though the central government of the PRC tends to rule over the country with a strong hand, each autonomous region is allowed to create its own laws, within limits, based on the needs of the unique minority cultures in their region. The two SARs, Macau and Hong Kong, are allowed to keep their own governments in all areas except diplomatic relations and national defense.

POPULATION DENSITY

With over 1.3 billion people, China is the most populated country in the world. Of the top 50 most populated cities around the globe, 1 in 5 is Chinese. The whole concept of population changes here. You'll find yourself referring to a city of one million residents as a small town and five million as just midsize. Villages might have a couple hundred thousand residents. There

a statue of Chen Yi, Shanghai's first mayor

© BARBARA STROTHER

© BARBARA STROTHER

shopping among the holiday masses at Yuyuan Bazaar in Shanghai

are times you'll feel the weight of this hefty city population, such as while you're trying to push your way through the masses who are all shopping for Spring Holiday, or when the rush-hour crowd carries you like a helpless stick in a river through the subway entrance. More than likely, though, you won't have to deal with China's population masses on a daily basis.

Ironically, though China's cities are so densely populated, the country as a whole is not. An estimated 65 percent of its people are considered rural, a number that has been slowly decreasing over the past two decades. In addition, vast tracts of land are uninhabited due to natural environments too harsh to support communities.

Almost all of China's premier cities line the coast along the eastern to southern seaboard, causing population maps to look something like a bright sliver of a crescent centered on its southeastern shore. There are only a handful of key cities that are farther than a couple hours' drive from the sea. China's wealth tends to follow that same crescent. As a general rule, the farther from the sea you go, the poorer the areas are. In the eastern provinces of Zhejiang and Jiangsu, some farming families are living large with colorfully ornate Barbie-style houses up to four or five stories tall, while those that live off the land in the hinterlands barely scrape by with a pitifully low standard of living.

WEATHER

In a country this vast, the weather can vary extremely from one side of the country to another. Except for its extreme mountainous corners, though, one thing's for sure: when it's summer in China, it's *hot*. On the coast it's hot and muggy. In Beijing it's hot and dusty. Even in Tibet with its grand elevation, the sun beats down and will fry you to a crisp in no time if you're not expecting it.

Winters, on the other hand, provide more diversity across the nation. Northeastern lands stay frozen and sparkling white for many months while the south doesn't ever see a single snowflake. In tropical Hainan Island you can get a golden tan while blizzards rage across subarctic Inner Mongolia. Fall brings pleasant relief from summer's intensity and spring brings its blossoms in Chinese gardens throughout the land, making these seasons the most pleasant times to be in the Middle Kingdom.

FLORA AND FAUNA
Flora

China's vegetation is incredibly varied. Straight and narrow poplars and silvery aspens line the dusty roads of Xinjiang to the west, towering alpine firs cover snowy mountains in Heilongjiang to the north, and tropical palm trees sway in the breeze on the sunny beaches of the South China Sea. Bamboo forests, delicate orchids, and giant lotus floating on calm ponds uniquely symbolize China.

Agriculture and landscape play a leading role in Chinese culture. The peach and plum, strong symbols involved in Chinese mythology, bring out throngs of Chinese to walk the orchards when in spring bloom. Part of the Chinese sense of regionalism is to boast of the agricultural products from your hometown, and the Chinese know what is grown where. Travel with a Chinese friend to the interior of Hainan Island and they will insist you try the five-finger greens that can only be found growing wild here; a trip to Turpan won't be complete without sampling the dried apricots, mulberries, and raisins that prosper in this desert locale.

© BARBARA STROTHER

a tranquil Chinese garden pond in Hangzhou

Gardens also play a very important role in Chinese history and culture. We're not talking about rows of lettuce and cucumbers, though there are plenty of those types too. Chinese gardens are ornate places filled with winding paths, arched bridges, rock sculptures, ponds with giant carp, and gorgeous flowers. Many of the Chinese gardens date back hundreds of years, though today the Chinese cultural priority for flowers and greenery is reflected in their amazing city landscaping. We were always amazed when a gorgeous design of annuals was allowed to grow for just a few short weeks, then was dug up and replaced with bright new blooms before the old flowers showed any sign of wilting.

Fauna

Who can think of China without thinking of its most loveable native, the panda? Like so many facets of life in China, each region has its own famous beasts: majestic reindeer in northeastern mountains, double-humped camels in northwestern deserts, giant pandas in central bamboo forests, the rare freshwater dolphins of the Yangtze River, long-haired yaks in Tibetan villages. You'll see some of these creatures at work, especially if you travel off the beaten path, or at rest in city zoos. You might even see some, whether you want to or not, right at your dinner table.

© BARBARA STROTHER

riding camels in Xinjiang province near the Kyrgyzstan border

Social Climate

For the most part, Chinese society today is quite harmonious, due in part to the heavy-handed government that does not permit dissension and disorder among its population. With the help of the present economic boom, most of the population have a general contentment about their lives and a positive outlook on their future. You will find pockets, however, that are less than content. When bulldozers roll in to tear down old homes and overtake farmland in the name of economic development, residents and farmers get angry. And when a Chinese Muslim walks into the 1,000-year-old mosque where his ancestors prayed to Allah for generations and finds a Han Chinese construction worker smoking and spitting inside while he does repairs, there's sure to be an ugly exchange. Although you're not likely hear about protests and demonstrations in China's official media, they do happen all the time.

The more time you spend in areas with high numbers of marginalized populations, such as minorities and some religious groups, the more tension you'll see in the local social climate. Uighurs and Tibetans resent the control of the central government; local minority groups are the target of ingrained distrust and are often branded as troublemakers regardless of their personal character. And even in the most modern cities, you'll see a subtle but ubiquitous disdain for migrant workers from those who are of a more comfortable economic class. Northerners consider themselves perhaps a bit more intelligent than southerners; one city competes against another to be the best.

For the most part, tensions in China's social climate don't play a significant role in the life of a foreigner in China, unless you are in some way aligned with one of these less-accepted groups. Although it probably won't

DEFINING THE TERM "EXPAT"

The term "expat," short for "expatriate," simply refers to one who is residing away from his or her home country. This word can be used as a noun, as in "Will there be other expats at the karaoke bar?" or as an adjective, as in "This Irish pub is the main expat hangout in town." The Chinese equivalent is technically *waiguoren*, "people from outside countries," though you are much more likely to hear the affectionate term *laowai*, "old outsider."

affect you directly, it can be infuriating when you witness blatant discrimination and the powerlessness of the victims to do anything about it.

CHINA AND FOREIGNERS

China has a long history of being closed to outsiders, closely guarding its borders for centuries, uninterested in the outside world. In the years of colonialism and concessions, other nations courted China for a time before all were kicked out and the doors locked shut during the early days of the communist PRC. But things have changed over the years. At first China slowly cracked the door open for a trickle of outsiders, and now has pushed the doors wide open and put out the welcome mat: "Foreigners welcome and wanted" (as long as they bring their skills and their bank book with them).

In many ways the Chinese are enamored of all things western. Their pop culture is now a strong blend of Chinese culture with a western twist. American movies and music are hugely popular in China; it is not uncommon to meet a local who has a more extensive collection of American DVDs than any westerner would dream of. McDonalds, KFC, Pizza Hut, and Starbucks are an ingrained part of life, as are U.S. sports heroes, especially NBA players. All of this adds to a general affinity for westerners. While the

© BARBARA STROTHER

taking a break at the Starbucks in the no longer forbidden Forbidden City

attraction tends to be stronger toward Caucasian westerners, the popularity of superstars like Michael Jackson and Shaquille O'Neal has brought about an almost-equal fascination for African Americans. Foreigners from other parts of the world, such as people from the Middle East, Latin America, or other Asian countries, will be treated well enough, although they might not get the same red-carpet treatment as Caucasians receive.

The Chinese are generally friendly and always very curious. They are often fascinated by foreigners, especially outside the key cities with high foreign populations. Strangers will want to take their picture with you, the foreigner. They'll watch what you do, what you buy when you shop; they'll have conversations with their friends about you right in front of you. You'll be sought out for English practice and asked for clarification on grammar rules. On our first trip to Shanghai in 1993, large crowds gathered to watch us when we stopped on the Bund to take a group photo. Nowadays Shanghai is too inundated with foreigners to care all that much—unless your group happens to include a number of cute little foreign kids.

Foreign Population in China

The number of foreigners currently living in China's cities is difficult to determine. Several different government agencies grant permission for foreigners to reside in China, whether as foreign experts, part of the labor force, members of the press, or students, and these agencies often do not collaborate their statistical information. And even if they know, they're not telling. Add to that the many who arrive on tourist visas and work illegally, as well as illegal immigrants who come in from less prosperous neighboring countries like Russia and North Korea, and the numbers get even harder to determine. One thing for sure is the number is continuously growing. Shanghai alone issues nearly 1,000 new work permits every month. Foreign student enrollment at China's colleges is at an all-time high, fueled both by China's growing global importance as well as the relatively low cost of higher education compared to western nations. The number of foreigners is just a drop in the bucket compared to China's 1.3 billion, but in the few key cities where most foreign populations are concentrated, the ratio feels much higher. On the other hand, traveling to less popular areas may make you wonder if there are any foreigners living here at all. You'll see plenty of foreign faces in China, though, attributed mostly to the more than 100 million tourists that come every year.

HISTORY, GOVERNMENT, AND ECONOMY

There are few countries in the world that have a history as long and rich as China's. The Middle Kingdom has played its part in the world history scene with pomp and circumstance, flair and fervor. From the colorful courts of Kublai Khan to the triumphs and tragedies of Chairman Mao's communist revolution, the eras of this ancient nation have been anything but dull. To gain an understanding of China and where it is going, you should first learn something about where China has been.

China's ancient dynastic history is a story of emperors and warlords competing for control of an ever-expanding geography. China's modern history is dominated by two stories: The first is a tale of China's difficulty engaging foreigners eager to trade and quick on their triggers; the second is a tale of China painfully remaking itself as an autonomous Communist state free from foreign influence. Today the Chinese government is still

totalitarian, but shows more and more signs of political freedom. As for economics in practice, red China is now one of the most capitalistic countries in the world, where entrepreneurs are redefining the global economy one deal at a time.

History

Chinese history is typically organized according to dynastic periods (10–15 of them, depending on which historian you ask). This makes the study more memorable but paints a somewhat inaccurate picture of China as a single country ruled by a single emperor who passed leadership on to other strongmen once his dynastic clock had run out. In actuality, the geographic borders of China have varied across the centuries, as did the influence wielded by those in power.

Like European historical eras (i.e. the Tudor period), Chinese dynasties are named after the royal family that ascended to power. And similar to the concept of the divine right of kings, emperors in China were called Tian Zi (son of heaven) as a nod to the divine approval of their reign. When a dynasty ended, it was understood that the royal family must have fallen out of heaven's favor.

THE CHINESE DYNASTIES
Xia and Shang Dynasties

The mythological birth of Chinese civilization begins with three legendary figures: Yan Di, the Fiery Emperor, ruler of the elements; Huang Di, the Yellow Emperor, ruler of the Yellow River valley; and Shang Di, the Heavenly Emperor, ruler of the spirit world. Together these three were responsible for human's creation, and today some still consider them to be active in the affairs of humans. When Robert Morrison translated the Bible into Chinese in 1807 he chose the name Shang Di to refer to the Christian God.

The Xia Dynasty (20th–16th centuries B.C.) might be better regarded as mythology than history, because the Xia were believed to be direct descendants of Yan Di, Huang Di, and Shang Di. Textbooks describe the Xia Dynasty as the beginning of urban life in China, but little else is known about this era. Society was thought to be hierarchical with much of the population living in slavery, and the rulers were thought to practice human sacrifice as part of their worship.

The Shang Dynasty (16th–12th centuries B.C.) ruled a small geographic area centered in modern-day Shandong Province, but its cultural and

© BARBARA STROTHER

exploring the ancient city ruins of Jiao He in the desert near Turpan

technological influence extended throughout Asia. Archaeological evidence shows that they created a written pictographic language (the basis for modern Chinese characters) and developed organized religion based on communicating with dead ancestors. The technological development of bronze tools, weapons, and chariots empowered Shang warlords to extend their rule across an area about the size of five modern-day provinces.

Zhou Dynasty (1122–256 B.C.)

The Zhou family enlisted the support of neighboring tribes and eventually overthrew the Shang. They expanded geographically by conquering territory adjacent to the earlier Shang borders. These areas became more civilized, and the rule of law replaced the harsh rule of the Shang warlords. The Zhou developed a sophisticated bureaucracy that led to peaceful civilization and a rise in population. Consequently the Zhou Dynasty endured the longest of all the dynasties. But with the development of iron came warfare, and the Zhou Dynasty eventually gave way to the Warring States period, characterized by small tyrant kingdoms fighting each other for over 200 years.

The warlords apparently had good military advice, because during this time Sun Tzu's book *The Art of War* was released. A traveling scholar named Confucius also emerged, who taught that harsh legalistic rule should be replaced by humanitarian leadership. Although wars were not eliminated, Confucian ideals of benevolent intellectual leadership and filial piety were widely embraced and have since been the model of leadership throughout Asia.

Qin Dynasty (221-206 B.C.)

Emperor Qin Shihuang ended the Warring States period by winning the wars (how else?) and uniting the various tribes into a single Chinese empire. It is from the name "Qin" that outsiders first began calling the country "China." Emperor Qin was not a big fan of Confucius's ideals regarding scholarship and respect for authority, so he ordered the burning of all books and the execution of scholars. Paranoid about retribution in the afterlife, he constructed thousands of terra-cotta warriors to be buried with him. He was also worried about invaders from the north and started construction of the Great Wall. Although the Qin Dynasty was the shortest, no other dynasty did as much for modern-day tourism in China.

Han Dynasty (206 B.C.-220 A.D.)

In a trend later to be followed by Sun Yatsen and Mao Zedong, a peasant named Han grew angry at official abuses and incited a peasant uprising that dethroned the brutal Qin rulers. Han had the brilliant idea of replacing harsh rulers with intellectuals. He instituted a university system and selected bureaucrats based on calligraphy skills, knowledge of Confucian texts, and other esoteric criteria. The Han made much progress in agriculture, textiles, paper, and warfare. Today the Han ethnic group comprises about 92 percent of China's population.

The Han Dynasty eventually fragmented into the so-called Period of Division, which lasted about 400 years. It was during this time of relaxed government rule that Buddhism came across the Silk Road from India. In response to this foreign competition, Daoists and Confucians stepped up their recruiting efforts as well, resulting in a renaissance of religion throughout Chinese society.

© BARBARA STROTHER

Sui and Tang Dynasties (580-907 A.D.)

The Sui Dynasty (580–618) briefly reunited China, but they were uneventfully succeeded by the Tang Dynasty, who extended the rule of China as far south as

reenacting an old poetry and drinking custom with floating shot glasses

modern-day Vietnam and as far west as modern-day Uzbekistan. The Tang made many advances in transportation and culture. Through diplomacy and military might, the Tang Silk Road trade expanded, and the Grand Canal emerged as a vibrant trade route between Beijing and Hangzhou, which to this day is still used by diesel sampan boats with their hulls so full their decks appear to be going under.

These transportation advances also facilitated cultural growth, especially in art, poetry, and music. Stringed musical instruments came across the Silk Road and have remained an important part of Chinese music ever since. Tang Dynasty art also reveals an improvement in women's rights that would unfortunately not last long. Tang art is filled with active women, and the plump ones were considered the most attractive. Perhaps as a nod to these culturally enlightened ancients, China's original rock band, Tang Dynasty, can be heard blasting in nightclubs throughout Asia and across the globe.

Song Dynasty (960-1279)

The Song Dynasty was a time of great economic development in China. To protect themselves from raiders and to facilitate transport, large ships called junks filled the harbors of China's port cities. The junks functioned as floating Wal-Marts, and along with the advent of paper currency, rapid economic development and urbanization occurred. But women lost ground in the Song Dynasty as they were bought and sold as servants, concubines, and prostitutes. Ideas about female beauty changed, and men who preferred slender dainty women initiated the cruel practice of footbinding, which lasted until the Communist Revolution. Song Dynasty government officials allowed commerce to flourish, focusing their attention on scholarly pursuits including literature and calligraphy. Even though the Chinese had just invented gunpowder, they were unprepared when the Mongols arrived at their door.

Yuan Dynasty (1279-1368)

China's neighbors to the north, the Mongols, decided to invade their neighbors after centuries of fighting amongst themselves. In 1279 Kublai Khan conquered Beijing and added China to the empire his grandfather, Ghengis Khan, had already established, stretching from Siberia to Hungary. China's Empress Dowager Xie had built a large army, but they were no match for the Mongol hordes, and neither was the Great Wall, which was built to keep the Mongols out. In a textbook example of revisionist history, the Chinese historians named this era the Yuan Dynasty, which makes it sound like a period of Chinese rule and takes away some of the sting of foreign occupation.

It was during the Mongol rule of the Yuan Dynasty that Marco Polo visited China and famously observed that the Chinese detest the rule of outsiders. But like the United States in Iraq, the Mongols turned out to be much better at conquering than ruling, and their own infighting weakened them, leading to their demise. Perhaps they were too cozy in the Forbidden City that they built. After numerous attempts to overthrow the Mongols, a militia led by the Zhu family succeeded in driving them back to the northern steppes in 1368.

Ming Dynasty (1368-1644)

During the Ming Dynasty, China's navy and merchant ships brought numerous technological innovations into the country. Movable type was invented, resulting in large-scale book production including the classics *Peony Pavilion* and *Journey to the West*. Matteo Ricci, the Italian missionary, noted an "exceedingly large" circulation of books with "ridiculously low" prices, not all that different from today's multistoried Chinese bookstores brimming with new books for just a few yuan. A fine arts renaissance also occurred, which is best represented by the famous Ming Dynasty blue-on-white porcelain. Ming literally means "bright" or "clear," which amply describes their cultural development. At this time China was the most advanced society on earth, but the inept government lacked the funds to finance a proper military because they had too many of their relatives and friends on the payroll. When foreign invaders from Manchuria attacked, the Chinese were once again easily conquered by outsiders.

Qing Dynasty (1644-1911)

During the Qing Dynasty, another period of rule by outsiders, Manchu rulers quickly imposed their will on the Chinese. Property was seized, and Chinese were prohibited from owning weapons, even bamboo, because it could be fashioned into weaponry. Chinese men were required to adopt the Manchu hairstyle, the queue—a shaven head except for a long ponytail. Conservative values were enforced, and Qing rulers closed theaters and banned numerous books and dramas, although one of the most famous works of Chinese literature, *Dream of Red Mansions,* was written at this time. To pacify the powerful educated Chinese, the Qing restored the literati to an elevated societal position and encouraged educated men to serve in the imperial court, including foreign Jesuit missionaries. While Manchu rulers were busy extending the borders of the empire to include Xinjiang and Tibet, western colonial powers had a keen eye on China's natural resources, especially tea.

IMPERIALISM, OPIUM WARS, AND THE REBELLIONS

Spanish, Portuguese, and Dutch trade ships had been visiting China's port cities since the Ming Dynasty. By the 19th century, trade was dominated by the British government–owned East India Company, which was impatient with the Ming rulers' reluctance to adopt European trading practices. By this time, Europeans had developed an appetite for Chinese silk, porcelain, and tea. To expand their trading operations, the Brits hatched an international dope-dealing scheme where they produced opium in India, imported it to China, and traded it for Chinese goods, especially tea.

Chinese officials weren't thrilled that their people were becoming drug addicts, so they complained to the Queen of England. The Portuguese also objected to British trade practices and banished them from their colony of Macau, forcing the Brits to settle in the uninhabited muddy islands of Hong Kong. The political situation deteriorated and resulted in the first Opium War (1840–1842). The Chinese were outgunned and the war was resolved with the first of many amply named Unequal Treaties. Among other things, the treaties required exorbitant silver payments from the Chinese and the establishment of foreign "concessions," geographic areas where foreigners were immune from Chinese law, in each port city.

The Taiping Rebellion (1854-1860)

Qing Dynasty rulers also had their own internal threats to put up with, the most notorious of which was the Taiping Rebellion. A peasant named Hong Xiuquan believed he was the brother of Jesus Christ, and he thought he was given a heavenly mandate to establish a kingdom on earth. Although Taiping literally means "heavenly peace," Hong's plan was to establish his kingdom through brute military force. From their base in Nanjing, Hong and his pals conquered territory in 16 provinces, resulting in the deaths of over 20 million people before the Qing rulers finally shut them down.

The Boxer Rebellion

From 1861 to 1911 the Manchu Dynasty was controlled by a wickedly selfish woman, the Empress Dowager Cixi. In 1898 she encouraged ignorant young men from the countryside to attack foreign businesses, missionaries, and locals who had converted to Christianity. In their spare time the young men practiced boxing and other martial arts, and this event was known as the Boxer Rebellion. The Boxers spread their violence beyond Beijing to other cities, and after two years the foreigners had had enough. In June 1900, an army of 20,000 troops was assembled from numerous western powers, and within two months the Boxer Rebellion was squashed and China fell victim to another unfair treaty. With better equipment the Chinese military might have mounted a better defense, but Cixi had already squandered state resources. In one infamous incident Cixi took funds that were allocated to build warships for the navy and instead spent them on the construction of an immobile marble ship (which you can still see today at the Summer Palace in Beijing) for her entertainment.

Sun Yatsen and the Last Emperor

After decades of diplomatic failures and disillusionment with the Manchu rulers, the masses eventually backed a revolution led by a western-trained doctor named Sun Yatsen. Sun recruited the help of military generals and secret societies who functioned like the Italian mafia. As seen in the movie *The Last Emperor,* the child emperor was dethroned, and power-hungry generals, warlords, and gangsters fought with each other, giving the masses little hope that the country would be improved. Consequently, the period from 1912 to 1928 is referred to as the Warlord Period. Although Sun failed to create a new society, his success in ending centuries of rule by aloof emperors earned him the nickname "the father of modern China"—a Chinese George Washington.

© RYAN SHAW

Sun Yatsen's mausoleum in Nanjing

CIVIL WAR

With the emperors long gone and warlords and generals failing to stabilize the country, many Chinese looked to the glorious Soviet Union for guidance. In 1921 the Chinese Communist Party was founded and, with the bold leadership of Mao Zedong, gained a wide following, especially among the rural peasants who were attracted by Mao's promises of equality, prosperity, and freedom from oppressive landlords.

Another group organized itself around the principle of nationalism (as opposed to imperialism) led by Soviet-trained Chiang Kai-Shek. This group, known as the Kuomintang or simply the Nationalist Party, successfully recruited urban factory workers who were tired of being exploited by the factory owners, many of whom were British or Japanese. Chiang also enlisted support from the underworld, including Shanghai's powerful Green Gang. The Nationalists and Communists began a long struggle for control of China's future.

a towering Mao statue on a university campus

© BARBARA STROTHER

In 1934 Nationalist troops encircled the out-gunned Communist troops around Hunan Province and nearly wiped them out before the Communists slipped away. In their legendary escape, known as the Long March, communist troops traveled 6,000 miles by foot to a new base in Shaanxi. Of the 80,000 troops who began the arduous yearlong journey, only 6,000 made it to Shaanxi.

Long before World War I, Japan had seized the Chinese territories of Taiwan and Manchuria. They tried provoking China into an all-out war through minor invasions, such as the bombing of Shanghai in 1932, but the Chinese refused the bait. Eventually losing their patience, the Japanese launched a full-scale invasion and began conquering major cities, including Beijing and Shanghai, but no city suffered worse than Nanjing. The "Rape of Nanjing" lasted seven bitter weeks in the winter of 1937. Japanese soldiers committed every imaginable cruelty including torture, more than 20,000 rapes, 300,000 murders, and horrific medical experiments. If you can stomach it, the Massacre Museum in Nanjing today serves as a sad reminder of this dark time.

The saying that "there is no better bond of friendship than a common enemy" proved true in China as the Nationalists and Communists formed an alliance to drive out the Japanese. With the help of the American military, their efforts were successful, as the Japanese had no fight left in them after the atomic bombs were dropped on Japan in 1945.

After outing the Japanese, Mao Zedong continued to build his support base in the Chinese hinterland while Sun Yatsen and his wife Song Meiling traveled abroad to raise support for their plans for a new China. The United States urged the Communists and Nationalists to put their guns down and start anew with a two-party system, but neither side liked the idea, and civil war broke out lasting from 1947 to 1949. Despite being better armed, the Nationalists were disorganized and lost favor with the people due to corruption and infighting. Rather than suffer a certain military defeat, they fled the mainland and settled in Taiwan. Mao's Communists quickly filled the vacuum, marking October 1, 1949, as the official birth date of the People's Republic of China. To this day, the Republic of China (Taiwan) considers itself a sovereign nation, but Beijing sees it as a breakaway province that should be reunited with the mainland.

COMMUNIST RULE
The Great Leap Forward and the Cultural Revolution

The new government ended the opium trade, improved infrastructure, and advanced women's rights. But it also cut ties with foreign businesses, seized

all land and buildings, ended diplomatic ties to the West, persecuted the religious, and harshly punished those bold enough to oppose it. In Mao's Great Leap Forward all agriculture was organized into giant collectives and millions of peasants were put to work building bridges, roads, and other worthy infrastructure projects. But the central planners in Beijing were incapable of managing the complexities of such a grand project and the Great Leap ended with the Three Hard Years (1959–1962) of famine, resulting in 30 million deaths.

© BARBARA STROTHER

PLA bags and hats are the latest kitschy trend.

Without a doubt the most infamous failure of communism under Mao was the Cultural Revolution (1966–1976). Fearing the loss of power to influential political rivals, Mao induced impressionable youths to join a new pseudomilitary group called the Red Guards. The Red Guards terrorized society's most productive members, especially doctors and intellectuals. If they couldn't flee the country, they were forced to work in farms and labor camps, while their jobs were filled by unskilled peasants. (Imagine having a serious medical problem and instead of seeing a trained professional being examined by the local turnip farmer!) Few people dared criticize Mao's policy failures, but as soon as he passed away in 1976, government officials quickly punished Mao's closest allies, the "Gang of Four," including Mao's wife, who was sentenced to death but instead committed suicide.

Reform, the Open Door, and Deng Xiaoping
Mao united China and freed its citizens from foreign domination, but much of what makes China great today should be attributed to the work of Mao's successor, Deng Xiaoping. Deng's sensible reforms transformed a backward agricultural country into a global superpower. Deng's success can be traced to his political ability to liberalize government policies while pacifying those who controlled the military and the Communist Party. After Deng took the reigns, China opened up to foreign businesses, and, of course, foreign currency.

Government

China political affairs are dominated by the Chinese Communist Party (CCP); the People's Liberation Army (PLA); and the national government, which is headed by the president. To effectively rule the country, a new president must win the confidence of the CCP and the PLA, which takes time. Mao and Deng served in the PLA and thus had little trouble winning the confidence of its generals, but none of the presidents after them have had the same credibility. In the past, there was little, if any, distinction between the Party, the state, and the army, but in recent years they have grown independent of each other.

GOVERNMENT STRUCTURE
The Chinese Communist Party (CCP) determines policy at all levels from national down to local. A Party Congress is held every five years to elect new leaders. Unlike the glory days of the revolution when the masses

eagerly joined the Party, today a mere 5 percent of the population belongs to the Party. Since China is moving further toward a market economy, the advantages of being a Party member are diminishing. Eight other token political parties exist but exert no real influence. The national government is headed by the National People's Congress, which is the legislative body that meets once a year to enact the policies that were already predetermined by the Party. Each province and city also has its own local government officials who form and enforce policies for their respective regions.

The People's Liberation Army (PLA) includes the army, navy, and air force. With 2.8 million members, it is the largest military in the world, but its equipment is supposedly outdated (much to the relief of China's nervous neighbors). Like militaries around the world, it plans to reduce its forces and rely more on high-tech weaponry. In many places the PLA functions more as police than soldiers. Historically the PLA has been used to defend China from invaders (i.e. Japanese), to seize additional land (i.e. Tibet), to squash rebellions (i.e. Xinjiang Muslim separatists) and even to subjugate its own citizens (as seen in the 1989 Tiananmen Square incident).

To pacify its minority groups, China has given some regions a token level of self-rule. This applies to the Autonomous Regions of Xinjiang, Tibet, Ningxia Hui, Guangxi Zhuang, and Inner Mongolia. The Special Administrative Regions of Macau and Hong Kong are also governed differently from the mainland. When the colonial powers returned these islands back to Chinese rule, much of the former political and economic systems were left intact. For example, gambling is illegal on the mainland, but Macau's numerous legal casinos make it the Las Vegas of the East.

CHANGING EXPECTATIONS OF GOVERNMENT

Unlike other regimes that ruled China as a group of elites, the Communists desired to govern according to peasant values. The unequal distribution of wealth that plagued the dynasties was to be eliminated. People were to be kept safe from alien invaders and local gangs, but most importantly, people were to have equal incomes, property, housing, education, and daily needs. The "iron rice bowl" policy was instituted, which guaranteed lifetime employment.

Today the Chinese have lowered expectations of their government. Under the economic reforms instituted by Deng Xiaoping, much of the burden of providing for people's daily needs shifted to employers. Under the model of pure communism, these companies were state-owned, so the government was the employer. People now must take responsibility for their own needs, including housing, health care, and retirement, unless they work for the state or for large companies. In some ways, large companies have taken over the state's socialist role, providing generous benefits such as on-site dormitory housing, although the law no longer requires it. Just as in the West, most residents of China have grown apathetic about government and see it as mostly irrelevant to their daily lives.

HUMAN RIGHTS

In 1989 students from all over Beijing gathered in Tiananmen Square to protest official corruption and demand democratic reforms. Art students erected the goddess of democracy statue modeled after the Statue of Liberty, and some students went on a hunger strike. Although they gained the support of the people and had the attention of the international community, after a few weeks the government had had enough and sent in tanks and troops who used deadly force to end the demonstration. Official figures are secret but it is estimated that 2,000 demonstrators were killed. Student leaders who didn't flee the country were jailed, and the officials who sympathized with the students found their careers abruptly ended. The students learned the hard way that totalitarian regimes are not easily overthrown, though the incident did get the attention of the officials, and many democratic reforms have been implemented since 1989.

Amnesty International claims that the Chinese government routinely abuses the basic human rights of its citizens. People who are most likely to

Worship is only allowed at official registered churches.

© BARBARA STROTHER

be punished include those who criticize the government (especially in the media but also on the Internet), those who organize secret meetings (such as unregistered house churches), and those who make contact with "hostile" foreign organizations (such as one of the Free Tibet groups). Violators are labeled "counterrevolutionaries" and subject to detention (for reeducation, of course) and seizure of property, and reports of torture and physical abuse frequently surface. The death penalty is exacted (sometimes publicly) for criminal offenses such as theft, embezzlement, and drug trafficking.

As an outsider, it is difficult to discern whether today's China truly is a widespread abuser of human rights or if they are just rightfully enforcing their laws. Stories of human rights violations in China are sometimes proven to be over-sensationalized at best and pure fabrication at worst. The real truth, if you could ever get at it, is probably somewhere in between the sensationalist claims of human rights groups and the denial of the Chinese officials.

GOVERNMENT AND EXPATS

Every westerner who has accepted a job in China faces interrogation—by his family members before he leaves! What are you going to eat? Don't they eat dog there? What about your safety? Aren't you worried about living in a communist country? In many stories about China that foreigners hear, the government is the villain. The reality is that unless you are an entrepreneur starting your own business, you'll have little or no interaction with Chinese government officials. After the customs agent stamps your entry visa, and you register with your friendly neighborhood PSB, you'll have no more interaction with your Big Red Brother. You probably won't file a Chinese tax return, because your employer will handle that for you. You'll see plenty of traffic police, but you probably won't drive, so you'll never get a speeding ticket or have to stand in line at the Department of Motor Vehicles.

Economy

No country has ever experienced the level of economic growth that China is currently enjoying. After growing about 10 percent annually for 25 years, China has the third-largest economy after the European Union and the United States, and foreign trade accounts for a third of China's GDP. The per capita income is $1,368 per year, though a typical college graduate earns about $500 per month. That doesn't sound like much, but with a cost of living 50–75 percent lower than the United States, it goes a long way.

IS IT REALLY COMMUNIST?

After your first five minutes in "communist" China, you'll encounter capitalistic street vendors selling everything from mobile phones to haircuts to stinky tofu. In no time it will be obvious that the government can't possibly control such a vast economy. And when the black Lexus runs the stinky tofu vendor's oversize tricycle off the road, it will be apparent that there is an unequal distribution of wealth. So, on a practical level, this whole "communist" label seems to be a misnomer.

The Chinese prefer to describe their current system as a "socialist market economy system." The socialist label means that all central government plans are designed with the best interests of the people as the focus, while the "market" label refers to increased freedom for businesses to produce the goods and services that are desired in the Chinese market and abroad. This blend of control and freedom is often called a "mixed economy," and compared to the massive government intervention in western countries the differences are not that great. The central government used to own all of the large companies, but most have been sold off to the highest bidder. The only enterprises still owned by the government are in the heavy industries, media, telecommunications, and tourism, and definitely not stinky tofu vendors.

BLACK CAT, WHITE CAT

"Poverty is not socialism; to be rich is glorious," declared Deng Xiaoping as he broke from Mao's socialist ideals and implemented capitalistic reforms. He explained, "It doesn't matter if a cat is black or white, so long as it catches mice." Mao freed China's economy from the colonial powers and, looking to the Soviet Union for inspiration, started the country on the fast track to industrialization. The failures of the Great Leap Forward and the Cultural Revolution revealed the soft underbelly of communism, and set the stage for Deng Xiaoping's free market reforms in the 1970s and 1980s. Deng's policies changed the system from a centrally planned economy to a mixed economy, which helped China become the main economic powerhouse of the East. The reforms were incremental and can be thought of in three distinct eras: Opening Up, Rapid Development, and Deep Reforms.

Opening Up, 1978-1984

Agricultural collectives were disbanded and farmers were freed to make their own decisions about what to produce. The iron rice bowl ended and people went to work for private companies. Special Economic Zones (SEZ) were established in Shanghai, Shenzhen, Zhuhai, and Xiamen that attracted foreign companies with their tax breaks, cheap labor, and other incentives. Most of the foreign firms taking advantage of this new "open door" policy entered into joint ventures with Chinese companies, many of them state-owned.

Rapid Development, 1984-1991

Deng privatized many of the large state-owned businesses in the 1980s (often selling them to his cronies at a great discount), and eliminated price controls, including controls on wages. Previously the government determined how much everybody earned in each position, but now employers began to determine wage rates.

Deep Reforms, 1992-Present

Financial and educational systems were modernized to follow standards in western countries. Sustainable-development measures were put in place to ensure that business interests were "harmonious" with the environment. Efforts were also made to develop the western regions, including Tibet and especially Xinjiang with its precious oil reserves.

GLOBAL BUSINESS

Business leaders from Japan, the United States, Taiwan, South Korea, and elsewhere believed the old marketing idea that if you could capture just 1 percent of the Chinese market, you'd be rich, and they opened businesses in China. Some of the companies export their goods to China from abroad, such as Washington State apples. Other firms set up production facilities within China. They either sell these products to Chinese consumers (and avoid paying Chinese import tariffs), or they export the products abroad, especially to the United States (to take advantage of China's cheap labor costs). Most of these companies formed joint ventures with a Chinese partner. Foreign manufacturing firms can be found in every major Chinese city, but are concentrated in the Special Economic Zones. Shanghai is the preferred location for foreign firms to locate their regional headquarters, with almost a thousand such firms including Bosch, McDonald's,

Global business spans the skyline along Pudong's financial district in Shanghai.

and Ford. Shanghai is also the preferred location for foreign research and development sites.

ECONOMIC CONTROVERSIES

China's increased integration into the world economy has not been without controversy. Some of the major economic issues include intellectual property violations, sweatshop work conditions, income inequality, environmental pollution, currency manipulation, the underground economy, and overpopulation.

Intellectual Property

Foreigners and locals have flocked to China's famous markets, which are loaded with counterfeit goods such as fake Gucci purses, Nike shoes, Microsoft software, and Hollywood DVDs. There will occasionally be a token crackdown by the police, but the penalties are not severe enough to keep the vendors off the streets. Western companies who are not being compensated for their intellectual property just don't have enough influence to get the Chinese to protect their intellectual property.

Sweatshops

The western media has been very critical of working conditions in Chinese factories, labeling them "sweatshops" and arguing that the employees are forced to work too hard and paid too little. The Chinese business managers counter that sweatshops provide jobs for people who otherwise wouldn't have the opportunity to earn money. Young men from the countryside move to the cities and work in sweatshops to earn enough money to pay dowry fees for a wife, or to buy a house back in their village. The more hours they work in a given week, the sooner they get home. Chinese managers also argue that they can't afford to pay higher wages because the American retailers they ship to (Wal-Mart, Target, and others) demand low prices.

Income Inequality

In a booming economy, incomes rise faster for the rich than for the lower and middle classes. Many of China's nouveau riche got that way because of *guanxi*, connections to government officials and/or investors. The "opening up" policies have been very good to them, but those without connections or skills have not reaped as many rewards from China's economic boom. Today wages are still as low as a dollar a day in places. As the income gap between rich and poor grows, the poor are getting restless. Every year the official number of recorded public demonstrations has increased. Most Chinese people are experiencing rising standards of living, but as the gap between the haves and have-nots continues to widen, the country is in danger of political instability. It is ironic that the unequal distribution of wealth that Mao eliminated by force through communism has reoccurred, bringing China right back to where it started in 1949.

The Environment

Most of China's pollution concerns relate to acid rain, dirty rivers, and desertification, mostly caused by industrial pollution. Much lip service is given to protecting the environment in China, but making money is a higher priority than preserving natural resources for future generations. Damage to the environment is especially worrisome in China because only a small part of its land can be used productively. Geographically, China is the fourth-largest country in the world, but only about 15 percent of the land is arable; the rest is dominated by the Himalayas, the Tibetan plateau, the Taklamakan Desert, and the Gobi Desert. Like most developing nations, the leaders of China have paid little attention to protecting the environment. While they are still quite busy patting themselves on the back for their economic progress, a sustainable-growth movement appears to be gaining influence.

Currency Manipulation

The central government no longer manipulates prices, but they do manipulate the currency. Most countries allow their currency to "float" with an exchange rate that fluctuates based on market conditions around the world. For close to ten years, China opted for a "pegged" system, where one U.S. dollar was worth 8.28 yuan regardless of conditions in international markets. In 2005, China pegged the yuan to a basket of foreign currencies and the exchange rate dropped 2 percent to 8.11. The result of this currency manipulation is that the yuan is kept artificially weak. This is bad news for foreign businesses whose products become too expensive for Chinese consumers, but good news for Chinese companies whose goods remain affordable for foreigners. This is also good news for expats living in China. A weak yuan means a strong dollar, so your dollars will buy more.

The Underground Economy

With China's recent admission into the World Trade Organization, the country is trying to modernize its finance sector, but today the underground economy is alive and well. Cash is still paid for just about everything: salaries, rent, bills, pirated DVDs, you name it. Cash makes it easy to cook the books (assuming there are books to cook), and this deprives the state of the tax revenue, for which they are hungrier than ever (since most of the cash-cow state-owned-enterprises have been privatized). The informal nature of the economy also hinders foreign investment. Perhaps the biggest problem of the underground economy is that "sin industries," such as intellectual property piracy, gambling, drugs, and prostitution, can flourish easily.

Overpopulation

Overpopulation is another serious problem facing China. Too many people can put a strain on the country's resources and leave a large footprint on the environment. The country not only has a lot of people, but they are all concentrated along the eastern seaboard. This is largely because commerce happens in this area and the deserts and mountains of the interior are so inhospitable. To grasp the population density, imagine all what it'd be like if all 300 million Americans suddenly moved to Florida. The 1979 one-child policy, which isn't always enforced, was supposed to solve the problem, but it has created another problem. Since male sons bring more honor to a family, millions of female babies have voluntarily been aborted. Now three decades later, there is a shortage of women and quite a few restless young men.

CHINA'S ONE-CHILD POLICY

Chinese officials aren't pleased that their country is the most populous nation in the world. Along with masses of people come the problems of providing for those masses. In an attempt to curb the rapid population growth, the government instated its infamous one-child policy back in 1979, allowing only one baby for each family. Abortions, forced birth control, and steep fines for subsequent pregnancies help to keep the Chinese in compliance, though most Chinese approach the law with a sense of patriotism and duty.

You've probably heard about this policy already, but you may not be aware of just how many exceptions there are to the rule. Minorities of the autonomous regions are not required to follow the policy, and rural farmers have fewer rules concerning the number of children they're allowed. For wealthy families who can afford to pay the fines, having more than one child becomes something of a status symbol. Expensive private schools for China's upper-class citizens boast much higher numbers of siblings than the general population. China is also reworking its one-child policy to possibly let an only child born to a mother and father who were both only children to have more than one child, in an attempt to save the lineages that would disappear if the third-generation child were to die young. On the other hand, couples that faithfully abide by the policy in their child-rearing years get an extra stipend in their retirement years, and an even higher amount if their only child is a girl.

PEOPLE AND CULTURE

There is arguably no country as culturally rich and diverse as China: ancient, colorful, and about as different from the West as, well, as East is from West. It's the rich cultural experience that draws foreigners to want to live in China in the first place, and when the culture shock hits, its what makes many rush home, each with a newfound love of their native country. At times frustrating and at times utterly delightful, Chinese culture is nothing if not thoroughly unique.

China is well known for its cultural icons: chopsticks, painted opera faces, elegant scrolls of calligraphy, ornate temples, acrobatic martial arts. An elderly man puts on his old blue Mao suit to play mahjong at the park. A young businesswoman buttons the high collar of her *qi pao* (traditional dress) that's made from pinstriped suiting rather than shiny silk. A Buddhist monk tightens the sash around his mustard-colored robes as he rises from his prayers. A Mongolian couple puts on pointy felt boots to check

on their herd of sheep. Each of these people, in their own way, represents a tiny piece of the grand puzzle of Chinese culture.

The Chinese also have unique cultural approaches to relationships. Conformity is valued over independence; parents are to be honored and obeyed at any age. Relationships are king, and preserving the balance is more important than asserting one's rights. In China it's not what you know but whom you know and what you do to build those associations. It takes years to learn the intricacies of Chinese social culture, which means that no matter whether you stay in China for one month or one decade, you'll continually discover new things.

The People

ETHNICITY

What does it mean to be Chinese? The majority of the Chinese population, nearly 92 percent, belongs to the Han ethnic group. When most people picture a Chinese person, they visualize a Han. But the remaining 8 percent of the population consists of 55 different national minorities, over 100 million people, occupying 60 percent of China's territory. Each has their own customs, costumes, architecture, arts, religion, and language—a beautiful cultural kaleidoscope. Social customs are often what most distinguish minorities from the Han, because often their physical appearance is not that different. Most of these minorities live along China's borders, such as the Mongolians in the north, the Uighurs of the northwest, the Tibetans of the Himalayas, and a large and diverse variety along the southwestern borderlands. Increasingly you'll find them running restaurants and other businesses throughout China's major cities, and it is no longer unusual to see Muslim Chinese, with pillbox hats or headscarves, walking down the cosmopolitan streets of Shanghai.

Chinese minority groups are given a fair amount of autonomy, including exclusion from the one-child policy. Five of China's "provinces" are actually "autonomous regions" (Guangxi, Tibet, Ningxia, Xinjiang, and Inner Mongolia) where the minority residents are allowed self-governance, within limits. As for their religions, such as Tibetan Buddhism, the same rules apply as any other worship in the nation—no foreign leadership, no secret meetings, and every event must be registered with the government.

Though many foreigners are appalled at the way the Communist Chinese government forcefully took Tibet, today the province is reaping huge benefits as the central government pumps money into their

THE AVERAGE ZHOU

There are less than 450 family names in China and 90 percent of the population shares the top 100 most common names, including Zhou (pronounced like Joe), Zhao, Sun, Li, Wang, Qian, and Zhang. *Lao bai xing*, literally "old one hundred surnames," is a term that refers to the general population of China, the common people. More people share the top three most popular names (Li, Wang, and Zhang) than the entire population of the United States.

infrastructure, transportation, and schools. Likewise, though many nationalities have suffered discrimination and even persecution over the years of Communist rule, the PRC has also helped to preserve their heritage, such as creating written language for groups that previously only had a spoken language. Today the government even grants affirmative-action perks for minority individuals, such as preference for government positions and university placement.

CLASS

China has the bright distinction of bringing more of its people out of poverty than any other nation in the history of the world. A new middle class, defined as those making more than $10,000 annually, is emerging across China. In fact, the majority of city dwellers consider themselves middle class even if their income doesn't meet the official mark. While the growing economy continues to raise the standard of living for all Chinese, unfortunately the gap is getting larger between the haves and the have-nots. In other words, what Communism originally tried so hard to eradicate—class distinction—is coming back with a vengeance. To make matters worse, the newly wealthy tend to flaunt their wealth, driving luxury cars, sending their kids to prestigious private schools, and filling their closets with Gucci and Versace (the real kind, not knockoffs). On the other hand, China's poor are still very poor, with the migrant workers of the cities and many rural farmers making barely enough to just scrape by.

PATRIOTISM, REGIONALISM, AND DISCRIMINATION

The people of China tend to be quite patriotic, vehemently defending the actions of their government against the accusations and rebuffs of outsiders. In their patriotism, they have a tendency to consider themselves a little better than other Asian nations (especially the Japanese), though these attitudes don't show up in personal relationships.

There is also a deep cultural focus on regionalism in China. The Chinese have always strongly identified with the province, and even city, they hail from, which is intensified by the many local dialects and cuisines that distinguish one area from another. This regionalism is due in part to the historical belief in ancestral worship, which tied a person to their ancestral hometown, where the spirits dwelled who could bring both pleasure and pain to their lives if not properly worshipped there. Like patriotism, regionalism in China can lead to an attitude of superiority toward those that are from less-affluent (or less-educated, or less-refined, and so on) areas within the country. In addition, some Han Chinese

BEING A LITTLE *DIFFERENT* IN CHINA

RACISM IN CHINA
You probably won't experience direct racism in China, but you may experience some discrimination if you're not Caucasian. Chinese employers are apt to choose the candidate with the fairest skin, especially if there are chances to feature a western employee in the company's marketing material.

HOMOSEXUALITY IN CHINA
Homosexuality is a very sensitive issue in China. In more cosmopolitan cities you will find just a few bars and nightclubs that cater to the tiny homosexual community in China. But beyond that, the subject is still mostly taboo.

VEGETARIANISM IN CHINA
Despite the abundance of vegetables in every Chinese restaurant in America, very few places in China cook without meat. Larger cities will have places designated as vegetarian, though they are few and far between.

OBESITY IN CHINA
Westerners who are overweight need to be prepared for the comments they will receive in China, where it isn't taboo to talk about a person's size. You may have both strangers and friends ask you why you are so big.

RELIGION IN CHINA
China grants a fair amount of religious freedom to its foreign residents, as long as you abide by their laws not to evangelize the locals. You can bring in your own personal religious reading material, but not bulk materials meant for the masses. A private conversation between friends about beliefs won't be punished, but stronger evangelistic efforts will be.

may be quick to stereotype minorities as troublemakers and criminals. Though these stereotypes are sometimes driven by the facts of criminal activity, plenty of innocent minorities do tend to get wrongly discriminated against, guilty by association.

Customs and Etiquette

ETIQUETTE

While it's always important to be versed in the local etiquette to avoid offending hosts when abroad, you might find yourself feeling offended, as well. Many western etiquette principles—such as don't stare, don't point, don't talk with your mouth full, don't spit, don't pee in public places, don't push, don't cut in line, don't take so much for yourself that those after you won't get any, don't fight for the best seat, don't ask inappropriate questions—aren't valued in China. You'll have to have a flexible attitude to take the western taboo–breaking in stride, and before long, you'll hardly notice it when your business partner in her designer suit dribbles shrimp shells out of the side of her mouth as she talks during lunch.

While the Chinese may not follow the same etiquette rules that westerners do, there are a few things that they find incredibly rude that we are often unaware of. For example, you should use both hands to receive a business card from anyone. Showing respect to elders and superiors is also very important to the Chinese. You should always allow them (insist, even) to enter or exit a door before you, and be sure to address them with the correct term of respect depending on their age in relation to yours. Touching the rim of your glass below theirs during a toast shows respect as well. Chinese people will expect these gestures and feel slighted when ignorant westerners fail to show proper respect.

All gifts, invitations, and the like should be refused at least twice before you accept. Presents that are wrapped should be opened in private unless the giver insists you open it immediately. A token gift of fresh flowers or a nice tin of high quality tea is an appropriate gesture if you are invited to someone's home for dinner or an overnight stay. Always remember to remove your shoes before entering the home; many hosts will provide slippers for their guests' use.

CUSTOMS

Some of the Chinese customs will confound you; some will delight you. We were always particularly fond of their custom of giving away wedding chocolates; our kids appreciate the custom of giving children red envelopes full of cash on the holidays. Knowing—and adopting—the Chinese customs will make your time there much easier and more memorable. And there is no place that is as rich in custom as sharing a meal together at a banquet or restaurant.

Dining Customs

The best way to look more like a local is to learn how to act like one at a restaurant. When you are seated, your table will be given just one menu for the entire group. If you are the host of a large group that covers more than one table, it is customary for whatever you order to be multiplied by the number of tables in your group, so that every table gets exactly the same dishes.

You'll be expected to pick just one starch, or what the Chinese would refer to as a main food, which includes rice, dumplings, steamed buns, savory pancakes, or noodles. Although we can't imagine eating Chinese food in the United States that isn't piled on top of rice, the Chinese custom is to eat rice *after* you've finished all other dishes, just to fill up.

Many restaurants in China have aquariums and tubs filled with your potential dinner swimming and slithering about. If you order a meal with one of these delicacies, you may be required to either pick the one you want, or at the very least verify that the creature is still alive and healthy before the chef hacks into him. We found this out the hard way when we were encouraged to look into a plastic bag our waiter gingerly brought to our table and saw a very angry and very large snake hissing back at us. If they show you your critter before they cook him, control your urge to gasp and just give a quick nod to show your approval.

A shared meal in China is always very literally shared. All food will be delivered to the middle of the table and everyone will help themselves, using their own chopsticks to delve into the communal dishes time and again. If you are extremely cautious about the spread of germs, you can request serving spoons, though it is not the traditional Chinese way.

It is polite to hold a bowl up close to your mouth as you eat from it, rather than letting it rest on the table. Similarly, soup can be drunk from the bowl. If you struggle with chopsticks, Chinese soupspoons are a ubiquitous option. Few restaurants have forks, and knives are never used at the table. If the food comes too big to take in one bite, you are expected to hold it with your chopsticks and nibble bite-size pieces off of it. Gristle, bones, and shells can be quietly dropped onto the table

CHINA'S KITCHEN

China's many cuisines are categorized by the provinces and cities where the culinary style was first developed. Restaurants in China almost always choose just one style to specialize in. Here are a few broad categories that you will run across most frequently.

NORTH: BEIJING, MONGOLIAN, AND DONGBEI

Northern foods have a reputation for being bland but filling, based more on wheat-based breads and noodles than the rice-based diet of the south, and relying heavily on cabbage, garlic, leeks, and onions. The most famous foods from northern China are Beijing Duck (sliced roasted duck served on thin pancakes with spring onions and plum sauce) and Mongolian hot pot (order several raw ingredients and a pot of hot broth will be placed at your table; drop in the ingredients yourself, then fish them out when they are done). Dongbei (northeast) food has a Korean influence, including their taste for dog meat.

EAST: ZHEJIANG PROVINCE AND SHANGHAI

The fish of Hangzhou's West Lake, Shanghai's hairy crabs and *xiaolongbao* dumplings, Shaoxing's stinky tofu and yellow wine – these are just a few of the diverse dishes from the eastern coastlands. Known for fresh ingredients (especially seafood), simple seasonings, and fancy presentations, this regional cuisine is considered the oldest – and most refined – in China. Shanghai in particular is known for its sweet tooth, adding a little more sugar to its dishes than other cuisines.

SOUTH: CANTONESE AND DIM SUM

The Cantonese (residents of Guangdong Province) are infamously known for "eating everything that has legs except the kitchen table." In the deep south you may be served dog, monkey, insects, or even an endangered species. On a more palatable note, the Cantonese are also known for their world-popular dim sum, or snacks. In typical dim sum restaurants carts are wheeled around for you to choose from their variety of small plates and bamboo steamers filled with pork dumplings, shrimp rolls, custards, and other two-bite delicacies.

next to your plate or into an unused bowl, but preferably not on your plate directly. Never leave your chopsticks sticking straight up in your food—this symbolizes death.

Concerning drinks, waitresses customarily bring a free pot of hot tea before the meal. Tea is considered an appetite stimulator, not refreshment, so expect the teapot and the cups to disappear when your food arrives. At cafeterias, you are expected to use your soup as a drink. Glasses of water are not provided with meals and ice is extremely rare, though chilled soft

SOUTHWEST: SICHUAN AND YUNNAN

The climate of the southwestern provinces, especially Sichuan, is particularly hospitable to growing chili peppers. Sichuan cuisine (Szechwan in the States) loads every dish with hundreds of chili-pepper pieces, making the predominant color a deep, intense red. Yunnanese restaurants, on the other hand, take their inspiration from neighboring Vietnam and Thailand with specialties like pineapple-fried rice, fried bananas, and exotic mushrooms.

XINJIANG AND THE NORTHWEST

At northwest-style restaurants (Xinjiang, Ningxia, and Lanzhou) you'll find Muslim-influenced cuisine of hand-pulled noodles in spicy vinegar, savory rice pilaf, round flat breads, and a predominance of lamb – by the leg, on a stick, grilled, fried, or roasted. You may also find dancers and musicians performing their art in Middle Eastern style, which makes for a very festive atmosphere.

© RYAN SHAW

Eating stinky tofu in Shaoxing: It doesn't taste nearly as bad as it smells.

drinks, beer, and bottled water are usually readily available for sale. The beer is always cheapest (unless it's imported), but you'll have to request it cold (*bing de*) since many Chinese still prefer their drinks room temperature. If you order water, you may get a cup of hot water—a common drink in cold northern climates.

The cry of *gan bei!* is a toast that signifies everyone should drink down whatever alcohol is left in his or her glass. You can politely refuse to do so and just take a sip, though your companions may chide you. The Chinese

© BARBARA STROTHER

Chinese alcohol can be quite potent, so be careful how much you drink!

find it incredibly funny to get a foreigner drunk, especially if you're their boss, so watch out—their *bai jiu* (hard liquor) is rather potent!

Banquets are times to impress, and that means the most exotic foods. You may be treated to duck's bill, baby pigeon, fish-head soup, chicken feet, cow's lung, pig intestines, scorpions, squids, and a whole lot more. Take only a very small amount of each dish because you won't believe how much food they will keep bringing. You'll know the meal is over when the complimentary slices of fruit arrive. You will have to ask for the check (*mai dan*) when you are ready to leave.

In China, whoever does the inviting is the one who also does all the ordering and all the paying. Splitting the cost of a meal is rude by Chinese custom, though Chinese who are familiar with foreign ways may be open to it. Instead, the accounts are balanced when your guests later invite you out for a meal.

If it's your birthday, you're expected to treat your friends to a meal rather than being treated. We discovered this the first time we invited a large group of friends to celebrate the birthday of a fellow American, who was incidentally quite low on cash at the time. Lots of people came—and ate—without pitching in a single *jiao* (dime), much to our chagrin.

ALL THE TEA IN CHINA

In China tea comes in a variety of forms, including loose leaves, tiny balls, and beautiful flowers. There are five main categories of tea in China.

GREEN
This tea, the most common in China, keeps its color because it is not fermented before it is dried. The pride of all green teas is the Long Jing (dragon well) tea that hails from Hangzhou.

RED
This is what is called black tea in the West. It is fermented before drying, making it black, but creates a reddish-brown liquid when seeped.

BLACK
Chinese black tea is hardened into compressed bricks, making it easy to transport to remote areas where it is popular among minority groups. It is also referred to as brick tea due to its shape.

OOLONG
Because it is made after partial fermentation, the color of Oolong tea is between green and black. Oolong is grown in Taiwan and Fujian Province.

SCENTED
These teas are made by adding fragrant flowers, such as jasmine or chrysanthemum, often creating a very beautiful presentation in a clear glass. Though quite popular among foreigners, jasmine tea is often snubbed by the Chinese, since the jasmine is sometimes used to disguise a lower-grade tealeaf.

© BARBARA STROTHER

a window display at a tea shop in old Shanghai

Social Values

To be successful in your relationships in China, it is imperative to play by the rules of the Chinese social paradigm. Understanding the role of *guanxi* (connections) and saving face, two of the most important social values in China, will help you know what to expect in your relationships with the Chinese. At times this may require you to override your western beliefs about appropriate behavior in certain social settings, but the payback for the sacrifice will be great.

SAVING FACE

It is of utmost importance to the Chinese to never cause another to look down on you, to never look ignorant or incompetent, to always be completely respectable and respected. While westerners also value not losing face, it is nowhere near as significant a concern as it is to a typical Chinese person. For this reason, nine times out of ten a Chinese individual would rather give you a wrong answer than admit he doesn't know the answer, or will avoid answering a question that may make you upset. Stop a stranger on the street for directions, and she will give you elaborate details on how to get to your destination even if she has no idea where your destination is.

Saving face plays an important role in the nitty-gritty confrontations of everyday life. Direct confrontation and challenge is not the Chinese way and will deeply offend and humiliate, no matter how simple the issue is. This can be counterintuitive to us westerners who are used to demanding what we believe we deserve and challenging anyone that offends us. Whether you choose to challenge them directly (thus causing them to lose face) or find an indirect way to express your concerns, you may get what you want in the end either way. But the damage the relationship will suffer could prove to be insurmountable. The simplest way to avoid this is to make up excuses or tell little white lies and always try to find something to praise. Here's a quick example: A friend, whom you can't recommend professionally, asks you to write him/her a letter of recommendation to give to your boss. Rather than revealing the true reasons why you are not willing to write that letter, you can simply give an excuse, such as your printer isn't working or you've just been given extra work and won't have any time, in order to prevent your friend from losing face.

There are times when you can use the Chinese value of "saving face" to your advantage. Foreign teachers find it the most productive way to discipline a young Chinese classroom. One round of the song "Lee and Lilly sitting in a tree, k-i-s-s-i-n-g…" will bring naughty little Lee and Lilly to tears—but they'll be better behaved than they ever have been before.

GUANXI

Guanxi, literally "connection," signifies a relational system based on repaying favors and taking care of one's friends. It is the backbone of how many Chinese relationships function. If you have *guanxi* with an individual, they are going to do what they can to take care of you and the same is expected of you. Whether helping your *guanxi* partner get a job, introducing them to your other "connections" in advantageous positions, or helping them out of a tough situation, building *guanxi* can someday benefit you when you are the one in need. The flip side of the *guanxi* system is that it can leave you feeling used when an acquaintance's previous generosity and hospitality later seem like downpayments on the unduly large favor they eventually ask of you.

If you are concerned about what may be lurking behind someone's offer of generosity, don't accept it. Or if you accept it, be prepared to give something back to them. You will find that this is the way many Chinese people approach relationships. A cheap Christmas gift once given to our neighbor's son was immediately met with multiple gifts and cash for our sons. You often can't out-give the Chinese, nor should you always try. You may be putting undue burden on a less-affluent Chinese family if you give them a generous gift.

Gender Roles

Mao's Communist Revolution may have done some serious damage to the nation over the years, but one thing it did quite well is to increase the status of women. The PRC has always treated women as equals, expecting them to labor in the fields alongside the men to achieve the communist ideals of the glorious working class. Today most Chinese women have careers. Though the highest-ranking positions in business and government are still predominantly filled by men, women can and do play significant roles across all private and public sectors. Staying home to raise a child and tend the house is not common practice in China. Indeed, taking care of the baby is a duty that the grandparents are expected to fulfill, or nannies can be hired for cheap. And for wealthy double-income Chinese families, prestigious boarding schools take little ones as young as two during the week and return them to their parents for the weekends.

XIAO HUANG DI: LITTLE EMPERORS

One child, two parents, four grandparents: China's one-child policy has resulted in the unforeseen effect of having spoiled kids doted on by six admiring adults. Many families in China are raising Xiao Huang Di, or Little Emperors – a Chinese term to describe children who have never had to learn to share their toys with their brothers or sisters and never had to get along with their cousins. You'll notice the Little Emperors around you, mostly younger kids, screaming for their Häagen Dazs ice cream, shouting at their parents when they don't want to do what they are told, sassing grandma when she asks her little queen not to climb so high on the playground.

It is yet to be seen how this trend may impact the social fiber of the nation as these young generations of emperors, who have become accustomed to the world revolving around them, grow older. Now that the first generation of Xiao Huang Di are entering adulthood, more and more parents and elderly are complaining of the lack of respect and care from their grown children. Parents are suing their adult kids over these issues, and the government recognizes that this is a growing problem in contemporary Chinese society, a shift away from traditional values.

Within a typical modern Chinese home, the division of labor between men and women is not so different from what you would expect in the western world. Women tend to carry most of the domestic responsibility, but we were often invited to friends' homes where the men were better cooks than their wives. Raising children also falls heavier on the shoulders of the women, but modern Chinese men take very active roles in raising their kids. This sense of domestic equality tends to lessen, however, the more rural and traditional the family is, and domestic abuse is unfortunately a more common occurrence.

Religion

Communist China is officially an atheistic state. During the early days of communism and the Cultural Revolution, the state sought to eradicate all religious belief, but religion has deep roots in China and their efforts were unsuccessful. In 1982 an amendment to the constitution allowed freedom of religion within certain boundaries. Today China is experiencing a spiritual revival of all religions across the nation as temples, churches, and monasteries long vacant are being restored and returned to their original purposes. Buddhism, Daoism, ancestor worship, Confucianism, Lamaism, Islam, and Christianity are all flourishing, and often the Chinese mix and match many of these belief systems without feeling the need to delineate which, exactly, they adhere to.

ANIMISM AND ANCESTOR WORSHIP

The earliest spiritual roots in China revolved around animism and ancestor worship, and these influences are evident in the prevalent superstitions and veneration for the dead that still exist. It is common in China to burn paper replicas of money, cars, and cell phones to their ancestors, gifts for use in the netherworld in the hopes that these spirits will bring prosperity and blessing in return.

CONFUCIANISM AND DAOISM

Confucius taught an ethical code of social behavior, not a spiritual faith, yet many have made Confucianism into a pseudoreligion. Daoism, on the other hand, is China's only truly indigenous religion. The Dao, meaning "the way," has been described as the way of nature, or the spiritual operating force of the universe, though they claim that if you can describe the Dao then you don't really know it. In Daoism all things have balance, a yin and yang, which can be achieved through a mystical sense of inaction and letting things develop as they may. Active Daoists today use the martial art *tai qi* to achieve an inner state of harmony with the Dao, as well as the worship and appeasement of a pantheon of good and evil spirits.

BUDDHISM

Buddhism infiltrated China from India by the 5th century and remains the most popular religion among the Chinese. In classical Buddhist belief, nirvana (a high state of enlightenment) is achieved when you can eradicate the suffering that desire creates using meditation, self-denial, and right conduct. After the massive destruction of the Cultural Revolution, it was rare to find any active Buddhist temples

© BARBARA STROTHER

a worshipper at the Lin Ying Buddhist Temple near Hangzhou

or monasteries, and many monks were killed or forced to do hard labor. Today restored Buddhist temples and monasteries are busy with the activity of incense-burning and kow-towing constituents in prayer.

The Tibetans formed their own strain of Buddhism, essentially a marriage of Buddhist tenets with the Shaman religion that preceded them. Tibetan Buddhism, also known as Lamaism, focuses on the mystical practices of ritual postures, spoken mantras, and sacred art. Though the religion is considered a highly compassionate one, the gods portrayed in its art are often fierce and evil beings that rape women and tear men apart with blood and gore. Lamaist Buddhism is also practiced by Mongolians and has seen a growth in its popularity around the world in recent years.

ISLAM

Islam was peacefully introduced to China through Arab traders at southern seaports, though today the religion is most prevalent in Northwestern provinces. In cities along the ancient Silk Road the Muslim Uighur and Hui minority populations have faithfully preserved their Islamic way of life, worshipping Allah and following the teachings of the prophet Mohammed. The Chinese Muslims are not as rigid and fanatical in their practices as other Muslim nations, which can most readily be seen in their freedom to drink alcohol.

CHRISTIANITY

China's Christian history dates back to the 7th-century Nestorian Christians, though a strong missionary presence didn't take hold until the 1800s. Christian missionaries followed in the footsteps of opium merchants, and although they did good works like running schools and orphanages, they were eventually blamed for much of the negative influence of the West at that time. All missionaries were forced to leave when the Communists established the PRC and have been forbidden since.

China's regulations provide for one official catholic organization, the Catholic Patriotic Association, and one official protestant organization, the Three Self Patriotic Movement (TSPM). Chinese Christian churches must abide by laws requiring self-propagation, self-governance, and self-support, forbidding foreigners from leadership, financial support, and evangelism (although the Chinese can evangelize other Chinese). Chinese law also forbids unofficial assembly for any group, spiritual or otherwise, meaning all Christian gatherings must take place in a registered location.

While the government puts the official number of Protestants at 10 million and Catholics at 4 million, some estimate the true number to be as high as 100 million and 20 million respectively, due to the vast number who are part of the unofficial underground Church. Many Chinese Christians, balking at the control of the church by an atheistic organization and fearing religious persecution, have taken to secretly meeting in people's homes rather than under the watchful eye of the government. It is the (sometimes brutal) crackdown on this illegal practice of secret meetings that results in what the rest of the world protests as strong religious persecution in China.

Arts

LITERATURE

The canon of Chinese literature reads like a list of golden oldies rock 'n' roll bands: the Five Classics, the Three Character Classics, the Four Books, the Eight Great Literary Masters, and the beat goes on. Though it's too much to cover in detail here, there are a few titles every expat should be aware of due to their abiding presence in modern Chinese culture.

The earliest Chinese classic is the *I-Ching,* which teaches the ancient art of divination. The ancient philosophy of Laozi's *Tao Te Ching (The Book of the Way and Its Power)* expounds the spiritual teaching of the Tao (Dao). Confucius proposed self-sacrifice, personal morality, and social responsibility in his writings and became the most influential philosopher of Chinese history. The definitive text on military strategy, Sun Tzu's *The Art of War,* written over 2,500 years ago, is still popular today among strategists in business and board games.

© BARBARA STROTHER

Confucius

Among Chinese novels there are four key classics. *The Dream of the Red Chamber,* also known as *A Dream of Red Mansions,* is a love tragedy considered by some to be one of the finest literary works of all time. *Water Margin* depicts the lives of 12th-century bandits while *The Journey to the West* introduces the beloved Monkey King as he travels with a Buddhist monk, a pig-monster, and a water demon. *Romance of the Three Kingdoms* delves into the political turmoil of the fall of the Han dynasty, recently immortalized in a popular PlayStation game of the same name.

Poetry plays an integral role in Chinese classical literary art. The Tang Dynasty produced the two most famous of all Chinese poets, Li Bai and Du Fu. While Du Fu wrote of deep grief, Li Bai and his poetic pals used wine-drinking games as impetus for creativity.

Though the Cultural Revolution and widespread censorship that followed the 100 Flowers Movement put a damper on literary freedom for decades, modern Chinese literature is once again pushing the envelope on creativity and indulging in a newfound freedom.

VISUAL ARTS

Historically China's visual arts have focused on ink-wash landscapes and natural elements, such as birds and flowers, which grace traditional Chinese scrolls. Fine crafts include work in cloisonné, porcelain, lacquerware, embroidery, and jade carvings. Calligraphy, the marriage of visual and literary art, is the oldest art form in China. Through the centuries the Chinese have developed several different types of artistic scripts that take years to master. Sometimes what looks the sloppiest to untrained foreign eyes is actually the disciplined work of a master calligrapher. Like its literature, China's modern art tends to try to make bold visual statements with a freedom of expression that is somewhat new to this communist state.

MUSIC

Traditional Chinese music, with its preference for nasal voices and high-pitched tones, is often described by foreigners in terms of cats (cats fighting in a cymbal shop, cats being tortured, cats being murdered, you get the picture). While it's true that some Chinese music is an acquired taste, there is much out there that is perfectly enjoyable, especially pieces using the traditional instruments of the violin-like *erhu,* the flute-like *dizi,* and the lute-like *pipa.*

China's popular music is a mixture of a heavy dose of western pop stars and Asian ones, with a majority of Chinese music stars hailing from Hong Kong and Taiwan. China's popular music scene is still years behind the West but is fast gaining ground, and Chinese pop stars like Coco Lee and Jacky Cheung enjoy demi-god status just as much as their western counterparts. One of the bands to emerge from China to world acclaim is the Twelve Girls Band, which uses Chinese traditional instruments in contemporary music to create a unique sound.

CHINESE OPERA

Chinese opera is a unique dramatic form that uses singing, dancing, acrobatics, mime, swordplay, and traditional music to tell its stories. The best known and most refined style of Chinese opera is Beijing Opera, though there are more than 300 individual forms named for the region where each developed. The Sichuan Opera is known for "face changes," a highly refined skill of suddenly changing an artist's look (with face paint or a facial screen mask), leaving the audience wondering, like a magician's show, "How'd he do that?" The Shaoxing Opera, one of the newest forms, breaks from the strong male tradition by primarily using female performers.

FILM

Modern films of the mainland, perhaps because they are still somewhat censored to safe subject matters, are often beautiful period pieces full of tragedy with a technical focus on skilled uses of color, texture, and light to create moods. The film industry of Hong Kong, on the other hand, tends toward violent, gory, and chaotic ghost stories and kung fu pieces or, on the lighter side, slapstick. China has produced several film stars loved the world over, including Hong Kong's Jackie Chan, Chou Yun-Fat, and Jet Li, and the mainland's most famous actress, Gong Li.

ARCHITECTURE

Chinese traditional architecture has an elegant style dating back to ancient times. Characteristic traits include sloping tile roofs with upturned eaves, elaborately decorated brackets and carved roof figures, and rooms built around open courtyards. The common raised thresholds were designed to keep less-intelligent evil spirits, who apparently do not know how to step over, at bay. Feng shui plays an important role in traditional architecture, determining details like which direction doors should face to maximize the inflow of good luck and keep evil spirits away (see the *Housing* chapter for more information on feng shui).

Some regions within China have unique architectural styles, from the tan, boxy earthen homes of the Uighurs to the round felt tents of the Mongols, cave houses in the hills near Xi'an, and large communal round wooden Hakka homes. Throughout China's cities, however, you'll find a mix of modern architectural styles, from the plain concrete boxes of Russian communist influence to a present trend toward gaudy and elaborate classical European architectural styles, and futuristic skyscrapers that compete for the admiration of those that stand in the shadows below.

Sports and Games

SPORTS

In America we have the right to free speech and assembly; in China they have the right to sports. The government of the PRC takes sports so seriously that they've written it into their law, guaranteeing opportunity for all its citizens to get physical. And with their reputation on the line in the 2008 Beijing Olympics, it has become a top priority for the State to produce world-caliber athletes.

The number-one sport in the country is soccer, which the Chinese claim to have invented. They also claim to have invented golf, which is quickly growing in popularity among Chinese yuppies. Table tennis has played an important role not only in recreation but also in modern politics: It was a table tennis tournament in 1971 that was the catalyst for opening diplomatic relations between the United States and the PRC. It will only take one good beating in table tennis by a seven-year-old for you to realize how important the game is to the culture. Basketball has gained a tremendous following in China over the past decade; courts are filled at all hours with young men hoping to be the next Yao Ming.

GAMES

Among Chinese table games the one that is most well known is mahjong, similar to the Gin card game but using carved tiles instead of cards. Mahjong has a rough reputation among the Chinese since the game is used for gambling. The Chinese also have their own version of chess, *xiangqi,* with rules and characters that are similar to the western version. *Xiangqi* typically uses wooden disks carved with the piece's title, so you'll have to learn to recognize about a dozen Chinese characters to play. Knowing how to play either— or both—of these popular games is a great way to interact with the locals, who are always delighted to discover a *laowai* (foreigner) that can play.

© BARBARA STROTHER

Foreign English teachers enjoy a game with their students.

PLANNING YOUR FACT-FINDING TRIP

If you are considering a move to China and haven't been there yet, put down this book and call your travel agent immediately. All the reading you can do is in no way sufficient to paint a true picture of the real thing. You will never know if you will love or hate the unfamiliar foods, squat-toilet bathrooms, complex language, and overly friendly curiosity of the Chinese until you've spent time with them on their turf. (Okay, you probably won't love the bathrooms, but will you be able to handle them?) And if you will have a choice of locations within China, roaming around the country is the best way to get a feel for which part of this vast nation best fits your style and your needs.

Planning a fact-finding trip to China is not quite the same as planning a vacation to China. The focus of your trip needs to be on doing the research you'll need to do to make your move as smooth as possible, but you

should be able to squeeze in a little fun along the way as well. The good news is, once you make your move to China, you'll have plenty of time and opportunity to do all the traveling around this amazing nation that'll make your friends back home severely envious of you.

Preparing to Leave

WHAT TO TAKE
Documents

A passport with a Chinese tourist visa is required for your arrival in mainland China, although North Americans and Europeans can stay in Hong Kong up to 90 days without a visa. (For more information, see the *Visas and Residence Permits* section of the *Making the Move* chapter.) If you have travel insurance, bring your documentation, including information on what to do if you should need an emergency medical evacuation. If you happen to be coming from a country that has yellow fever, you'll be required to show proof of immunization when you arrive in China. You'll also want to make sure you are up to date on all of your other travel shots. (For detailed information on immunizations, see the *Health* chapter.)

Clothing

In this area, we recommend traveling very light. It is easier to buy extra clothes there, should you need them, than bothering with bulky luggage—unless you are very large or tall, in which case you won't find clothes that fit in China. Bring a good pair of comfortable walking shoes because you will be putting them hard to work daily. You may want to pack a poncho if traveling during the summer rainy season, although umbrella peddlers will suddenly appear as soon as the first drops start to fall.

Miscellaneous

Other items you may want to consider packing include a small calculator to help with the exchange rate, a detailed travel guide, a pocket-size phrasebook, insect repellent, hand sanitizer, and a few tissue packs for toilet paper. If you love to shop, consider bringing an empty extra suitcase to cart home all the treasures you're bound to pick up on the way. (You could also buy one there.)

Be sure to bring a journal for jotting down notes about your fact-finding research, and a thin plastic file holder can organize the magazines and materials you pick up along the way. A camera, whether still or video, is great for both remembering what you've seen and showing friends and family what your new life may look like, especially if you have kids back home who will be moving with you.

Business cards are an important part of both the business and social culture in China, so you'll want to have a small stack with you. If you don't already have business cards, get some simple name cards that include your email and other contact information printed before you go. Keep in mind that proper Chinese protocol requires you to give and receive business cards with two hands as a gesture of respect.

MONEY
How Much to Bring?

Just how much money will you need for your journey? This greatly depends on your itinerary and your standards. Smaller cities come quite cheap, but the main tourist drags of Beijing, Shanghai, and the like are not the bargains they once were. Hong Kong has even become one of the most expensive destinations in Asia. Comfortable but low-frills mid-range travel can be done for about $50–70 a day; if you can get by on street food, local hostels, and public transportation instead of taxis, you can get by on much less. But if you intend to stay at five-star international hotels, take multiple flights, and enjoy China's haute cuisine, plan on spending at least $250 a day. Be sure to bring plenty of spending money on top of this.

Currency and Exchange

You'll want to bring the bulk of your money in cash. Travelers checks are only accepted at some hotels and banks and are sometimes a bigger hassle than they're worth, although they do have the added protection against theft. Credit cards are a fairly new idea in China, and only a handful of businesses, such as high-end hotels and fancy restaurants, are equipped to take them. You will,

© BARBARA STROTHER

Eating sidewalk snacks is a great way to go easy on the budget.

however, want to bring your ATM card, as ATMs have become very common in China. (It sometimes takes a try at several machines before you find one that will take your card, however.) Most high-end department stores and large supermarket retailers have ATMs that are both bilingual and dependable.

You can exchange your dollars for renminbi at the airport, which you'll need to do since you can't use U.S. dollars in China. Most banks can also change money—the standard procedure is to take a paper number as you enter the bank (much like at deli counters in the States), and watch the electronic signs above each teller for your number. The simplest place to change money, though, is at your hotel; you'll need your room number and your passport to use their services. You'll need your original exchange receipt if you want to change renminbi back into dollars at the end of your trip, so hang on to it.

Precautionary Measures

Keep an eye on your money and bags at all times. If traveling to areas with heavier crime rates, you'll want to use a hidden money belt or pouch for the bulk of your cash. Hotel rooms provide small safes, which is a good place to store your valuables when you're not in your room. Put your wallet in a buttoned pocket if possible, or fasten the pocket containing your wallet with a safety pin when going into crowded areas such as buses, subways, and popular markets.

WHEN TO GO

The best time to visit just about anywhere in China is either spring or fall. Northern winters are unbearably cold, and even the south can chill you to your bones since all public buildings south of the Yangtze River have no central heat. Summers are hot throughout the country, and many cities experience their rainy season during summer. Fall offers wonderfully mild temperatures and pleasant weather; springtime has the added benefit of the trees and gardens in bloom. But if the primary purpose of your trip is to consider a long-term move to a land of extreme temperatures, you may want to visit during their worst season. Don't try to imagine how it will feel to wait at a bus stop in the biting winter winds of Harbin or to walk to summer classes in a hot and wet Hong Kong monsoon; go experience it for yourself. See if Tianjin's winter grays depress you. It is what you'll have to deal with if you move here, after all, and firsthand experience is one of the best ways to prepare yourself mentally for your relocation.

CHINESE FESTIVALS AND HOLIDAYS

A colorful time to travel or more hassle than it's worth? Either way, these are the key events of the year:

Chinese New Year/Spring Festival: This is China's most significant holiday with at least five days off work. On the eve of the New Year, cities resemble war zones, as fireworks fill the sky with bursts of color, sonic booms, and lingering smoke. It is customary to visit family and bring gifts during this holiday. Late January or early February.

Lantern Festival: When dusk falls, people walk the streets with paper lanterns. Mid-late February.

Tomb Sweeping Festival: This is a day dedicated to tending relatives' graves. Some people burn paper replicas of money for great grandpa to enjoy in the netherworld. First week of April.

Labor Day/May Day: This international holiday celebrates the workers of the world. Many Chinese prefer to spend their weeklong vacation doing sightseeing travel. May 1.

Dragon Boat Festival: For this festival, people watch dragon boat races and eat the traditional *zongzi*, a triangular delicacy of sticky rice wrapped in a large leaf. Typically in June.

Mid-Autumn Festival/Moon Festival: This romantic night may be meant for gazing at the moon, but it is perhaps most popularly celebrated by eating moon cakes. Late September or early October.

National Day: This state holiday of 3-5 workdays or more celebrates the creation of the People's Republic of China. October 1.

Chinese holidays can be a fun time to travel when the cities are decked out in their finest with all kinds of festivities to take part in. The flip side of holiday travel is the masses of Chinese traveling beside you. Public transportation will be packed; tickets and hotel rooms will be hard to come by. Prices skyrocket as the demand increases, with no room for bargaining. Often the frustrations of traveling during these times outweigh the fun. If you must travel during a major holiday, book everything well in advance, and try not to roam around the country until everyone is back at work again.

JOINING A TOUR GROUP

Some travelers to China prefer to join a package tour, especially on their maiden voyage. Although these trips can be expensive, a package tour will guarantee a certain level of quality in accommodations, food, and transportation, as well as the comfort of a bilingual guide. If you want to cover a lot of territory, a package tour may end up being cheaper than what you could put together on your own. And if you want to visit a restricted area, such as Tibet, you'll have to be officially part of a tour group to get the necessary government permits.

On the other hand, if you forego the group tour to set out on your own, you will get a richer experience of what life in China is really like. Package tours have a reputation for using the places that are most fit for big groups of foreigners, such as large restaurants with bland food and foreign hotels that tend to keep you distanced from the fascinating world outside its doors. Being on your own or traveling with just a few friends, however, will allow you to be much more flexible and spontaneous. You'll be able to make your own choices about when to splurge and when to save, rather than letting a tourist company make those decisions for you. You will also be able to customize your daily itinerary based on what you want to see in preparation for your move. Most tour groups will not be open to spending time in local grocery stores, driving through expat neighborhoods, or touring an international school.

Arriving in China

CUSTOMS

While it is possible to slip in one of China's backdoors by ship, train, or four-wheel drive, most likely you'll make your arrival via an international airport. Before your plane arrives, the flight attendants will hand out the forms you'll need to clear customs and immigration. Be sure to document any expensive equipment you are bringing into the country, or they may try to charge you duty on the item when you leave.

Although lines for customs and immigration can be long at some airports, the process is relatively easy. Just wait your turn to approach the window, hand over your passport and forms, and you'll be on your way within a matter of moments. Random individuals are chosen for bag searches; if you're not particularly suspicious-looking, they'll most likely wave you by.

Nothing pornographic, or even slightly risqué, will be allowed in. Large amounts of religious materials will be confiscated—anything that looks like it's meant for the masses—but there is no problem bringing in religious books for your own personal use. More than two bottles of wine or 400 cigarettes will be charged duty taxes. All medications should be in their original container; prescription drugs should have the original prescription. China takes drug offenses seriously; do not give them any reason to suspect you may be involved in illegal drug activity. Drug dealers are executed in China, even foreign ones.

TRANSPORTATION

When you've successfully made it through with bags in hand, it will be time to step out of the gray zone of the airport and into the hustle and bustle of modern-day China. Most airports are located a considerable distance from the city center, but you'll have several ways to get into town. Metro lines service a few of the major airports. Inexpensive airport buses are common, although you will need to know the city fairly well to know which bus will take you to your destination. Only the luxury hotels offer airport shuttle buses. The easiest way out of all airport areas

© BARBARA STROTHER

First step: Find the taxi queue.

is simply to hop in a taxi. You'll have to find the taxi queue and take the next one in line. Fares to and from airports can be steep—you should budget $50 to be safe. It's best to have a business card or a fax with the hotel's name in Chinese characters to show your driver; the majority of cabbies in China do not speak any English, and some struggle to understand foreigners who speak Chinese.

Sample Itineraries

China is a big, big country. You can't experience all of China in one trip, but with enough cash for airfare and energy for an intense pace, you could cover quite a bit. We recommend, however, focusing your itinerary to just a handful of cities or a couple parts of the country, leaving the discovery of the rest of China to future trips. The best itinerary will allow you to contrast the energy and modern amenities of big city life with the cross-cultural appeal of life in a smaller city. It should give you a view of the countryside, if only through the window of a bus or train, and plenty of time to check out the local expat scene, housing options, and supermarkets. And don't forget to allow some time to break from researching for a little fun.

If you already have a job opportunity in China, you'll want to focus your itinerary on the location of the position. If your future is not bound to one particular city, the sample itineraries will give you a broad experience of the key highlights of China. If your trip is solely for the purpose of fact-finding, one week should give you plenty of time to do the research you need to do. If, however, you want to look at multiple areas around the nation, or if you want to include a fair amount of tourism and sightseeing, you'll want to extend your trip to a minimum of two weeks or even a full month to cover a lot of ground. Regardless of where your itinerary—or your future—leads, your trip will give you a good feel for what life in China is all about.

THINGS TO DO
Daily Life Research

You'll want to make sure you experience as much of daily life in China as you can. For starters, spend some time wandering around grocery stores. Try a mega-mart like Carrefour as well as a little convenience store. If you have an iron stomach, stop by an open-air wet market where vegetables still smell of dirt and tonight's dinner is still breathing. (However, stay far away from the live bird area, which can give you the deadly avian flu.) These are also good environments for you to try communicating in Chinese, even if you don't know any—use that phrasebook!

Be sure you schedule some time to check out the housing scene if your employer won't be providing housing for you. This can be as simple as looking at the postings in the windows of the real estate agencies you pass or as complex as pre-arranging a couple days with an agent to visit numerous properties and discuss the financial and contractual obligations.

Other places you may want to visit include international schools for your kids, local health facilities, both upscale shopping malls and cheap clothing bazaars, and the city's restaurants and clubs where expats tend to gather. If you're thinking of attending university in China, check out the foreign student dorms and the cafeteria, and try to sit in on a class. If you already have a job or if you have an employer in mind, you'll want to tour the facilities and get to know the part of town they are located in—this may become your stomping ground in the near future.

Challenging Experiences

It would also be good to test out a few experiences that are quite different from what you may be used to. Use public restrooms. Order a meal in a restaurant where no one speaks any English. Take as many modes of public transportation as possible, although it's easy just to rely on taxis. Try a bus at rush hour. Rent a bike from your hotel (or simply buy a temporary one, since they are so cheap) to pedal around town. Hop on the subway. And *always* fit in at least one train journey; make it hard seat (for short journeys) or hard sleeper (for long journeys). These are the best ways to interact with the locals, and it's the little interactions you have with the Chinese, and the new friendships you make along the way, that will give you the most satisfying journey in the end.

Tourist Stuff

Although setting your specific itinerary will depend on the areas you think you may end up living in, there are a few places that really shouldn't be missed. The list is endless, but here are a few options to get you started. Any visitor to China will want to see the Great Wall, which most tourists access via Beijing. Xi'an's terra cotta warriors are also usually high on the list, as well as Shanghai's metropolis and historic Bund. The beauty of

SQUAT POTS

If you have a weak stomach or get grossed out easily, you may not want to read further. However, Chinese squat toilets are something you'll deal with when living in China, and they can be nasty.

Squat toilets are so called because you don't sit on anything: You simply squat over an opening. The nicest ones are porcelain, have indented spots to show you exactly where to put your two feet, and have a flush handle. Typically they'll include a nearby trashcan for disposing of used toilet paper to spare weak plumbing systems of extra waste. You'll find this type in public places like restaurants, although more modern establishments will have western toilets.

The worst squat pots don't even have a pot. You'll step up between stall walls (sorry, no doors) to a raised platform, and squat over a long trough that extends to all the stalls. There's no individual flush (so try not to look down), but occasionally a flood of water will race violently down the trough to wash everything away. You may encounter these in places like older bus or train stations, and they are much more common in little towns and rural areas than in the cosmopolitan cities.

Using the squat system isn't too hard to master, although for a western woman who never knew it was possible to take care of business without sitting on a toilet, it can be a bit daunting at first. You'll *always* need to provide your own toilet paper, which is why you'll find cheap little tissue packs sold everywhere you go. And don't get too excited if you find a western-style toilet in a public place. Many Chinese people prefer to squat, so the seat may be marked with the footprints of those who've squatted where you are getting ready to sit.

© RYAN SHAW

Taking a horse to the Great Wall provides a nice alternative to a tour bus.

Hangzhou and Suzhou must be seen sometime, although these could be saved for future excursions; the same goes for the seaside resorts of Dalian, Qingdao, and Xiamen. Hong Kong is a world unto itself, Chinese at heart, but in so many ways unlike the rest of the mainland.

ONE WEEK

With just a week in China, we recommend you choose just one region to stay in, making your base in a major city and taking day trips from there. (One possible alternative would be to explore two major cities with one domestic flight between them.) In this example, you stay one week in Shanghai, with the bulk of your time spent exploring the city, but still fitting in a quick two-day tour of Hangzhou, and possibly a day trip to Suzhou or one of the nearby ancient river towns.

You can use this Shanghai sample itinerary to model similar trips in other areas. With one week based in Beijing, you can explore the key expat living areas of the city and include fun day trips to the Great Wall, Tianjin's antique market and European concessions, and Chengde's odd mix of temples. If you'd prefer to keep to the South, a week based in Hong Kong will keep you busy checking out schools, housing, and employment options, and you can add a day trip to charming Macau and a two-day trip by train up to Guangzhou by way of Shenzhen and Shekou, which will give you a feel for the "real" China.

Day 1

If you leave home on a Friday night, you can expect to arrive in Shanghai roughly on Sunday morning local time. By the time you go through customs, exchange some money, and check in to your hotel, you'll have just enough time to grab a bite to eat and make your way to the Sunday afternoon expat service at Hengshan church. Even if you're not a religious person, this is the place you'll find the greatest number of foreigners gathered at one time in the city, and a good way to meet new friends. From the church, make your way eastward down Huai Hai by bus (and if it ever turns off Huai Hai, hop off at the first stop and walk back to Huai Hai), heading to Xintiandi. When you've gone part of the distance, be sure to get off and walk a little to see all the posh upscale stores, glamorous residences, and crowds at ground level.

Xintiandi, on the eastern end of Huai Hai Street, is a nice place to end your day. You'll have your choice of high-end restaurants, both Chinese and international, as well as trendy nightclubs where you may want to stay and play for a while if you're not too exhausted from all your travels. Before you head back to your hotel, be sure to pick up one of Shanghai's English-language magazines, such as *That's Shanghai* or *City Weekend,* given out free at area restaurants, for tons of great information about the city and what's happening while you'll be there.

Days 2-3

Monday and Tuesday should be dedicated to your fact-finding research. Try to schedule appointments for a realtor take you around to the apartments or villas in the areas you are most interested in. Tour the local international schools, talk with potential employers, or tour the university campus if you are considering studying abroad. Be sure you squeeze in time to check out the local shopping and dining areas around the neighborhoods you're looking at. You may want to end the day at a mega-mart like Carrefour, where you can get a meal in the dining court and wander around the shop to see what's available and at what prices. If on these days you have numerous appointments that you'll have to reach on your own, consider renting a car and driver for the day (just ask your hotel for help). Be sure you leave plenty of time between scheduled appointments, especially if they are located in different parts of the city.

Day 4

After two days of research, you can have a little fun on Wednesday. Start your day on the west end of the Nanjing Road pedestrian shopping area, and make your way gradually east to its end at the Bund. While you walk around the waterfront enjoying the views, sign up for a river cruise for later in the evening. Hop on the passenger ferry that will take you from the Bund to the Pudong side of the river; it leaves every 10 minutes or so. Just outside the Pudong ferry terminal, snack on a lamb kebab from one of the Muslim vendors with grills on the back of their bikes, a delicious and dirt cheap little snack. From here you can walk to the Jin Mao building. Head up to the Hyatt

© BARBARA STROTHER

Around Shanghai, you'll find several quaint old river towns worthy of a day trip.

inside, where you can enjoy the views from the lobby on the 54th floor or have a nice meal at one of the (pricey) restaurants that overlook the city.

From Jin Mao, the futuristic T.V. Tower is a few long blocks to the north. The admission price here is based on just how high up you want to go; the views from the top decks are unbelievable. To get back to the Puxi side of the city, follow the signs to the pedestrian tunnel (due west of the tower) where you can get a psychedelic light show while you are transported back to the Bund on this subterranean ride. If you've timed this well, you shouldn't have long to wait before you can board your evening river cruise up and down the Huang Pu.

Days 5-6

Thursday and Friday are good days to escape Shanghai to get a feel for life outside such a big city. Although you could spend these two days in Nanjing, Suzhou, Ningbo, or even Putuoshan Island, we recommend Hangzhou. A two-hour train ride in the morning will get you into Hangzhou with time to check into a hotel (preferably one close to the West Lake, such as the new Hyatt) and grab a bite to eat. If you are considering moving to Hangzhou, you'll want to make sure you see the things you are most interested in: for students, Zhejiang University; for parents, Hangzhou's international school; for those in need of a place to live, a tour of housing options with a local real estate agent. If you have time for tourism, Hanghzou has tons to do for tourists. You'll want to explore the lakefront area and take a boat to the islands in the middle of the lake. The silk museum or tea museum are other options, as are climbing one of the pagodas around the city or shopping the silk market. Ask your hotel for a tourist map or *In Touch Zhejiang* magazine for more details.

The downtown area to the east of the lake is loaded with great restaurants and shops, and the area is relatively easy to navigate by foot. When the sun goes down, head to the outdoor night market downtown for a fun shopping experience. Night owls will enjoy the lively bar scene along Nan Shan Road, which is also a good spot to run into expats who live in Hangzhou. Return to Shanghai by train or bus on Friday night to get well rested for Saturday, your last full day in China.

Day 7

You'll want to take stock of your remaining questions to plan your time for this day. If there are places you couldn't see or people you didn't have a chance to meet with, now's the time. You may also want to wander around Old Town, explore the Yuyuan Garden area with its famous old teahouse, or check out the museums along People's Square. Saturday could also be spent exploring Suzhou's ancient gardens or wander the narrow paths of one of the old river towns in the countryside surrounding Shanghai. If you go to the tourist bus station at the Shanghai stadium, the helpful ladies there will show you which buses are leaving next and where they are going. Just be sure you also find out what time the bus returns to Shanghai because you don't want to miss it. You'll want to be well rested before your Sunday morning flight back home. With the time zone difference, you'll most likely leave China on Sunday morning and arrive back home by Sunday evening.

TWO WEEKS

If you have two weeks to spend in China, you can cover quite a bit more ground. Boarding a Friday night flight to China, you could start your tour on Sunday morning with Hong Kong's high life. The easiest variations on this sample itinerary would be to swap out the time in Guangzhou or Xiamen and replace these legs with flights into other cities of interest, such as Chengdu, Qingdao, or Xi'an.

Day 1

Once you get checked-in to your hotel on Sunday, wander around Central by foot and double-decker tram. Make your way up to the top of Victoria Peak on the Peak Tram. Stroll around the summit for its amazing views, and grab dinner or a drink at Café Deco overlooking the city. Afterward, catch the Star Ferry to Kowloon for Nathan Road's nightlife or the Temple Street night market.

Days 2-3

Start Monday off with your fact-finding research. You may consider taking a look at the housing situation in various areas around the city, looking into schooling options for kids, or meeting with potential employers. Be sure you stop in a grocery store and a Watsons drugstore to get a feel for what's available. Finish up your research on Tuesday, or if you've seen enough, take a helicopter or hovercraft for a day trip to Macau.

Day 4

On Wednesday morning say good-bye to the Hong Kong high life and hop on the light rail up to the mainland. You can pass through Shenzhen, meeting with a realtor or checking out the expat hangouts around Shekou, before taking the two-hour train or bus to Guangzhou.

Days 5-6

Spend Thursday and Friday checking out life in Guangzhou—by now, you'll be an expert on doing your fact-finding research. Be sure to save a little time to wander Shamian Island. Taking the overnight train to Xiamen on Friday night will save your daylight hours for sightseeing, as well as the cost of a hotel night.

Days 7-8

For your weekend in Xiamen, reserve one day for fact-finding and one day for tourism. Xiamen's Marco Polo Hotel is a good place to find out what's going on in the local expat community; look for a *What's On Xiamen* magazine while you're there. Spend your fun day on quaint little Gulangyu Island and kicking back at the beach.

Days 9-11

Schedule a Monday morning flight to Shanghai. Three days in Shanghai will give you a feel for the Shanghai vibe; for a break from the big city bustle, hop on a train or bus for a day trip to neighboring Suzhou. Take the overnight express train Wednesday night from Shanghai to Beijing.

Days 12-14

Arriving in Beijing on Thursday morning will give you three full days in the capital to explore the expat life in its neighborhoods, shops, and schools. Squeeze in a little time to tour the Forbidden City, eat some yummy Beijing Duck, and take in a day trip to the Great Wall before you'll leave for home on Sunday morning.

ONE MONTH

If you can afford to take the time, a month will let you experience China the way it deserves to be seen. Even with this much time, you won't be able to see it all, but you will get a good introduction to all the key expat locations. On a one month tour, you could experience much of the hinterlands, minority regions, and hard-to-reach locales, but since your trip is meant to expose you to the cities that you may call home, we recommend following a path that will cover China's most prominent cities along its eastern and southern coastlines. If you have days left to spare after touring the areas listed, spend them traveling farther west along the coastline to the areas rich with the culture of many of China's minority populations or farther inland to the natural beauty around Yangshuo and Guilin.

In any city that you may eventually move to, you'll want to schedule several extra days for specific fact-finding research—use the one week itinerary as your guide to how much time you'll need. But even your time spent on purely sightseeing ventures around the country will not only be fun, it will also show you the culture and language of China as well as the difficulties of being a foreigner in this foreign land.

Beijing and the North

Start from Beijing, where you can do the must-see sights of the Forbidden City and the Great Wall. Pass through Beijing's neighboring port city, Tianjin, and on to one of the very pleasant northern sea towns, such as Qingdao or its smaller cousin, Yantai. If you are interested in China's religious heritage, swing by the holy Taoist mountain of Taishan or walk in Confucius's steps in his hometown Qufu.

Inland

Heading inland, check out Xi'an's terra cotta warriors and other ancient relics. Fly down to Chengdu, where you can check out the city or head out of it for a few days of gorgeous scenery. A bus to Chongqing will get you ready to board a cruise down the Yangtze River to Wuhan.

The East and Shanghai

Following the Eastern coastline, Nanjing figures prominently in recent history, although only a day or two is necessary there; be sure not to miss the melancholy museum of the Japanese massacre. On the way to Shanghai, Suzhou is famous for its elegant ancient gardens and canals. The energy of cosmopolitan Shanghai will keep you hopping for a few days; follow it with a few laid-back days relaxing along the paths and gardens of famous West Lake in Hangzhou's central city.

The South and Hong Kong

Farther south but still on the coast, you can enjoy Xiamen's Mediterranean-style coastal charms. From there, head on to the Pearl River Delta, where you can spend some time in a number of prominent cities, including Guangzhou, Shenzhen, and Zhuhai. In Hong Kong, you'll want to spend a few days island-hopping and bargain shopping. (Be sure to save Hong Kong for last if you do not have a multiple-entry visa for the mainland.) Across the water lies Macau with its unique mix of Portuguese and Chinese culture. Moving farther along the coast, Hainan Island is considered the "Hawaii of the East," with palm-lined golden beaches and sun all through the year.

Practicalities

Once upon a time not so long ago, foreigners were required to stay only at lodgings that were approved to receive them. Today, a traveler's choices in China are infinite. Where to sleep, where to eat—every major city has hundreds of options. We've given you a few choices to consider for the major entry points of Beijing, Shanghai, and Hong Kong, just to get your travels started. These options were included either because they are famous, strongly recommended by travelers, or have staying power. For restaurants we've specified a few famous places, as well as general districts known for their dining options. We recommend you get a very up-to-date travel guide, such as *Lonely Planet China,* to help plan the rest of your journey, as there is simply not enough space to make recommendations for the entire country.

Hotel Essentials

While there is a vast range of choices for lodging in China, most Chinese hotels are basic at best and way below western standards at worst. However, larger cities will have plenty of international chain hotels to choose from, with high standards and prices to match. China uses a star rating for its hotels, ranging 1–5 stars, although some hotels boast more stars than they have actually earned. Don't trust the rating; take a look around and ask to see the room before you commit. You should negotiate the price on every hotel room. The published rate is only the starting point; discounts of 10–50 percent or more can be easily had with a little bargaining. The exception to this rule is during the major holidays when the increased demand for hotel rooms will make the high prices nonnegotiable.

Some Chinese cities have hotels with local flair, like this one in Turpan.

© BARBARA STROTHER

Typical Chinese hotel rooms will consist of two twin beds. Rooms with beds big enough to share, such as a double or a king bed, are much less common. Extra beds can be brought into the room for a fee.

For check-in you'll need your passport showing the type of Chinese visa you have. You'll have to fill in a form with this information, which will be passed on to the local Public Security Bureau (PSB) so they can keep track of visitors' movements. (If you stay with a friend instead of at a hotel, your friend will have to register your stay with the PSB.) You'll also need a cash deposit, even if you'll be paying by credit card when you check out. (Ask before relying on plastic—many hotels three stars and below do not accept credit cards.)

BEIJING
Accommodations

Beijing is huge, about the same size as Belgium, so location is quite important in your choice of accommodation. Most prefer to be near the center of the city near Tiananmen Square, the Forbidden City, and the Wangfujing pedestrian street. Other options put you near the airport or train station so that you can make a quick getaway.

For high luxury with a price to match, the **St. Regis** (21 Jianguomenwai

Ave., tel. 10/6460-6688, fax 10/6460-3299, www.starwoodhotels.com/stregis, $390 double) is considered by many to be Beijing's best hotel. The modern and sleek **Kerry Center Hotel** (1 Guangha St., tel. 10/6561-8833, fax 10/6561-2626, www.shangri-la.com/beijing/kerrycentre/en, $301 double) aims to please the business traveler crowd.

For a different experience, try **Haoyuan Guesthouse** (53 Shijia Hutong, tel. 10/6512-5557, www.haoyuanhotel.com, 550元/$68.65 double), a Qing-dynasty hotel located in a traditional *hutong* with a pleasant tree-lined courtyard.

The **Holiday Inn Lido** (Jichang St. and Jiangtai St., tel. 10/6437-6688, fax 10/6437-6237, www.beijing-lido.holiday-inn.com, $256 double) ranks high for offering vast amenities but low for its location, which is far from the central city's attractions but close to the airport. For a good value place, **Hademen Hotel** (2A Chongwenmenwai Ave., tel. 10/6711-2244, www.hademenhotel.com, $62 double) is located near the train station and a subway stop.

Dining

We've listed a few not-to-be-missed locales, but you'll find plenty of great eateries anywhere you go. Upscale hotels will also have several good dining options with the added benefit of an English menu. To sample the world's best Beijing Duck, you can find several locations around the city

© BARBARA STROTHER

No trip to Beijing is complete without a little yummy Beijing (Peking) Duck.

TIME FOR TEA?

When it's time to give your feet a break from all your fact-finding wanderings, China's teahouses are pleasant places in which to relax. Some offer traditional teas in a very sophisticated ambience, while others specialize in colorful and fruity *boba* teas (with or without the black tapioca pearls) and novelties such as swings instead of seats. It is typical at traditional teahouses first to order your preferred cup of tea, and then snacks like watermelon seeds or dried kumquats are often provided free of charge. Some places even offer a large snack buffet with enough variety to make a light meal. For those who prefer coffee, Starbucks has taken China by storm over the last few years; ironically there's even one inside the Forbidden City.

of the famous chain **Quan Ju De Roast Duck Restaurant,** but the most famous is at 32 Qianmen Avenue (tel. 10/6302-3062). This is where George Bush, Sr., and Fidel Castro have dined. In the Chaoyang district along Sanlitun Street, the two main streets of the **Sanlitun area** are littered with expat cafes and bars. For a fun place to try a large sampling of dishes, **Donghuamen Night Market** (northern end of Donganmen Ave.) offers some strangely delicious—and some just plain strange—foods.

SHANGHAI
Accommodations

Most tourists to Shanghai will want accommodation in Puxi, the main part of the city to the west of the river. This is where you'll find the famous Bund, Nanjing Road Pedestrian Street, Yuyuan Gardens and bazaar, and a whole lot more. Pudong, the newer part of the city to the east of the river, is the home of the financial district, making it a good option for those wishing to look into corporate opportunities. No matter where you choose, rooms fill up fast in Shanghai. Book as early as you can.

The **Peace Hotel** (20 Nanjing Dong St., tel. 21/6321-6888, www .shanghaipeacehotel.com, $189 double) is Shanghai's most famous hotel and, thanks to its green roof, the most recognizable building along the Bund. Art deco–style rooms give a strong sense of the history this place has seen. Conveniently located in the Shanghai Center on West Nanjing Road, the **Portman Ritz-Carlton** (1376 Nanjing Xi Rd., tel. 21/6279-8888, www.ritzcarlton.com, $393 double) is considered the best hotel in Puxi, with prices to match.

© BARBARA STROTHER

Tired of Chinese? Get a juicy burger at Shanghai's Blue Frog.

Several elegant historic mansions have been converted into rooms and restaurants at **Ruijin Guesthouse** (118 Ruijin Er St., tel. 21/6472-5222, www.shedi.net.cn/outedi/ruijin, $135 double). These were once the stomping grounds of Zhou Enlai and Ho Chi Minh. Shanghai also offers a chance to sleep in the tallest hotel in the world: the **Grand Hyatt** (88 Shiji Dadao/Century Blvd., tel. 21/5049-1234, www.hyatt.com, $462 double) starts on the 54th floor of the towering Jin Mao building in Pudong and goes up a mind-boggling 33 floors from there. You'll pay a little extra for a view of the Bund far below; corner rooms cost even more.

Dining

Shanghaiers love to go out, whether to catch a quick bite with friends or to party the night away at posh clubs. Cheap food can be found at little Chinese restaurants along side streets, but Shanghai is well known for being top-notch epicurean, both in Chinese cuisine and a vast array of cuisines from around the world.

Located on the 54th floor of the Grand Hyatt in the Jin Mao building, **Grand Café** (88 Shiji Dadao/Century Blvd., 54th floor, tel. 21/5049-1234, reservations required) offers incredible views of the city through its glass walls and an excellent international buffet. There are several other upscale restaurants here as well.

The best place to get Shanghai's famous *xiaolongbao* dumplings is

Nanxiang Steamed Bun Restaurant (85 Yuyuan Lu, tel. 21/6355-4206), located on the other side of the pond from the teahouse at Yuyuan bazaar. There's always a line, but it's worth it.

There are plenty of dining choices in **Xintiandi,** a trendy pedestrian area with a collection of high-end restaurants, Chinese or international cuisine, in renovated old buildings. Located on the eastern end of Huai Hai Street, it's also a pleasant place to stroll when the meal is done. In the French Concession, **Maoming Nan Lu** (South Maoming St.) boasts a number of pubs popular with partying expats. Try the **Blue Frog** (207–06 South Maoming St., tel. 21/6445-6634) for great American-style bar food in a stylish environment.

While you're checking out a **Carrefour** (Gubei Area, 268 Shuicheng Nanlu, tel. 21/6209-8899, or Pudong Jinqiao Area, 279 Biyun Rd., tel. 21/5899-1899) mega-mart for what's available shopping-wise, you can usually grab a bite to eat in the food courts and fast food restaurants in the center it's located in.

HONG KONG

Hong Kong, though made up of hundreds of islands, is divided into four main sections: Hong Kong Island, Kowloon, the New Territories, and the Outlying Islands. Most visitors will probably want to be located near the activity of northern Hong Kong Island known as Central or southern Kowloon in its bustling tip called Tsim Sha Tsui.

Accommodations

Dubbed Hong Kong's poshest, **Peninsula Hong Kong** (Salisbury Rd., tel. 852/2920-2888, www.peninsula.com, HK$2,900/US$374 double) is an architectural presence on the watery tip of Kowloon in Tsim Sha Tsui and boasts unrivaled colonial elegance. Conveniently located in the Central district of Hong Kong Island, the suites at **Ice House** (38 Ice House St., tel. 852/2836-7333, www.icehouse.com.hk, HK$850–1,800/US$110–232 depending on the size of the room or apartment) are a great choice for long-term visitors and families who could benefit from the in-room kitchenettes and work desks.

If you're looking for super-budget accommodations, you may want to start at **Chungking Mansions** (Nathan Rd., Kowloon, HK$150–300/US$19–38 double). This is not one hotel but a block full of old, cheap hostels.

Dining

On Victoria Peak, **Café Deco** (118 Peak Rd., tel. 852/2849-5111) overlooks the ciy. Stop by famous **Yung Kee** (32–40 Wellington St., Central, tel. 852/2566-1624) for delicious Cantonese dim sum, served in the afternoon, or for a plethora of Cantonese delicacies at lunch or dinner.

Tsim Sha Tsui has Kowloon's own collection of international eateries. Nathan Road is at the heart of this area, located at the southern tip of the Kowloon peninsula. Check out the Chunking Mansions area for several great Indian restaurants; other options include Korean, Japanese, Malaysian, Parisian, and more. On Hong Kong Island, located along a pedestrian alley between Central and Mid-Levels close to the Peak Tram, the **Lan Kwai Fong** neighborhood has tons of pubs and bars great for a late night out.

DAILY LIFE

MAKING THE MOVE

So you've done your research. You've learned about the Chinese culture and the lay of the land, you've discovered the work you want to do or the program you plan to study. You may have even picked up a little Chinese and fancy yourself ready for the lingual challenge. Now what? What are the steps it'll take to get you settled on the other side of the world?

If you're lucky, you'll have an employer that will be managing your move, making all the arrangements to transport you and your household overseas. On the other end of the scale, you may have to handle every last detail completely on your own. Either way it will still be up to you to decide exactly what to take and what to leave behind. When we first moved to China, we brought a lot of the wrong things and not enough of the right things. The first time a good friend came to visit, we were quick to request that he bring us things like thick socks and a stockpile of deodorant, and convinced him to bring home our unused sewing machine. You can do your friends a favor if you pack a little more wisely than we did.

© BARBARA STROTHER

Only tourists pass

本镇居民通道

Only local people pass

Getting ready for the big move can be a busy and complicated time. If you have children, the younger ones may not understand what all the commotion is all about; the older ones will understand it all too well. Add to that all the detailed paperwork and processes you'll need to manage, as well as saying good-bye to family and friends and perhaps a family pet, and making the move can be quite a stressful time. Just make sure you don't get so caught up in the details that you miss out on the joy and thrill of this incredible adventure you are embarking on.

Visas and Residence Permits

DAILY LIFE

The first step in making your move to China is to get a visa. Welcome to the web of Chinese red tape—and oh, what a web they weave. Unless you are only trying to get a tourist visa, you'll want to leave plenty of time for obtaining all the documents you'll need. Two months is a safe bet, though the process can be expedited if necessary. The Chinese embassy typically takes around a week to process the application before it can be returned to you. Keep in mind, however, that most visas are only good for entry within three months of their issue date, so you don't want to get your visa too far in advance.

OVERVIEW

Chinese visas are classified based on your purpose for being in China, such as tourism, education, or employment. To stay long term in China, you'll have to be connected to an organization (the company you work for or the school you attend), which pretty much rules out the possibility of retiring there or just hanging out for longer than a tourist visa will allow. And if you're thinking of starting your own business in China or working in the country on a self-employed basis, you're going to have a very difficult time getting the entry visa you'll need, since all work visas must have a corporate sponsor. (Currently you must first get a Chinese business partner who can register the business in China, though with the current push toward opening up the nation for foreign business, these regulations may soon change.)

If any of these difficult situations apply to you, our best advice is to hire one of the visa services in Hong Kong. Though expensive, they can sometimes work miracles (though if you're a highly ethical person, you may not want to ask just how they were able to obtain that visa for you).

Visa applications are no longer accepted by mail; you'll need to walk it

VISA TYPES

Visa Type	Name	Issued for	Length of stay	Residence permit needed?
L	*Luxing*, "travel"	Tourism and family visits	Typically to 30 days though longer requests may be granted	No
F	*Fangwen*, "visit"	Short-term study, lecturing, business visit, cultural exchange, job training, etc., of less than six months	Typically to 30 days though longer requests may be granted	No
X	*liuXue*, "study abroad"	Long-term studies or job training of more than six months	Residence certificate typically valid for one year, renewable annually	Yes
J-2	*Jizhe*, "reporter"	Foreign correspondents on a short trip for a reporting task	Variable	No
J-1	*Jizhe*, "reporter"	Resident foreign correspondents	Residence certificate typically valid for one year, renewable annually	Yes
Z	*renZhi*, "job/post"	Those coming to China for employment and their family members	Residence certificate typically valid for one year, renewable annually	Yes
D	*Dingju*, "reside"	Those expecting to permanently reside in China	Residence certificate valid for 10 years	Yes

in to the nearest Chinese consulate or embassy, or have your travel or visa agent do it for you. You'll also need to pay the application fee, which varies depending on your citizenship and the number of entries into China. All visas are classified as single entry, double entry, or multiple entry. If you are in China on a single-entry visa but would like to leave the country temporarily (including visiting Hong Kong or Macau), you can have your visa entry type switched at your local Public Security Bureau (PSB) before you go. The PSB will also help you out if you need an extension on your visa or residence permit. Staying past your expiration date will result in a 500元 ($62) fine for every extra day; if you need an extension, contact the local PSB at least a week in advance.

© BARBARA STROTHER

TOURIST AND SHORT-TERM-STAY VISAS

The simplest visa to get is a single- or double-entry L visa for tourists, which will allow you to stay in the country for 30 days, or longer if requested. Multiple-entry L visas are valid for six months or more, though you'll need to prove why you'll be visiting so frequently (i.e. proof of real estate purchase or a sick relative). Hong Kong and Macau have their own guidelines for tourist visas and allow many nationalities to stay up to 90 days without any visa at all (check the *Hong Kong and Macau* chapter for more information). To obtain an F visa for short-term study or a business visit up to six months in duration, you'll need to submit an invitation letter from the host company or university. If you will need to return regularly for business purposes and have documents to prove it, you can get a multiple-entry F visa good for up to two years. Check the Chinese embassy website (see *Contacts* in *Resources*) for more information on what kind of documents will suffice.

RESIDENCY VISAS

Residency visas (D, J-1, X, Z) are only good for getting you into the country; you'll need a residency permit to stay in the country. Each type of residency visa requires different paperwork. To get a Z visa (issued to those

VISA SPECIFICS

Visa Type	Documents Needed for Application (subject to change)	Number of Entries Available	Cost for U.S. Citizens	Cost for Non-U.S. Citizens
L	Application with photo	Single entry:	$50	$30
	Passport	Double entry:	$75	$45
	extra documents needed for multiple-entry visas, see China Embassy website for details	Multiple entry, 6 mos:	$100	$60
		Multiple entry, 1 year:	$150	$90
F	Application with photo	Single entry:	$50	$30
	Passport	Double entry:	$75	$45
	Company invitation letter	Multiple entry, 6 mos:	$100	$60
	extra documents needed for multiple-entry visas, see China Embassy website for details	Multiple entry, 1 year:	$150	$90
		Multiple entry, 2 years:	$150	$90
X	Application with photo	Single entry:	$50	$30
	Passport	Multiple entry:	$150	N/A
	Form JW201 or JW202			
	Enrollment letter from school			
	Physical exam certificate			
J-2	Application with photo	Single entry:	$50	$30
	Passport	Multiple entry:	$150	N/A
	Company letter			
	Foreign Affairs Office letter			

coming to China for employment), you'll need to submit a Work Permit or a Foreign Expert's License, obtained by the company in China you will be working for, and a letter of invitation from your employer, as well as the marriage certificate and birth certificates for accompanying spouse and children, respectively. Long-term-study X visas require an enrollment letter and educational application form from the Chinese school. Journalist visas (J-1 or J-2) require both a letter from an employer and a letter from the Foreign Affairs Office. To get a D visa, you'll have to first get a permit from a local government in China before you can apply (if you have family members in China, they can obtain this document for you). Unless

Visa Type	Documents Needed for Application (subject to change)	Number of Entries Available	Cost for U.S. Citizens	Cost for Non-U.S. Citizens
J-1	Application with photo Passport Company letter Foreign Affairs Office letter Physical exam certificate	Single entry: (Residence permit automatically allows multiple entries)	$50	$30
Z	Application with photo Passport Company invitation letter Work permit or foreign expert license Letter from employer Marriage certificate Children's birth certificates Physical exam certificate	Single entry: (Residence permit automatically allows multiple entries)	$50	$30
D	Application with photo Passport Residence Approval certificate, issued by the PSB Physical exam certificate	Single entry: (Residence permit automatically allows multiple entries)	$50	$30

DAILY LIFE

you have close relatives who are Chinese citizens, D visas are extremely difficult to get and are typically only rewarded to those who have already resided in China for some time and have made sizeable contributions to the country financially, culturally, or technologically.

RESIDENCE PERMITS

It is not the visa but the residence permit that gives you the legal right to live in China. Once you arrive in China, you'll have 30 days to secure your residence permit. Your initial visa will expire within a few months, but your residence permit will function like a multiple-entry visa, allowing you to leave the country and return without an additional visa as long as the permit is valid. Three types of residence permits can give you the legal right to live in China. Permanent residence permits, a.k.a. the new "green cards," accompany the D visas and are renewable every 10 years. Temporary residence permits are for those staying more than six months but less than one year, such as visiting scholars or those coming for job training. The Foreigner Residence Permit, typically good for one year and renewable annually, is standard issue for the majority of foreigners working in China, though some (such as company executives, legal representatives, or investors) qualify for a permit that is good for two years. With a valid residence permit you are allowed to leave the country and return, even if your initial entry visa has expired.

Physical Exam Certificate

Technically you are required to have a physical examination certificate for residence permits; the Chinese embassy lists them as required documents for residency visas. We spent a lot of money getting all the health tests completed but were never asked to submit the paperwork. If, like us, you'll be entering on a tourist visa and then switching to a residency visa after you arrive, you may save a bit of money if you wait to see if they will actually require the physical and then get it done in China. Some provinces actually require that the physical exam be done at a local Chinese health facility. The best bet is to wait until you're told when, and how, to get it.

CHANGING VISA TYPES

It is illegal to be employed in China on an L or F visa (in other words, tourists and students cannot work in China). If discovered, illegal employees are fined, fired, and often deported. If you get a job offer while you're in China as a student or tourist, or if you come as a tourist and decide to stay for schooling, you can switch visa types at the PSB in most provinces. There are some locales, however, that require you to leave the country to obtain the new visa; most people accomplish this with a quick trip to Hong Kong. Either way, just don't start work or classes until you have the correct visa in hand.

Along the same lines, it is illegal to engage in any news-reporting activities, such as journalistic interviews, if you are in China on a tourist visa. China likes to keep a close watch over the media, and you can be detained for engaging in journalistic activities without having a J visa.

FAMILY MEMBERS

Accompanying spouse and children are given the same type of visa and residence permit as the one who will be employed or studying in China, though each family member will have to fill out an individual application and pay the application fees. If the stork should find you in China, you'll need to bring your new baby's birth certificate to the local PSB for registration.

China does not recognize gay or lesbian unions, nor do they extend any familial benefits to unmarried heterosexual couples. Significant others will have to apply for their own visa and residency with their own sponsorship.

If you have an employment visa and residency based on a family member's employment, you may find your own employment while in China. However, your new employer will then have to register your employment and file the necessary paperwork to make it legal.

ONCE YOU'VE ARRIVED

After you've moved into your new digs, you'll need to register with your local Public Security Bureau within 10 days. Bring your passport and all other documents showing your residence status. Your residence permit will be tied to your physical address, so should you decide to move, you will need to register the move with your local PSB before the relocation date, and then register with your new PSB office after you've arrived at your new location. Failure to register with your friendly neighborhood PSB can get you deported.

You should also register with your embassy or consulate, either online, by fax, or in person when you arrive. If a natural disaster strikes or political unrest breaks out, you will be on their radar screen, and they can and will do all in their power to help you.

Foreigners and the Law

One final word of warning: The Chinese government does not appreciate foreigners breaking its laws, and they will let you know that. We were once interrogated like serious criminals, forced to sign a confession, and required to pay a hefty fine when our kids' residence permits had inadvertently lapsed. Staying past your visa expiration or working without the appropriate visa will be punished. China even has laws forbidding entry to those "suffering from mental disorder, leprosy, AIDS, venereal diseases, contagious tuberculosis or other infectious diseases;" if found out, visitors with any of these conditions will be kicked out. Our only question with these laws is, what if it was living in China that made you crazy to begin with?

Moving with Children

When we first announced we were taking our twin two-year-olds to the Middle Kingdom, our friends and family were worried. To some, the idea of moving children to China sounds downright frightening. And we have to admit, there were times that it was frustrating and even frightening to have our little guys with us, though for the most part we were pleasantly amazed at what a great place China is to raise kids.

If you are preparing for a move to China with children, we think you're in for a real treat. The Chinese love kids, and little ones are given quite a bit more freedom to just be kids than they are in the West. School-age kids have great experiences attending top-notch international schools and making friends from around the world. Of course you'll have different trials living overseas than you would at home, and each age group presents its own challenges and rewards.

PREPARING KIDS FOR THE MOVE

Making a move overseas is stressful for every member of a family. The littlest ones have the hardest time understanding what is to come, but they can be prepared by talking about what the move will mean as much as possible. Try to read books and watch shows about moving and about China (we had *Big Bird goes to China* just about memorized before we left). Bring along as much as possible from home that they are attached to, such as favorite blankets, toys, or movies, to keep things in their life somewhat familiar.

School-age kids and teenagers can get ready for the move in some of the same ways, by learning about China and packing personal items that mean the most to them. These older kids will struggle with losing friends and having to make new ones. Be sure to keep email and mailing addresses of their friends, and budget for phone calls to old buddies and grandparents during the adjustment period. Giving older kids the opportunity to be involved in the decision-making, such as what house or apartment to choose, which room will be theirs and how to decorate it, and which school they will attend, helps as well. The choice to move to China may be out of their control, but allowing them some freedom to make other decisions will help them feel like their whole life is not out of their hands.

One good exercise to do during the move is to take stock of the things (personal items, events, relationships, routines, hobbies, sports) in your kids' lives that define who they are, the things they enjoy the most. Be proactive in helping them find these things in China, or find good replacements, which will make the adjustment period much shorter.

MOVING WITH BABIES

One of the best things about living in China with a baby is the abundance of inexpensive domestic help. The majority of expats in China have at least one part-time *ayi* (literally "Auntie," a term used for any female providing domestic support). *Ayis* can handle everything from cooking, laundry, and cleaning to taking care of pets and, most importantly, child

FOREIGN BABIES ABROAD

The Chinese *adore* children – especially those that are very young, very cute, and very Caucasian. If you've ever wondered what it's like to be famous, just take a blond baby to a small Chinese town. They'll stare and point and follow you, they'll stalk your family with cameras like paparazzi. They'll try to touch your kids and pick them up and even take away their toys just to hear the cute little foreign kids cry. Many expat parents get in a routine of shielding their kids in public, ready to protect them from any grabby hands. If you've got extroverted children who love attention, they'll be in heaven, but if your little ones are afraid of strangers, they may find themselves in Chinese hell.

The Chinese believe that it takes a village to raise a child. While this has its perks, such as times when you and your mate can enjoy the rare uninterrupted dinner conversation because your kids are off playing with the restaurant staff, it can also be frustrating. In some ways the role of parental authority is weak in China. If a stranger wants to offer your child a candy or a snack (or, speaking from experience, a drink from their bottle of beer), they most likely won't ask you if it's okay first. If they feel you are not treating your child correctly, they won't hesitate to get involved, such as grabbing an icy drink out of the hands of a thirsty toddler (according to Chinese custom, cold drinks can bring harm to a small child). At times this lack of respect for your authority as the parent will clash with your own cultural beliefs about parenting.

Although at times frustrating, the pleasure of seeing your kids experience a foreign culture firsthand far outweighs the nuisance of the cultural differences. Just be prepared to accept it as part of the cross-cultural experience.

care. Some expat families with two working parents find it such a benefit to have the help of inexpensive *ayis* that they hire one for each child in the family. Even if you only use an *ayi* to come a few days a week for laundry and cleaning, you'll be able to spend more time with your kids and less time on domestic chores.

One of the worst things about living in China with a baby is the lack of equipment. Restaurant high chairs and public diaper-changing stations are extremely rare. Public transportation doesn't allow for car seats; bumpy public sidewalks and a lack of elevators are not conducive to strollers. Child safety is not high on the priority list of many Chinese manufacturers or architects. At least department stores and supermarkets now carry a decent selection of baby items, though you'll pay much more for the quality imported items. Unlike the States, good used items are very hard to find.

MOVING WITH PRESCHOOLERS

Life with preschoolers in China is often much easier than in the West. Cheap toys are sold everywhere; kiddie rides are around every corner. Potty training can be easier in a nation where bathrooms are not requisite to taking care of your business (if you're male). On the other hand, emergency runs to public bathrooms in China can be terrifying to adults, let alone kids who are already not so sure about this whole toilet thing to begin with.

China provides a rich cultural and educational experience for any age.

© BARBARA STROTHER

Bring a few of their favorite things from home, and beyond that, they may just have to grow up a little quicker than they normally would. Our boys had to learn quickly to sit in seats without booster chairs and sleep in big beds without a railing. Chopsticks can be a challenge to someone who's hardly learned to use a fork, but luckily Chinese soup spoons are available at every restaurant.

MOVING WITH ELEMENTARY-AGE KIDS

The elementary age is a great time to move to a foreign country. At this age kids are not yet so settled into their friendships as to create a catastrophe by leaving them, and still of an age to pick up a second language with amazing quickness. As long as you are moving to a major city, they'll have plenty of great school choices. Plus they'll retain much more of the memories of their time in China than the younger ones will.

As far as packing for this age, there are a few things that are hard to find in China. If you'd like to have your own educational materials (whether for home-schooling or for supplements to regular school), materials for this age are hard to find in any subject, though the classics in English (adult classics made for kids, not kids' pop classics like Harry Potter) can always be picked up at large bookstores. Additionally, boys' clothing is best brought with you, unless your boy *likes* to wear jeans with embroidered teddy bears.

MOVING WITH PRE-TEENS AND TEENS

Though perhaps the most difficult to move, this age can have more amazing experiences in China than their younger siblings. School trips may take them to exotic locations; sports games may let them experience new Asian cities. The new friends they meet will be people they visit for years to come, jet-setting to Singapore or Australia to connect with old high school buddies. And learning Chinese language and culture will help them tremendously in the global business world of their future careers.

Being exposed to the multiculturalism of international schools can be both a blessing and a curse, however. Although you may be an American family that believes that children shouldn't ever drink alcohol, your kids will be exposed to new ways of thinking as they interact with friends from other countries who've grown up with wine or beer on the nightly dinner table. China does not enforce a minimum drinking age, meaning kids can get alcohol easily. The upside is that you won't have to worry about your teen's friends drinking and driving, because it will most likely be a taxi or personal driver who's taking them around town. Drugs do exist in China, though on nowhere near the scale of America, so you will have much less to worry about. And the violence that has been plaguing American schools will be a faint memory in this land of gun control.

Your teens won't miss American movies because they'll be able to pick up an unlimited supply of cheap pirated DVDs from the nearest sidewalk vendor, but they may miss their favorite music. Being out of the country also leaves them a little out of the pop-culture loop, making it hard to return home without feeling like an outsider. Repatriation for teens is an especially tricky time and should be proactively treated with care.

Moving with Pets

If you are considering bringing Fluffy with you to the other side of the world, there are a few things you'll need to know first. Only those with residency visas are allowed to bring a pet to China. When you and your pet arrive at the airport, customs officials will require a health certificate and vaccination certificate from your vet verifying that Fluffy is fit and his shots are current. Then you'll have to pay 280元 ($35) at the Quarantine Station, though the quarantine will actually take place at your own residence. Within a month or two an official will stop by your house to evaluate your pet's health, including a stool check. If Fluffy passes, you can pick up your verification of vaccination, which you'll need to get him registered. All dogs (whether coming from overseas or purchased in China) are supposed to be registered; some larger cities require multiple photos of your dog, permission from your neighbors, and a fee up to 2,000元 ($250) to complete the registration process. When it's time to move back home, you'll need to bring your pet and the vaccination certificate back to the Vaccination Office, where you'll get a Certificate of Health. The airport veterinarian will check this paper before letting your pet leave the country.

Each airline has different requirements and fees for transporting pets, so do your research first. You may pay more to fly your pet to China than you would a child. Book early because planes often have a limited number of spots for animals.

LIFE IN CHINA WITH A PET

What will life in China be like for you and your pet? Some things will be easier, especially if you have household help that can clean the litter box and walk the dog while you're traveling. On the other hand, only a minority of foreigners in China can afford a villa with a private yard, so your pet may have to adjust to apartment-dwelling. Pet supplies are sold at the big supermarkets, though you won't find variety. If your pooch insists on moist canned food or if your cat refuses to use a box without the right kind of litter, you're going to have problems in China. As for veterinarians, local vets are cheap enough; those in big cities may even speak English and use U.S. medications. Some foreign veterinarian firms are moving into the market for those who prefer western veterinarian practice (with prices that match), though they may not be in your part of town. Keep a first-aid kit for your pet in case you can't get to your vet quickly in an emergency.

GETTING A PET IN CHINA

If you decide to leave your pet behind, you can always get a new one in China, such as one of the beautiful birds kept in ornately carved cages, or go native and even get a grasshopper or two, kept for their song and the luck they bring. Finding a pet in China won't be too hard—in fact, they'll come to you. Entrances to subways or areas around parks are common places for people to sell caged mice, hamsters, and baby bunnies for just a few bucks. Flower and bird markets have all kinds of pets to choose from, much more than just birds (but if you're in southern China, please make sure it's a pet market and not a fresh-food market!). Unfortunately Chinese pets for sale are often unhealthy, diseased, or just too young to be away from their mothers. It can be difficult to keep these animals alive for long. We personally went through 13 pets (albeit half were caged grasshoppers) during a 16-month stay in China, and only the cat was still alive when we left.

Recent years have seen the growing popularity of expensive purebred dogs. It is not uncommon to see elegant Afghans, perky Pugs, and more exotic species being walked down China's sidewalks. You'll still want to check out the living conditions of the pet before you buy it, if possible. Even purebreds purchased in China tend to be sickly.

What to Take

Deciding what to take will, of course, depend on how long you will be in China and what sort of a shipping budget you are working with. To get you started in your selection process, there are three broad categories that will help you decide what to pack: availability, an initial supply of necessities, and personal items. For everything else, try to leave it behind.

Most expats find their Chinese homes much smaller than their western homes, with very limited storage. Unless you are relocating with a long-term position in a corporation that provides a significant shipping budget, it's just not worth the cost and effort to bring too much.

AVAILABILITY

China is a shopper's paradise: cheap clothes, handbags, watches, and scarves; gorgeous Chinese antiques and trendy Ikea-style furniture; elegant Asian art and funky Chairman Mao tchotchkes. There's enough retail therapy to keep you happily out of your

A giant toy market in Beijing bustles with activity.

shrink's office for years. But even with the great deals and amazing finds, there will be some items you'll want that, no matter how hard you search, you just won't find. Or you'll find it but it will be of such inferior quality or high price that you'd be better off just bringing it with you from home. Here are a few items in this category.

Leisure Items
• Reading material in English
• Board games
• Musical instruments (common instruments like guitars can be purchased cheaply in China, though you get what you pay for)
• Bike helmets and specialized sports equipment (such as camping or rock-climbing gear)

Cooking/Baking Items
• Barbecue utensils
• Oven thermometer (if you are lucky enough to get an oven, it won't have dials marked in Fahrenheit)
• Baking pans, pie plates (the Chinese don't bake)
• Quality potato peeler and can opener

CUSTOM MADE IN CHINA: CHINESE TAILORS

It can be difficult for foreigners to find clothing that fits in China. Because the Chinese are so thin and often short, average-size westerners struggle through the XXXL racks to fit a frame that would only be considered a Medium back home. Only petite shoppers get to enjoy all those Chinese markets full of cheap clothing. For the rest of us, don't despair; help can be found in your local Chinese tailor.

Chinese tailors work inexpensively and quickly, turning out simple items in just a few hours. A friend and I once had a pair of pants and a couple scarves custom made while we enjoyed a long lunch – and paid less than $15 for it all. You can even get a suit custom made in less than 24 hours, though for complex items like suits and *qi pao*'s (traditional Chinese dresses), quality tailors may take two to three weeks to get the details right.

Chinese tailors are amazingly versatile in their skill. They can work from a photograph, or duplicate a favorite piece of clothing you already own. Give them the dimensions of a friend or relative back home and they'll create a one-of-a-kind, custom-fit gift for someone who has never even set foot in the country.

Most tailors carry a small selection of fabrics, though you can buy your fabric elsewhere if you don't see what you like. Many cities have indoor markets with multiple tailors' shops congregated together. Silk shops in touristy areas or upscale department stores will also offer tailoring services, but you will pay quite a bit more for their quality work than for the little mom-and-pop tailor shop in your local neighborhood. A tailor's quoted price will include the fabric and the labor. At upscale shops that cater to the rich and foreign, high quality suits and *qi pao*'s can cost you well over $100; tiny shops that serve the local community can turn out a short silk *qi pao* for as little as $5 and a thin suit for around $25.

Both tailors and the ubiquitous street-side menders (look for hand-run sewing machines on the sidewalks near older residential areas) will mend torn clothing and broken zippers, or adjust a hem to your height, starting at just one or two kuai ($0.12–0.25) for simple tasks. Repairs like this are cheap enough to make you swear off ever doing your own mending again.

© BARBARA STROTHER

Food Items

• Maple syrup, salad dressing, yellow mustard, pancake mix, western-style pickles, BBQ sauce, any Mexican food, real coffee, mayonnaise that isn't sweet, Thanksgiving foods (stuffing, cranberry sauce)
• Spices—if you have favorites, bring them

Bathroom Items

• Deodorant (bring lots!), dental floss, tampons, perfume (major shampoo brands are readily available, including dandruff shampoo)
• Make-up—it is available at department stores but is expensive and often of the "whitening" variety

Clothing Items

• Clothing in large and tall sizes, bras above size 34
• Thick socks (socks are plentiful but very thin)
• Large-size shoes (above 9 for women, 11 for men); if high-quality shoes are important to you, bring your own—Chinese shoes don't last long
• Men's swim trunks, if you don't like to wear Speedos

Household and Children's Items

• Construction paper, index cards, cardstock, quality markers/pens/sharpies, felt (most other common office supplies are readily available)
• Items for the minor holidays such as Easter-egg dye (Christmas decor will be easy to find)
• Smoke detectors, carbon monoxide detector
• Quality toys (cheap toys are everywhere, but name-brand toys like Legos are only at department stores and carry a high price tag)
• Books and educational materials for older kids in English (there's plenty for preschoolers, though you won't find the classics like Dr. Seuss)
• Insect repellent (non-aerosol)

PERSONAL ITEMS

The few personal items that you will need to keep with you are mostly documents, such as birth certificates, immunization records, diplomas, marriage certificates, extra résumés, your will, banking and financial information, drivers license, health insurance documentation, and so on. There are also personal items you'll want for their sentimental value; you never know when—or how hard—homesickness will hit you. One of the best ways to get yourself through is to have a stash of items that make you feel those good "home" feelings again, things that celebrate who you are and where you come from, such as:

• Photos of your family, house, pets, and hometown—these are also great to share with new Chinese friends to show what your life was like "back home"

• CDs or mp3s for relaxing (or partying!) with music that is familiar to you—you'll be able to pick up plenty of mainstream CDs in China, including lots of oldies from the '60s and '70s, so just bring your favorite and hard-to-find selections

• Your kids' most favorite toys and DVDs (don't bother bringing VHS tapes; VCRs are obsolete in China); like CDs, English DVDs will be very easy to come by, at least until the government gets serious about cracking down on piracy

ONE-MONTH'S SUPPLY

There are a few things you will need to use immediately before you've had time to find where you can buy them. Items that you may find embarrassing to shop for (i.e. feminine hygiene products, condoms) are better brought with you in the beginning to help minimize the stress of the transition. If you are moving with a small child, think through what you will need for the first month and be sure to bring enough diapers, wipes, rash ointment, formula, and anything else you normally keep in the diaper bag. While many popular brands of hygiene items, such as shampoos and soaps, are readily available, you may want to bring a small supply of your favorite brands until you can determine where to buy them in China.

A WORD ON ELECTRONICS AND ELECTRICITY

Electronics are plentiful in China. It is easy to pick up digital cameras, mp3 players, computer components, and more. But contrary to what most foreigners expect, the prices are no cheaper and often considerably more expensive than in the United States, even for items manufactured in China. According to Chinese law, all foreign-branded items that are made for export but consequently sold in China must include an import tax. Additionally, you'll have to deal with lack of instructions in English, low product support for repairs, and voltage/outlet problems when you leave China. As a general rule, if you're only going to use the item in China, buying it there ensures the proper electrical components. But if you will be using the item long term, even after you've left China, then you're better off buying it before your move.

The voltage in China is 220. Most buildings will have outlets that will fit several configurations of plugs; adapters are easy to pick up at local markets if you have a plug that does not fit. Transformers are available for converting the voltage on small appliances, though it is not always easy to find the one you need (which is why we eventually sent back our unused sewing machine and an older camcorder whose charger was not compatible). If it is possible to buy your appliance there, it is often better to do so, rather than having to deal with finding and using a transformer.

Shipping Options

If you are only going to be in China on a short-term basis, you may be able to fit what you need to bring within the confines of your airline luggage allotment. If not, assess the extra weight and do a comparison between your airline's cost for excess baggage weight and the cost of mailing the extra items to your address in China.

If, however, you are moving to China on a long-term commitment, you may be looking at moving your entire household. We strongly recommend that you keep it as light as possible, planning on buying new stuff in China (which is cheap) rather than paying to have everything shipped over (which is expensive and a big hassle). You'll pay steep customs fees on some things, such as furniture and other "luxury" items. On the other hand, going light will give you reason to do more shopping while you are there. Hunting for antique furniture bargains is a favorite pastime for many expats.

There are some tricks to getting your stuff to China without having to pay expensive shipping. For example, we invited a good friend to travel with us during our move and used his extra luggage space for more of our stuff. If you know friends or family will come visit you when you are overseas, you can leave boxes or suitcases packed and ready for them to bring along as part of their luggage if they are willing to do so. This trick also works in reverse, a great way to get some stuff home and save on shipping when you leave the country.

SHIPPING AND RELOCATION COMPANIES

If you need to ship much more than the airlines, or the local post office, can take, there are many relocation and shipping companies that can handle the job. Typically they will pack all of your belongings, get them ready for the high seas, and see them off at the port, then deliver them to your new home and unpack them. Household shipment from middle America to the Middle Kingdom will put you out around $6,000 for a two-bedroom apartment up to $9,000 for a four-bedroom home, varying greatly based on the size of your shipment, extra services, and your specific destination.

You can save some money if you pack the boxes yourself, though often this job is best left to the professionals. You'll want to contact several companies that specialize in international relocation to get quotes. You have your choice of using western-based companies that will subcontract the work when your shipment arrives in China, or a China-based company that will subcontract the initial packing and loading work. While some people prefer the comfort of working with someone who is from their own country, others prefer to trust the Chinese professionals who really know the complex customs laws and processes. There are also a few major companies, such as Crown Relocations, that have offices and staff in both locations.

You should plan on three months for your oceangoing shipping process from start to finish. Airfreight can be used for those items that you will want immediately. Standard airfreight will arrive in 7 to 14 days; express shipments will get the most crucial items to you in two to five days. You'll pay dearly for these options, especially express, so use them wisely.

DOCUMENTATION

Make sure you are fastidious about all the documents you must fill out with your shipment; otherwise you may be fined steep fees and/or your belongings may be impounded for several months while the problems are sorted out. Your international moving company will provide you with a whole folder full of forms and will let you know what other documents you will need that are specific to your situation.

Getting your stuff into the country is only half the battle; you'll need to get it all back out again (unless your move is permanent, of course). You'll need to hang on to all those original customs forms. The process for exporting your household goods out of China is about as complicated as importing them into China, and you'll have to prove you brought this stuff with you or you'll owe duty. Other paperwork to hold onto includes receipts for antique furniture purchased in China and verification that the antique is less than 150 years old (and therefore legal to export), as well as all receipts for significant purchases made while living in China.

LANGUAGE AND EDUCATION

China has always been a rich place for education. In ancient times, government officials were selected based on their intellectual prowess, and today placement exams are major life events that determine future prospects for high school and college students. On international standardized tests Chinese students routinely outscore their western counterparts in math and science. Today there are more Chinese people studying English than there are people in the rest of the world whose first language is English. Around 100,000 foreigners are currently studying Mandarin and other subjects across China in universities that have begun generating the same level of respect as those in the West. Foreign children living in China now have multiple international schools to choose from in every major city. Living in a new country and learning a new language is tough, but we think students of all ages will find China's educational opportunities quite rewarding.

© STUART STROTHER

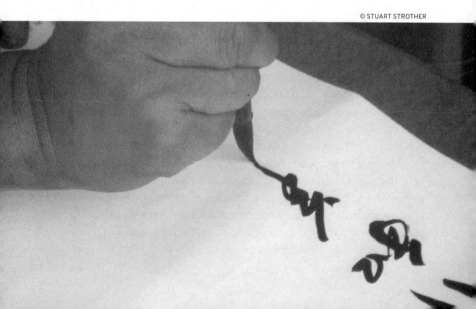

Learning Chinese

If you're like most expats who've decided to move to China, one of your biggest concerns may be how you will communicate. Chinese is one of the most difficult languages in the world to learn—but that doesn't mean it's impossible. The written characters seem incomprehensible at first, but after some study you'll easily recognize many of them based on their pictographic roots. How can you forget that 三 means three? Thankfully, Chinese grammar is also very simple. It follows the same subject-verb-object pattern as English and there are no fancy verb conjugations, irregular verbs, or difficult past and future tenses. With enough study and practice, anyone can successfully learn to speak, read, and even write Chinese. An American friend of ours is frequently asked by perplexed locals, "How did you learn to speak Chinese fluently? Isn't it too difficult to learn?" He always replies, "Well… you learned it, didn't you?" If a billion Chinese people have proven that it's possible to learn Mandarin, then there's hope for the rest of us.

Most Chinese will not expect you to be able to speak with them, so they'll be surprised and delighted if you can communicate beyond simple greetings. Putting forth the effort to use their language sends a powerful message of respect and goodwill. And because language and culture are intricately tied together, the more Mandarin you know, the more you'll understand the culture of the Middle Kingdom.

If you took three years of college-level Chinese classes and learned everything, most people would consider you fluent. The benefit of learning in college is that you'll learn all four language abilities: speaking, listening, reading, and writing. Textbook smarts and street smarts, however, are two different things. Whatever classroom instruction you receive should be supplemented with real-life conversations with native Chinese speakers. This will help you with your pronunciation and you might even learn some idioms and the latest slang words. Most westerners who are fluent in Chinese got that way only after studying Chinese in China diligently for at least two years.

HOW MUCH CHINESE DO YOU NEED?

How much Chinese you need to know depends on where you'll be in China, what you'll be doing, and how long you'll be there. If you are in Beijing, Shanghai, or Hong Kong, there are so many English speakers that it's possible to get by without learning much Chinese at all, especially if English is the language of your workplace. We know a few expats who've had the luxury of living and working in an expat enclave in China for over ten years and have never learned to communicate beyond a simple thank you or excuse me. We also know quite a few expats who were extremely motivated and achieved conversational fluency after only two years in China.

If you're just going to be in China for a short-term assignment, you should strive to learn at least "survival Chinese," just enough to shop, eat out, travel, and make a little bit of small talk. After survival Chinese, you might strive to be fluent in "phrasebook Chinese," meaning you've learned all the words and phrases in a typical traveler's pocket phrasebook.

If you're making a long-term career move, however, then you need an aggressive study plan that will move you toward proficiency as quickly as possible. Expats who speak Chinese make thousands of dollars more than those with the same skills and no language ability.

WRITTEN CHINESE
Characters

The written Chinese language is universally understood by those who speak Mandarin, Cantonese, or any of the other Chinese dialects. Many of the characters are also used in Korea, Japan, and Vietnam. There are about 3,500 simple Chinese characters, which can be combined to form at least 10,000 additional complex characters. For instance, combining the simple character for "person" (人) with the character for "tree" (木) results in a complex word (休) that means "to rest." In this example the Chinese language makes sense because a tired person would certainly find rest under the shade of a tree. Chinese characters originated from pictographs, and if you look carefully at the characters above, you can see the resemblance to a crudely drawn stick man and a tree. Notice that when these two simple words were combined, their form changed slightly so they could more easily fit together. Chinese words are designed to fit inside a box shape.

When separate words are combined to form a complex character, the individual parts are called radicals. Radicals hint at the meaning of the word, the pronunciation of the word, or both. Modern dictionaries list about 200 radicals, which are arranged according to the number of strokes. The character for "person" (人) has two strokes, while the character for "big" (大) adds a third horizontal stroke, making it look like the person is now stretching out their arms to show how big the fish was that got away. Incidentally, the strokes always start at the top left and work their way down to the bottom right. If you want to give your calligraphy teacher a major

© BARBARA STROTHER

practicing calligraphy

headache, go ahead and make the strokes out of order. In the example above the radicals are side by side, but they can also be on top of each other. Plenty of words combine more than two radicals, such as 众, which means "crowd"—this is easy to see because the word is made up of three radicals that individually mean "person." In Chinese, just as in English, three's a crowd.

Nowadays Chinese characters on a page are mostly written starting from the top left then moving horizontally to the right, just as in English. But beware that sometimes the characters are written vertically from the top to the bottom, or even horizontally from the right to the left. Just when you think you're getting the hang of things you'll come across some tricky writings like these.

Simplified Characters

Back in the 1950s and 1960s, the government mandated that many written characters would be simplified to have fewer brushstrokes. Previously a complex character such as 愛, meaning "love," required 14 brushstrokes to write. The simplified character, 爱, requires just 10 brushstrokes. Supporters argued that simplification would promote literacy. Critics claimed that simplification would dumb down the language. For instance when the word for love was simplified, the 心 radical meaning "heart" was eliminated. They complained, "How can you have love with no heart?" Simplification was adopted in the mainland and eventually in Singapore, but those in Hong Kong, Taiwan, and Macau still use traditional characters. The foreign community is perhaps the greatest beneficiary of simplification because written Chinese is now less difficult to learn.

Pinyin

Unlike English words, you can't sound out the pronunciation of Chinese words just by looking at them, so the pinyin system (literally meaning

HOW ABOUT A CHINESE NAME?

You'll need a Chinese name when living in China. You'll use it to fill out some documents, and people will have something to call you. It's not every day that many of us to get to choose our names, but before you go crazy, there are some conventions to know.

Chinese names most often consist of three syllables. The family name comes first, followed by one or two words that make up the given name. For the family name, foreigners typically choose a traditional Chinese family name that sounds like their English last name. Given names in Chinese can be just about any two words, but you should pick a cool name that describes you or sounds like your English name. One of the easiest ways to find a Chinese name is to look for the way your name has already been translated in Chinese – if you share your name with someone famous, most likely there's already a Chinese translation.

Stu became "Situ" after watching the movie *Stuart Little*. Situ also happens to be a respected family name in China, similar to the way the surname "Kennedy" demands respect in the States, and this made the name a great choice for doing business in China. Barbara discovered "Ba Ba La" after buying a pair of Barbara Brand shoes in China. Because it is not a Chinese name, it sounds foreign and strange to the Chinese, but this made it easy for Barbara to recognize her name in Chinese conversations when she was a novice at Mandarin.

In addition to considering the meaning of the name and how closely it sounds like your English name, you also may want to weigh in how complicated the characters are to write. You'll have to use your Chinese name on some documents, so if you're not comfortable with the script, you'll want to choose characters that don't have strokes that are too complex to memorize. Before finalizing your selection, run it by a few Chinese people to make sure the name isn't too cheesy and to make sure it's not a homophone for something offensive.

"phonetic spelling") was developed to help foreigners learn how to pronounce Chinese words. When we ignorant foreigners see 你好 we have no idea how to say it, but if we see the pinyin, *ní hǎo,* then we can give it the old college try. A pocket phrasebook with English, Chinese, and pinyin is an invaluable tool to help you start communicating like an old pro. You'll see pinyin next to the Chinese characters on street signs and product labels, and sometimes the pinyin spells out some pretty funny English words, such as *maxipuke,* the pinyin name of a brand of popular playing cards.

For a person who just wants to learn to speak Chinese without learning to read and write, pinyin will serve them well. We don't recommend this approach, however, because knowing how to read and write the characters is a crucial step not only toward language literacy, but also toward cultural literacy. Besides, learning the characters can be a lot of fun, like solving a puzzle or deciphering a secret code.

Writing with Computers

Computer software can now easily handle Chinese characters with programs such as NJ Star. With NJ Star you use a keyboard to type in the pinyin pronunciation of the word, then you'll be given many characters to choose from that match your pinyin entry. Some websites will allow translating between English and Chinese, such as Alta Vista's Babelfish site (http://babelfish.altavista.com). For a variety of language tools, including a searchable dictionary of more than 30,000 words, check out www.mandarintools.com.

SPOKEN CHINESE

When a Chinese word is written in pinyin, the diacritic marks above the vowels tell the speaker which of the five tones to use when pronouncing the word. The first tone is called the flat tone, signified by a flat line above the vowel, and it sounds a little high-pitched, like a man trying to imitate a female voice. The second tone is called rising because the pitch rises at the end of the syllable, such as when a person says "yes?" in response to a knock on the door. The third tone is the difficult tone that falls then rises, like when a person hears an unbelievable bit of gossip and responds "what?" The fourth tone is the falling tone, which sounds like you are impatient or angry. The fifth tone is a relaxed pronunciation and is mostly reserved for the last word of a sentence. It may seem a bit confusing, but

THE FIVE TONES

In Chinese, a single sound can have different meanings depending on the tone. Check out the different meanings for the sound "ba."

Pinyin	Character	Meaning
bā	八	eight
bá	拔	to pull out
bǎ	把	to hold something
bà	爸	pa, dad
ba	吧	an auxiliary word that functions like an exclamation point

don't fret—with time, practice, and exposure to native speakers, it will eventually come naturally to you.

The Chinese language has a huge number of words that have exactly the same sound, which is the source of an incredible amount of frustration for those of us trying to learn the language. For instance, the word for "kiss" is pronounced *wěn* and written 吻. The word for "mosquito" is pronounced *wèn* and written 蚊. In this example the words have different diacritic marks, but in a normal conversation you may struggle to figure out which tone was used.

Some words have exactly the same sound and tone but different meanings. In this case the context of the conversation determines the meaning. For example, the sound *wěn* can also mean "to cut one's throat." So if your sweetheart offers you a *wen,* we hope you can figure out by the context of the conversation (or at least by knowing the current status of your relationship) whether you're being offered a kiss, a mosquito, or to have your throat cut.

CHINESE GRAMMAR

Learning to speak and write Chinese is much more difficult than most other languages, but thankfully the grammar is much simpler. The basic sentence structure is the same as used in English: subject-verb-object. In Chinese there are no irregular verbs, such as in English where the past tense of "go" is "went." In fact there are no verb conjugations or verb tenses at all. To ask a question, just add 吗 (*ma*) at the end of your sentence; similarly, to make a verb past tense, you just add the 了 (*le*) particle after the verb. If you don't know how to say a word's opposite, you just add the word 不 (*bù*) before the word. For example, if you know how to say "good" (好, *hǎo*), you can then just say 不好 (*bùhǎo*) to mean "bad."

WHICH CHINESE?

When most people say Chinese, they mean Mandarin, a label that signifies this is the language spoken by the mandarins, the scholar bureaucrats who ruled imperial China for two thousand years. But the Chinese call Mandarin "Putonghua," which literally means "the general language." In mainland China most people speak Mandarin because it's the official language, used in public schools, though every region has its own local dialect as well.

In southern China most people speak Cantonese as their first language. There are eight major dialect groups within China including Cantonese

LANGUAGE COMPARISON

Area	Official Spoken Language	Preferred Spoken Language	Written Language
Mainland	Mandarin	Mandarin	simplified
Hong Kong and Macau	Mandarin	Cantonese	traditional
Taiwan	Mandarin	Mandarin	traditional
Singapore	Mandarin	Mandarin	simplified

(also known as Yue, which is spoken in Hong Kong, Guangdong, Guangxi, and Hainan), Wu (spoken in Shanghai, Zhejiang, Anhui, and Jiangsu), Xiang (spoken in Hunan), Minbei (spoken in Fujian), Minnan (spoken in Hainan and Taiwan), Jinyu (spoken in Shanxi, Shaanxi, and Henan), Hakka (spoken by a nomadic group who settled in southern China), and Gan (spoken in Jiangxi and Hubei). A large number of the overseas Chinese migrated from southern China, so Cantonese and Hakka are commonly spoken in Chinatowns around the world.

WHERE TO LEARN

If you're serious about becoming fluent, you should enroll in regular classes that are held more than once a week.

Before You Leave

If possible you should start learning Chinese in your home city before moving to China. More and more western universities now offer 2–3 years of Chinese classes, or you can sign up at one of the language schools that can now be found in virtually every major western city. Berlitz, for instance, has language schools in over 50 U.S. cities.

University Programs

The best way to achieve fluency is to enroll in a university program in China. You'll have to make financial sacrifices to do this, but it will be well worth it. At least one university in each large city has a Mandarin language program for international students.

Language Schools

You'll also find privately run language schools that cater to foreigners. You

learning Chinese calligraphy techniques at Zhejiang University

© STUART STROTHER

can enroll in a group class or sign up for individual one-on-one instruction. Some crash courses are as short as 10 days, but most classes meet two or three times a week for a month. If you don't know any Chinese at all, after completing an intensive one-month beginner's course you'll know about 250 words. This isn't too bad considering you need to know about 800 words for basic daily life, but you're nowhere near the 3,000 needed to read a newspaper. Language schools come in all shapes and sizes, so you should be able to find one that meets your needs. Foreigners who enroll in a school tend to learn at a much more rapid pace than those who just study on their own. The formal class setting provides structure and people tend to be motivated to work hard at something after they've invested money in it.

Language Partners

An alternative to language school is to find a language partner. It can be more convenient and there's usually no expense involved. Most language partners expect you to help them with their English half the time, and then they'll help you with Chinese for the rest of the time. Be careful, though, because a lot of the so-called language partners have ulterior motives such as having you help them get a visa, a job, or even a lover. Since there are many more Chinese than foreigners who want to partner up, you can afford to be choosy. If you're not learning from your partner, move on until you find someone you click with.

HSK

The Hanyu Shuiping Kaoshi (HSK) test is a Chinese-language proficiency test. Just like Chinese students who take the TOEFL test before studying in the United States, foreign students take the HSK to be placed at the appropriate level within a Chinese university. Foreign workers use their HSK scores to prove their Chinese-language ability to prospective employers. There is a preliminary level and then three official levels scored on a scale of 1 to 11. Elementary is 1–3, intermediate is 4–8, and advanced is 9–11. A minimum score of 6 is required to be admitted to study in a Chinese university program taught in Mandarin. You can take the test in China or at a number of overseas locations.

General Education in China

The Chinese school system is structured very much like the U.S. system, with elementary, junior high, and high schools. Beyond that, there are universities, some of which allow foreign students to enroll, and technical schools.

The official school calendar is established by the central government each year and typically begins around September 1, ending around July 15 for summer break. The other major break is for Chinese New Year/Spring Festival, which typically runs January 15–March 1.

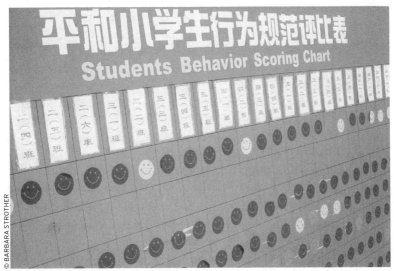

© BARBARA STROTHER

In many Chinese schools, behavior is graded like academics.

COLLEGES AND UNIVERSITIES

China's higher education system consists of technical schools and universities. The tech schools prepare students for careers in fields such as manufacturing, cosmetology, and cooking, while the universities function just as in the United States. There is no community college or junior college system, but some private schools are filling in the gap, such as the Australian Informatics College. Unlike the universities, the private schools often don't require minimum test scores.

More than 50 Chinese universities accept foreign students. Beijing is the top destination for most, with Qinghua and Beida Universities at the top of the list. Shanghai is the second most popular study city, and Fudan and Jiaotong are the preferred schools. Another popular choice is Zhejiang University in Hangzhou, China's largest.

Students come from all over the world and study just about every topic including the arts, agriculture, and traditional Chinese medicine, but Mandarin remains the most popular. You needn't know any Mandarin to enroll in language classes; you can start out in a beginning class. Most foreign students who plan to study other subjects often start out with a year or two of Mandarin first.

A 2004 *China Daily* article estimated the number of foreign students at 86,000, with 35,000 from South Korea, 16,000 from Japan, 7,000 from the United States, and 6,000 from Europe. The article predicted the number to grow to 120,000 by 2008. Many of the universities have built modern dorms to house foreign students, and some have even housed them at local hotels because they lack the appropriate space on campus.

The Chinese university system is almost identical to the U.S. system, with bachelors, masters, and doctorate degrees awarded. Be aware that at this point in time, a degree from a Chinese university may not be recognized by a western employer, and credits from a Chinese university might not transfer into a western university.

As in the United States, the academic calendar consists of a fall and spring semester, and most schools also have intensive summer programs. Admission is typically limited to the fall semester, which generally start around September 1, so you'll need to apply in the spring—you'll need to submit your completed application before the end of June at the latest.

The cost for one year of undergraduate study at Beida is a minimum of $6,000. Tuition is about $3,000. If you live on campus, your dorm room (if you can get one) will rent for around $1,200, and you'll shell out another $1,200 for the cafeteria meals (if you can survive for a year eating

Chinese school lunches). Realistically, you'll need a few thousand more for traveling and for the psychological benefits of having a western meal once in a while, not to mention all the karaoke and discos your classmates will drag you to.

Foreign Universities

While living in China, it's also possible to take courses from a number of foreign universities that have alliances with Chinese universities. The alliances could be as simple as just exchanging a couple of students or professors each year, or as complex as a joint-venture agreement with permanent facilities. The China Europe International Business School in Shanghai, which offers the highest-ranked MBA in Asia, was formed through such a partnership. Johns Hopkins University has a permanent site in Nanjing, and Penn State offers classes in multiple Chinese cities. In Ningbo, the University of Nottingham has built a large campus. So while living in China, it is possible to further your education through a university with accreditation that is recognized in the West.

ELEMENTARY AND SECONDARY SCHOOLS

Because both parents typically work in China, the children start their schooling in a preschool (called "kindergarten" in China) as early as two years old, unless the grandparents are able to watch the children. There are quite a few private English preschools available, whether run by foreigners or Chinese. At six years old, every child is required to be enrolled in elementary school, which lasts until age 12. Junior high follows and lasts three years. The kindergarten, elementary, and junior high schools are assigned based on where the child lives, but at the end of junior high, a rigorous standardized test determines which high school the child will attend. Do well on the test and a child will surely be invited to a "good" high school where he'll be prepped for college. Have a bad test day and he or she might be relegated to trade school and perhaps a life of mundane factory work and low wages. After high school, students take another exam that determines which university they'll be admitted to, if any. Those who perform poorly on the exam can't attend college and will be off to trade school and eventually the factory floor.

With the exception of a few small fees for books and the like, public education through high school is free for locals, though foreigners will have to pay a nominal fee to enroll their children.

International Schools

Unlike some foreign posts where home-schooling is the only option for expat children, there are top-notch international schools in every major expat destination in China, typically covering preschool or kindergarten

---

AN INTERVIEW WITH TIM AND BETTE KRENZKE
INTERNATIONAL SCHOOL TEACHERS

For more than eight years, Tim and Bette Krenzke have worked at Concordia International School Shanghai (CISS), where Tim teaches 1st and 2nd grades and Bette teaches kindergarten. Before moving to China, Tim and Bette were university professors in the United States. Although they had no previous international experience, Tim and Bette were able to fulfill a lifelong dream of working overseas when they learned of an opportunity to help start a new school. Today CISS has grown to 700 students, and Tim and Bette consider Shanghai their home. When you look into their happy, sparkling eyes, it's easy to see how much these two love what they do for a living.

What were your impressions when you first arrived, and how have they changed over time?
In the beginning we were quite scared because of all that we had read about China, but we quickly learned that what we had read was either outdated or plain wrong. We have grown to appreciate Chinese culture and understand why things work the way that they do. We're quite impressed with the planning and achievement of goals that the government is making, and citizens are beginning to enjoy the benefits of those accomplishments. There is a genuine desire among the Chinese people to take their rightful place in the world. On top of it all, we are living in one of the safest countries in the world! We have come to love China and will always think of it as our second home.

How does teaching in an international school compare to teaching in the States?
The best part of teaching in an international school is the families who send their children to us. We primarily have families who are intact and who have one parent dedicated solely to supporting their children's education. One of the biggest disadvantages is that there are no teacher stores here, so you have to be willing to make a lot of teaching aids yourself.

What have been some of the greatest struggles living in China?
One of our greatest frustrations at first was expecting everything to work just the way it did in the United States. That isn't going to happen! You have to say to yourself, "It's not better or worse, it's just different." Once you accept the differences, you are in for the time of your life! It takes everyone almost 4-6 months to adjust to these

up to 12th grade. The English-language schools tend to follow either an American or British curriculum, with the latter often offering the International Baccalaureate college-prep program. The student population at the international schools is incredibly diverse—when our children attended

differences, but once you can consider this your home as well, you know you have arrived.

What have been the greatest rewards?
Getting to know people from all over the world. We now have met people from every continent, and many of them keep in touch through email, even though they are no longer in China. Another reward is getting to travel to places that we only dreamed of seeing.

What encouragement would you give to parents of school-aged kids who are considering their first move overseas?
Kids are resilient and adjust much more quickly than adults do once they are settled in school, so choose a school that is consistent with your philosophy of education. (You do have a lot of choices in large cities like Shanghai!) Bringing things with you that make your child – and you! – feel at home in the new environment will help the adjustment time. Even more importantly, if a spouse stays at home, he or she has to get out of the compound and pursue personal interests. The working spouse and children adjust more quickly than the at-home spouse, so it is vital to keep active and stretch his or her comfort zone.

Any last words of advice?
First, learning Chinese is essential, not only to communicate and get around, but also to make contacts with the Chinese people. You will be richly rewarded with wonderful memories of people whose faces light up when you say just a few simple words. Second, try not to get too spoiled. If you're located in a major city like Shanghai, you'll enjoy a standard of living that is way beyond what you would ever have in the United States. Take time to do something for the people living around you. There are still many needs in China, and expats can make a tremendous difference if they get out and look around for ways they can be of service.

Tim and Bette Krenzke

COURTESY OF TIM AND BETTE KRENZKE

an international school in Shanghai they had classmates from more than a dozen different countries. Unfortunately, current Chinese government regulations only allow those with a foreign passport to attend the international schools, so your children probably won't have too many local Chinese classmates unless these rules change.

There are plenty of advantages to putting your kids in an international school. For one, your children's classmates will come from families of diplomats and business leaders, so you won't have the typical parent worries about gangs, violence, drunk driving, and so on. It's been our personal experience that the teachers have better qualifications than what we've experienced in the public schools in the United States. It's not uncommon for an elementary school teacher at an international school in China to have a doctoral degree, and quite a few of the teachers are seasoned veterans who've decided to finish out their careers on the international scene. Another advantage is that the schools regularly put on community events that will give your family the opportunity to get plugged into the expat community. The main disadvantages of international schools are the high price, which can approach $20,000 per student per year in the most prominent cities (though cheaper locales will be closer to the $10,000–15,000 range), and the lack of integration with the local Chinese community.

Most international schools want to increase their enrollment, so they offer the kinds of programs that parents value to compete for new students. Many of the schools offer after-school programs and clubs in art, music, drama, and especially sports.

Local Schools

You can also enroll your children in a public or private Chinese school, which will cost considerably less than the international schools. Your children will probably excel in math and science and will quickly learn Mandarin. Be aware, however, that if your child can't speak Chinese, the adjustment process will be quite stressful for your littlest ones. Since most Chinese schools start teaching English very early on, your older child may have classmates who can converse in English. However, other than the English teachers, not many other teachers or staff members will speak English.

Private schools in China follow the same division of ages and grades as the public schools in China. Many of these private schools are semi–boarding schools, where the kids stay on campus all week but return home to their parents on the weekends. This is true for all ages, even some preschools, though boarding is not required.

ELITE WORLD CITIZENS OF HIGH CALIBRE
精品　高素质　国际化

© BARBARA STROTHER

DAILY LIFE

Private Chinese schools strive to produce top-notch students.

While the cost of attending a Chinese school will be nowhere near what you'll pay at the international schools, you'll still have to pay fees for books, meals, and administration. These fees will be nominal for public schools but are much higher at private schools, where you may pay a quarter to a half of what you would pay at an international school in the same city.

It is quite rare for expats to send their kids to public school in China, as most fear that their child would receive an inferior education. In a private school you are much more likely to find top-notch teachers and more western educational values (such as creativity and a rich learning environment) than in public schools, which often focus on rote memorization and have dismally blank concrete walls. Hong Kong's schools are the exception, however. There are also a handful of mainland public schools, primarily located within special economic and development zones, that enjoy a good reputation among the local community. If you are interested in considering public school, you'll want to tour the facilities during a school day to see firsthand if this will work for your family.

Home-Schooling

Home-schooling has grown in popularity around the world, which gives families the freedom to travel extensively and spend more time interacting with a foreign culture.

HEALTH

In many ways the Chinese have a much healthier society than Americans. At a time of day when most Americans are hitting their snooze button, many Chinese are hitting their local park for tai chi exercises and ballroom dance practice, followed by their daily commute by bicycle. Chinese meals are often high-vegetable, low-meat, low-sugar affairs that keep the cholesterol and the weight down. And traditional medicine shops do a brisk business in dried snake, seahorse, and ginseng root, believed to work wonders for one's vitality and longevity.

Adopting a traditional Chinese lifestyle may add a few years to your life, but there are plenty of influences that will take away from it as well. Diseases tend to float around rural China with fluidity. Food-borne illness can leave you running for the squat pot a little too frequently. And if contaminated food doesn't do you in, the traffic might. Nevertheless, when you need it, you'll find adequate health care available, from international medical facilities in major cities that employ only western doc-

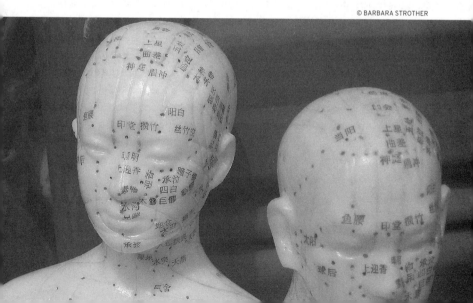

tors and imported drugs, to inexpensive local public clinics where your antibiotic prescription may come with a few vials of murky green traditional medicine. And if a health situation proves too serious for the local facilities, medical-evacuation choppers offer transportation to the nearest place that can help.

Hospitals and Clinics

The greatest horror stories you'll ever hear about China are about what happens behind hospital doors. Nowadays most of the stories about recycled needles and contaminated medical environments are simply urban legend, though substandard and even harmful health care does still exist in places without foreign influence. The best way to keep from becoming one of these horror stories is to do your research. Look around the facility, ask lots of questions of the staff, and seek out reviews of other foreigners who have firsthand experience.

The health facilities in China's prime cities can be divided based on their management, whether foreign-run (including joint-venture facilities) or domestic-run (including both private and public facilities). The public system is further divided into district-based clinics and city-based hospitals, many of which have VIP wards for foreigners and wealthy locals.

If you find yourself in need of specialist care, many medical facilities (both foreign and domestic) have specialists on staff that they will bring in as needed. China also has numerous small hospitals that specialize in one area of medicine, which you will be referred to if your situation demands it.

FOREIGN-RUN HOSPITALS AND CLINICS

Hospitals run by foreigners are the most expensive option for health care in China, but they are also the most trustworthy. You'll pay dearly for their services, so you'll want good insurance first. A procedure at an international facility can regularly cost more than ten times the same procedure at a public hospital. Fortunately the international health institutions are more likely to accept your insurance (check first!), so you won't have to pay out of pocket and wait for reimbursement. Some of these facilities also require membership before you can take advantage of their facilities.

Hospitals and clinics that are wholly foreign-owned are typically staffed by expatriate doctors; joint-venture facilities are often managed by a foreign company but staffed by foreign-trained Chinese personnel. There

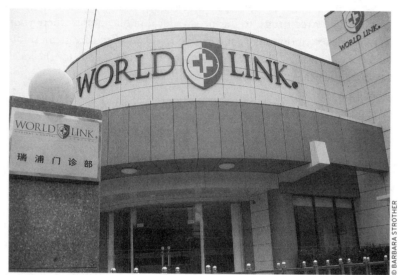

the Worldlink Clinic in Pudong, Shanghai's primary foreign-run health system

shouldn't be much difference in medical treatment between the two, but philosophy of practice can differ greatly, such as how much information to give a patient or to what degree a patient is allowed to make choices in their treatment. Staff at foreign-run hospitals and clinics will be fluent in English; they may also speak a variety of other languages. You'll find several foreign-run hospitals and clinics in China's biggest cities, though smaller key cities may have just one or none at all.

DOMESTIC-RUN HOSPITALS AND CLINICS

Any foreigner can take advantage of the public hospitals and clinics in China, paying the same amount as the locals do to get the same treatment. These facilities do not take appointments; just show up and join the waiting crowd. You'll pay the basic fee when you arrive at the registration desk, then pay again before each test or treatment you require. You'll have to contact your insurance company later for reimbursement. Fortunately an increasing number of hospitals in larger cities are now accepting credit cards for payment.

Chinese medical care often includes the choice of western or traditional Chinese medicine. If you prefer Chinese medicine alone, most towns have hospitals that are solely dedicated to it, though just about any Chinese doctor at any medical facility in China can (and will) prescribe a traditional option in addition to his western recommendations.

Be aware of the cultural differences in medical practices between China and the West. Chinese doctors often refuse to supply copies of medical records, lab results, or X-rays. Some have been known to strongly discourage patients from seeking a second opinion, and refuse to listen to requests from patients concerning their own treatment. While domestic-run health care can be a bargain, you might pay for it in lack of service-oriented professionals.

Rural hospitals can be as backward as the backwoods they're located in. Foreign residents in smaller cities tend feel more comfortable traveling to the closest larger cities for treatment, while others prefer to head directly to Hong Kong's trustworthy medical facilities for all their health needs. You'll have to judge your situation for yourself to determine what options you are most comfortable with.

City-Level Hospitals

Public city-level hospitals are thought to offer better overall medical service than the smaller district-level clinics. They keep advanced and specialized medical equipment and prescription medications. Some also offer VIP wards (called *gaogan bingfang*), where you can pay extra to be treated in a comfortable private room with English-speaking staff more attentive to your needs. In fact, foreign medical firms like Global Doctor run clinics in many of these VIP wards. Though the docs are often still Chinese and have a Chinese way of doing medicine, they will be thoroughly western trained. You'll get sound medical care, but you may not get the autonomy we enjoy in the United States, such as the ability to make your own decisions about childbirth methods.

District-Level Clinics

District-level clinics offer the convenience of being close to your neighborhood and having much shorter wait times than larger hospitals. A typical visit at a district-level facility, such as a check-up or minor ailment, should only take 10 or 20 minutes, whereas visiting a city-level hospital for the same reason could take three or four times longer. Fees are less at your local clinic, though so will be the amount of English spoken. Some expats make the mistake of dismissing this option before checking it out, but you never know when you'll find a nearby doctor you like who speaks English and is thoroughly trained. If your ailment is more complicated than a simple cold or rash, however, you should go directly to a city-level hospital with more advanced technology.

OTHER TYPES OF CLINICS

By the looks of some Chinese smiles, you might think that there are no dentists in China. On the contrary, whether or not the locals choose to take advantage of them, China has many fine dental and orthodontic services, often charging a small fraction of the cost of their American counterparts. Many large hospitals include dentists and orthodontists, as well as other specialists such as ophthalmologists. Major cities offer eye-care centers with western-trained professionals; some cater specifically to English speakers.

CHOOSING A MEDICAL FACILITY

We recommend checking out all the options in your area before you actually need them. You'll want to confirm that gloves are always changed between patients and needles always come from sealed packages, and make

TCM 101: A PRIMER

You pick up a pack of normal-looking pills at the local pharmacy labeled "stomach care tablets." But hidden in the fine print, the active ingredients include starfish, ginger, oyster shell, and a few obscure roots and rhizomes. Welcome to traditional Chinese medicine, a.k.a. TCM.

In the States, TCM has a reputation of being strictly an alternative therapy, but in China it is an integral part of the modern health care system. You'll likely have ample opportunity to try a little of this 3,000-year-old folk medicine while there; here's a little basic information to get you started.

THEORIES

Five Elements: All of your body's organs are associated with a specific element, such as wood for the liver, fire for the heart, earth for the spleen, metal for the lungs, and water for the ears. Medicinal herbs are also similarly categorized. If an herb causes dry skin, it would be called a "fire" herb. To control the "fire" ingredient you'd add a "water" ingredient; to help a "wood" problem in your body, you'd take a "water" herb.

Meridian System: In TCM, the Meridian system is made up of lines that show the connections between organs and other areas of the body. If an acupuncturist puts a tiny needle into one point on your body, it is believed to benefit the other parts of the body that lie along the same meridian.

Yin-Yang: a belief that all things should be balanced, represented by the popular black-and-white symbol. To have optimal health you must reach your balance point, and certain foods are believed to do this. While Asian ginseng helps your Yang, American ginseng helps your Yin. Dried duck gizzards, on the other hand, will balance out the Yin and Yang of any recipe.

sure you don't see anything with blood on it left sitting around. You'll also want to know how the hospital is managed, such as what types of payment and insurance are accepted, if you can specify which doctor you would like to see, and how long the typical wait time is. Find out what they charge for visits and for a few common medical procedures. The U.S. Embassy's website (www.usembassy-china.org.cn/us-citizen/medical.html) lists recommended medical providers by city and includes some listings for dental, orthodontic, and ophthalmologic clinics.

If you'll be working for a Chinese employer who is providing health benefits, check to see if they require that you use a specific facility. If you would prefer to not use their choice, be sure you are aware of the financial consequences of using a different facility. When we worked at a Chinese school, we were able to take advantage of the school's own clinic for most of our medical needs, such as common colds and immunizations for our

DIAGNOSTICS

TCM practitioners are trained in observing subtle changes in the body, and may examine your tongue, ears, and face, the tenderness of your abdomen, how you smell, or how your voice sounds. Then they'll classify your symptoms into external or internal, yin or yang, cold or hot, and psychological or physical, and prescribe a treatment plan accordingly.

TREATMENTS

Acupuncture: The practice of sticking tiny needles into various points of your body to stimulate healing. Some swear by it, others just swear when getting it.

Moxibustion: Instead of needles, herbal leaves are burned on or near a point along the body's meridian system to stimulate acupuncture points.

Herbs and Food Therapy: A mixture of natural ingredients to fit your specific needs. Classical mixtures come in all forms: pills, syrups, plasters and liniments, tablets, liquid extracts, and tea infusions, as well as foods to add to your dinner menu to get your *qi* back in balance, such as bird-nest soup for beautiful skin and strong spleen, and apricot kernels for the lungs. Seahorses alone are beneficial for the kidneys, circulation, swelling, frequent urination, wheezing, and impotence – the Viagra of the sea.

Qigong, Tai Chi, Chinese Martial Arts: The Chinese martial arts serve as exercise but more importantly focus on balancing your *qi*, your internal energy or life-force, performing physical movements that bring a certain sense of spiritual balance.

© BARBARA STROTHER

Maybe these critters contain your cure!

kids. When we had problems beyond their scope, they would refer us to the district clinic or tell us which city hospital could best help us. At our nearby district clinic, our helpful doctor spoke English, the wait time was low, and the fees were minimal. The city-level hospital, however, proved both time consuming and difficult to find answers to our questions, though the facility was quite clean and modern.

When you've decided which health facility to primarily rely on, be sure to keep their business card in your wallet. In an emergency, you'll want it to show a taxi driver to get you to your hospital. Don't bother waiting for an ambulance to take you there; ambulances in China do not come with sophisticated medical equipment and the drivers often have no medical training.

Insurance

Currently China has no uniform system of private health insurance, so you'll want to make sure you are adequately insured prior to your move to China. Many U.S. policies do not cover services received outside the United States. If your insurance does cover Chinese medical expenses, you will typically have to pay up front and file for reimbursement later, though foreign-run hospitals may take your insurance.

You'll want to make sure that your insurance policy covers emergency medical evacuation, since it can cost well over $50,000 should you need it. Check your policy for psychiatric treatment as well, since stress and depression are common among expats as they learn to adjust to a new environment without their close friends and family nearby.

You may consider choosing a provider that includes the services of SOS International. As the world's largest medical assistance company, SOS maintains relationships with over 150 hospitals across China that they have approved for treatment of foreigners, as well as the Chinese military and commercial airlines to arrange for medical evacuation when needed. Their convenient 24-hour hotline operators can answer medical questions and recommend where to get quality medical assistance in any corner of the nation (see *Resources*). For those who will not be covered by insurance offered by an employer, you can buy a personal SOS membership with the option to add travel insurance as well as expatriate medical insurance or study abroad medical insurance. You can also buy a one-week SOS membership for one of their half-dozen clinics just when you need it most.

If you are thinking of saving money by not carrying any medical insurance, here's the situation. If during the time you are in China you will only suffer very minor ailments, such as colds or the occasional rash or stomach flu, and you don't mind going to the cheap local Chinese clinics, you could save a ton of cash. On the other hand, if you find yourself with a serious medical situation (such as injuries resulting from one of the frequent traffic accidents), you'll have to pay upfront for all the expensive tests and treatments. If you can't pay, you may have a very difficult time getting the medical attention you need. And if it's serious enough to warrant a medical evacuation to better facilities in Hong Kong or the United States, let's just say we hope you have a very, very wealthy uncle, one who loves you dearly.

Pharmacies and Prescriptions

You shouldn't have to walk far to find a pharmacy in China. In most cities you'll find one every block or two, marked by a green cross. You can also pick up medications at hospitals and foreign health clinics, both of which charge more but have stronger safeguards against the possibility of getting counterfeit medications. The foreign clinics will carry the imported medications you are used to, but you'll pay much more for them than you would back home. On the other hand, many common Chinese medications (even prescription drugs) sell for just a few dollars.

AT THE PHARMACY

Finding a pharmacy may be easy, but finding English in that pharmacy will not be. You'll be lucky to find one that keeps a bilingual medical dictionary, or that has any staff who can speak a lick of English, let alone medical terms. Fortunately many of the Chinese medications will have the drug's generic name in English on the box, although all directions and precautions will be in Chinese. When you do find the drug you need, be sure to keep the box to show it to the pharmacy the next time you need it.

A typical pharmacy sells Chinese versions of western medicine.

© BARBARA STROTHER

The process of getting prescriptions filled in China is similar to what you would expect in the United States, except it is solely paper-based. You'll need your doctor in China to give you a prescription paper, which you will then take to the pharmacy (no computerized records of prescriptions are available, and don't expect to have your doctor call in a prescription for you). Chinese pharmacies will not recognize a prescription brought from your home country; you'll have to take that prescription to a local doctor to obtain a new Chinese prescription.

Pharmacists can help diagnose basic medical symptoms and prescribe over-the-counter medications. Unless you already speak Chinese, the trick will be in how to communicate your symptoms, and how to know for sure that the pharmacist has understood you correctly. A pharmacist's advice is best sought for ailments that are visual, such as rashes. Better yet, just bring a bilingual friend with you to translate.

OVER-THE-COUNTER DRUGS

Chinese pharmacies carry over-the-counter medicines that are similar to what you'll find in the States. If you are partial to a certain brand, however, you should bring it from home. Your local convenience store and supermarket may also carry a small amount of over-the-counter medications, but don't expect the variety you see in similar stores at home.

It used to be that many drugs requiring prescriptions in the United States were available over-the-counter in China, a convenient way to avoid having to go to a doctor if you knew all you needed was an antibiotic. With recent changes to the law, many of these drugs now require a prescription, although you can sometimes find a pharmacy that will sell them to you if you agree to sign a waiver releasing the pharmacy from any responsibility for your risk.

AVAILABILITY OF PRESCRIPTION DRUGS

If there is a prescription you know you will need while in China, you should verify its availability before you go. If you have a membership with one of the medical services for foreigners such as SOS, Worldlink, or Global Doctors, check with them before you go. Some medications are not yet available in the mainland, but just about anything can be picked up in Hong Kong. Some common prescription drugs, such as birth control pills, are available over-the-counter in China, though you may have a hard time locating them in smaller or more remote cities. It is best to assume that you won't be able to get the medication you need and plan accordingly. If you decide to bring a stock of your needed drug with you, be sure to keep the original prescription handy in case you are stopped by customs.

DAILY LIFE

© BARBARA STROTHER

preparing natural prescriptions at a traditional-medicine pharmacy

HERBAL MEDICINE

If you are interested in trying traditional Chinese herbal medicine, look for a pharmacy that specializes in it. You'll know them by their jars of brined snakes and ginseng on display.

Diseases and Preventative Measures

China has plenty of diseases floating around, though most can be avoided by using vaccinations and a healthy dose of wisdom.

VACCINATIONS
General

As with any travel, you should make sure your diphtheria, polio, and tetanus immunizations are current before you leave. Vaccination requirements and recommendations specific to China should be obtained from your doctor or the Centers for Disease Control (www.cdc.gov, 877-FYI-TRIP) for up-to-date information. As a general rule, immunizations for Hepatitis A and B are recommended. Hepatitis A, caught through contaminated water or food and poor sanitation, is quite widespread, and China is considered high-risk for Hepatitis B, spread through contaminated blood, needles, and syringes.

Tuberculosis (TB), spread through respiratory droplets, is a prevalent problem throughout China. The vaccination is only recommended for children younger than five and adults at very high risk since it prevents serious complications of the disease but may not protect you from getting TB in the first place.

Rural or Subtropical Areas

Typhoid is not an issue in China's modern cities, but if you plan to travel off the beaten path, poor sanitation and contaminated food and water may put you at risk. The vaccine is only needed if you'll be spending considerable time in rural areas.

Japanese encephalitis is a threat in rural areas and is also carried by mosquitoes. Although very rare, the disease can be quite deadly, especially to children; on the other hand, the immunization is quite expensive. We were fortunate to get the vaccine free for our children at the Chinese school where we taught; you may also want to wait until you get there and try a Chinese hospital for a cheaper vaccine. (Don't try this with the most important vaccines, however, since you risk not being able to find a hospital that carries them.)

Malaria, spread by mosquitoes, is only a threat to those bound for Hainan Island or southern Yunnan Province. If traveling or staying in these areas, you'll want to protect yourself from mosquito bites.

If you'll be arriving in China from a country that has Yellow Fever, Chinese immigration will require proof of immunization before they'll let you in.

SARS

The Severe Acute Respiratory Syndrome (SARS) outbreak of 2003 was a scary time for people around the globe, but none so much as the residents of China. SARS originated in China and rapidly spread around the world via airline travelers, infecting over 8,000 people and killing over 800 in 33 countries. The threat has passed and China has been declared SARS-free for the moment, but a single case can lead to another outbreak. After being sufficiently shamed over the initial outbreak, the Chinese government has put a rapid detection system in place that should protect them from a similar outbreak happening in the future. Scientists around the globe are currently working on producing a SARS vaccine that should be widely available within the next couple of years.

AVIAN FLU

Avian Flu, a.k.a. Bird Flu, is a deadly disease that is passed from infected fowl to humans mainly through contact with body fluids, such as when butchering an infected chicken or coming into contact with bird feces at a live animal market. From 2003 to 2006, about 200 people contracted the disease and more than half of them died from it. Most cases of bird flu have occurred in Vietnam and southern China. Medical science experts are concerned that if the virus mutates into a form that is easily transferred between people, there could be a pandemic that would leave hundreds of thousands dead in its wake around the globe.

At the time of writing, both China and the United States claimed to be in an advanced stage of testing effective vaccines, though no vaccine is currently available to the public. A drug called Tamiflu is believed effective in treating it, which has led many governments to stockpile the drug in case of a pandemic. China is not currently stockpiling Tamiflu, though in the case of a national outbreak, they are prepared to manufacture the drug themselves, disregarding international patent laws. Ironically, Tamiflu is created from ingredients that come from China and are used in traditional medicine, such as star anise.

The best way to protect yourself from bird flu at this point is to simply avoid contact with live birds, including any water or surfaces that could become contaminated by infected birds. Eating poultry, as long as it is well cooked, poses no threat.

AIDS

The first reported case of AIDS in China was in 1985. In twenty years, that one case has grown to an estimated 840,000 HIV/AIDS patients, according to China's government statistics (meaning the number may be much higher if you factor in unreported cases). Among China's infectious diseases, AIDS now ranks fourth in number of deaths, and that number is rising. Many of the initial cases were a result of contamination through poorly managed blood donations; nowadays the disease is mostly spread through sexual interaction and dirty needles.

The best precaution against AIDS (as well as Hepatitis B and C) is to avoid the activities associated with these diseases, such as unprotected sex and drug use. Be aware that the quality of Chinese condoms can be dangerously less than American standards. You should also safeguard yourself from contaminated blood by refusing any needle or syringe that was not opened from a sterilized package in your presence, and perhaps even bringing your own needles and syringes if you'll be spending time in rural areas without modern medical care. If you are already HIV-positive, the Chinese government doesn't even want you to bother coming. Chinese law prohibits anyone "suffering from mental disorder, leprosy, AIDS, venereal diseases or other infectious diseases" from entering the country. While you may be able to slip in on a tourist visa, you'll be required to get an HIV test if you'll be in China longer than six months.

Environmental Factors

MOSQUITOES

They are annoying. They buzz around your ears in the dark and their bites make you itch like mad. And in the rural backwaters of China, mosquitoes can also give you potentially fatal diseases like malaria and Japanese encephalitis. Even in the city mosquitoes can get into your house, hotel room, or college dorm, coming in through the drains if you keep your windows closed. Luckily there are several ways in China to keep the little buzzers at bay.

For walks in the woods or along waterways, keep a travel-size can of bug spray with DEET handy. Inside your home or hotel room, China's plug-in repellents with replaceable pads work wonders. We cannot verify that the chemical they emit won't be hazardous to your health, however, since they aren't available yet in the United States. One cool bug-repelling device that sells for less than $2 is a battery-operated bug zapper that resembles a plastic tennis racket—except the metal strings have an electric charge. It kills flies and mosquitoes mid-air with a satisfying pop as their small bodies go up in a tiny flame. While good at killing bugs, this racket is not, we discovered, a good way to play a trick on a friend by daring him to touch the electric lines, unless you like to see grown men cry.

FOOD AND WATER

Any travels overseas invariably include some sort of trouble for the tummy, and China is no exception. Caution must be taken to wash all fruits and vegetables, especially since human manure is still used as fertilizer in some parts of China. Lettuce and leafy vegetables that hide stubborn dirt can be placed in a quart of water with a couple drops of bleach; rinse with drinking water before consuming. Overall it's good to follow the standard advice of, "Wash it, boil it, peel it, or forget it."

DIRTY FOODS

When we returned home from China, it wasn't the immense beauty or the ancient culture that I missed most – it was the food. Not just any food; the dirty food. Food of dubious origin sold from the back of a bike by illegal street vendors, food from grungy little two-table "restaurants" down dark alleys. *Dan Chao Fan* (Egg Fried Rice) never tasted as good as when it was made in a wok that was due for its annual washing.

A trip to China would not be complete without savoring some of the delicious and dirt-cheap sidewalk foods, such as grilled lamb kebabs, tea-boiled eggs, spicy squid-on-a-stick, and roasted sweet potatoes from mobile drum-barrel ovens. Nonetheless, extreme caution should be taken. Look for food that is cooked over a flaming fire or sizzling griddle while you watch, not pre-cooked. Stay away from meat that has been sitting out in the sun or exposed to flies. Be sure that any foods kept in water, such as pineapple-on-a-stick, has not been soaking in tap water; if in doubt, buy a bottled water and give the fruit a thorough rinse before you indulge. And if you are concerned about the cleanliness of your chopsticks or bowl, use hot tea to do a quick rinse.

Tap water is not recommended to drink in China, and in fact, most Chinese don't drink the water. The problem with tap water isn't so much bacteria as it is chemicals and minerals, such as lead. You shouldn't have a problem with using the tap water to wash vegetables or brush your teeth. For drinking water, bottled water is available everywhere. Hotels provide each room with bottled water and a daily thermos of boiled water. Apartments come furnished with water dispensers, and new bottles will be brought to your door with a quick phone call to the management company. Ordering cold water at restaurants will typically get you either a bottle of mineral water or a glass of water that has come direct from a bottled water dispenser (though if you are in a smaller city or rural area, we wouldn't recommend drinking a glass of water of unknown origin).

Traveler's diarrhea does happen in China, but not nearly as often as you would expect. The truth is, in this country so focused on starches (with rice, noodles, or dumplings at every meal) more foreigners experience problems with constipation than the runs. If it comes too quick, eat more rice and drink some tea. If it doesn't come at all, boost your intake of fiber and water and get some exercise—or down a couple of venti lattes at your nearest Starbucks, now found scattered throughout every major Chinese city. One of our colleagues drank tap water in small quantities daily in the hopes that its contaminants would help her stay more regular.

THE ELEMENTS

China is a land of extremes, and those extremes can take their toll on your health. Heatstroke and sunburn are common in areas as diverse as the tropical south, arid northwest, and the intense sun of the high Himalayas. On the other extreme, hypothermia and frostbite are possible in the frigid northern winters and the high elevations of China's dramatic peaks. Altitude sickness is a serious problem in Tibet that can be fatal if precautions are not taken. Use wisdom to protect your health in all of China's natural extremes; sunblock, hats, and plenty of liquids to protect from the sun; adequate warm clothing and gloves to protect from the cold; and rest when your body is telling you to slow down.

POLLUTION

China claims the infamous distinction of having 16 of the 20 most polluted cities in the world. Efforts to improve the situation, like locating factories beyond the city limits, are unfortunately offset by increased car ownership, trading vehicle emissions for factory emissions. Beijing and northern industrial cities struggle most with pollution, though no city is immune; even the smallest mountain villages can produce a fair amount of dirty air when coal is used for heating and cooking. Some days the pollution indexes (which are reported daily or weekly by the media in most major cities) exceed the World Health Organization's maximum level by three or four times.

If you already have heart or respiratory problems, you may have a very difficult time adjusting to the air in China's cities. To contradict the effects of the air pollution, use a humidifier and an air purifier, try to keep your home as dust-free as possible (not an easy task!), and keep plenty of green plants around to pump fresh oxygen into your air. If you long for a deep breath of the good stuff, drop by one of the oxygen rooms offered at some hospitals, hotels, and serviced apartments (though Beijing doctors recommend that you don't leave your home at all when the city's pollution index is soaring).

SMOKING

Factories and vehicles aren't the only ones polluting the air in China; smokers are playing their part as well. This is a nation with a serious nicotine addiction problem. One third of all cigarettes smoked per day worldwide are smoked in China, and 3,000 Chinese die every day from smoking-related diseases. As the top pro-

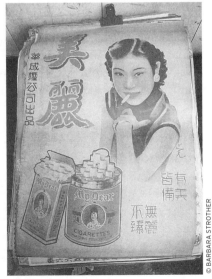

ducer and consumer of cigarettes, China is blowing a lot of second-hand smoke. Fortunately the government is starting to do something about it. Some cities are starting to follow Shanghai's lead to ban smoking in public places, such as schools, supermarkets, teahouses, restaurants, cinemas, public transportation, and, long overdue, hospitals (where, incidentally, 60 percent of doctors smoke). Unfortunately, though the laws are on the books, little is done to enforce them. If, on the other hand, you are a smoker, you'll still find plenty of freedom

Smoking is a widely accepted social practice in China.

in China—not to mention cigarettes so cheap and plentiful that it makes nonsmokers wonder if they should start the habit just to take advantage of the bargain.

SPITTING

Regardless of the numerous No Spitting signs, fines for lawbreakers, and even anti-spitting squads, almost everyone spits in China. Male, female, young, old; you'll hear them hocking up loogies all around you. It's not only disgusting (especially when you lean up against something and come away with a green glob of goo on you), it's also the means for spreading tuberculosis and SARS. On its par is the frequent "farmer's blow"—holding one nostril closed to blow the contents of the other nostril onto the ground below. There's not much you can do about the spitting and the blowing, of course, except be careful where you walk, sit, swing your arms, and rest your bags. And don't forget to wash your hands frequently.

Safety

ACCIDENTS
Traffic

They say in China the most dangerous thing you can do is walk across the road. With 600 fatalities and 45,000 injuries due to traffic every day in China, crossing the street (or riding in a taxi, or hopping on a bus, or pedaling your bike down the road) is not to be treated lightly. Use the growing number of pedestrian overpasses and underground crossings to get to the other side of a busy street; their entrances are sometimes hidden inside a nearby shopping mall. It takes some time to learn to cross a street like the Chinese do; the best way to maneuver it is to wait for a group, putting the locals between you and the oncoming traffic.

Household

In addition to traffic dangers, expats face a greater chance for household accidents in Chinese houses and apartments. Sometimes gas appliances are not sufficiently ventilated resulting in a build up of lethal carbon monoxide, and there have been American citizens who have died in their Chinese homes because of this. Pack a carbon monoxide detector with you before you come, and make sure you have good ventilation when your appliances are installed.

It goes without saying that no matter where you live, in your home country or abroad, you should always keep smoke detectors and fire extinguishers in good working order throughout your house. Create a fire-escape plan for the whole family and do a few trial runs until everyone is comfortable with the routine. Pick a meeting place outside the scope of potential danger. In China the emergency number to reach the fire department is 119; ambulance/medical emergency is 120 (though taxis are faster).

NATURAL DISASTERS AND OTHER CATASTROPHES

Trains collide, airplanes crash, earthquakes destroy, political unrest breaks out, and wars start. We sincerely hope that none of these catastrophes will touch you during your time in China, and chances are they won't. Nevertheless, you should be prepared for the worst. The best thing you can do to help yourself and your family in the chance of such a major event is to register with your embassy or consulate (see the *Once You've Arrived* section of the *Making the Move* chapter for more information). If they don't know you're there, they can't warn you of rising political unrest, or advise you of when is the right time to get out of the country. If they know you live in the area hit by a natural disaster, they'll be eager to make sure you are okay.

CRIME

Foreigners are seldom the victims of violent crime in China. The country as a whole has a low crime rate. Most expats feel safer in China than in their hometown; just knowing that in China individual gun possession is unheard-of makes a huge difference. The most crime you'll need to worry about in China is pickpockets, con artists, and other scammers. The riff-raff of China don't want to hurt you; they only want to share your wealth (with or without your consent). Take the usual precautions to guard your money and your belongings, and be wise when it comes to doing business on the streets. If you do find yourself the victim of a crime, dial 110 to get the local police (a.k.a. PSB, Public Security Bureau), or just chalk it up to experience. Major cities staff the 110 call center with English speakers.

If, on the other hand, you are the law-breaker, watch out! Playing with the communist government is a very foolish thing. Don't assume that because you are a westerner, the worst they will do is deport you. They have the right to sentence you to the same punishment a Chinese offender would receive. There are currently hundreds of foreigners serving prison terms in China, many for economic crimes like tax evasion and fraudulent business deals, as well as selling pirated DVDs and other counterfeit goods. But serious crimes, including drug trafficking, can be punished by the death penalty, and foreigners have been executed in China for such activity. In a country where even white-collar crimes like government corruption are punishable by public execution, you just don't want to get on their bad side.

a nimble little police car in Nanjing

© BARBARA STROTHER

Crimes Against Women

As a female traveler, I've had my bottom pinched by Russians and my lips kissed by an Argentine I had just met. I've been propositioned in Costa Rica and frisked by a passing Turk. I've had a family in Iran insist I sleep in their compartment to protect me from the single men on the train. But in all my time in China, I have never been inappropriately treated by a male. While caution should always be exercised, most American women feel much more comfortable walking alone after dark in China than they would anywhere in the States.

The majority of crimes against women in China happen within the context of relationships. China has been on the slow end of believing that date-rape is truly rape, and instead tend to consider it simply a private matter between the couple. Domestic violence is a serious problem in China, especially in rural areas, but this won't affect you directly unless you are a single woman—or man, for that matter—who is in a serious relationship with a Chinese national.

CHILD SAFETY

If you're off to China with kids in tow, there are a few safety concerns you should be aware of. To start with, many of the most basic safety restraints that we would never live without in the West aren't even available in China. Seat belts are ubiquitously absent in the back seat of taxis. Infant car seats can be purchased, but will be quite impractical unless you have your own car or a regular hired car-and-driver at your disposal. Bike helmets and protective sports pads are also difficult to find because the Chinese don't use them.

One of the best things about living in China with kids is the abundance of children's activities. Tiny cars, mini merry-go-rounds, blow-up bouncing rooms, obstacle courses—all these and much more can easily be found as your family explores a city. But before you give in to the desperate pleas of your little guys, take a second to look things over. For one, equipment is just not maintained in China; you never know when something will break. Call me overprotective, but I would never let young children ride a roller-coaster at any Chinese-run amusement park. For two, just because someone calls it an activity for kids does not mean that you can trust it to be safe for them. When we agreed to let our boys try a park's archery range, we didn't realize the arrowheads were razor sharp. And for three, the Chinese aren't great at taking safety precautions. You'll find plenty of pedal boats and bumper boats on ponds and lakes, but you won't find any life jackets.

Child abduction is not a common problem in China. Though your kids will probably not be taken from you, you might very well misplace them. The swarms of pushing crowds in busy areas can easily separate you from your children. Stay close, keep emergency contact info on your child at all times (hidden in a shoe or sewn into a coat or backpack), and be sure your older ones know exactly what to do if they can't find you. We always discuss a recognizance plan with our kids before subway rides on the off chance that we get separated while trying to enter or exit the train. Luckily China is a place that adores children, especially foreign ones. Most kids that go missing are eventually found having a grand old time with a group of delighted Chinese adults.

Tourism can pose additional threats to kids. We once spent two days cursing ourselves as foolish parents as we hiked up and down Yellow Mountain with our three-year-olds (nobody told us we'd be on the edge of slippery sheer cliffs the whole time!). And I can still feel the fear when I remember taking them on a sightseeing ski-lift ride in Nanjing where one wiggle could have slipped them through the bars and sent them dropping to the treetops below us. In both cases we didn't realize the potential life-threatening danger to our children until we were past the point of no return. It won't take too many harrowing experiences like these before you'll get a good feel for what is appropriate for your kids.

Travelers with Disabilities

If you are a person with a disability and are considering a move to China, you will want to think long and hard about that decision. China has only recently started to entertain the idea of building with persons with disabilities in mind. Though there is a much stronger push now to provide wheelchair-accessible facilities, they are currently very few and far between. Photos in train brochures show beautiful attendants pushing smiling elderly men in wheelchairs along the station platform, but you won't find enough space to maneuver a wheelchair on most trains, nor accessible bathrooms. Stairs are everywhere in China; elevators are rare. Even the most popular tourist destinations such as the Forbidden City and the Great Wall have not bothered to make a way for the tourist with disabilities.

When you do find the rare accessible facility, it will often have a less-than-politically-correct translation, such as the wheelchair ramp recently noticed marked "pathway for deformed man." The Chinese also have a cultural tendency to unabashedly stare and point and ask strangers questions that make westerners uncomfortable. It takes a very strong and even stubborn person to face the physical and emotional difficulties of living in China with disabilities.

EMPLOYMENT

Thirty years ago, the first expatriate workers in China were English teachers employed by the universities. Today teachers still make up a significant part of the expat workforce, but the opportunities for foreigners wanting to work in China have widened considerably thanks to the economic boom that Deng Xiaoping's reforms in the 1970s triggered. Foreign-owned and Chinese companies alike are hiring expats with skills in sales and marketing, engineering, management, and other areas. And these days teaching doesn't just mean being an English teacher; instructors for international schools are in higher demand to teach the children of all the expats bringing their families. Whether you work for a local firm or an international firm, are an executive or a teacher, you should expect your time in China to be both extremely rewarding and extremely frustrating. If you have a good attitude and can maintain your sense of humor, working in China will give you the kind of cross-cultural experience that today's globally-minded employers value.

© BARBARA STROTHER

DAILY LIFE

The Job Hunt

Expatriates working in China will have vastly different experiences depending on whether they work for an international or a Chinese employer. Generally speaking, the international companies, schools, NGOs, embassies, and the like treat their employees according to labor customs in the home country, while Chinese employers follow local human-resource standards, which might mean lower pay and less-generous benefits. In recent years, however, the Chinese have been rolling out the red carpet as well as they can to keep their foreign workers happy, but the red carpet just isn't as plush as the carpet rolled out by the international firms.

BUSINESS
Where to Look

The best place to find a job in China is to use your personal contacts who work for a company that needs someone with your exact skill set. If you aren't blessed with such *guanxi,* then I suppose the Internet will do. American and multinational companies advertise heavily on www.monster.com, while Chinese companies tend to use www.zhaopin.com, but you might need a little Mandarin to navigate that site. If you're already in China, you can also check out the classifieds in your city's English magazines. Such listings are more likely to be part-time or contract work and much less likely to include a nice employment package, such as free housing or paid travel for your return trip home.

What Employers Want

Foreign-Invested Enterprises, as international firms are called, employ about 85 percent of the expat workforce who aren't working as teachers. About 40 percent of the jobs have been in sales and marketing; about 20 percent in engineering; 10 percent in management, including accounting and finance; and IT jobs make up about 5 percent. The typical FIE has high-priced expats at the top while the hourly employees are most likely to be locals, especially in manufacturing. Companies doing global business will staff their front office (sales, marketing, etc.) with expats while the back office and operations will be locals. Foreign companies desiring to sell their products in local markets often hire senior managers from the local labor pool.

Early on expats primarily worked for foreign firms, but more and more are hiring in at local firms, even the State-Owned Enterprises. About

15 percent of the non-teaching expats work for Chinese companies, primarily employed as engineers or managers in high-tech manufacturing firms.

To a business, the ideal expatriate worker has the right mix of hard skills, soft skills, and language skills. Hard skills in demand include technical skills (including both IT and complex manufacturing processes), financial skills (including CPA credentials and expertise with GAAP), international marketing skills, and legal skills, especially lawyers familiar with international trade laws. Of course, having a college degree is an important step in gaining hard skills and more than 90 percent of expatriates have college degrees and quite a few have advanced degrees.

Having the right hard skills and credentials may land you an interview, but the soft skills like flexibility, maturity, people skills, and cross-cultural competency are what will help you secure a job offer, especially sales and marketing jobs that entail regular communication with Chinese customers. Not everyone can cope with the stress of living and working in a cross-cultural setting, so lots of expats end up going home before their contracted time is up. The expat "failure rate" for China has been reported to be as high as 70 percent. Human resource personnel know the average Joe won't cut it in China, so expect to be scrutinized heavily before being offered the job. Employers want someone who can project a positive image for the company and they certainly want to avoid the expense of sending an employee home early.

Having the right mix of hard skills and soft skills will qualify you for an excellent job in China, and promotions and pay raises will come quicker and easier than you'd expect back home. But if you want to start out ahead, the best thing you can do is learn Chinese. The best-paying jobs require a conversant level of Mandarin. Positions that require Mandarin fluency listed on websites such as www.monster.com tend to pay as much as $30,000 more than the same job without the language requirement. Even if you aren't quite fluent, any Chinese language ability will be beneficial in this job market.

The Hiring Process

Like any job search in today's Internet society, you'll probably apply for jobs in China via email, hopefully followed by phone interviews. If you are applying for a position with a major corporation, you'll have a series of in-person interviews and probably undergo a few weeks of training before being sent abroad. Because this gets expensive for the company, they often prefer to hire from within, unless the position requires a high skill level that you happen to fulfill. Management- and executive-level hiring will probably be handled by a third-party HR firm, not the actual employer.

Landing a job with a Chinese firm will be done via email and phone. The company probably won't fly the candidate to China for the interview; they prefer to fill these positions with people who already live in China. But for high-level or high-skill positions, an international HR firm in the United States might do the hiring.

Working for an International Employer

Expat compensation from an international employer can be quite generous because you might qualify for more than one type of pay. First, the base pay is given according to the normal wages in the home country. Cost-of-living allowances might also be offered (even if you're able to get by on less). And you might even get the "hardship" pay, especially if your destination will be outside the key expat cities of Hong Kong, Shanghai, and Beijing. Expats who work for international firms are typically paid 125 percent of the typical salary in the home country. Additional incentives can be earned (such as bonuses and stock options) for achieving productivity measures. If you're really lucky, you'll be promoted before you go, with the possibility of higher pay. And let's not forget the legendary benefits package that you might get including luxury housing, health and life insurance, travel, a few more days (in some cases, weeks) of vacation, private car and driver, and private-school tuition for the kiddies. Many expat compensation packages are no longer as generous as they were in the good ol' days, but working for an international employer can still be an excellent way to go.

Working for a Chinese Employer

Chinese employers won't even come close to offering the same lucrative packages that international businesses offer, but they'll still pay you more than they'll pay their own countrymen. You might expect to earn one-and-a-half to two times the amount a local would earn in your position. In addition, many Chinese employers will provide free housing, cafeteria meals, Internet access, travel bonus money, and reimbursement for your airplane fare, among other little perks.

TEACHING
Where to Look

English teaching jobs or university teaching jobs tend to be filled via email and telephone contacts with the school directly or through a placement

关注每一个学
理解每一个学

TO LOVE, CARE AND
UNDERSTAND STUDENTS.

© BARBARA STROTHER

Private high schools can be excellent places to teach.

agency. To search for English teaching jobs on the Internet, try www.
teach-in-asia.com. Some agencies, like Appalachians Abroad (based at
Marshall University) match teachers with Chinese schools, provide pre-
departure training, and only charge a modest fee for the service. On the
other end of the spectrum, some organizations, particularly those with a
religious affiliation, provide the same placement service but require that
their teachers raise a significant amount of funds prior to placement in
a Chinese school. Since these organizations typically provide teachers
to Chinese schools under a volunteer or a low-pay arrangement, these
funds will pay your living and travel expenses as well as health insurance,
training, and ongoing support from the organization.

International school teaching jobs tend to be filled at the major job
fairs each year in London (February and May), Vancouver (February),
and Fairfax, Virginia (June). Candidates need a government-issued public school teaching certificate and should plan on attending the fair to
participate in on-site interviews. To search for international school positions on the Internet, try www.tieonline.com.

What Employers Want

English teaching jobs typically require that you are a native English speaker and have a college degree—any subject will do, it doesn't have to be in English (yeah, they're desperate). American English is preferred, but the Queen's English will suffice. To land a position teaching English at a top university, you'll probably need a TESOL certificate. Having a master's degree isn't necessary to get a teaching job but it will earn you anywhere from $100 to $500 more in monthly salary. English teachers have primarily worked in the colleges, but quite a few high schools and middle schools have started hiring foreigners as teachers now. There are also now a fair number of jobs at the new private language schools. Just be careful though, because a lot of these schools are new, unregistered, and unproven, so they might not provide you with stable employment.

To teach subjects besides English at the universities, you'll probably need a master's degree, and more and more they want PhDs for full-fledged professorial work. Most of this work is still compensated according to local standards, which is still enough to live on in China, but nowhere near what a college prof would earn in the States. If however you are a highly regarded scholar who can bring prestige to the school's reputation, you'll be compensated according to international standards. At Zhejiang University, for instance, they recently shelled out $1,000,000 to hire a Nobel prize–winning scientist for the summer.

Teaching at an international school in China is an excellent option for those that already have U.S. teaching credentials. The schools are run according to the standards in the home country, so if you have the appropriate college degree, and a teaching certificate from any U.S. state, you're qualified to teach at an international school. Because the school pays for the teachers' housing, they prefer to hire husband and wife teams.

English-Teaching Contracts

An English-teaching contract is a short document that specifies the teacher's workload and the compensation provided by the school. The contract will probably be signed by the school principal and faxed to you while you are still in your home country. Although the contract is a legally binding document, it's impossible for the teacher (and the school) to know whether the other party will fulfill their promises, so you should check their references first. If the school is legitimate, then they'll be able to put you in contact with people who have previously taught there. That way you can find out what you're getting into before you make the plunge.

A typical contract will specify the number of teaching hours; 15 is considered full-time, but if you have a higher salary, you might be expected to go up to 20 hours or more. To first-time teachers, that doesn't sound like much, but you'll still have plenty of non-classroom work filling your schedule including grading, lesson planning, meetings, and participating in events like English Corners.

The contract will also specify the teacher's monthly salary, which should be paid for the 10 months that you'll be teaching and the 11th month when you'll be traveling and/or returning home. A good contract will also specify that the pay is "after tax," meaning that the school will pay your income tax separately rather than deducting it from your salary. On a one-year contract schools pay for round-trip airfare; for less than a year, they may pay half or less. Since some teachers have been known to leave before the contract is fulfilled, the schools prefer to reimburse you for half of your ticket when you start, and then pay you the other half when you finish teaching. Your contract should also specify free private or shared lodging, health care, cafeteria meals, and travel bonuses.

Perhaps most importantly, your school should provide you with the necessary paperwork to get a Z work visa. If they tell you, "just come over on a tourist visa, and we'll work it out when you get here," you take the risk that the school may be unregistered and you'll be an illegal worker. On the other hand, since your Z visa will be tied to your specific employment, coming on a tourist visa buys you and your employer a little time make sure the arrangement will be a good fit for both of you. To stay legal, however, you should have the Z visa in hand before you actually start your regular teaching schedule.

All the items above should be clearly spelled out in your contract, but it's unlikely that all of your other questions might not be fully answered, such as "Will I have broadband Internet in the room, or will I have to use the library?" or "Can I eat three meals a day in the cafeteria or just lunch?" Keep in mind that most English teachers do the work as a one-year adventure rather than a permanent career move, so they don't mind a little bit of uncertainty in the contract. As long as the contract is satisfactory to you and the school has good references, you should be fine. On the other hand, the Internet is filled with stories of teachers who were victims of a bait-and-switch scam, where their salaries were lowered, or they were housed in tiny dormitories, or their airfare wasn't reimbursed, and so on. To avoid getting scammed, consider using a proven placement agency, and always check the references.

Employment Laws

To enter China you need a letter of invitation, visa, health certificate, and work visa notification letter. Once you get the letter of invitation from your employer, you can apply for the appropriate visa (see the *Visas and Residence Permits* section in the *Making the Move* chapter). If you have obtained a job while in China on a study or tourist visa, you'll have to get your visa changed before you start work. If discovered working on a tourist visa, you'll face serious consequences including a fine and possible deportation.

Labor laws, set by local governments, typically limit the workday to eight hours, and the workweek to 44 hours, but these laws are not regularly enforced. With the exception of prison labor, employment is "at will," meaning workers are free to quit their job if they feel underpaid or abused. A recent *Businessweek* article points out that as China continues to grow as the workshop of the world, the newest problem isn't worker abuse but a labor shortage. There are so many factories demanding more and more labor that workers are now able to command higher wages. Nonetheless, without a minimum wage or independent labor unions (which are illegal), some workers are not well protected from exploitation, though this is more of an issue for low-skilled local workers than foreigners.

FOREIGN EXPERT STATUS

Back in the 1970s and 1980s foreigners in China were openly charged higher prices than what the locals paid. When China started opening up to the outside world, some astute bureaucrat realized that the dual pricing system might be a significant hindrance to attracting foreign talent to come work in the Middle Kingdom. Rather than eliminate the dual pricing system altogether they decided to grant preferential treatment to the "foreign experts" while still sticking it to the fat-cat tourists. So the experts were issued the "foreign expert" cards that look like thin red passports. The cards are supposed to allow the expert to receive part of their pay in foreign currency and generate discounts at hotels, and on bus, train, and airline tickets, but these economic benefits are pretty rare nowadays. The government issues the cards directly to the employer and when you leave your job you are supposed to turn it back in to your boss.

DISCRIMINATION IN HIRING

HR managers in the United States work extremely hard to keep their companies out of costly discrimination lawsuits, but since Chinese society is not as litigious, Chinese employers are more open to discuss topics that are taboo in the United States. A job posting from a Chinese company might specify the ideal age and even list some of the personal characteristics they prefer. Don't be surprised if you find a job posting like, "tall beautiful single women wanted as account managers." In fact, most Chinese employers require that you submit a photo with your application.

If an employer asks your age they are probably interested in a person with a certain level of life experience. If the employment ad notes a married person with children is desired, that indicates that the employer is looking to hire someone who will stay in the position for a long time. If you are a young person who is newly married you might be discriminated against because the employer fears you'll miss lots of workdays when the babies come.

Such discriminatory hiring practices are more likely to occur with a Chinese firm than with an international firm. Hiring practices at an international company would typically follow the same laws and customs of the home country.

MOONLIGHTING

We've met quite a few foreigners doing business in China whose original reason for visiting China was for some other purpose, especially studying or teaching. There are an unlimited number of opportunities to cash in on your English-language skills or the foreign way you look (unless, of course, you're of Asian heritage). Don't be surprised if you are stopped on the street and offered work as a movie extra, model, translator, narrator, or tutor. Although blue-eyed blonds tend to be the more sought-after as subjects for the camera, even Asian foreigners can get acting gigs when studios need someone who is a native English speaker.

You should be able to make some good pocket money if you can pick up some moonlighting work. Our kids were once paid to play with pool toys; the resulting photos were used on product packaging that would eventually make their way to Target stores in the States. A couple of Russian girls we know were paid $1,000 per day to do high-fashion runway modeling in Shanghai, even though they had no previous modeling experience (their height and long blond hair helped). Some employers request that their workers not moonlight, though many expats find ways around this, justifying it by their need for the extra dough.

Self-Employment

A few brave expat souls are seeking their fortunes as entrepreneurs in China. In such a booming economy where the heavy hand of government does not easily enter into the expat community, starting a business in China can be a rewarding experience. Of course the big money is being made by western manufacturing companies who have opened factories in China to take advantage of the cheap labor. But what about the little guy? Are there small business opportunities in the Middle Kingdom? You bet.

The difficulty with wanting to start a business in China is that if you aren't already there, you'll have no employer to get you a work visa. The best way around this is to get a "starter" job, or even register for a semester of classes as an exchange student, either of which will give you your entry visa. Then, once you are there, you can work on the legalities of getting your visa type switched when you need to—it's easier to do it in person.

BUSINESS OPPORTUNITIES
Expat Services

With the western expat community in China fast approaching a quarter of a million people (most of whom live in just the three biggest cities), some of the best small business opportunities focus on serving this niche market. These people need help finding and setting up households—consequently a thriving new relocation industry has sprung up focusing on the needs of expats. They also have diverse shopping needs (where can you get Pampers in Xi'an? Or orange marmalade in Xiamen?), and a number of imported-items stores have opened up for business specializing in the things expats crave and are willing to pay for. And without the comforts of home, for-

HIRING LOCALS

Quite a few expats hire locals for services including domestic help, drivers, *kuai di*s (couriers), language tutors, and the occasional construction worker to help with repairs or remodeling around the house. All of this employment is customarily handled off-the-record, without the formalities of work permits, taxes, and the like. And the workers prefer it this way since many of China's laborers are unregistered workers from the countryside who don't possess official work permits for employment in the big city. And don't worry about what may seem like very low wages – expats tend to pay more than market wages, and unregistered workers are earning much more than they could back home.

DAILY LIFE

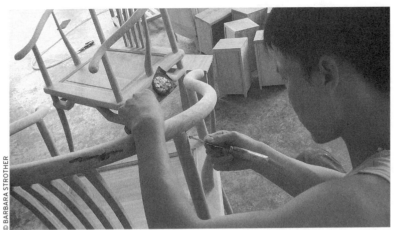
A carpenter custom finishes a traditional-style chair.

eigners are also desperate for entertainment and comfort food. Some expat entrepreneurs have found success opening places for expats to hang out and have a beer and a cheeseburger or a western-style breakfast.

Another expat need that seems unmet is in professional services. Expats in China often don't know where to go for legal advice, document notarization, or to have a will drawn up. How about a marriage? Or a divorce? And how about all those American companies that need advice on how to break into the Chinese market? A westerner with legal and business savvy could do quite well running a small business helping foreign residents and businesses accomplish these tasks.

Language or Cultural Services

Another wide-open business opportunity is serving the Chinese population who are interested in your language and cultural expertise. Your native English-language ability might be your most marketable skill in China. With a little bit of business savvy, opportunities in tutoring, translating, or acting/modeling could certainly be developed into viable businesses. We once ran a micro-business recruiting English teachers to come to China to work in Shanghai high schools. If you want a quick start, check out the Internet advertisements for English-language schools that are up for sale. Why not jump right in?

STARTING A BUSINESS

Once you've decided to take the entrepreneurial road, your next decision is whether to be an upstanding, law-abiding citizen and register your business,

AN ENTREPRENEUR'S LIFE
AN INTERVIEW WITH MARK SECCHIA

Although most business expats in China are working for "the man," some have found success going it alone and forging their way as small business entrepreneurs. When Mark Secchia was required to do an internship for his MBA at China Europe International Business School in Shanghai, he decided to use the opportunity to start his own business instead. With fundraising and business plan in hand, he and a few colleagues founded Sherpas, a service that delivers meals from Shanghai's gourmet restaurants to their customers' front doors.

Mark knows what it's like to take on the difficult task of starting up an entrepreneurial venture in China. Weathering the China challenges, Sherpas now has more than 60 employees and delivers meals from more than 80 restaurants. Ever the entrepreneur, Mark has since started a second business, Plastic Film Sourcing (PFS), which exports hundreds of millions of Ziploc-style bags to customers throughout North America.

What first brought you to China?
I first visited in 1989 back when Americans couldn't even use Chinese money — we had to use special tourist money. The place was exciting, cheap, dusty, crazy, loud, and confusing. But I moved to China because of love. Not because of my (eventual) love for the country, but because my girlfriend moved here to teach English, and I followed. It was only supposed to be a one-year trip, but nearly 10 years later, we are married and still here.

What gave you the idea for Sherpas?
My wife and I would both get home at about 8 P.M. on weekdays. We didn't really like to cook, so we ordered a lot of deliveries. At that time, it was only Chinese food and pizza that were available for delivery. So we started calling other restaurants, and most of them said the same thing: They don't do delivery, even though lots of people ask for it. So I saw the supply and the demand and figured there was a market for it.

What have been the biggest challenges of running a small business?
In 1999, opening a company was a lot more difficult than it is now. Just trying to understand where to register the office and how to handle the administrative details was a nightmare. Now there are dozens of companies that can do it for you for a few thousand dollars. Back then there were only a few, and their fees were much, much higher. So to avoid the high fees, we actually stood in the lines and got the permit approvals ourselves. It was a long, very confusing process. Once we got up and running, the actual food delivery part of our business was the hardest part to solve. Getting the order correct, not shaking it up, not tipping it over, not letting it get cold — they were all very difficult to do. Our couriers were not used to understanding the importance of food presentation and how important it was for the food to maintain its temperature. Sounds trivial, but it almost killed us in the beginning.

Can you give us some idea of the financial aspects of starting a business in China?

It took us 18 months to get cash-flow positive. I started losing my hair and gaining weight around month number 12. It is a big responsibility knowing that our staff was living on their salaries month-to-month, and we needed to get cash to them every month. The staff was fiercely loyal to me and the company, and if I could not pay them for it, it would be the biggest failure of my life. It actually took about four years before I could start to pay back my investors. In my business plan, I thought it would take two years. Luckily, for the growth of my business, my suppliers finance our growth. This is because we take the food from the restaurant and pay them back in about 45 days. So as we worked at about a 20 percent growth rate for the past few years, it has not affected our cash flow.

What other jobs have you had in China?

In order, I used to be an English teacher, a project manager for Amway, sales manager for *That's Shanghai* magazine, and the general Manager of *City Weekend Magazine*. Mixed in were a few entrepreneurial failures that my ego prevents me from listing.

How have your impressions of China changed over time?

I now think of it as controlled chaos. Things tend to work out fine – you just have to let go of the desire to understand the "why" of everything.

What do you miss about life back in the States?

I sorely miss college basketball and, of course, my family.

What do you think are the most difficult challenges as an expat in China today?

The drinking and partying. We arrived in our early 20s, and there wasn't much else to do on the weekends except congregate and head to the bar. This is a dangerous routine that has impacted the health of many of those around me. Have fun – just go slowly.

If someone wanted to follow in your footsteps, what words of advice would you give?

It is easy to get the feeling that this economy is like a bullet train whizzing by and you just can't find a way to slow the train down enough for you to hop on. Just look for an opportunity. They are everywhere. Ignore the hurdles. Realize that when operating in China, forgiveness is easier to obtain than permission. Just get out there, and chase your dream.

Mark and Laurie Secchia

COURTESY OF MARK AND LAURIE SECCHIA

DAILY LIFE

Some expats have opened international restaurants like these.

or whether to operate under the table on a cash basis. While the latter option may seem ridiculously unethical, keep in mind that as an "emerging" economy, that's just how much of Chinese business gets done.

Opening a legitimate business in China is a very complex matter. We'd advise you to start with a trusted local partner because Chinese laws place many restrictions on foreign ownership of a business. Next you'll need to register with the Ministry of Commerce, the State Administration of Industry and Commerce, and the various tax authorities at the national, municipal, and local government levels. You'll also need proof of sufficient start-up capital before you get the green light. For instance, a new wholesale company needs proof of 500,000元 cash ($62,000), and a new retailer needs to show proof that they have at least 300,000元 ($37,000) in start-up money. Playing by the rules, while difficult, is necessary for a legitimate business to start out on the road to long-term success. To play by the rules, however, you first need to know what the rules are, which are way beyond the scope of this book. If you are seriously considering starting a medium- to large-size business, we recommend you contact one of the numerous corporate consulting firms that specialize in this kind of work.

A large percentage of small- and medium-size businesses are unregistered. If the business is tied to an obvious physical location, such as a restaurant or a retail shop, you will pretty much have to register. If, on the other hand, your business is service-oriented, you will likely face very little pressure to register.

This would be the case with any consulting work, leading tours, and virtually all language-related work. We know of a few English-language schools with physical classrooms run by expats who have chosen not to register. They just figure it's better to ask for forgiveness than to ask for permission. As with any business start-up anywhere in the world, you first need to research the viability of your plan. Talk to other expat entrepreneurs in your city and learn from them the ins and outs of running a small business.

Important Chinese Business Practices

GUANXI

As someone who will be working in China, you will need to be very aware of how *guanxi* will affect your business relationships (see description of *guanxi* in the *People and Culture* chapter). First of all, *guanxi* can be hard to break into. Even if you have the best possible product, price, and service, you may not get the sale if your competitor already has an established relationship with your potential client. Or your competitor may have better *guanxi* to offer, especially if they have a relative in a strategic government office or have a large budget to use on "gifts" for clients. Business in China is best done when it is *not* all business. Patience, and much effort put toward relationship-building, is in order. Getting to know your client (what is his family like? what are her hobbies?) and treating them to dinners, gifts, and special privileges is an important part of building business in China.

SAVING FACE

As you interact with the Chinese in business, never forget the concept of saving face. If you suggest a better way to do a task, a Chinese businessperson may refuse to accept your ideas, regardless of how good they may be. To some, accepting your ideas would be to admit that they are either intellectually inferior to you or that they haven't been doing their job well enough to begin with. You may feel like they won't heed your suggestions simply because they aren't their own original ideas—and you'll be right. If you find yourself working with someone who is like this, and your ideas are important to you, you may need to get creative in how you suggest them so it won't cause them to lose face. Make them think it was their idea to begin with.

LANGUAGE

Some people describe the language of business with the adage, "I buy in my language, and sell in your language." Over the past few years the Chinese

ONE FOOT IN TWO CULTURES
AN INTERVIEW WITH
CHINESE AMERICAN BUSINESSMAN DAVID LIN

David Lin was born in Taiwan and finished elementary school there, but spent his teenage and young adult years in the United States. He speaks Mandarin fluently, and although he blends in just fine in China, David's outlook is 100 percent American. David works for a major U.S. software company as a senior manager for business development within the greater China region. He lives in Beijing with his wife and three children.

How is the information technology industry in China?
China's IT industry is a few years behind the United States. We consider it an emerging market with more regard for hard goods (like servers and gears) than soft goods (like software and services). Services fetch a good price in the United States, but the Chinese expect them for free. Piracy is a huge issue in the software space as the law governing internet protocol is emerging. People are not used to paying more than a few dollars for anything that comes on a CD.

How does business in China differ from the United States?
The big difference is learning the Chinese way of conducting relationships. *Guanxi* (connections) and *mianzi* (face) are everything. Getting results is less important than how you get there and who was involved in the process.

It's the China Century, every Global 1000 company is vying for the market, and business opportunities are everywhere. More people are learning Chinese around the world and keeping up with news from the Middle Kingdom. China needs managers, teachers, leaders, artists, and just about every profession out there one can think of to help it become a great nation.

Can you tell us what it is like as a Chinese American in China?
Having shared the same language sure gave me a foot up. I am very American in my worldview and value system, but since my parents were both born and raised in China, I understand the local culture. I have received feedback at work that I am too American. Indeed, I think like an American, and I prefer the efficiency and pragmatism of the American culture. This is part of a special challenge for Chinese Americans. On the outside I look Chinese, so they treat me as one of them; but as soon as they start relating to me, they get this funny feeling that I am a foreigner. I blend in well and love to see people scratching their heads trying to figure me out. Chinese treat foreigners differently, whereas I get the real scoop on things. I am also happy that I don't get the "foreigner's markup" when I shop!

What were your impressions when you first arrived in China?
Awed and impressed. I had some conceptions of China but boy, was I surprised on my first scouting trip to Beijing and Shanghai. The cities were modern and cosmopolitan. We hung out with some very hospitable expat friends and realized that we could have a comfortable lifestyle – not quite what we had in the United States, but far better than our expectations.

DAILY LIFE

How have those first impressions changed over time?

China is a complex place. What I have come to understand is that the Chinese are an extremely wounded people. From poverty to the Cultural Revolution to the sudden catapult into the market economy, people have lost the ability to trust and to be honest. Tensions are rising between the rich and the poor. While Wall Street celebrates 9 percent GDP growth, I am concerned about where this great nation is headed. Yes, new buildings continue to go up in the already modern skyline in preparation for the 2008 Olympics, but Beijingers have yet to figure out what service is all about. However, I have also had

© HENG ZHANG

David Lin

encounters with strangers who have touched me with their kindness, and I have made many dear friends that would do far more for me than many of my old friends back in the States.

What have been some of the greatest rewards for your family living in China?

Making new friends and seeing our children pick up the language and culture. After an initial semester in an international school, we moved them to a local school, partly to save on the outrageous tuition but also to let them learn more Chinese and appreciate the Chinese culture. After about two years of struggles, they are fluent. The youngest is in preschool and talks with a Beijing accent. I also feel that we are making a difference with the local friends around us. Family life and marriage are two big issues here, and people come to us to ask for help and counsel.

What do you miss about life back in the States?

The quality of life, clean air, the great outdoors, and efficient systems. I also miss Mexican food, Costco, and shopping. It's so much easier to buy things in the United States, where I can count on quality at a good price, order online, and return things easily. Prices for name brands are usually more in China than in the United States. Finding English books is a chore. Our family loves to read, and we really miss the library.

If someone wanted to follow in your footsteps, what words of advice would you give?

Study the language, and prepare the family. If there are children involved, make sure they are involved in the decision process. Be realistic on the length of time it takes to adjust to a new environment, and try not to take on too much. Give yourself time; go for the long haul. Round up support for living abroad. We were blessed to have good friends and a strong community here.

China is one of the most dynamic places on earth today. It's not only the most populous nation and one of the biggest markets, it is also rich with history, culture, and cuisines. Here you'll have opportunities to grow in your career, learn about a new culture, and speak a new language. This is an exciting place to be. Often I have thought to myself that I should have come sooner.

business lunch, expat style

have perfected the art of manufacturing consumer goods and exporting them to places like the United States where they'll eventually be purchased by consumers who speak English. Because the Chinese wanted to sell to us, they've learned our language. So if you are the buyer in a business exchange with the Chinese, you'll do fine in English. But as Dylan observed, the times they are a-changin', and westerners can't expect to always get by with English only. If you hope to sell to the Chinese, your Mandarin better be more advanced than *nihao* and *xiexie,* or you may be sent packing with your tail between your legs and no sale.

WINING AND DINING

In the West, business deals are made based on the merits of the contractual relationship. In the East, you won't even get around to contractual concerns until you've finished a number of rounds of wining and dining. Even if the business deal makes sense to you and your Chinese counterpart, you'll still have to participate in a number of banquets in addition to the obligatory business meetings. And don't forget the *guanxi* of banquets—for every banquet they host for you, you're expected to host one for them. Some Chinese businessmen won't trust you until you've gotten drunk with them, smoked their cigarettes, and had at least one John Denver karaoke marathon with them, which may or may not end with an offer of a prostitute. It's their way of building a relationship, and a strong personal relationship leads to a strong business relationship. If you prefer not to participate in something for health, religious, or other reasons, just explain that to your host. They'll understand, but you'll still have to put forth a lot of other effort to build the relationship.

© BARBARA STROTHER

DAILY LIFE

Language skills can boost your career, whether English for the Chinese or Chinese for the foreigners.

CONTRACT LAW

Just as in America, contracts are legally binding in China. When a contract is breached, the offended party can seek financial damages and an order from the courts that would force the other party to make good on its original promises. To some Chinese a contract might be seen as more of a suggestion than a binding agreement. The biggest difference in contracts between the United States and China is in how contract disputes are resolved. If arbitration fails then the courts must resolve the dispute. American judges resolve contract disputes based on the principle of "good faith." If your company signed a contract to purchase 1,000 widgets then you are obligated by good faith to honor your promise and purchase the widgets. Chinese judges might rely more on reason than the principle of good faith. If your company suddenly has no reasonable need for the widgets, then you might not be expected to purchase them, even though you previously promised to do so. Most business transactions work out just fine, but if you do find yourself in a contract breach situation, be prepared for the worst.

If, on the other hand, you are the one reneging on a business contract, you need to take careful steps to bring about a peaceful resolution. There are a number of American businesspeople currently serving prison time for business deals gone bad, and you don't want to join them. Since China's admission to the WTO corporate criminals are facing stricter penalties, especially in internationally sensitive areas such as piracy and intellectual property violations.

FINANCE

For more than half a century, the Chinese economy has been a cash-based system. Few people had personal bank accounts, and no one had a checkbook or credit card. The only sources of credit were loans from relatives, friends, village elders, and loan sharks. But today, like everything else in China, the financial system is changing. People are taking their life savings out of ginger jars and depositing them into bank savings accounts. Thanks to the rise of e-commerce, credit cards are starting to gain popularity, and banks are now issuing more mortgages, student loans, and even personal loans to the credit-worthy.

For decades, foreign currency hasn't circulated outside the expat enclaves, but this is expected to change since the central government recently relaxed the laws that forbid locals from holding foreign currency. All this progress comes with certain challenges. The exchange rate is slowly inching lower, meaning your dollars won't go as far. And that old infuriation that's second only to death—the income tax—is now a harsh reality in

© BARBARA STROTHER

China. We've made every effort to fill this chapter with useful practical information that's up to date, but keep in mind that the rules of finance are constantly changing, and the interpretation and enforcement of the rules still varies from place to place. Use this chapter as a guide, but hire professional help if your finances are complex.

Cost of Living

The living standard for all Chinese people has risen dramatically in recent years, but unfortunately so has the cost of living. China's three most cosmopolitan cities, Shanghai, Beijing, and Hong Kong, now rank as some of the most expensive places to live in the world—but this statistic is based on a comparable western lifestyle. Buying a car and a house with a yard in Chicago is much, much cheaper than doing the same in Beijing; but the difference is you don't *need* to buy a car or a house in Beijing, and you can get by nicely with much, much less. Compared to the United States and Europe, living in China can still be a bargain. In the second tier cities, such as Tianjin, Hangzhou, or Qingdao, your cost of living will be about two-thirds lower than in Beijing, Shanghai and Hong Kong, and in inland cities such as Chengdu and Xi'an you can easily live on less than half of what you'd need in the Big Three.

Besides location, the other major cost of living factors to consider are housing and lifestyle. Housing in China can cost as much or more than what you'd pay in the West. The good news is that most employers provide housing, so there's a good chance you won't have to pay a dime for the item that keeps China's cities on those most-expensive lists. If you do have to pay for your own housing, do plenty of research into housing costs in your city to make sure you can afford it before accepting the position. Your lifestyle expectations will also greatly impact your cost of living. If you're willing to live like the locals and don't mind riding a bus or bike instead of catching cabs, eating noodles instead of steak, and taking trains instead of airplanes, the Middle Kingdom can be an incredible bargain.

HOW MUCH MONEY DO I NEED?

In the early days, employers provided housing (often including utilities), health care, and transportation for their expat workers, so you just had to figure out how much money you needed for food, clothing, souvenirs, travel, entertainment, and other daily necessities. Employers today still consider China a hardship post, but not as "hard" as before, so the benefit packages have been scaled back in recent years. This is especially true for those who go to China for one purpose, such as studying or teaching, then hire on with a business. (These types are often labeled "local hires," and since the employer knows you're already somewhat acclimated to the culture and lifestyle, you won't receive the same benefit package as an expat recruited from abroad.)

Prior to accepting your new job, do some research into the prevailing wages for your position and the cost of living in your assigned city. There are plenty of opportunities to work in China, so you needn't settle for a low-paying job or one

A menu board shows prices for western foods.

© BARBARA STROTHER

with sub-par benefits. China won't always be a bargain, so choose a position with a decent salary, and you should have an excellent lifestyle and even be able to save a few bucks for your future.

Minimum

In deciding how much money you need to live on, we suggest no less than 3,000元 (around $350) per month for a single person, which will get you a bare-bones existence, if you don't have to pay for housing. This amount will get you the same standard of living as a lower-middle class local in most cities or a low income local in first-tier cities. Even though this income is the same as the locals, an expat's expenses will be higher than those of a local, especially when you consider the cost of imported foods, international phone calls, western restaurants, and the tendency to depend on taxis rather than navigating the complex local public transportation system. So for 3,000元 a month, you'll be able to afford some budget travel and a few western meals once in a while, but you'll have to go without many things that your expat peers will be enjoying. It's not much fun eating noodles and rice while your expat comrades are enjoying barbequed ribs, apple pie, and cold Heineken at Tony Roma's. Living on the cheap might also hinder you from hanging out with Chinese peers, because the Chinese who run in expat circles are typically well-educated and their own incomes are well above 3,000元.

COST OF LIVING COMPARISON BY REGION

The economic boom in China has been accompanied by rising prices, and the cost of living in major Chinese cities now surpasses the cost of living in many western cities. Despite the rising prices, most expats still find China an affordable place to live because they receive free housing from their employers. Every year, Mercer Human Resource Consulting compares costs in major world cities. Some of the results of their cost of living comparison are shown below. The Cost of Living Index number shows that what $100 would buy in New York, only costs $90.40 in Shanghai.

2005 Ranking	City	Country	Cost of Living Index
1	Tokyo	Japan	134.7
3	London	United Kingdom	120.3
9	Hong Kong	Hong Kong	109.5
13	New York City	United States	100
19	Beijing	China	95.6
30	Shanghai	China	90.4
44	Los Angeles	United States	86.7
52	Chicago	United States	84.6
63	Shenzhen	China	81.3
65	Guangzhou	China	80.6
78	Washington, D.C.	United States	77.4
83	Atlanta	United States	76.1
131	Tianjin	China	62.5

DAILY LIFE

Average and Luxury

For an average lifestyle in a first-tier city, we'd recommend 5,000–10,000元 ($625–1,250) per month, which will give you the freedom to purchase a few imported foods, eat out at western restaurants, visit the cultural sights in your city and afford travel to the far corners of China. You're probably not going to live in China all your life, so you'll want to travel and take in China's amazing sights while you can. As the Chinese say, "No man is a man unless he's climbed the Great Wall."

If you plan to do a considerable amount of traveling, shopping, and eating out, and you prefer not to economize your lifestyle, you'll need a salary comparable to your salary in the United States. Modern conveniences in the Middle Kingdom generally carry modern price tags.

For a luxury lifestyle, the sky's the limit in China. If you require a luxury

With a growing upscale market, China is not always a bargain.

villa-style house and will send a couple kids to an international school, housing and schooling alone will cost you well over $100,000 a year.

MONTHLY EXPENSES
Housing and Utilities

If your employer doesn't provide your housing, then you should expect to pay no less than $1,000 per month to rent a modest two-bedroom flat in the big three cities of Beijing, Shanghai, and Hong Kong. In other cities rents will be less. On the high end, a western-style suburban house in a gated community can rent for $10,000 per month or more.

Common utility expenses are: electricity (80元/$10 per month), gas (60元/$7.50), telephone (60元/$7.50), water (40元/$5), cable television (25元/$3.10), and bottled water (10元/$1.25 for each five-gallon bottle, delivered). Of course these figures fluctuate, especially in the north where you'll use more gas or electricity to heat your home.

Food and Other Necessities

Food can be very inexpensive in China. If you don't mind a steady diet of rice and vegetables, a single person can live on $100 or less per month. For our family of four, a typical weekly shopping outing at Carrefour for groceries and household necessities runs around 500元 (about $63). That

YOU PAID HOW MUCH FOR THAT?

Everyone who has ever moved overseas has probably worried about the cost of living in the new country. In China, you can expect most things to cost less than in the United States. Here's a list of common items that you might purchase and their prices (in 2006):

Item	Cost in the United States	Cost in China
Bus fare	$1	$0.12
Big Mac sandwich	$2	$1
Gallon of gas	$3	$1.50
Box of Cap'n Crunch	$4	$8
Pack of cigarettes	$4	$0.50
Pint of beer from the corner store	$5	$0.25
T-shirt	$10	$2
Haircut at a barber shop	$12	$1
Pack of 25 Pampers diapers	$12	$15
Mid-range restaurant meal for two	$24	$5
DVD	$15	$1
Ten-minute taxi ride	$15	$2
Mid-range mp3 player	$60	$75
Mid-range hotel room	$75	$50
Low-end bicycle	$80	$20
1,000-mile train ride	$300	$100
New compact car	$10,000	$5,000
Cadillac Deville	$25,000	$50,000
1,200-square-foot (365-square-meter) apartment in major city	$400,000	$120,000

figure could be much lower for someone who could do without the western foods we like, such as breakfast cereal, bread, soft drinks, cold cuts, imported canned goods (tuna, corn, etc.), imported dairy products, and imported chocolate (the local variety just doesn't do the trick for us).

Medical Expenses

Medical expenses vary widely. Large local employers (especially schools) typically have a clinic with a nurse and a physician who will see you for free or for a nominal fee. The district hospitals and clinics are also quite cheap. I paid less than 100元 ($12.50) each for two visits. On the other hand, the western health care system frequented by the diplomatic and business community is priced according to western standards.

Schooling and Household Help

If you put your children in a Chinese school, you'll have to pay fees to cover books, meals, board (if needed), and administrative costs. The costs vary widely among the schools but are nowhere near the high cost of the international schools, which cost between $12,000 and $20,000 per child per year, with schools in second tier cities on the lower end. The cost to attend a private Chinese school is about a third what you'd pay at a comparable international school. For help raising your children or help around the house, you can hire an *ayi* for about $100 per month. *Ayi's* fees are higher in larger cities, and in places like Hong Kong, it is customary to provide housing for your *ayi*.

Entertainment and Travel

The cost of entertainment and travel also varies widely. Traveling from Shanghai to Beijing by plane costs around $150 round trip, while the same trip by sleeper train is only $50. To travel really cheap you can take a long distance bus, which will cost less than the train but will be twice as grueling. Entertainment, on the other hand, can be just as satisfying on the cheap, if your idea of fun is watching DVDs (which you can get for less than a buck) or eating out with friends at cheap Chinese restaurants (where you can feed a whole group for less than $20). But if your entertainment includes symphony concerts, designer fashion shows, or partying until dawn with a continuous stream of mixed drinks in hand, you'll need to have a nicely padded wallet.

Tipping will be among your entertainment and travel expenses, as this practice is slowly creeping its way into Chinese commerce. At five-star hotels the porters expect to be tipped, but it's not expected at four-star and lower hotels. Waiters at high-end restaurants appreciate tips, but check your bill first, because a 10–15 percent service charge may have already been added, in which case a tip is unnecessary. Tour guides and interpreters expect about $1 per day per person in your group, and hired drivers (but not taxis) expect of tips about half as much as the guides and interpreters. A word of advice regarding guides: They sometimes (gasp!) steer you to places where they're paid kickbacks. So if you hire a guide, clearly communicate where you want to go and consider reducing the tip if your expectations weren't met.

Shopping

The beauty of shopping in China is that you can purchase almost anything here (except certain foods from back home that you'll come to miss). After all, most of the world's goods are made here before being shipped out to the shops in the four corners of the globe. And yes, it's true what you've heard about the low prices. On the other hand, for those with high tastes and a high cash flow to match, China's shopping districts are filling up with international designer stores that are the real deal but offer no deals, like Tiffany, Gucci, and Coach.

Mega-marts like Carrefour, Wal-Mart, Trust Mart, and Metro can be found all over the big cities and even in some of the smaller ones. As in the United States, these stores are chock-full of the types of goods consumers demand in their everyday lives. There are also plenty of smaller mom-and-pop

BIG-BOX RETAILERS IN CHINA

Store	Ownership	Specialty
Carrefour	French	The biggest and best mega-stores selling clothes, bikes, hardware, electronics, household goods, and a huge grocery section including imported foods. The ground floor usually consists of specialty retailers.
Auchan	French	Similar to Carrefour but with larger wine selections.
Metro	German	A cash-only bulk warehouse-style store requiring a membership.
Wal-Mart	American	Carries few imported items and mostly caters to local shoppers.
B&Q	British	Home improvement.
OBI	German	Giant home improvement store.
Isetan	Japanese	High-end department store selling apparel, food, household goods, and various other products.
Ekchor Lotus	Thai	A slightly less-impressive version of Carrefour.
E-Mart	South Korean	Hypermarket with quite a few Korean products.
Trust Mart	Taiwanese	Huge hypermart. Look for the pet fish in the meat department.

© BARBARA STROTHER

night market bargaining, communicated by calculator

shops that tend to offer better service than the big stores. (Try to avoid the mega-marts after work or on weekends because these places are often maddeningly chaotic with throngs of rush-hour shoppers.)

Your city will probably have some specialty markets where similar goods are sold by multiple vendors under the same roof, such as shoe markets, electronics markets, antique markets, and of course the fresh food markets (which we fondly referred to as "hepatitis markets" because of the filth). These markets are open during the day, but the really fun markets are the "night markets" where city streets or sidewalks are closed off to make way for hundreds of vendors with their silks, pirated DVDs, name-brand knockoffs, and fake antiques.

BARGAINING

Bargaining is expected in markets and small shops, but not in large department stores or supermarkets. The best way to discover if there is room to bargain is to ask, *"Keyi pianyi yidian ma?"* (can you go a little cheaper?), a hard phrase to memorize but one that will save you lots of dough. They'll reply with either *"bu keyi"* (nope) or *"keyi"* (sure), in which case you can proceed to bargain. The rule of thumb is to cut a seller's price in half and eventually settle on a price around two-thirds the original quote. A good way to learn what a fair price is for something is to check out the price in two or three different shops. As you walk away, the sellers will probably offer the true price for the item.

In the beginning you'll be overcharged quite a bit, but don't worry about it. If the price sounds good to you, go for it, and don't worry that the next foreign shopper might pay half the amount you paid. Have fun and be happy that you are helping the local economy. As your Chinese-language skills improve, they'll see that you aren't a fat-cat tourist, but someone who is really in the know. They'll give you better prices just for speaking the language.

Some belligerent foreigners, who don't understand that bargaining is just a ritual between the buyer and seller, get angry and criticize the quality of the good or insult the seller with their words or body language. Try to remain polite—negotiating is a fact of life in Chinese commerce, and it is all part of the ritual. You'll know you've arrived as a bargainer when after fierce, and seemingly angry, negotiation, you enjoy a good laugh with the seller and they toss you a freebie and offer you a cup of tea. Now you are starting to fit in.

Banking

Despite how modern China has become, cash is still king in the Chinese economy. Consider your check-writing days over, and except for high-end tourist hotels and the mega-marts, most businesses won't accept your credit cards either. You'll have to get used to carrying around wads of cash with you. Whether or not you should open an account at a Chinese bank depends on how you are paid, and how you plan to manage your cash flow needs. The risk that your home will be burglarized is pretty minimal, but since it's fairly simple to open a local bank account, why take chances? Unless you have reason to believe the authorities will seize foreign assets again like they did back in 1949, your money is safe in a Chinese bank.

OPENING AN ACCOUNT WITH A CHINESE BANK
Renminbi Accounts
To open an account with a Chinese bank, just show up with your cash, your passport, and any other Chinese identification you might have, including your residence card and foreign expert card. Fill out the forms, make your deposit, and you'll be ready. You'll be given an ATM card, but don't expect to be issued a checkbook. Your initial deposit should be in cash to simplify

matters. Once your account is established, you can deposit checks from foreign banks, but it'll take up to four weeks for them to clear.

Multicurrency Accounts

Opening a renminbi account is pretty straightforward, but if you want to open a "multicurrency account" you'll have a little more paperwork and you'll probably be charged a start-up fee. With these accounts you'll have the flexibility of getting dollars when you need them, such as for an extended trip out of the country. At the government-owned Bank of China (the largest bank), the minimum deposit to open a multicurrency checking account is foreign currency equal to the value of 100元 (about $12). For savings accounts the minimum start-up deposit is foreign currency equal to 500元 (about $60). To deposit more than $5,000 cash you'll need to submit the "currency declaration form" that your flight attendant offered you on the way over. If you need to make a large withdrawal, visit your bank the day before to give them time to get the foreign currency. Multicurrency accounts can be set up for U.S. dollars, Hong Kong dollars, British pounds, Euro, Japanese yen, Canadian dollars, Australian dollars, Swiss francs, and Singapore dollars.

The interest rate on your savings account depends on how long you commit to leave the money in the bank; the longer time, the higher the interest

MANDARIN MOOLAH

You probably know what bucks, greenbacks, and smackers are, but how about kuai, *qian*, and *jiao*? This list should help you figure it all out.

Pinyin	Characters	What's it mean?	Value in 元	U.S. equivalent term
Renminbi	人民币	Literally, "the people's money"	1	U.S. Dollar
Yuan	元	Slang for *renminbi*	1	"buck"
Kuai	块	Slang for *renminbi*	1	"buck"
Jiao	角	Literally means "horn"	1/10	dime
Mao	毛	Slang for *jiao*, literally means "feather"	1/10	dime
Fen	分	Literally means "point"	1/100	penny
Qian	钱	Money		

rate. Interest rates on multicurrency accounts also vary according to the type of international currency that was initially deposited. The highest rates are for Australian, British, and U.S. currencies; the lowest rates are for Swiss, Singaporean, and Japanese currencies (the yen earns the lowest at 0.01 percent, perhaps as a result of the grudge the Chinese still hold more than half a century after the Japanese invasion of China).

INTERNATIONAL BANKING

China's financial sector has opened up somewhat and the authorities

Agricultural Bank of China

© BARBARA STROTHER

DAILY LIFE

now allow certain foreign banks to operate in the country. Today you can physically conduct all of your banking at a branch office of an international bank such as the Standard Chartered Bank or HSBC, both headquartered in London, or the New York–based Citibank. These banks aspire to be just like your neighborhood bank back home and offer just about every financial service you might need, including multicurrency accounts, renminbi accounts, foreign exchange, credit cards, ATMs, loans, and even mortgages for purchasing real estate in China. If you plan to bring a large amount of money to China, you may prefer to open an account with one of the international banks while you are still in your home country.

FOREIGN CURRENCY

The State Administration of Foreign Exchange in Beijing has established some very tight foreign exchange policies. For instance, only 19 foreign currencies are convertible into Chinese yuan, and reconversion from yuan back to the foreign currency requires a copy of the original exchange memo. When you're ready to leave the country, you'll have difficulty converting your yuan back to dollars if you've earned your money from a cash-based job and/or if you've misplaced your paperwork.

The yuan–dollar exchange rate has hovered around 8:1 for more than a decade. Despite what you may have heard about a new "floating" exchange rate for the yuan, don't expect dramatic changes any time soon. Only minor changes (less than 2 percent) are expected from time to time, so don't expect to make money buying and selling Chinese currency. Be aware, however, that banks, hotels, and airports charge an exchange rate that can differ slightly from the official rate, but the difference is never in your favor. The airport rate is typically 5 percent worse than what you'll find at a hotel or bank.

Black Market Exchange

Strict currency regulations make it difficult to exchange renminbi for dollars at official sites. Prior to exchanging their renminbi for dollars, foreigners must show proof that they either earned the renminbi as wages, or that they previously exchanged their dollars to get that renminbi. Because of these regulations, a small black market for foreign exchange has emerged to cater to both locals and foreigners who don't have the right paperwork to get the cash they want. You may be approached by illegal moneychangers, especially near the tourist hotels, offering attractive exchange rates. Because some of their renminbi notes are only as authentic as their fake Gucci bags, it's best to avoid them and just exchange your dough at the official banks.

ATMS

ATMs are pretty common in China, especially if you use a Visa ATM card, or a card that's compatible with the Maestro system. If you use an international card you probably won't be charged a transaction fee, but they'll probably give you a below-market exchange rate. And don't forget that your bank back home will charge you $5 for each transaction, even if the transaction isn't completed. If your ATM card is from an account at a Chinese bank you'll only be charged a nominal fee of around 2元 ($0.25).

Most ATMs have limits of 1,000–3,000元 ($125–375) per transaction, but some will allow you two or more transactions in a row. Considering the fact that the finicky ATM will spurn your advances a third of the time (even for ATM cards from Chinese banks), the fees you end up paying can be 5 percent or more. To avoid the heavy fees, you may need to get a larger share of your pay in cash. We typically kept a few thousand renminbi stashed in a homemade book safe in our house, and hoped our *ayi* would not suddenly get the urge to read our English books!

FOREIGN CREDIT CARDS

Don't cut up your credit cards just because you are moving to China. Take at least one with you, and forget all the cool advertisements about

MasterCard and American Express, because if any card will be accepted, it's going to be a Visa card. Although credit cards will be of no use to you in the everyday street economy of China, they can be quite useful for online shopping, booking airline tickets, and paying at hotels and international restaurant chains.

CHECKS

Most banks will not accept foreign checks unless you leave them some collateral such as your bank card. Because almost no one accepts checks as a form of payment, you can generally count your check-writing days as over when you reach the Middle Kingdom. Some expats receive financial support from their home country in the form of checks. With a check you won't be able to walk away with cash from the teller window; the Chinese bank will only deposit the funds into your account once they've received the funds from your home bank, which can take as long as 3–4 weeks. The funds can either be deposited into your account as renminbi or as dollars if you have a multicurrency account. Checks are treated like cash deposits when it comes to exchange rates, and there should be no fee associated with depositing them. In the end, however, it might be simpler to keep your U.S. bank account open and have checks sent there, then access the funds through an ATM in China.

TRAVELERS CHECKS

Travelers checks are not that useful for expats, because they are only redeemable at high-end hotels and certain banks. Considering the fees you pay when you get them (around 5 percent), the lousy exchange rate you're likely to get, and the inconvenience, they don't seem like such a great idea. But if you worry about misplacing your money (haven't we all done that?) or if you're concerned about burglary or an *ayi* with sticky fingers, you might prefer travelers checks for some of your money. We've used them when leading large student groups and it seemed safer to carry $15,000 in travelers checks than in cash. For die-hard fans, you can get more travelers checks in U.S. dollar denominations at major Chinese banks.

ELECTRONIC FUND TRANSFERS

You can wire money to China from a U.S. bank (or any bank for that matter). You'll just need to give the U.S. bank the cash and the account number of the bank in China, and pay the fees. Western Union can also do this (for a fee), but you might have better results using Bank of China, which has branch locations in New York and Los Angeles, or an international bank, like HSBC, that has locations in the United States and in China. If you first open an account with a Bank of China branch in the United States, you'll be able to avoid the $2,999 cap on wire transfers for non-account holders, but you won't be able to access your account in China other than by ATM, since Bank of China accounts in China are not linked with those in the United States.

If you do a wire transfer you'll pay at least $20, so our recommendation is instead to deposit the funds into your U.S.-based bank account and access the funds in China via an ATM. Just leave a few deposit slips with your parents or someone else you trust and they can easily add funds to your account when you need it.

Getting Paid

The way you are paid as an expat working in China depends on the type of employer you work for. You might receive all of your pay in China; all of your pay could be deposited into your bank account back in your home country; or you might receive a portion of your pay in China while the rest is deposited into your account back home.

Keep in mind that U.S. dollars do not circulate in China's markets, so they won't do you much good unless you are leaving the country soon. Chinese authorities want the renminbi to remain the unit of exchange, and they don't want money leaving the country. They want you to spend your dough in the country rather than export it. So go ahead, shop a little—it's good for the economy!

IN CHINA

Technically, central government regulations specify that employers, whether foreign or domestic, cannot pay their China-based employees in foreign cash, but they can pay foreign currency directly into your Chinese multicurrency bank account or into a foreign bank account. But in reality, if you get paid in cash, your employer can choose to exchange a percentage of your renminbi pay into U.S. dollars for you. They will inform you what the maximum amount is that you can exchange into dollars, which you will need whenever you leave China, including travel for vacation or business. Just make your request well in advance of payday to give your company enough time to go to the bank. Our old employer preferred to pay 70 percent of our pay in cash renminbi, while the rest was in U.S.

ZHONGGUO RENMIN YINHANG

中国人民银行

拾圆

10-yuan notes

dollars. We could always exchange the dollars for renminbi if we needed them, but sometimes it was convenient to have dollars on hand, especially for traveling abroad or reimbursing a visitor who brought us items we had requested from home.

If you work for a Chinese company or university, then you'll probably receive all of your pay in China, and you'll probably be paid in cash, in renminbi. Every two weeks you'll have to show up at your employer's cashier window where you can sign for a brick of money. With all large transactions it is customary for the recipient to count the money before signing for it. Remember to be discreet, because your brick of cash may be many times thicker than your Chinese counterparts around you.

If your experience is like ours, you'll sometimes be pleasantly surprised that your pay is a little more than you had expected. It's probably not an error—Chinese employers often surprise their employees with small bonuses, especially around the time of the local holidays. Be grateful and don't wait around for an explanation. Also, don't be surprised if you get a regular pay raise and nobody explains why. In China, you've got to accept that there are some things you'll never understand.

IN THE UNITED STATES

Most international businesses still consider China a hardship post, and even with some scaling back, they give their employers generous pay and benefits, including housing and transportation allowances. They know you won't be able to spend all your income in China, and you'll end up saving a lot of it, so they'll give you the option of depositing a portion of your pay in your home-country bank account. A couple we know who taught at an international school returned to the United States after their three-year stint in China having saved enough to pay cash for a house. Check with your human resources department to find out what pay options are available to you. If you *are* the human resources department, you can learn the official regulations from the Local Labor and Human Resources Agency, the government agency in charge of such matters. Keep in mind, however, that the official party line is not always an accurate representation of how business is done in China, so you might be better off getting advice from a management consulting firm such as BCG, PriceWaterhouseCoopers, or China Consulting Association.

WHAT IF I DON'T GET PAID?

Some expats who work for unprofitable Chinese companies or cash-strapped universities have been met at the cashier's window with dull stares and apologies of *"mei you, mei you"* (don't have, don't have). If payday's on a Friday, you probably won't be able to complain to management until they return on Monday. How you resolve the situation depends on you. If you consider your work in China to be humanitarian work, then a delayed paycheck is little more than an inconvenient nuisance compared to the greater good that you are accomplishing. But those of us who feel that our work should be fairly compensated should let our employers know that missing a payday is unacceptable. If you let them delay your pay once, you can count on it happening again. You'll have to confront your boss, and no matter how tactful you are, such a confrontation will result in a loss of face for your boss. As a result, your relationship might never be rosy again.

You can also try your luck in China's relatively young court system, but don't get your hopes too high, especially because your boss will probably have more *guanxi* in the local community than you. Some expats whose pay has been withheld have gone on strike, refusing to work until paid. If the problem persists, you may want to look for other employment or return home if there are no other options. Don't feel bad, you'll be in the fine company of hundreds of other expats who went home early when their high expectations were dashed in the Middle Kingdom.

Taxes

China has tax treaties with the United States (and plenty of other countries) that are ostensibly set up to prevent individuals from being double taxed, but the treaties are also designed to help each country catch the cheats. As you can imagine, penalties for tax evasion are far more severe in China than in the United States. In the United States you'll get a slap on the wrist and a fine, but in the Middle Kingdom you'll earn a free vacation at the "behind bars" resort. And since spring 2006 the tax bureau has been connected to the immigration bureau, so if you're going to be busted, it's likely to happen at the airport, just when you were planning to leave. Wave good-bye to your loved ones—it might be a while before you see them again!

As an expat in China you might be required to pay taxes both in China and in your home country, especially for atypical income such as property taxes and royalties. Ask your employer to help you sort out your tax liability *before* accepting the assignment. You should understand, however, that your taxes can be infinitely complex, and the more you try to go "by the book," the higher your tax bill will be. Some feel its best to let sleeping tax collectors lie.

CHINESE INCOME TAXES

Back in the glory days of communism, nobody in China paid income taxes. The government was content to earn its money from the income generated by the state-owned companies. The people were left alone, but of course

LET'S ALL PAY TAXES!

If you've been in China for...	
90 days	You are now a "tax resident" and must pay Chinese income tax (unless you are a citizen from a country with an income tax treaty, such as the United States).
183 days	You are now a "tax resident" and must pay income tax on all of your income earned in China (even if you are a citizen of an income tax treaty country).
5 years	Your total worldwide income is subject to Chinese income taxes.

most everyone was dirt poor as well. Now that capitalism has conquered red China, the standard of living has vastly improved, but alas, now everyone must pay the despised Individual Income Tax (IIT). Most fringe benefits are not subject to the IIT, including travel and relocation allowances, housing (unless you are paid a cash stipend), health care, language school, and the educational allowance for dependent children.

The IIT in the mainland is a progressive tax just like in the United States. The first 4,000元 ($500) of your monthly salary isn't taxed, but for wages up to 20,000元 ($2,500), you are taxed 20 percent (after a 375元/$47 standard deduction), for wages 20,001–40,000元 ($2,500–5,000) the tax rate is 25 percent (after a 1,375元/$170 deduction), and so on. The highest tax bracket is income over 100,000元 with a marginal tax rate of 45 percent. When you consider that 100,000元 is only about $12,000, 45 percent seems quite high; China's IIT rates are among the highest in Asia. The rates are lower for people classified as "individual entrepreneurs," and the tax brackets are higher in high-cost cities such as Shanghai. Some expats who work as teachers avoid taxes by splitting their work between two schools and keeping their earning below the 4,000元 threshold with each employer.

Workers in Hong Kong pay a 16 percent flat income tax on annual income. Similar to the U.S. system, the gross annual income figure is adjusted downward based on deductions such as the personal deduction of HK$100,000 (US$12,500) and the child deduction of HK$40,000 (US$5,150). Those who split their work between Hong Kong and the mainland prefer to pay income tax in Hong Kong due to the lower rates, and some are successful at manipulating tax residency loopholes and avoid paying taxes in either place.

Unlike the United States where income taxes are paid once a year, in China they are paid each month. Employers typically handle the tax burden for their employees. They'll withhold the tax from your salary and pay the State Administration of Taxes on your behalf, so you'll never have to personally file your taxes.

Nevertheless, since tax laws are constantly changing (they call it "reform") and tax avoiders face harsh penalties, we suggest you consult a tax expert if your situation is complex. Companies such as Deloitte Touche Tohmatsu offer all sorts of legal and financial consulting, including tax advice, but as always, it's best to start with your company's HR department.

U.S. INCOME TAXES

U.S. citizens who live and work in China still find themselves under the thumb of the IRS. According to the tax treaty between the United States and China, you are entitled to tax credit; generally the amount of tax paid in China can be used as a "tax credit" when you file your taxes in the United States. So if you owe Uncle Sam $5,000 this year, but already paid Uncle Mao $1,000, you just have to pay Sam $4,000. The principle of reciprocity supposedly keeps international tax matters simple. On a practical level, many U.S. expats who work for non-U.S.-based companies (such as teaching at a Chinese university) choose not to report any income because they know their employer will not report any income to the IRS. The income is typically too low to warrant any U.S. taxes anyway.

If you plan to file a tax return in the United States, the best way to reduce U.S. taxes on your Chinese income is to claim the Foreign Earned Income Deduction. You can treat $80,000 of your income as not taxable. To qualify you must earn your income abroad and pay taxes abroad (i.e. to China). Use IRS Form 2555 to claim your deduction and submit your Chinese tax documents.

Investing

So, you've heard of all the capitalists striking it rich in this great bastion of socialism and you want a piece of the action too, eh? It is true that millionaires have sprung up like bamboo after the rain, but most of these *nouveaux riche* got that way through entrepreneurial exploits creating businesses to serve the needs of a more affluent society, or manufacturing goods for export. The really lucky ones, like He Ping, the son-in-law of Deng Xiaoping, used their *guanxi* (connections) to strike up sweetheart deals with powerful Party officials. As a so-called "emerging" market, there are still plenty of opportunities for investors to earn a reasonable return, but speculators should beware. As with anything Chinese, or Asian for that matter, investing is a complex matter with many subtleties unappreciated by the typical westerner. But if you follow our advice here, you're sure to strike it rich—well, maybe not, but at least you'll have some practical information and perhaps avoid a few pitfalls.

While economic growth in China is expected to remain triple (9 percent) what it is in the United States (3 percent), don't set your expectations too high, and in all of your investing, don't forget the basics of buying stock. When you buy a stock, you are handing over your hard-earned money to a company that is supposed to use your money for things like purchasing new equipment that will help them earn more money by manufacturing more stuff. There have been cases in which businesspeople have pocketed the newly invested funds rather than using the money to expand their business. The lines are somewhat blurry between making a bad investment and getting scammed, so be careful and consider yourself warned.

CHINESE STOCK MARKETS

Deng Xiaoping, that closet capitalist, understood the value of allowing businesses to raise investment capital from the people, so his economic reforms included the creation of two stock exchanges in Shanghai and Shenzhen.

Hong Kong

Hong Kong has long had its own stock exchange and the free flow of investment cash was an important part of the prosperous little island's success. Companies whose stocks are traded on the Hong Kong exchange are known as H-shares. If the company is controlled by the Beijing government, the stock is known as a "red chip." H-shares and red chips are valued in Hong Kong dollars and enjoy a much rosier reputation than stocks traded on the Shanghai or Shenzhen exchanges. There are no citizenship restrictions on purchasing shares of stock for companies listed in the Hong Kong exchange.

Shanghai and Shenzhen

In Shanghai and Shenzhen individual company stocks are either classified as A-shares or B-shares. Most of the A-share companies are controlled by the Chinese government. They are valued in yuan and can only be purchased by Chinese citizens or "qualified foreign institutional investors," meaning large financial services companies with at least $10 billion in assets, such as Merrill Lynch. B-share companies have their stock valued in U.S. dollars and can be purchased by locals or foreigners. Whether deserved

the soaring world of high finance in China

© BARBARA STROTHER

or not, the B-share companies have a poor reputation and are thought of as struggling companies whose best chance at making money is by having some deluded foreigner purchase their stock. In other words, you can't buy A-shares and you shouldn't buy B-shares, so you'll just have to figure out another way to strike it rich in China.

Of course not all of the B-share companies are dogs, so if you really want a piece of the action you can open a trading account with a Chinese broker just like in the United States. Since most stock trading happens electronically now, you might consider opening an account with one of China's electronic brokerages like CITIC Securities or the more fashionably named Great Wall Securities. Just make sure you can read enough of the website's Chinese, and be prepared for that warm feeling you get from making a charitable donation!

FOREIGN STOCK MARKETS

The best way to directly invest in China's economy is by purchasing Chinese company stocks that trade on international stock markets. Numerous Chinese companies are listed on the New York Stock Exchange such as China Eastern Airlines or China Unicom. A handful of others trade on

CHINESE STOCK MARKET PERFORMANCE COMPARED TO THE UNITED STATES

Security	Description	2005 Return	Average Annual Five-Year Return
Shanghai Stock Exchange Index	Index of about 800 Chinese companies listed on the SSE	-17 percent	-13 percent
Hang Seng Index	Index of the 33 largest companies in Hong Kong	14 percent	1 percent
S&P 500	Index of 500 leading companies in the United States	6 percent	-13 percent
China Unicom	Widely held Chinese stock	4 percent	-61 percent
Lenovo Group	Widely held Hong Kong stock	40 percent	-10 percent
General Electric	Widely held U.S. stock	1 percent	-34 percent

the NASDAQ exchange and hundreds are available over the counter. The bottom line is that numerous Chinese stocks can be purchased using a typical U.S. broker as easily as you would purchase a U.S.-based company's stock. In this scenario your dough is subject to U.S. investment laws, so it is presumably safer.

MUTUAL FUNDS

Besides the obvious "buy low—sell high" advice, you might consider the old "diversify your investments" advice, in which case you should put your money in a mutual fund whose investments are primarily in Asia generally or China specifically. Some of the larger U.S.-based financial services companies offer mutual funds consisting of Chinese-only securities, and there are also a few mutual funds that hold securities from all over Asia. Fidelity's China Region mutual fund, for instance, holds stocks from Taiwan, Hong Kong, and the mainland in many major industrial sectors. It has earned about a 12 percent return over the past five years. In such a mutual fund, the return on your investment should mirror the overall Chinese economy's performance, so you shouldn't lose your shirt, but you also won't strike it rich.

COMMUNICATIONS

You'll be pleased with the communications systems in China. When you pick up a telephone, it'll work (even though you might not fully understand what the caller is saying). When you mail a package, it'll get there—maybe not as quickly as you'd like, but it'll get there. Mobile phones work better in China than they do in North America, and when you use the Internet it'll most likely be broadband, not dial-up. Books, magazines, and newspapers are plentiful and can be pretty interesting (if you don't mind a small dose of propaganda). Hundreds of television channels beckon for the attention of couch potatoes, and nowadays there's quite a bit of English-language programming. For hundreds of years expatriates in the Middle Kingdom resolved themselves to a life of isolation, but today it's never been easier to stay in touch both within the Kingdom and with the outside world.

Telephone Service

Just like in the United States, ordinary telephone service is everywhere and it works quite well. You can expect phone lines to already be installed in your home, and your landlord will probably have already turned the service on for you. Just don't expect the wall jacks to be conveniently located. If for some reason your landlord hasn't already turned on the phone service or you are the rare expat that purchases a brand-new home that hasn't been wired, you can contact China Telecom, the local telephone company, and ask them directly to turn it on.

LANDLINE SERVICE

It costs about 200元 ($25) to have new landline telephone service installed and about 25元 ($3) per month for service. In most cities you won't be charged for the calls you make, instead you'll receive a flat-rate phone bill each month. A few cities have measured-rate service where you are charged for local calls. In Xiamen, for instance, China Telecom gives you 80元 ($10) in credit each month. If you gab a lot and reach the 80元 limit, they'll turn off your service until you go downtown and pay your bill. You can always

COMMUNICATIONS COSTS IN CHINA

Landline telephone	200元 ($25) installation, 25元 ($3) per month
Local telephone calls	0.2元 ($0.02) per minute
Long-distance calls within China	0.7元 ($0.09) per minute
Calls from China to the United States	8元 ($1) per minute
New mobile phone	350-4,000元 ($43-500)
SIM card	100元 ($12)
Mobile phone airtime	50元 ($6) for 100-200 minutes (depending on the company)
Rented mobile phone	80元 ($10) per day
Airmail postcard	11元 ($1.35)
5 lb. package to the United States	300元 ($36.90)
Internet access	5元 ($0.60) per hour dial-up, 150元 ($19) per month broadband
Newspaper	2元 ($0.25)
Cable TV	25元 ($3) per month

LET'S PLAY CARDS! *by Gary Zhou*

This handy guide will help you make sense of the different telecom cards for sale at the ubiquitous street kiosks.

I.P. card	The fancy abbreviation is for "Internet protocol," which refers to the fact that the voice signal is converted to digital packets and sent across the Internet. The quality might be lower, but so is the price. You also have to dial a lot of codes before calling. You can use the IP card for direct dialed domestic or international calls from payphones and regular telephones.
I.C. card	The original cards actually had tiny "integrated circuits" built in, but nowadays it's just a simple magnetic strip that you swipe at the payphone or just dial a string of codes like the IP card. The rates are higher than the IP card, but you don't have to dial as many codes, and supposedly the quality is better.
Mobile phone card	All mobile phone service is prepaid, so you'll have to buy one of these to add airtime to your account.
SIM Card	Small electronic chip that gives your mobile phone its own unique ID.

pay extra to avoid getting your phone cut off. In high-end housing including villas and serviced apartments, you'll probably never see a phone bill; it will be built into the cost of your monthly rent.

In general, you can expect telecommunications expenses in China to be less than half what you'd expect to pay in the States. Long-distance domestic calling rates average about 0.7元 ($0.09) per minute. Direct-dial calls from your Chinese home back to the United States should be about 8元 ($1) per minute.

CALLING CARDS

If you worry about gigantic phone bills giving you sticker shock at the end of the month, you should consider purchasing prepaid phone cards. These cards are readily available at most newsstands and convenience stores. The rates might still be somewhat ambiguous, but at 50–100元 ($6–12) per card it is easy to control how much you spend. The I.C. and I.P. cards are the most common calling cards.

A typical 100元 ($12) China Telecom I.C. card is good for about 200 minutes of local calling, about 120 minutes of long-distance calling within China, or about 12 minutes of calls back to the United States or other

© BARBARA STROTHER

Call and they will come (with their bamboo ladders) to install the phone services.

countries, but it is only good at public payphones. Although everyone has a mobile phone in China, the I.C. payphone cards are still useful because of the "dead zones" where there is no mobile signal (like subway stations). An I.C. card might also come in handy if your mobile phone's battery goes dead.

Another prepaid card is the I.P. card, which can be used from a payphone or landline. A typical 100元 ($12) I.P. card is good for about 330 minutes of local calling, about 250 minutes of long-distance calling within China, or about 50 minutes of international calling. The hassle of the I.P. card is that you'll have to dial a long string of numbers (as many as 35 digits!) to connect your call.

VOIP

The cheapest way to make international calls is to use VoIP (voice over Internet protocol) service. To make free Internet calls, you and the person you're calling will have to download the software, and then you can make voice calls as long as you are both online. You can also use the service to call traditional phone numbers, but you'll have to pay a small fee for this service (but it's still way cheaper than direct-dial long distance). Leading companies include U.S.-based Skype (and their Chinese partner TOMO) and 263.net. Apple computer users use iChat for VoIP.

VoIP companies are under fire from the large state-owned telecom companies who stand to lose a lot of money when their customers replace costly long-distance calls with free Internet calls. Some local telecom companies have even blocked the VoIP companies. Government officials also worry

USEFUL COMMUNICATIONS NUMBERS

110	Police
119	Fire
120 or 999	Ambulance, medical emergency
114	Local Directory Assistance
115	International Assistance
117	Time
121	Weather
163 or 169	Free dial-up internet

about VoIP because they see encrypted voice calls as a security threat. VoIP has gained momentum around the world so don't expect it to go away. We'll just have to wait and see how it all shakes out in the Middle Kingdom.

HOTLINES

In every city there are informational hotlines, accessible from landlines or mobile phones. These hotlines can connect you to emergency services, directory assistance, or weather information, to name a few. In larger cities most will be available in English. The national number for police is 110; ambulance is 120; fire is 119; and information operators is 114. There may also be a medical emergency hotline number that will connect you to western medical personnel—of course if you are not already a paying customer, you can't expect too much help. There are also translation service hotlines that will help you communicate with the locals for a subscription fee. All these hotline numbers are listed in the Yellow Pages; if you're lucky, your city will have an English-language version.

Mobile Phones

There's a saying that "even the beggars have mobile phones in China." More than 400 million Chinese people have a mobile phone, about one for every three people. This is due in part to their extreme affordability. Since Chinese cities are so densely populated, they need fewer cell towers to provide user coverage, resulting in cost savings they can pass down to their customers. Mobile phone service is both high quality and low cost, so you shouldn't have any problems. Make sure you pick from the top three

DAILY LIFE

companies (China Mobile, China Telecom, and China Unicom), and choose a phone with style, because in China, the ubiquitous mobile phone makes a statement about your personality. If you really want to fit in, hang a toy Hello Kitty or Pikachu off the antenna, the bigger the better. And get your thumbs warmed up—your Chinese friends prefer to communicate with text messages because they cost half as much as voice calls.

Buy a new card and pick up a mobile teddy while you're at it.

BUYING A MOBILE PHONE

Signing up for mobile phone service is pretty simple. Unlike the United States, you won't have to sign a service contract; in fact you'll be delighted that there is no paperwork whatsoever. But you also won't be given a free phone. You'll have to purchase the phone, which will typically cost between 350元 and 4,000元 ($43–500). If your city has an electronics market, start there—they'll have the best selection and the coolest newest phones. Every major shopping center and all the mega-stores like Carrefour and Wal-Mart also have mobile phone counters, as do the mom-and-pop shops, and, no guarantees, but you'll even find people selling phones from the back of their tricycles (like everything else in China).

There's also a bit of phone recycling among expats. Before you arrive, ask your host if they know of anyone who is leaving who wouldn't mind off-loading their phone. If you really want to go on the cheap, ask one of your young hip Chinese friends (assuming you have one) to find you a secondhand phone. Since these hipsters demand the latest styles, you can easily pick up last years' model for next to nothing.

SIM CARDS AND AIRTIME

When you buy a new phone you'll also need to purchase a SIM (subscriber identity model) card, available anywhere the phones are sold for about 100元 ($12). This 0.5–square inch computer chip slides into the back of your phone and uniquely identifies your phone's number to the mobile network. Ask the vendor to show you their available numbers so you can try to pick one that's easy to remember. Of course all the lucky numbers (with lots of 8s) will already be taken.

After purchasing the phone and the SIM card, you still need to buy the airtime, which runs 50元 ($6) for about 100–200 minutes (depending on the company) or 100元 ($12) for about 200–400 minutes. Airtime cards are sold just about everywhere. After you've paid for it, just scratch off the silvery stuff to reveal the numbers, type them into your phone, and you're ready to start flapping your gums again.

The city where you buy your SIM card is now the "hometown" for your phone, and while your phone will work all across the Middle Kingdom, you can only add airtime to your phone from cards purchased in your hometown. (Yeah, you guessed it; we learned this the hard way.) So if you'll be hitting the road on some cross-country trip, make sure you buy a couple extra airtime cards before you leave home. When you use the phone while traveling, you don't have to worry about expensive roaming charges because most mobile phone service is considered "nationwide coverage" even though they don't label it as such. Airtime is typically good for three months, then you lose it if you don't use it.

USING YOUR MOBILE PHONE FROM BACK HOME

Your U.S.-based mobile phone probably will not work in China, unless it is compatible with the Global System for Mobile communication standard (GSM) and you've set up international access with your U.S.-based carrier. Many of the mobile phone companies have reciprocal agreements, so even if you are "roaming" in China and make a few calls on your GSM phone, you won't be billed directly by the Chinese company. The calls will show up on your home-country carrier account and you'll be charged an arm and a leg.

GSM might be a good option for short-term visits, but if you are making the move, just leave your fancy mobile phone at home and plan on getting a new one in China. Even for visits as short as a month, you are still better off just buying a cheap China-based phone. Another option is renting a phone from one of the shops in the major airports (about 80元/$10, per day).

Internet Access

In China, Internet access is more advanced than in the United States where the Internet was invented. Our Chinese friend from Anhui laughed and shook his head when we told him most American households still use dial-up access. In China, most computer users have leapfrogged dial-up and gone straight to broadband. The typical Chinese computer connects to the worldwide web using a broadband DSL connection and a pirated version of Microsoft software ($1 from the same guy down the street who sells DVDs from the back of his bicycle).

STAYING IN TOUCH WORLDWIDE

Whether you live in China or anywhere else in the world, you can make it easier to stay in touch with your friends and family back home by subscribing to certain worldwide communication systems. Most travelers know that you can check your email in any Internet café on the planet as long as you have a web-based email account such as through Hotmail, Yahoo, or Ureach, to name just a few. What you might not know is that a lot of these companies also offer Internet-based phone numbers and fax numbers. They'll assign you a U.S.-based telephone number so you can easily receive faxes and voice messages through your email account.

You can also set up a permanent P.O. box in the United States and request to have your snail mail and packages forwarded to your China address either as they arrive or periodically. The post office will charge you fees for boxing your mail and forwarding it to you. This system makes it easier for your loved ones to send you stuff, and when you move around, you won't have to mail out those annoying change of address notices. If you receive a lot of packages from private shippers like UPS then you might consider getting a permanent P.O. box with a private company such as Access USA. It charges a small setup fee, a monthly fee, and then charges about $25 per kilogram to express deliver your mail to you.

© BARBARA STROTHER

Not sure your mail will reach your letterbox in your remote location?

DIAL-UP

Connecting to the Internet is easy; just plug your computer directly into an ordinary phone jack and dial up one of your city's free Internet numbers, a paid service number, or a prepaid card number. Free Internet numbers include 163 or 169 (use this same number as your login ID and password). If neither of these numbers works, ask around for the local free Internet numbers. If you want a quicker connection, you can use one of the pay-as-you-go services. Just like the free dial-up, you just need to know the telephone number and the user ID. In Beijing, for example, dial 95700 (using that same number as the ID and password) and you should be connected right away. The charges (about 5元/$0.60 per hour) will automatically be added to the telephone bill. You can also purchase an Internet IP (*hulianwang*) card (different from voice IP cards, so be sure to specify when you buy it), scratch off the annoying silver coating, and dial up according to the instructions on the card. IP cards are sold everywhere (especially at subway and sidewalk news kiosks), and each hour of use costs about 5元 ($0.60).

BROADBAND

Every major city has multiple broadband internet service providers. Ask your pals which company they'd recommend, but generally speaking there's little difference regarding service and price. Of course you could play it simple and just go to the nearest China Telecom office and sign up for service. DSL service costs starts at around 150元 ($19) per month and varies depending on the speed. For about 350元 ($45) you can buy a DSL modem at the electronics markets. Tell the shopkeeper you want to purchase an ADSL (asymmetrical digital subscriber line), which is what the techies call them. If you're in high-end housing, your landlord will probably already have DSL set up for you.

Broadband companies have also begun rolling out "broadband wireless fixed access" (BWFA), which will allow you to connect to the Internet with your laptop from any location in the city. Unlike WiFi, which is typically constrained to a hot spot like a cafe, BWFA will work wherever your mobile phone will work. The telecom carriers are currently building BWFA networks and by 2007 you should be able to purchase access in China's major cities.

INTERNET ON THE ROAD

Most Chinese hotel rooms have extra phone jacks that you can use for dial-up Internet access. You'll need to know the city's free numbers, the hotel's access numbers, or use an IP card. If you'd rather travel light and leave the laptop at home, you can surf the web and check your email on the computers at your hotel's business center—most hotels, four-star on up, have business centers and usually charge less than 10元 ($1.25).

You can also visit one of the local Internet cafés. Worried government censors shut down the Internet cafés from time to time, but they keep popping back up, so you shouldn't have a problem locating one. Every city has Internet cafés, but you'll be amused that few of the customers actually use the Internet, preferring instead to play PC games. The typical Internet café is dimly lit, grimy, and full of heavy smoke; and most are hard to find unless a local takes you. The charge is about 3元 ($0.37) per hour. There are "upscale" Internet cafés with comfy settings, fancy drinks, and clean workstations, though these are very rare.

Postal Service

Your expat buddies may advise you not to use the Chinese mail system, complaining that China Post is a stereotypical government bureaucracy that will lose your letters, pilfer your postcards, and break your boxes. They may convince you to use FedEx, UPS, or DHL. However, we've mailed letters and boxes from post offices all across China for the last ten years with no major problems, and our advice is opposite from what you'd expect. You may want to think twice about using FedEx and UPS because they are still relatively new on the scene and still struggle with

© BARBARA STROTHER

Neither rain, nor wind, nor snow will stop the China Post.

LOWERED (FED-)EXPECTATIONS

In the United States, Federal Express has a reputation for being one of the most reliable overnight shipping companies; they've expanded into China just within the past few years. So when I needed a few last-minute things for some business meetings, my secretary in Los Angeles FedExed a package from L.A. to the hotel in Beijing where I'd be checking in a few days later. "It'll be waiting for you when you arrive," she said.

When I got to Beijing, there was no package, so I called FedEx. The manager said they wouldn't deliver the package unless I paid some money first. "How much money?" I asked.

"We don't know, so we can't give you your package now, but we need you to fax us a copy of your passport. We'll get back to you on the fee."

I sent the fax but after a few days, I still hadn't heard back from them, so I called again. This time the manager politely told me "The reason we won't deliver the package is because FedEx only delivers to companies, not individuals." Rather than admit he didn't know where the heck my package was, I could tell this guy was just making up excuses to save face.

I called again the next day, and the manager told me the problem was that I had to designate the content of the package as "personal goods" or "company samples." "Be careful," he warned. "If you choose wrongly – big trouble with customs." It seemed that even FedEx couldn't escape the long reach of the infamous communist bureaucracy. I chose "personal goods," but it didn't seem to make any difference.

This tit for tat continued almost daily for three weeks. Every day my secretary complained to FedEx in L.A., and I complained in Beijing, but still no package. Each day the excuses were more varied and bizarre, such as "The manager will be on vacation, so no one at FedEx is working today." My favorite was "FedEx can't deliver in Beijing, only to Shenzhen."

It should have comforted me that I could enter my tracking number on www.fedex.com and see that my lonesome package and I were in the same city. But alas, we couldn't meet. At this point I had stopped caring about the contents of my package, I just wanted to win. You see, the hardest part of being an expat in China is that you have less control over your daily life than you did back home. When things you take for granted back home – like a hot Starbucks cappuccino or a FedEx delivery – don't work, it takes some of the wind out of your sails.

Business took me out of the country for a week, and then on to Shanghai, where I would spend the rest of the summer house-sitting for a friend. "FedEx can't deliver to residences, only businesses," I was told, so I had them send my package to a friend's office. Eventually, after three long weeks, my "international express" package arrived and I was happy. Not happy to get my things – the business meetings were long over – just happy to win. This experience reminded me that the happiest expats are those who have learned to have a different level of expectations.

DAILY LIFE

the complexities of China's bureaucracy, especially with customs issues. If you are in a hurry use DHL, or China Post's new Express Mail Service, which is available in the larger post offices.

SENDING AND RECEIVING MAIL

Letters and postcards can be mailed within China for 1元 ($0.12) or less depending on the destination. Airmail letters or postcards to the United States currently cost about 12元 ($1.50). Package rates within China are just above 100元 ($12.50) per kilogram, and packages sent internationally via surface mail cost a little more than 200元 ($25) per kilogram. International packages can also be airmailed, but the rates will be at least quadruple the surface mail rates. Options like delivery confirmation and certified mail are not available in the Chinese postal system.

Sending or receiving packages can be a sensitive matter. To mail a package you'll always have to show your passport and fill out some paperwork. To receive a package at the post office, it's the same story, except for those lucky occasions when they decide just to drop off the box at your place, which is more likely if you use your work address instead of your home address.

When shipping a package, don't seal your box before you get to the post office because they'll want to open it up and make sure you're not exporting contraband. Our postal workers were always amused when they'd open our "reverse care packages" and see the Chinese novelties we were mailing back to our pals in the States like mahjong sets or electric mosquito zappers. Lately the postal workers have also been repackaging everything into industrial grade cardboard boxes and smothering the box with packaging tape.

If you are shipping something abroad, just write the address in English, and your package should arrive just fine. Airmail takes about 5–10 days to reach the United States from China. Surface mail can take as long as two months. If people are sending you mail from abroad, they can write your Chinese address in English and it will reach you. However, it might take a while longer without some Chinese on the parcel.

Media

Back in the 1940s and 1950s Mao and his pals developed a powerful Russian-style propaganda industry that rallied millions of China's peasants to join the cause. During the Cultural Revolution Mao motivated his Red Guards using passionate messages across radio waves, newspapers, posters, and of course the famous "little red book" that contained Mao's coolest sayings. For all their other faults, you gotta admire their PR skills.

THE GREAT FIREWALL OF CHINA by James Bezjian

When the Communists rose to power 50 years ago, the free press was replaced with a Soviet-style propaganda machine. The government has loosened a bit since the glory days of the revolution, but all media and communications are still subject to censorship today.

Television, movies, and print media typically paint a rosy picture of life in modern China, but every so often a journalist musters up enough bravado to criticize the policies of the Communist Party. Such dissidents are quickly labeled "counterrevolutionaries" and can face strict sanctions from the government. Yahoo! China recently made international headlines by releasing the real name of a blogger who wrote scathing critiques of the government. He was promptly put on house arrest.

The boom in Internet use in China has made censorship quite a bit more challenging for the government. The "Great Firewall of China" has been put in place and many websites are blocked, especially those related to Tibetan independence, democracy, religious expression, or pornography. Conspiracy theorists claim that thousands of government censors work in dark smoky rooms reading our emails and listening in on our phone calls (ever wonder where all that static comes from?).

Researchers at Harvard have collected a list of "blocked" websites that can't be accessed in China. The list is impressive, but let's be fair. How often do we get the "website not found" error message while web surfing back in the States? As with all stories about the Middle Kingdom, it is sometimes hard to separate fact from fiction.

Back in 2001 when the U.S. military spy plane crash-landed on Hainan Island, all English-language news websites were immediately turned off. Foreigners who had heard of the incident stayed informed of the situation by international phone calls and using the Spanish-language news websites, which hadn't been blocked.

Censorship exists in China, but to what extent, nobody knows for sure. Nevertheless it's far better to be safe than sorry. So try to avoid talking or emailing about taboo subjects. If you absolutely feel the need to discuss controversial matters, grab one of your expat friends and chat face to face over coffee, or just wait until you're back home to talk it over.

Since then all media has remained under the tight fist of the Party. Those who dared write or say anything critical of the establishment were labeled "counterrevolutionaries" and severely punished. But as Bob Dylan noted, "the times, they are achangin'." Since Deng Xiaoping's Opening Up policy of the 1980s the government has been gradually loosening its grip on the media. But with Hu Jintiao's recent ascent to the presidency censorship, especially of the Internet, appears to be back on the rise.

NEWSPAPERS

Major English-language daily newspapers include the *China Daily* and Hong Kong's *South China Morning Post.* Most Chinese cities also now have their own daily English newspapers like the *Shanghai Daily.* The topics include politics, business, international news, sports, celebrity news, and quaint stories about locals, more like a small-town U.S. paper. Unlike the *New York Times,* which can be two inches thick, Chinese papers are usually only about 16 pages long, even in the big cities, and sell for just 2–3元 ($0.25–0.40).

Reading these English papers will give you a sense that all is rosy in the world, especially in China. These newspapers are provided for students

Numerous newspapers and magazines are available at local newsstands.

studying English and for China's foreign guests. As such, you will never find any news that is critical of the Chinese government. Instead of weighing in on a controversial topic such as the Taiwan situation, the opinion/editorial columns will explore more pressing dilemmas such as which is the cooler sport, table tennis or badminton. If you are a sports fan, you'll be able to keep up with American basketball, but you might as well forget football and baseball. Instead, you might find yourself developing a strange new interest in cricket and rugby. To stay abreast of world affairs you'll have to use the Internet.

MAGAZINES

All print media is extremely affordable in China. Walk in any direction for five minutes and you'll soon find a newsstand loaded with newspapers and magazines. Even if you aren't fluent in Mandarin you might still enjoy a local magazine once in a while. Most of the magazine will be in Chinese, but often one or two articles will be in English, and surprisingly, most titles and picture captions are bilingual. (I guess they know we just want to look at the pictures anyway.) We especially enjoy the decorating, fashion, and sports magazines, but don't care too much for the ones devoted to guns, tanks, missiles, and other ways to kill people.

BOOKS

Books and literature have always been highly esteemed in Chinese culture. Today, you'll find numerous bookstores in every Chinese city. Small bookshops pop up in the quirkiest places, and like in the United States, you'll find bookstores near universities. The big cities have massive five-story bookstores that are worth a visit. Usually one whole floor is dedicated to foreign-language books. You'll find a decent number of the English classics, and a few of the most recent nonfiction bestsellers, but not much in the way of popular novels. Because of the increasing number of Chinese who are taking college courses in English, you'll also find a generous selection of textbooks and scholarly books in English. There are also special foreign-language bookstores in the major cities that have high-quality English books with high-quality prices.

TELEVISION

Television is dominated by the numerous CCTV (Chinese Central TV) channels. The programming consists of quirky game shows, sappy Beijing Opera—style soap operas, news programs (all good news of course!), and propaganda shows that highlight exciting new advancements such as a new pedestrian bridge, or a calligraphy contest at an elementary school. It seems like quite a few expats prefer to watch pirated DVDs rather than normal television channels, and without a daily barrage of news they can easily fall out of touch with current events.

You can get cable television that will get you English-language favorites like Star TV, ESPN, HBO, and MSNBC. The desktop decoder box costs as much as 1,000元 ($125), but you might get one free from your landlord or from your local cable TV company. Monthly fees for cable TV are only around 25元 ($3), which might already be built into the cost of your rent. If not, you'll have to tolerate the annoyance of paying by automatic bank draft from your local bank account each month.

Satellite TV is becoming more available, especially in the high-rise buildings where the landlord or management company has purchased a license for the entire building. In some cases the channels you get might be limited by the direction your home faces.

RADIO

Like television, most Chinese radio programming is targeted to Chinese listeners. Some of the stations play a mix of western music and Chinese pop music, especially sappy love songs adored by junior high girls. Numerous stations take their cues from the Chinese opera and broadcast humorous stories and high-pitched traditional singing. Quite a few expats prefer to build up their music CD collection (just $1 for pirated music CDs from the street vendors; or just a few bucks in music stores, where coincidentally, the music is probably also pirated).

You can also catch Voice of America broadcasts and BBC news broadcasts in the larger cities. The language might be simplified since the broadcast might be intended for locals who are studying English. Needless to say, living in China might cause you to fall somewhat out of touch with world affairs, but on the other hand, just think of how much you'll be learning about China!

TRAVEL AND TRANSPORTATION

The Chinese transportation network is as vast and diversified as the colorful nation it crosses. Many regions have their own unique way of getting around—from the ultra-fast maglev train in Shanghai to plodding donkey carts of the west, from swift Mongolian horses in northern hills to bamboo rafts plying inland rivers. On any given day airplanes can connect you to more than 160 cities, trains can deliver you to all but the most remote regions, and buses will take you all the way to little villages untouched by the modern world. And as the Chinese government continues to annually invest 15 percent of its GDP in transportation and logistics, the system is always expanding and improving. On the other hand, some of the quaintest traditional methods for getting around, such as rickshaws, pedi-cabs, and motorcycle taxis, are being outlawed in larger cities to keep up with modern times.

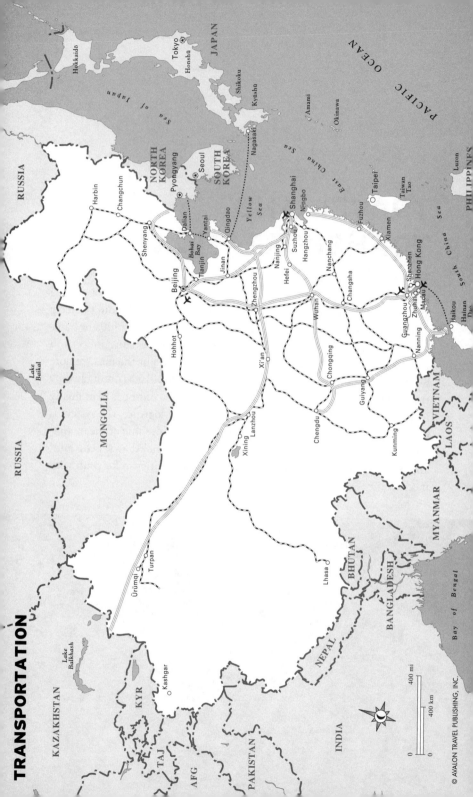

Much of your time in the Middle Kingdom will be spent in the middle of the masses on the move. A given day could include a complex chain of transport options. Our commute to church included a bike ride to a bus to the subway. To our favorite shopping district we took a taxi to a river ferry to the local bus. And did we mention cheap? You'll pay a tiny fraction of the cost of western countries to be whisked around in cabs, trains, buses, and boats.

By all means, get out there and experience the wealth of travel options in China—it will make your stay rich with unique experience. Hop in a rickshaw, sleep on a train, fly to remote regions, and store up memories, photos, and tales to tell for years to come.

By Air

Although it is possible to arrive in China via an eastern boat, northern train, or western four-wheel drive, more than likely your introduction to China will be via one of China's international airports. Direct flights from San Francisco, Chicago, Los Angeles, New York, or Newark take around 12 to 13 hours. Most international arrivals to the mainland come through Beijing, Shanghai, or Guangzhou, but more than 20 smaller cities have opened up to international flights from major Asian cities. These numbers should grow dramatically over the next few years since a new goal has been set to open as many as 53 cities to receive direct flights from the United States by the year 2025.

Within China, close to a dozen domestic airline carriers grouped into one of three main airline groups (Air China, China Eastern, China Southern) can shuttle you around the country's airports with reasonably efficient service. The longest distances can become quite pricey, with flights between Guangzhou and Urumqi at 2,840元 (about $350) economy one-way, or Shanghai to Lhasa around 2,880元 ($360) one-way, doubled for round-trip. Shorter flights, such as Beijing to Dalian or Guangzhou to Guilin, will run you less than $200 roundtrip.

To book a flight you'll find local travel agents and airline booking offices plentiful on China's city streets. Alternately, most hotels have a reservation desk staffed by English speakers who can make your travel arrangements for a small service fee. You can also book flights online (see *Resources* for web addresses). Prices are often given in one-way fares; double it for round-trip, add 25 percent to upgrade to Business class, add 60 percent to upgrade for first class. Kids under 12 get a 50 percent discount; babies under 2 pay just 10 percent of full fare. Optional insurance is available for 20元 ($2.50).

While Chinese domestic airlines now boast safety and service comparable to western airlines, take note that traveling by plane within the country is often more expensive—and more hassle—than it's worth. For shorter distances, or traveling any distance with children, we enthusiastically recommend taking the train.

By Train

The trains in China are a budget traveler's dream. Vast, reliable, and cheap, the train network can now get you to every corner of this giant nation and offer you a great view of rural countryside and picturesque villages. Attendants regularly wheel snack carts down the aisles offering potato chips, fresh fruit cups, instant noodles, meal boxes, warm beer, and hot water for tea; longer rides also have a dining car where Chinese chefs will whip you up a number of Chinese dishes. Not all train journeys offer the same level of cleanliness and comfort, however, so it is important to understand the Chinese system of ticket classes and train numbers.

In a socialist effort to rid itself of class distinction, Chinese train tickets opt for monikers that don't make a statement on the worth of the individual. There are no first- or second-class citizens here; only those that opt to purchase one of the following tickets: hard seat, soft seat, hard sleeper, and soft sleeper. The terms "hard" and "soft," consequently, do not literally describe the softness of your resting place—nowadays, all seats and bunks are padded.

TYPES OF TICKETS
Hard Seat

If you value comfort and cleanliness, you'll want to avoid the hard-seat section on all but the shortest train routes. Although dirt-cheap (about $3 for a five-hour ride from Nanjing to Shanghai; about $1.50 Shanghai to Suzhou, one hour), hard-seat cars are often packed tight with travelers sitting shoulder to shoulder on upright benches that are *supposed* to fit just three. On longer rides the floor fills up with discarded shells of nuts and tea-boiled eggs, watermelon rinds, litter, green spatters of spittle, and an occasional wetness from a toddler clothed in the traditional open-bottomed pants. And don't even think about using the hole-in-the-floor, handrail-on-the-wall, squat pot "toilets" after the first few minutes into your hard-seat

This way to the Line 1 metro stop in front of the Shanghai railway station.

journey. When the train jolts, the watery mess will splash from the floor up your pant leg. Hard-seat class is recommended for only three occasions—if you want to travel dirt cheap on a super-short trip, if you want to rub shoulders (literally) with the locals and experience the hardship of "real China," or if you have your heart set on a trip and all the other tickets are sold out. Have fun—just don't say we didn't warn you.

Soft Seat

Soft seat is a great improvement over hard seat. A ticket in this class with get you an assigned seat (no overbooking allowed) on a carpeted train car featuring lacy curtains, tablecloths, seat covers, air-conditioning, and clean bathrooms with choice of western toilet or eastern squat pot. Slightly more expensive than hard seat (in comparison, Shanghai to Nanjing runs about $6, double the cost of hard seat but still cheap), this class offers a pleasant environment for you and your friends to sip tea and play cards while watching terraced hills and rice paddies pass by. Unfortunately soft-seat cars are only available on a few of the shorter trains between major tourist destinations.

Hard Sleeper

For overnight journeys, hard sleeper is our favorite way to travel. Six bunks in an open compartment face a corridor with fold-down window seats.

Pricing is based on the bunk's position. The highest bunk is the cheapest, offering little headroom but a good option for tall travelers who can stretch their feet out into the corridor without bothering anyone walking by. The bottom bunk is the most expensive due to its conveniences: under-bed storage, easy use of the mini-table and hot water thermos, and a convenient place to sit during daylight hours. Unfortunately everyone else will also find your bottom bunk a nice place to sit, and you may long for the American ethos of personal space. Alternatively, many foreigners find the middle bunk the best option. With a middle bunk you can choose when to join your bunk-mates in a game of *xiangqi* (Chinese chess) and when to hide away comfortably on your bunk with your mp3 player and a good book. Sample fare: Beijing in the north to Guangzhou in the south, 22 hours, 458元 (about $57).

Soft Sleeper

If you greatly cherish your privacy, a soft sleeper ticket will buy your way into a two- or four-bunk compartment with locking door and the ability to control the lights, speakers, and vent. The newer trains also boast individual TV screens and outlets for laptop use. The luxury is reflected in the price, though, and for some destinations soft sleeper is as expensive as flying—but keep in mind you are also saving the expense of a hotel night when you sleep on the train. The most common soft-sleeper route is the Shanghai–Beijing express train, 12 hours, 499元 (about $62).

BUYING TRAIN TICKETS

Most major cities have a ticket window at the train station specifically for English speakers. Or, for a service fee, use a local travel agent or hotel ticket reservation desk. Biannual train guides with intricately detailed timetables and ticket pricing can be purchased near the ticket windows at the station. No English versions are available yet, and the guide is complex, but if you can work your way through it, you can come up with all kinds of exciting travel plans. For a quick reference, enter your destination at www.travelchinaguide.com/china-trains for information on the trains that cover your desired route.

Train tickets can't be purchased more than three or four days ahead of your travel date. The exception is during key holiday seasons, when the tickets will go on sale a few weeks ahead of time. These tickets are very hard to come by, however, since millions of Chinese will be crisscrossing the nation during the Chinese holidays to visit family and do touring of their own. As for return tickets, most can't be purchased until you reach your destination station (a stressful reality for anyone who has to get back to work in time), but as China's train system becomes computerized, some round-trip tickets can now be purchased at major train stations.

Kids get a discount on train tickets based on their height. The littlest ones can share your bunk, saving money and giving parents peace of mind that their tiny tots won't fall out of the bunk with the occasional jolts of the train. Compared to the discontent of being strapped into a plane seat, the freedom kids have on the train to walk around and climb on the bunks far outweighs the lack of good rest a parent may get being squeezed between their little snoozer and the edge of the skinny bunk.

TYPES OF TRAINS

All trains in China have an alphanumeric label based on their age and speed. Train numbers starting with a Z are the newest and fastest express trains in the fleet, each boasting its own "luxury" perks. Comfortable compartments (by Chinese standards) may offer amenities such as personal TV screens, individual reading lights, wireless Internet access, a place to plug in your laptop, a menu with both western and Chinese options, and even breakfast delivered in bed in the morning. Heck, they even give you complimentary noodles if it's your birthday (Birthday Song not included). The majority of Z trains have only soft sleepers, but the prices still are not that much higher than the cost of hard sleepers on older trains traveling the same route.

T trains used to be the fastest and most luxurious class of express trains before the Z trains were released in 2004. These T trains feature all classes of seats and sleepers and crisscross the country in every direction. The next step down, K trains, are a little slower, and cheaper still. Trains labeled with an N, or those without any letters at all, are slower, older, and cheaper. These trains don't ply the major tourist routes, so you might not even encounter them unless you're headed off the beaten path.

As a general guideline for overnight routes, T trains add a couple hours to the Z train schedules; K, N, and numeric trains add at least four to five hours with both a decreased price and a decreased comfort level.

Two words of advice for train travel: First, don't lose your ticket on the train because you will have to show it to exit the station at your destination. And second, travel light. You'll have to lug your bags down several flights of stairs to board the train. Escalators going up are common enough in China but down escalators are much more rare, even in train station areas where you'd think they would find it rather helpful to provide them. Besides, the baggage space is small—you may have to share your skinny bunk with your chubby Samsonite if it doesn't fit in the luggage area.

METRO

While you'll probably use the long-distance train system on breaks and holidays, daily you'll probably find yourself on a different sort of train—the metro. Residents of Beijing, Shanghai, Hong Kong, and Guangzhou (and to a lesser extent, Tianjin, Nanjing, and a handful of other cities with expanding subways in the works) will want to be intimately acquainted with the metro system in their city. Often

the daily commute via Shanghai's subway

faster than taxis and always cheaper, the metro is the most efficient mode of transport around China's crowded cities. Typical fares run between 2元 and 5元 ($0.24–0.60); tickets are purchased at booths or machines displaying metro maps that show the fares for each stop.

You'll find the Chinese metros to be quite English-friendly. Arrival announcements are made in English as well as Chinese, and route maps give the names of stations in pinyin as well as characters. The biggest drawback of the metro is the pushing and jostling that goes on as the masses force their way onto overcrowded trains at rush hours. As with any crowded subway system around the world, watch your bags and pockets for wandering hands.

By Bus

LONG-DISTANCE BUS

Long-distance travel by bus can be rather slow and uncomfortable. There are few times when self-arranged long-distance travel is best by bus. For instance, short distances such as Shanghai to Hangzhou can take the same amount of time by train or bus, but if you are located closer to the bus station than the train station, it may save time and money. Because the demand is less, tickets are cheaper and easier to come by than other modes of transportation. Besides, China's long-distance buses can get you to even the tiniest of mountain hamlets, which is their greatest appeal—offering unparalleled first-hand experience of the China your grandparents saw in picture books when they were children.

The buses plying the most popular routes will be relatively clean and comfortable, air-conditioned, some showing movies during the ride. If your destination is small or remote, however, you may get stuck on an over-packed, under-padded ratty old bus with farmers taking bags of live ducks to the market.

Sleeper buses offer reclining seats or two-tier bunks, a cheap way to spend the night and reach your destination at the same time. Check out the bus before you commit, though, because some of the sleeper buses look quite dirty.

All long-distance buses will stop for meal and bathroom breaks at places that will give you fodder for stories to impress your friends with your bravery and adventurous spirit for years to come. Our advice: bring your own snacks, and drink as little as possible on these trips, especially if you are female.

Tickets

Except for major holidays, you can just show up at the bus station and buy a ticket on the day you want to travel—just get there early enough to accommodate for the possibility of long lines and communication woes. Try to get as much information as possible on your options. They may sell you a ticket on the next departing bus, without bothering to mention that if you waited another half hour, you could upgrade your seat on the jalopy to an air-conditioned luxury bus for a fraction more. Tickets can be purchased at marked windows or directly from the attendant on the bus.

CITY BUSES

For those who don't live close to a metro line, the public bus system can take you just about anywhere in the city—that is, if you can find the route you need. Bus-stop signs list the routes, but without a lick of English or even pinyin, it can take quite a bit of effort to figure it out. City maps, however, list bus numbers along each street. If your English map doesn't show bus numbers, pick up a Chinese map at the nearest bookstore, train station, or tourist site and compare the two to find the route you need. Typically you won't have to wait more than 5 or 10 minutes for the next bus to come.

Public buses are dirt cheap, typically just 1元 ($0.12), unless you choose an air-conditioned bus (labeled with a K or a snowflake) for the exorbitant rate of 2 or 3元 ($0.25–0.36). We found these air-conditioned buses to be a great place for our toddlers to catch a quick nap while we enjoyed a cheap city tour sans heat wave. If there is no coin-drop when you get on, you'll pay the conductor. Just take a seat and she'll come to you. Some common routes feature double-decker buses, some with an open roof on the second level. Most buses stop running around 11 P.M.

When you do get settled into the Chinese neighborhood you'll call home, experiment with the local buses. You can always grab a cheap and easy taxi back home if you end up stranded in an unknown part of town. Riding buses through the neighborhoods is how we found some of our favorite restaurants, tailors, and markets. You never know what you'll discover. Be aware, though, that rush hour can be unpleasantly jammed full of shoving, elbowing locals who may be a little too interested in what's in your wallet.

By Boat

In China you may find yourself more often afloat than you would back home. Boats are a part of the spice that gives China its unique flavor, such as dragon boats on idyllic lakes, morning commutes by Hong Kong ferry, and gondolas still plying the ancient canals of river towns.

Not so long ago traveling by ship in China could open up a whole world of high seas adventures. Sadly, as roads, railways and air routes become more efficient, many of the old passenger ship routes are being discontinued. A few good routes still exist, though, protected by the poor accessibility via land to these destinations. Dalian's peninsular location provides numerous options for traveling via boat, as well as the many islands and inlets of the South China Sea around Hong Kong, Macau, and Hainan Island.

© BARBARA STROTHER

In some ancient river towns, gondolas still serve as water taxis.

RIVERBOATS

Riverboats, although sometimes excruciatingly slow, offer an unparalleled view into life along China's waterways as they meander China's inland rivers and canals. Along the Three Gorges from Chongqing to Wuhan, perhaps the most famous river cruise route, luxury cruise lines glide past gorgeous scenery that has already started to disappear beneath the controversial dam project. The Three Gorges cruise cabins are comparable to three- to five-star hotel rooms but with a much higher price. Other less-glamorous river routes, such as Nanjing to Shanghai along the Yangtze or Hangzhou to Suzhou along the old Grand Canal, offer slow passage in less-than-luxurious rooms with an up-close look at life along—and on—the river. For any Yangtze River trip, keep in mind that the closer you get to the sea, the wider the mighty Yangtze becomes, too wide to see anything except a dull expanse of muddy brown water in all directions.

CITY FERRIES

There are a handful of cities in China that use ferries in their everyday commute. Hong Kong, with its hundreds of islands, depends on its extensive ferryboat system to keep its island-hopping commuters on the move. On a much smaller scale, Shanghai's ferries can be the fastest—not to mention most scenic—way to cross between Puxi and Pudong if your origin and destination lie close to the river. At less than $0.25 a trip, you get to

Ferries can take you from the Shanghai Bund to Pudong.

© BARBARA STROTHER

DAILY LIFE

bridgetunneltraffic,andyoucaneven bring your bike or
motorcycle across the river with you if you'd like. Ferry routes are marked
on most city maps.

By Car

They say the most dangerous thing you can do in China is walk across the
street. Every day traffic accidents claim the lives of 600 people in China
and injure 45,000 more. Drivers breaking traffic laws cause more than
85 percent of fatal accidents. And as the national economy continues to
boom, car ownership is multiplying at a dizzying rate, filling the streets
with more inexperienced drivers and new vehicles than the roads can hold.
Despite the risks and the major traffic congestion, getting around on four
wheels—whether by taxi or private car—is probably the way you'll most
often get to where you need to go.

TAXI SERVICE

Compared to other major cities around the world, China's taxis are cheap
and plentiful. Beijing has five times more taxis than New York City. While
taking taxis daily would be cost-prohibitive in most countries, Chinese cabs
cost just a few bucks a ride. Taxi fares start around 10元 ($1.25) for the
first three to five kilometers and 2元 ($0.25) for each kilometer thereafter,
varying by city and type of taxi. Tips are never expected for a typical ride,
although daily rentals expect a little extra for their services and may want
you to pick up the lunch tab as well. Except for rainy days and rush hours
(and especially rainy rush hours), it should be easy to find a cab. Just step
up to your nearest street curb and start waving your hand. Any movement
will do since cabbies intently watch foreigners for the slightest sign that
their taxi services may be needed. If you tell the driver where you want to
go and he turns you down, it may be that he is holding out for a higher
fare, or it may be that regulations forbid him from taking the route needed
to reach your destination. Some cities limit the number of cabs that can
use busy tunnels or bridges on certain days and times.

One of the most difficult aspects of using cabs is the lack of English
spoken by drivers. If you find one that can say more than "Hello," consider yourself lucky—and get his phone number to request his services
regularly. Otherwise, the most foolproof way to communicate with a taxi
driver is on paper. Grab a business card from your hotel or a business near
your home for the return ride. Have a bilingual acquaintance jot down

A TAXI OF ANOTHER COLOR

When you hear the term "taxi cab," what do you picture? Something with four wheels, no doubt, perhaps a yellow car with rectangular lights on top. But in China's smaller cities and traditional neighborhoods, you may be surprised to find what the local taxi service looks like. In Turpan, donkeys pull you through the city in wooden carts covered in colorful rugs. Along Suzhou's canals and Beijing's *hutongs*, three-wheeled bicycles called pedi-cabs offer a comfortable bench seat for two behind a thick-calved pedaler. In Nanjing's Confucian Temple area, rickshaws take you to your shopping destination powered the old fashioned way – by foot of the coolie. River towns built around waterways offer gondola taxis and elsewhere motorcycles are enclosed in sheet-metal compartments resembling micro-minivans.

By all means, if your journey is a short one, use the local transport. They are a great way to celebrate the adventure of living in China. They may be slower, but they allow you more opportunity to take in the sounds and smells and back-alley sights of the world you are traveling in. You'll never think the same way about what it means to take a "taxi" again.

© BARBARA STROTHER

a motorcycle taxi in Beijing

your destination in Chinese. Or point to your destination location on a map—but do *not* make the assumption that your driver will be able to use that map to find his way around.

Scams

Most taxis have meters and do not try to rip you off. If, however, the meter isn't working in your cab, you have the right to refuse to pay. For the most part metered taxis are honest, to the point of offering discounts if they took a wrong turn or missed the right street. Watch out, though, for unmetered taxis such as pedi-cabs or the little *mian bao che,* literally "loaf of bread car," which are funny little vans that often hang out at train stations waiting for groups toting excessive luggage. Fares for unmetered rides need to

Traditional rickshaws can still take you for a ride in Nanjing's Confucius Temple area.

be agreed upon and negotiated before you get into the vehicle because, as one expat put it, "the price of a ride depends on the length of your nose." Make sure that the amount is the total, not a per-person rate (a favorite trick played on unsuspecting tourists), and carry small bills to pay the exact fare. If you spend any length of time traveling around China, you will eventually be the victim of a conniving cabbie. Disagreements with drivers over fares can get quite ugly; you're better off just letting it go.

If you do feel that you are being taken advantage of by a taxi driver, be sure to write down his license number, posted in front of the passenger seat, as well as the phone number for the cab company (also posted within the cab). If your disagreement is with a rickshaw or pedi-cab driver, or some other private taxi service, look for a nearby policeman to help you negotiate the situation. Often seeing someone in your party go after a man in uniform will make your driver immediately give up on his attempted scam. You can also call 110 to summon police help, which is staffed by bilingual operators in larger cities.

DRIVING

With the extensive and highly efficient public transportation available in China, driving your own car is both rare and really quite unnecessary. Driving is a tricky affair in China, and should be avoided by foreigners who value life and limb. A better way to get around by private car is to hire a driver. But if you have your heart set on getting behind the wheel, here is what you will need to know.

The first step to getting behind the wheel is deciding whether or not it is the right choice for you. Will you be in the country for a year or less? Then it won't be worth your time to muddle through the complex process of getting a license. Are you in China on a tourist visa? Then just forget about driving—only those with a foreign residence permit need apply. Can you read enough Chinese to maneuver the streets safely? Only a few locations have bilingual road signs. Where will you be driving? If your destinations lie mostly in the central city area, you'll spend most of your time searching for the elusive parking spot. How are your defensive driving skills? Since thousands of new licenses are issued each year, Chinese streets are filled with inexperienced drivers. We strongly recommend that you spend a fair amount of time observing the traffic situation in your Chinese city before you make your final decision.

Drivers Licenses and Traffic Laws

If you still have your heart set on getting behind the wheel, you'll have to get a local Chinese driver's license, as international licenses aren't recognized in China. First take your U.S. or international drivers license to an official translator and stop by a hospital for a physical exam (local clinics don't count). Next up is a written test, which in major cities is available in English; if not, you will be allowed to bring a translator with you. Bring a few passport photos for the application, your residence permit and passport, your translated foreign license, and money to cover the fees. When the process is complete you can return in a week for your coveted card. If you live in Beijing, it's easier just to pay FESCO (Foreign Enterprise Service Corporation, www.fescochina.com) to handle the whole process for you.

Once you've found your way legally into the driving seat, you'll find the rules of the road a bit ambiguous. Traffic weaves all over the road ambivalent to marked lanes. Chinese drivers feel they can do just about anything they want to as long as they use their horns to blaringly announce their intentions, such as going the wrong way down a one-way street, running red lights, playing chicken in oncoming traffic to pass a slower vehicle, forcing left-hand turns directly into oncoming traffic, and driving in bike lanes and even on sidewalks. The idea seems to be that if you see—or hear—them, you're supposed to just get out of their way. Speed limits are regularly posted, less regularly followed. Mobile phones are off-limits for drivers; seat belts are required in the front seats. Be aware that hidden traffic cameras are abundant in some areas, so even though you don't see any police, they are watching you, and they know how to find you. If you do find yourself the lucky recipient of a ticket, you'll be required to go to the traffic police station nearest the spot where you broke the law to pay the fines.

RENTING OR HIRING A CAR

Unlike the thriving rental industry in western nations, the car rental industry in China is in its infancy. Rentals between cities in China are not available to tourists and have only recently become available to the general population of foreign residents with Chinese drivers licenses. A

You don't need to know a lick of Chinese to understand these road signs.

few of the prime U.S. rental agencies are opening locations in China, such as Avis and Hertz, where cars can be rented for local use starting around 400元 ($50) daily.

The preferred way to rent a car in China includes hiring a driver as well, which is a great way to get around without having to personally hassle with the complicated traffic, tricky navigation, and nonexistent parking. Comfortable cars and vans can be reserved ahead of time through a travel agent or hotel desk; alternately, you can negotiate a flat day rate with any cabbie driving by. Many businesspeople opt for a long-term hire arrangement with a specific car and driver. In these arrangements you'll be chauffeured around for a specified number of hours per week for a flat fee, getting you and your spouse to work, bringing the kids home from school, or running around on errands and sightseeing activities. Extra hours require an extra per-hour rate, and the driver can use his off time to seek other fares. The monthly fee, depending on the quality of the car and the experience of the driver, typically starts around 50元 to 60元 ($6–7.50) per hour. Although there are agencies that will help you locate a long-term hire, fees can be steep. The best way to find someone is to ask for recommendations from others who have personal drivers.

BUYING OR LEASING A CAR

Since the bureaucratic challenge of bringing your own vehicle into China is hardly worth the money or effort, you may consider buying or leasing a car during your stay. The sale of privately owned cars is skyrocketing in China, as owning your own car is becoming a status symbol affordable to a growing number of Chinese. You'll see plenty of sedans and minivans made by Hyundai, Buick, and Volkswagen on the road, as well as lots of micro-cars made by Chinese companies like Chery. Even high-end luxury cars are on the rise, with plenty of Cadillacs, Range Rovers, and even Hummers (which, after tariffs, cost three times as much as in the States). New car dealerships are popping up around the country; bring your PRC license if you want to test drive. If you'd prefer used over new, secondhand car markets in major cities will have plenty to pick through—but the level of trustworthiness of the sellers is hard to gauge. As with many other major purchases, the easiest way to buy a used car is to pick one up from another expat who is on his or her way out of the country.

The costs associated with buying a new car include the price of the car, registration fee, emissions test, appraisal tax, road tax, user tax, license plate, and insurance. Sticker price for imported luxury cars such as BMW and Mercedes can be found in the $100,000 range; locally made cars are a little more affordable, such as the popular MPV in the $25,000 range or a Volkswagen two-door in the $10,000 range. Since the government controls the number of license plates issued each month, competition for new plates can drive the prices much higher—around $4,000 or $5,000 in competitive markets but a mere couple hundred RMB in more rural areas. License plates with lucky numbers, such as all 8s, fetch ridiculously high prices at auction. With monthly maintenance, tolls, and insurance, you can plan on spending about an extra $3,000 annually.

Recent changes to the law allow foreign residents who have been in China for over a year to apply for auto loans. Approved financial institutions include credit unions and the newly formed auto finance companies run by the likes of Toyota, GM, and Volkswagen.

Instead of buying a car, consider leasing. Benefits include a lower down payment and no responsibility for repairs and maintenance. Some companies even provide emergency service if you break down on the side of the road. You will need to provide an upfront deposit in the range of $1,200–$3,600, depending on the value of the car to be leased, as well as your ID card, passport, and local drivers license. Of course, the downside of leasing is that in the end, you don't have much to show for all those payments you made, and you'll have paid much more for the car than its original price. A car that costs $25,000 outright will end up costing you about $32,000 through leasing.

A WORD ABOUT MOTORCYCLES

Motorcycles and motor scooters can be quite cheap in China, starting around $200 for a scooter from your local Carrefour superstore or other large retailer. No license is required for the scooters—just keep them on the bike lanes and sidewalks. As for motorcycles, you will need a Chinese driving license. D licenses cover all motorcycles (including those with side-cars and motorized tricycles), while an E license covers just two-wheelers. In an effort to curb traffic problems, some cities have banned motorbikes outright from the central city and major roadways. Others have forbidden all bikes over a certain age. Additionally, the number of motorcycle license plates is fixed per city. If you buy a bike without a plate, you'll have to jump through quite a few hoops to get a license. Because of the changing laws concerning motorcycles, be sure you check out the latest situation in your city before investing in one. The best way to get the latest scoop is to find a local riding club, which can often be found listed in the classified sections of English-language city magazines.

By Bicycle

Car ownership may be on the rise in China, but bicycles are still the number-one way to get around. Most roads in Chinese cities include an ample bike lane, making it much easier to navigate by two wheels than in the West where city planners don't consider bikes a standard mode of transportation. You'll see whole families on one bike, or bicycles used as delivery trucks. A local appliance shop in our old neighborhood used traditional two-wheel bikes for deliveries, with a refrigerator strapped to each side of the bike and one stacked on top of the others. You might not carry your furniture around with you, but bike baskets make handy spots to throw purses, briefcases, groceries, or laptops. We once had a bike we affectionately termed our Chinese minivan: two extra seats for our two toddlers and three baskets made it possible for just one of us to take the kids to do the weekly grocery shopping.

The rules of the road for biking are simple. Stay to the right except to pass. When you hear the sound of a car horn or another bicyclist's bell, get out of the way. If you want to pass a pedestrian or another biker in front of you, use your own bell to signal your intentions. And think twice about riding double with a person of the opposite sex, which signifies that you are dating.

Bikes are very cheap in China—in both price and quality. The cheapest models start around $20. Luckily mobile bike repairmen sit around the sidewalks with carts full of spare tires and replacement parts ready to fix your flat or broken brakes for a few coins while you wait. (You'll find them next to street-side tailors doing the neighborhood mending with their ancient hand-operated sewing machines.)

One word of advice for buying a bike in China: Don't get one that looks fancy. Cool-looking bikes tend to disappear no matter how well you lock them up, but a plain- or old-looking bike is the best protection against theft.

DAILY LIFE

HOUSING CONSIDERATIONS

Most foreign workers in China have their housing provided by their employer directly or the employer hires a service that takes you by the hand and walks you through every step of the house-hunting process. Chances are you won't be tackling this process on your own your first time over, though those who tend to stay longer eventually desire a change—experienced expat teachers prefer to move off campus, and some of those who have decided to stay for the long haul choose to invest in buying a house rather than renting.

Searching for the right place to rent or buy in China can be an exasperating experience. Between doubts that your real estate agent or landlord are being honest with you, inflated real estate prices, and having properties you were interested in pulled out from beneath your feet before you've had a time to make a move, trying to find a place to call home can leave

© BARBARA STROTHER

you stressed out. The best way to relieve some of that stress is to become as educated as possible about the process. This chapter can serve as a general guideline, a good starting place, but you'll have to get to know the market in your specific city as well.

We strongly recommend that you don't try to find a permanent place to live right off the bat. If you can, plan to live in a temporary residence while you get to know your new city before you sign a long-term lease or purchase a property. Students and teachers at Chinese schools should plan on staying on campus at first; those with corporate budgets can stay at a serviced apartment until they find a place. If you don't fall into either of these categories, consider an inexpensive short-term furnished apartment rental.

Housing Options

Housing options in China primarily include apartments, dorms, and villas (houses), plus an occasional townhouse or traditional Chinese house. The majority of city-dwellers in China live in standard apartments, though some foreigners prefer a serviced apartment, which comes with all the bells and whistles of a luxury hotel.

STANDARD APARTMENTS

Standard apartments are the most common housing arrangements for both locals and foreigners alike. "Standard" is in contrast to "serviced," which are apartments that are run more like hotel rooms complete with services like daily housekeeping and room service. Standard apartments vary greatly in quality, size, and cost.

Unlike the American system of apartment rental where one company owns the whole complex, apartments in China are purchased individually after they are built. Though you may deal directly with the apartment's management company in paying your rent and other landlord-type issues, they are typically only performing this as a service to the individual who actually owns the apartment you are renting. There are, of course, companies who buy up blocks of apartments to rent them out, but it is very rare for one company to own all the apartments within a complex. It is also possible for foreigners to buy their own apartment.

The average rents for apartments vary considerably from one city to the next. Hong Kong, Macau, Shanghai, and Beijing have some of the highest rents in the world; on the other hand, you can rent a nice flat in smaller cities for as little as $100 to $200 a month. If you're in the market to buy, apartments are much cheaper than villas, starting as low as $30,000 in the hinterland on up to well over a million dollars for a swanky place in Beijing.

The Range of Standards

While there are no hard and fast guidelines to what is or is not a "standard" apartment, you should be aware of what lies at each end of the spectrum. The worst-case scenario will be the very old (and very cheap) apartments, which foreigners rarely choose unless they are quite broke. With these apart-

a traditional courtyard

ments, you may have a squat hole in your bathroom instead of a toilet. You won't have a bathtub and you'll be lucky to even get a shower curtain; often the entire bathroom—floor, walls, and ceiling—are tiled, with a shower-head sticking out of one wall, and the entire room is exposed to the water as you shower. You may be washing your laundry by hand and hanging it on poles sticking out your window to dry. The floors will be cheap lino-leum or shiny fake wood that's warped and nicked. You may not have any heating or air-conditioning. All the pipes will be exposed in the kitchen, and you'll have no appliances except a cheap, portable two-burner cook top sitting on a modest kitchen table. There's hardly any storage, and the rooms are so tiny they remind you of the walk-in closets back home, which are just a memory, because standard Chinese apartments won't have any closets at all.

Modern luxury apartments, on the other hand, may have large garden tubs, Italian marble and real hardwood floors, central heat and air, and broadband DSL access wired into the walls. Those that are designed with foreigners in mind will have a clothes washer *and* dryer, a built-in oven, a dishwasher, and lots of kitchen cupboards and storage closets, but you'll pay for these high-end amenities. Wall-to-wall carpeting is rare except in the nicest places, and you wouldn't want it anyways in a place that is not as nice (just look at the nasty carpet in any Chinese hotel room to see why!).

The nicer the apartment complex, the more amenities will be located within its walls, such as convenience marts, beauty salons, health club facilities, swimming pools, tennis courts, restaurants, pubs, and coffee shops.

The bulk of the standard apartments available in China will fall somewhere in between these two extremes, with prices to reflect this. For the most part, you won't know exactly what a place will be like until you see it, but you can guess by its price tag at which end of the spectrum it may lay. Generally, when the prices are quoted in yuan, and the complexes don't choose cheesy English names, you can be sure that you are now on the local economy (as opposed to the all-foreigners-are-wealthy economy). This will, of course, vary considerably based on which city you live in. A property advertised for $200 a month is likely to be decent in Xi'an, but a dump in Beijing. And the Chinese toilets? In major cities pretty much all apartments will come with western toilets, though in places farther removed from western influence, like Kunming, you may be surprised to find a squat pot installed into the marble floors of a beautiful new apartment. The apartments we've listed in the prime living locations of this book are all some level of international standard, though we don't guarantee that you'll get the dishwasher or the garden tub.

Floor Level Matters

Chinese apartments are categorized as tall (i.e. skyscrapers) and mid-height towers. Buildings over seven stories are required to have elevators, which

HOUSING TERMS IN CHINA

Detached villa: house
Attached villa: townhouse or duplex
Gardens: green space and landscaping
Private garden: yard
Serviced apartment: an apartment run like a hotel
DIY: Do It Yourself home remodeling
Undecorated: unfinished (no flooring, doors, appliances, cabinetry, fixtures, etc.)
Decorated: finished (has flooring, doors, cabinetry, fixtures); may be furnished as well
Furnished: comes with furniture, appliances, electronics, and decor
Unfurnished: no furniture or appliances but all else will be complete (flooring, doors, etc.)
Secondhand home: one that has been lived in previously

is why you'll see many places no higher than this in an effort to spare the extra expense (a great way to stay in shape if you live on a top floor, but not exactly convenient!). Apart from the obvious benefit of great views, there are several reasons to pay attention to the floor level of apartments. The higher the apartment, the more likely it is to be posh. Higher floor levels garner higher prices, and it is standard practice for every apartment listed in Chinese housing classifieds to advertise what floor they are on in relation to how tall the building is.

Many apartments have luxurious two-story penthouses on the top floor.

© BARBARA STROTHER

Most modern apartment buildings in China are built with luxury penthouses on the top floor. Often these penthouses are huge, with two stories, and might even include large rooftop garden areas. Driving around a Chinese city, look up and you'll see these penthouses, with huge walls of windows spanning both floors.

On the other end of the scale, apartments on the first couple of floors are more prone to burglary and have less privacy. Since gates and guards protect most housing in China, security isn't typically a problem, although there are areas, particularly Macau, where burglary has become more of a problem in recent years. The privacy may be more of an issue when an occasional landscaper or janitorial staff has no qualms about stopping their work to stare at you through your windows. If you have small children or pets, you may be willing to deal with these issues in exchange for the convenient access to the green space outside where kids and pets can play.

Direction Matters

Most westerners don't pay too much attention to which direction an apartment faces, but direction plays an important role in Chinese real estate. For one, feng shui dictates certain blessings, curses, and luck that are closely associated with directions. If you're not a feng shui enthusiast, you may not

GET YOUR FENG SHUI ON

Feng shui, which literally means "wind and water," is a mystical belief that architecture, layout, and decoration, when done right, can direct the mysterious *qi* power into your life for blessing and prosperity. Feng shui uses the *luo pan,* a geomancy compass, to follow the guidelines of the *bagua* octagon, which has the yin and yang in the center symbolizing balance, surrounded by different compass points that correspond to natural elements and important life issues. The northern compass point, for instance, corresponds to the water element and relates to your front door, your career, your ancestors, and your ears (yep, guessed it – feng shui is also used in traditional Chinese medicine). Whether you believe in feng shui or not, a basic understanding of it should give you a greater appreciation of the many idiosyncrasies of Chinese architecture.

According to feng shui principles, bathrooms and kitchens should be isolated so as not to disrupt the peace and quiet of the living spaces. Windows are placed not just to let in light but also to ensure the free flow of *qi* into and out of your home. The wealth corner must be decorated with items that symbolize prosperity; the love corner should have pairs of objects. A mirror in the dining room promotes abundance, but a mirror opposite the front door bounces the positive *qi* right back out of your house.

Perhaps the main idea of feng shui for your home is that the design will evoke simplicity, clean lines, and a lack of clutter. The bottom line is that feng shui results in homes with pleasant layouts, but whether it generates more *qi* or not, well, we'll leave that one up to you.

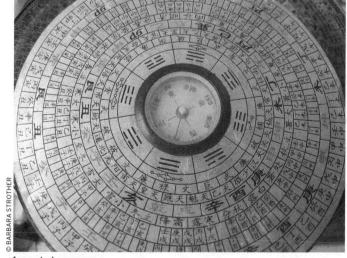

feng shui compass

old apartments next to new construction in Beijing

find this very important to you. It plays a stronger role in purchasing than renting, since it will affect resale value of the home. As a westerner, you'll probably take the second reason direction is important much more to heart: the direction you face can determine which TV signals you'll receive. So-called "cable" TV is actually transmitted via analog signal over the airwaves. If you're a sports or news addict, you may want to check first before you commit to a place where you'll never be able to get the big game on TV.

SERVICED APARTMENTS

Serviced apartments are rental flats most often found on the premises of four-and five-star hotels, though there are a few chains that run serviced apartments that are not hotels. They are designed for short-term rental, from just a few weeks up to a couple of years. Although some are not much more than glorified hotel rooms, most were designed with the same types of layouts you would expect in a simple apartment: a small kitchen, dining area, living room, and one or two bedrooms with a matching number of bathrooms. A few may also have a balcony but you should forget having a yard or green space. You won't get a yard with a standard apartment either, but standard apartments often have parklike green areas where you can walk your dog, let your kids play, or practice your *tai qi* in the morning. Serviced apartments rarely have such spaces.

Serviced apartments are quite a bit more expensive than standard apartments for the amenities they offer. Residents can take advantage of all of the hotel's amenities, from fitness centers, saunas, spas, and swimming pools to room service, breakfast buffets, restaurants, concierge services, daily housekeeping, and the like. These places are typically staffed by English speakers who can take care of your requests and needs, which can be quite handy when you are new to the country and don't yet speak any Chinese. The flip side to this benefit is that residents tend to stay isolated from the local community, taking longer to learn basic conversational Mandarin and rarely making Chinese friends, though it is within your power to overcome this.

Some upscale hotels have long-term serviced apartment rentals.

Serviced apartments are of course only available to rent, not buy. As a general guideline, you'll typically pay twice as much for a serviced apartment than for a standard apartment, but this can differ significantly based on location and what amenities the serviced apartment offers.

DETACHED VILLAS AND ATTACHED TOWNHOUSES

What most westerners would call a "house" the Chinese call a "villa." Whether detached with its own yard (always called a "garden" in China), or attached as a duplex or in a row of townhouses with small yards or shared green space, villas are typically the most expensive and most luxurious option in Chinese housing. Villas are always built within walled complexes with guarded gates, with an English-speaking management company that services the community around the clock. The villa market is new to China, having come in on the wave of China's new economic wealth in order to cater to the growing wealthy class and to the growing numbers of foreigners living in China.

Some villas are absolutely huge, even up to three, four, or five stories tall. They come in a large variety of styles, Mediterranean or mid-American, elaborate classical European or minimalist Japanese Zen. Most places offer three to five bedrooms, a private garage, western appliances, and gorgeous landscaping that you don't have to lift a finger to maintain. In addition, most villa complexes also have the added perks of swimming pools, playgrounds, a gym and sport facilities, gift and imported-foods shops, a pub, and a restaurant or two. Some have on-campus preschools (called "kindergartens") or classes for kids such as ballet and swimming, making them the best option for families with children.

As with serviced apartments, living in a villa complex tends to keep expats more isolated from the local Chinese community and less likely to learn the language. On the other hand, you'll be able to make friends with neighbors that come from all around the world.

Whether buying or renting, villas will take a big bite out of your wallet, which is why they are typically only used by executives and diplomats who receive them as part of their expat compensation packages. Some start as low as $2,000, but others rent as high as $15,000 or more per month.

OTHER HOUSING OPTIONS
School Dorms

A great number of foreigners living in China live on a school campus. English teachers are given apartments on the grounds of the school or college where they teach; most foreign university students live in the dorms.

If you'll be a university student in China, you can expect to have a tiny dorm room, sometimes shared and sometimes private. If you're lucky you'll have your own little bathroom; otherwise, you'll share a communal bathroom with the other students on your floor. At the best campuses, your room will have heat, air-conditioning, and a television in a comfortable but simple environment, with a cafeteria on the premises or close by and a launderette, with or without dryers.

As a teacher (regardless of what age group you'll teach), you should be given a small apartment on or near campus. Sometimes you'll have the apartment to yourself; sometimes you'll share a two-bedroom flat with another teacher. Your room arrangements are subject to negotiation; if it's important to you to have your own space, you can try to bargain for a better deal before the contract is signed. The housing will be provided free of charge but you'll have to pay the school for some or all of the utilities you use, though often cable TV and Internet access are also provided by the school. The flat will be fully furnished, and should come with a small washer and dryer (be sure to ask first!) as well as a microwave, cook top, small refrigerator, and bottled water dispenser.

Roommates and Home Stays

Another housing option to consider is to rent a room in someone else's apartment or to arrange a home stay. Both of these are great options for those who are serious about learning Chinese. Chinese housing websites such as www.soufun.com and www.515j.com have advertisements (some in English) from people who are looking for roommates. Alternately, you can search the classifieds in English magazines and websites for your city, which are more apt to come up with both English-speaking Chinese and foreigners looking for roommates.

You'll also occasionally find a classified from a Chinese family or individual who desires to have a live-in native English speaker and will provide a free room in exchange for the language practice they will get, especially for families that want their children to learn English well. Home stays are not as common in China, mostly due to the fact that such fraternizing with foreigners was forbidden before the very recent opening-up policies. If you are interested in this option and can't find anything available online before you get there, consider posting your own classified ad. Given the Chinese fascination with learning English, there are bound to be plenty who would love to host a foreigner but have just never considered it an option before. One word of warning, though: Be sure you clear it with the local PSB (Public Security Bureau) before you move in. Chinese people who are housing foreign guests, even for a night, are by law required to report it to the PSB, and besides, not all PSBs are clued in to the new freedoms that have been granted to foreigners.

Unusual Chinese Homes

Beyond the standard apartment and villa options, some Chinese cities offer more unique housing options. Beijing has its *siheyuan,* old brick houses built around courtyards down mazes of narrow roads. Qingdao, Xiamen, and all the other seaside cities that served as foreign concession ports have areas with remaining hundred-year-old European villas. In Inner Mongolia's countryside, people still live in yurts (felt tents), and close to Xi'an there's an area where homes have been built into hewn caves, complete with electricity but few other utilities. For those who are big on adventure, and in most cases with a big wallet as well, one of these unique options may appeal to you. Just don't expect it to be easy to find one or easy to live in.

Renting a Home

If your employer won't be providing your housing in China then you'll have the daunting task of finding a place on your own. Whether an apartment, villa, or townhouse, you'll have a wealth of options in location, size, amenities, and price.

USING REAL ESTATE AGENCIES

Real estate agents in North America are predominantly there to help their clients buy a home, but real estate agents in China help their clients with both buying and renting. In fact, the bulk of the work that a typical Chinese agent will do involves helping a client find a home to rent. Each agency has its own properties available, and you'll know you've found a real estate agency when you walk past a shop window that is covered with photos and details of apartments and villas. A few agencies in cities with large expat communities cater specifically to foreigners; the best way to find them is through online searches and through their advertisements in the local expat magazines.

The typical fee you'll pay for their services will be equivalent to one or two months' rent for the property you eventually decide on. For that fee you'll have someone who will take you around to see the properties you are interested in, answer your questions about the place, and help negotiate terms with the landlord. The real estate industry is not as regulated in China as it is in the States, however, so you will need to make sure that you are comfortable with the trustworthiness of the agent you'll be working with. Some may take advantage of your lack of familiarity with the way things work to pad their own pockets a bit. You won't be on an exclusivity contract, so feel free to try other agents as well, especially if you see a place you're interested in but the listing belongs to someone other than your agent. The fees you pay are a commission on the property you choose, so you technically won't have to pay an agent that is unsuccessful in finding a home for you (although some may try to get you to pay them for their time—you are the rich foreigner, after all).

FINDING A PLACE ON YOUR OWN

You can also forego the expense of using an agent and just do the legwork yourself. Expat magazines and websites for your city often have classifieds with places available to rent. If you're already there, you can start asking around for leads as well; many people know someone who has a place to rent, especially since China's newly wealthy trust putting their money into real estate investments more than putting it into the stock market or the bank. If you see a complex that appeals to you, stop in and see what's available.

By far the best way to get information is through the Chinese property-listing websites. Of course if you can't read Chinese well, you'll need to enlist the help of a Chinese friend to decode it for you. These online listings will tell you whether or not the home is being offered by the individual or by a company, and will give you the contact information for the landlord. Companies can be more trustworthy than an individual landlord when it comes to maintenance and other issues, although they will have much less flexibility to customize the rental agreement to your specific needs. Be aware, however, that when a potential landlord discovers that you are foreign, often the price immediately starts to rise. Price negotiations might be best handled by a Chinese agent before the landlord finds out you're not a local.

RENTAL TERMS

Most Chinese landlords are looking for a one- or two-year minimum lease agreement, though there are a few who are willing to do short-term rentals. Before you sign your new lease, be sure you are financially prepared to do so. Apart from the fees of one to two months' rent you'll pay your agent (if you used one), you'll also have to give your new landlord a security deposit. Some demand a six-month deposit, but you can probably negotiate just a one- or two-month deposit. Take your rent and multiply it by five to estimate the amount of cash you should have accessible to get into a new place. If you can't swing that much cash, skip the agent and bargain hard directly with the landlord for a smaller deposit amount. Monthly rental amounts are also negotiable, and in some places, the initial rental offering will be quite a bit higher than the landlord will take after some negotiations.

To pay your monthly rent, since China's monetary system does not involve personal checks, the typical process is for you to deposit your rent every month directly into your landlord's bank account. The specific payment details will have to be worked out between the two of you. There are a few other details that are open to negotiation, such as whether the apartment is furnished.

Furnished or Unfurnished?

Most apartments and villas for rent come completely furnished, including electronics. On the other hand, those rentals that are advertised as unfurnished may not even have basic appliances such as a stove or a fridge. If you would prefer to use your own furnishings, or if you're interested in an unfurnished location but need it to be furnished, it's all negotiable. Even if you'd prefer a different type of furnishing than what is there, you can try to get them to swap it out for you. Keep in mind, however, that if you're asking for them to remove the stuff that is already there, they'll have to do extra work as well as find a new place for the items, so expect it to cost you a little in the bargaining. Some landlords with

© BARBARA STROTHER

Getting an unfurnished place allows you to shop for furnishings to your taste.

unfurnished homes will let you pick out the furnishings within a certain budget, a great way to get the style you want without committing yourself to possessing a lot of junk you'll have to get rid of when you leave the country.

Utilities and Services

Within the majority of rental agreements, you will be responsible for paying for your utilities directly. Your landlord will probably have all of your utilities turned on before you move in. If not, contact the landlord first, will handle it for you, or else tell you what you'll need to do for the utility companies. Monthly utility bills will arrive in the mail each month, and can be paid at utility company offices, post offices, at banks, or, in some cases, inserting your I.P. card (the same I.P. card that is used for making phone calls) directly into the electric meter. The apartment complex provides trash receptacles, which are included in the responsibilities and expenses of the property maintenance company.

Common utility expenses per month are: electricity (80元/$10), gas (60元/$7.50), telephone (60元/$7.50), water (40元/$5), cable television (25元/$3), and bottled water (10元/$1.25 per bottle, delivered). These figures will fluctuate by region, season, and size of your home, especially in the

AYIS

Quite a few expats hire locals to work as *ayis*. *Ayi* literally means "auntie," and a typical *ayi* plays the roles of nanny and maid and, like an auntie, eventually feels like a member of the family. They'll clean, do laundry, cook, and wash windows. They'll do your grocery shopping and can often help you arrange any maintenance needed in your home. The nicer homes in China are built with *ayi* quarters, and the *ayi* typically stays the night during the week and goes back to her home on the weekends. Make sure you give her time off according to the Chinese holidays, and make sure you pay bonuses according to what's normal for your community (just ask your neighbors). To find an *ayi*, check with your real estate agency, or ask your expat friends' *ayis* for recommendations. Depending on the city, an *ayi*'s pay ranges $75-200 a month for a full-time *ayi*, half that for a half-time *ayi*. You'll feel guilty getting so much service for such a small amount of money, but the relationship won't always be easy. There's the language barrier and the strange food (river snakes, anyone?); she might not discipline the children according to your standards; and you might find her cleaning methods strange, such as when you catch her mopping the windows and the rugs.

DAILY LIFE

north, where you'll use more gas or electricity to heat your home. Electricity is 220 volts AC, 50Hz. Expect to buy some power strips, because the wall outlets are sparse, and while two-pin and three-pin sockets are standard, don't be surprised if your apartment has five or six different types of outlets.

Some landlords, especially in serviced apartments and high-end apartments, will provide a summary bill for utilities and request that you pay them directly. This seems convenient, but you'd be wise to request a peek at the original bills so you don't get overcharged. In older apartment buildings, some of the utilities might be shared, in which case you'll be asked to pay a share each month, or responsibility to pay the entire monthly bill will rotate between the households.

THE MOVE IN

Before you start unpacking your boxes, you should give your new home a thorough inspection. Chinese housing sometimes may be subject to shoddy construction, so test all the taps, flip each light switch, flush the toilets, and make sure every door and window can be opened, closed, and locked. If you have any valuables, then you should change the locks soon after you move in and keep all the keys to yourself. You should also register with the

PSB and your embassy or consulate (see the *Once You've Arrived* section of the *Making the Move* chapter for more information).

Owning a Home

Many foreigners are surprised to discover that they now have the option of purchasing a home—whether apartment or villa—in communist China. In fact, those that are investment-savvy claim that it's the only wise financial choice, given the rising economy and with it the rise in home values. On the other hand, for a foreigner buying a home in China can be a bureaucratic nightmare that is not for the faint of heart.

For all practical purposes, buying an apartment or buying a villa is the same process. In Chinese cities, building a home is not done by individuals but by real estate developers, who build the homes then sell each unit individually. Though rural Chinese do build their own homes, if foreigners wanted to try to build their own home, they'd face an incredible amount of resistance and would probably be told it's not possible (though China is a place where you can turn impossibilities into possibilities if you are determined; "not possible" is an easy answer that you will get all the time, even on simple things you know are quite possible because you've done them before).

We strongly recommend that you do not consider buying a home until you have spent a considerable amount of time in this country, long enough to learn its business ways and a fair amount of its language, and long enough to make sure you'll still love it here when the honeymoon stage has worn off and you're facing serious culture shock. Add to that the new anti-speculation laws designed to keep you in your home for at least two years, and you don't want to get stuck in a situation you're not happy with. That said, if you are convinced that buying a home is the right option for you right now, here are a few things you'll need to know.

THE RISKS

There are a number of risks involved with buying a home in China, including legal complexities, the chance of getting scammed (this country has more than its fair share of con artists and those who know how to manipulate the system to their benefit), the financial issues of the country's strict banking laws, and the possibility your property's value will drop as in the early 2006 real estate bust in Shanghai.

© BARBARA STROTHER

China's newest style of housing is based on North American suburbs.

When you buy a home in China, you are only buying the building structure, not the land itself. All residential land is actually on a 70-year lease from the government, after which time they have the option to reclaim the land and recompense you according to what they think is fair. Homeowners do not have the same kind of rights in China as they do in the West, and it is not uncommon for local residents to get bought out of their homes and forced to move. Beijing just doesn't care all that much about your attachment to your home. They care quite a bit more about making way for "progress," and if your property happens to be in their way, you have no guarantees.

The chance that your home will be taken from you is slim, but you may face poor quality issues. No matter how beautiful the home looks when you purchase it, the quality of the place may immediately start to deteriorate. Chinese construction tends to take shortcuts when possible, and items manufactured for domestic purchase are often of extremely inferior quality. Stuff breaks, and repairs can be shoddy and jerry-rigged. Finding a handyman you can trust to always do things right with all the right materials and tools is a treasure. The most you can do is be prepared to accept this as part of home ownership—or learn the skills of plumbing, carpentry, electrical work, and masonry, as well as the business of importing goods and materials.

BRAND NEW VS. SECONDHAND

The home-buying market in China is divided into two sections: homes that are newly built and those that have been previously lived in (referred to as "secondhand" in China). The buying experience can be quite different for each. In many cities, the competition for getting a brand-new home is so fierce that even before the houses or flats are built there are long lines of people waiting to buy. Some places have a lottery system, where you pay to put your name in and if you get lucky, you get to buy. Some places even charge you just to tell you the listed sale price on their homes. Buying a secondhand home is much less competitive, though if you see a place you like, you shouldn't take too long before you act.

With a newly built apartment or villa, you'll be getting what the Chinese call "undecorated." This doesn't mean it won't have art on the wall. In fact, with an undecorated place, you might not even get any walls! All you are guaranteed is an empty shell, though some will come a bit more finished. It will be up to you to "decorate" the home, which typically takes 2–3 months. You'll have to purchase (and have installed) all appliances, all cabinetry, all bathroom fixtures and light fixtures, and all flooring. You may have to oversee the building of walls where you want them and other construction details. You'll spend a lot of time at appliance stores and Do-It-Yourself (DIY) outlets such as B&O and Ikea. Secondhand homes, on the other hand, will be finished and sometimes fully furnished, although probably not to your liking.

HOW TO FIND A PLACE

The way to find a place to buy in China is not too different from the way to find a place to rent. Basically, you can choose between using a real estate agent or looking on your own, though the legal process becomes quite a bit more complicated with buying than renting, increasing the risks involved if you try to do it on your own. A third way to find a home to buy is to attend a home-selling convention, which some cities hold every quarter. At these events quite a number of properties are bought and sold. Some complexes schedule mini-bus tours from the convention grounds to their property to show off the homes for sale; others use photographs and detailed information. These events are in no way focused on foreigners, however, so you typically won't find a lick of English.

FINANCING AND MORTGAGE ISSUES

If you are purchasing a brand new apartment or villa, the developer will probably have an exclusive financing agreement with a Chinese mortgage company that you'll be required to use. More competitive financing terms might have been found elsewhere, but at least you'll have the convenience of your developer handling the administrative details, which should fast-track the process quite a bit.

If you decide to arrange your own financing, you can use a foreign bank such as Wing Hang, Bank of East Asia, Standard Chartered, or HSBC. Chinese banks that grant mortgages to foreigners include Bank of China, Industrial and Commercial Bank of China, and the Bank of Communications. Some of these banks only offer loans in renminbi, while the international banks offer loans in renminbi or dollars. For the renminbi loans, interest rates are based on a benchmark rate published by the People's Bank of China; dollar loans are based on the U.S. prime rate. Thirty-year mortgages are available, but more favorable conditions are offered for shorter terms. Few of these banks will finance the entire price of the home; most require a down payment of 20 to 50 percent.

OTHER RED TAPE

Real estate law changes every year, and because so many real estate deals end up in the courts, you should hire an attorney who has a proven track record helping expats purchase homes in China. You'll need permits for land use, construction, sales, and housing quality, and any error in the paperwork can invalidate your home purchase. Not every apartment or villa on the market can legally be sold to foreigners, and there are tax issues specific to expats. You'd hate to miss out on one of the tax breaks that are for foreigners only. Hiring an experienced lawyer should help you negotiate favorable conditions and minimize your chances of getting burned.

WHEN IT'S TIME TO LEAVE

When the time comes to pack up your bags and head back to your homeland (or on to new adventures), you can sell your home by listing it with a Chinese real estate agency. New regulations designed to drive out speculators require you to own your home for at least two years prior to selling it, or else you'll pay a stiff penalty.

After selling your Chinese home, you'll be stuck with a wad of renminbi that can be converted into hard currency after you jump through some

administrative hoops. First, you'll have to apply to your local foreign exchange bureau, who'll then send the request to the State Administration of
Foreign Exchange (SAFE). You'll need to submit a number of documents to
SAFE including receipts of foreign currency that you brought into China,
original home purchase documents, sale documents, and proof that your
property taxes have been paid. Once SAFE is satisfied, they'll give approval
to your bank to convert your loot into greenbacks.

Renting Your Home

If you want to hold on to your Chinese property, but don't plan to live
there, you can entrust the process to a real estate agent or to your complex's
management company and enjoy the proceeds from the rent from abroad.
Just be sure to pick an agency that has experience working with expats.

PRIME LIVING
LOCATIONS

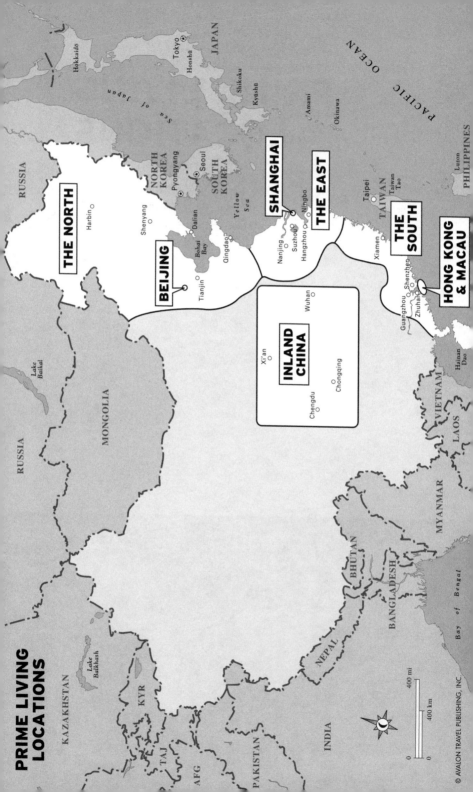

PRIME LIVING LOCATIONS

THE NORTH

BEIJING

SHANGHAI

THE EAST

THE SOUTH

HONG KONG & MACAU

INLAND CHINA

RUSSIA

MONGOLIA

KAZAKHSTAN

Lake Balkhash

Lake Baikal

JAPAN

Hokkaido

Honshu

Shikoku

Kyushu

Tokyo

NORTH KOREA

SOUTH KOREA

Pyongyang

Seoul

Harbin

Shenyang

Dalian

Bohai Bay

Qingdao

Tianjin

Yellow Sea

Sea of Japan

PACIFIC OCEAN

Amami

Okinawa

Taipei

TAIWAN

Taiwan Tao

Luzon

PHILIPPINES

Nanjing

Suzhou

Hangzhou

Ningbo

Xiamen

Shenzhen

Guangzhou

Zhuhai

Xi'an

Wuhan

Chongqing

Chengdu

Hainan Dao

VIETNAM

LAOS

MYANMAR

Bay of Bengal

BHUTAN

BANGLADESH

NEPAL

INDIA

PAKISTAN

AFG

TAJ

KYR

400 mi

400 km

© AVALON TRAVEL PUBLISHING, INC.

OVERVIEW

This *Prime Living Locations* section is designed with two types of people in mind. For those who have the opportunity to choose their destination in China, these chapters will help you make an informed decision. But most foreigners moving to China won't get to choose where to live; their employer will have already done that for them. For those of you who have been assigned to a specific location, the information on these pages will give you a solid introduction to what to expect in your new home away from home.

For the sake of this book we've divided the country into seven sections. China's major cities are covered in the *Beijing, Shanghai,* and *Hong Kong and Macau* chapters, while the *North, East, South,* and *Inland China* chapters cover the best places to live in each of these broad regions. Don't be surprised if you don't see your favorite vacation spot on these pages; quite a few places are great to visit but difficult to live in. We've chosen to cover

© KEVIN SELDOMRIDGE

the places that can offer the best quality of life for foreigners, based on factors like the size of the city's expat community and the accessibility of western amenities like imported groceries (i.e. butter, cheese, and cereal), high-quality housing, international schools, and western health care.

Beijing

Proud capital and seat of power, Beijing wields an amazing amount of influence over this vast nation. All provinces live by Beijing; they set their clocks by Beijing time and speak Beijing's Mandarin dialect in their schools, businesses, and local government.

This city is the heart and soul of the nation, and the presence of central government is strongly felt here. In fact, politics is one of the main reasons why many foreigners come to Beijing, from diplomatic positions at one of the many embassies to journalists who keep the world informed of what this mighty giant is up to.

Compared to Hong Kong and Shanghai, Beijing is much more "Chinese" than its cosmopolitan cousins. Though its immense skyline is decorated with copious glassy skyscrapers, this city still feels old, due in part to the gloriously stubborn existence of *hutongs,* the labyrinthine neighborhoods dating back hundreds of years. It's also the center of the Chinese performing arts, celebrating the rich culture of this ancient nation's unique culture with its Chinese operas, acrobat shows, and traditional orchestras.

Unfortunately Beijing is often weighed down by thick gray smog. Harsh winters and occasional dust storms blowing in from Mongolian deserts add to the challenges of Beijing residents. But the city is in the midst of massive change. As Beijing prepares for the 2008 Olympics, every corner and facet of this great capital is under scrutiny for how it will look and function when the world descends on its doorsteps. Vast improvements to infrastructure and industries supporting the tourist market are quickly turning this city into a world-class destination.

Shanghai

With over 17 million residents, Shanghai is not only the largest city in China, it's also the biggest in the world by some counts. In this flourishing commercial and financial center, East meets West in a striking blend of world cultures. Historic European buildings stand regally along its busy river, a reminder of its colonial past, while Asian temples and old-style

Chinese neighborhoods hint at the more ancient culture. The real heart of Shanghai is in its fast-paced business and social scenes. This city is all about energy, and it is hard not to feel the excitement pulsing behind its futuristic skyscrapers when you first arrive. This place is also all about money, and Shanghaiers have a reputation for focusing their lives on the pursuit of conspicuous wealth. Businessmen in thousand-dollar suits jet about in shiny new Buicks, Bentleys, and Hummers to high-powered business meetings; the young and beautiful get all decked out in designer labels and pack their way into the subway for yet another night out on the town.

Some compare Shanghai with New York, some with Paris—though don't go expecting either or you may be disappointed. As for expat amenities, Shanghai can't be beat among mainland cities. You'll be able to get just about anything you want here, though you may have to pay dearly for it. Your money will also buy you more choices here than in other parts of the country, from what kind of world cuisine to eat for dinner to what architectural style of luxury villa to live in (Mediterranean stucco or Bavarian village? Japanese zen or sleek ultramodern?). Shanghai offers more opportunities to forget, for just a little while, that you are living in China—something that foreigners in smaller cities long for when the culture shock and the homesickness come on strong.

Hong Kong and Macau

The return of Hong Kong to mainland China in 1997 and Macau in 1999 made these areas official Special Administrative Regions (SARs) of the People's Republic of China, although they retain their own laws, currency, and taxes. Though the British governed Hong Kong for 150 years and the Portuguese ruled Macau for 400 years, these spots have always maintained their Chinese character, along with a bit of European flair. Yet so many years of independence from the mainland have given Hong Kong and Macau a unique flavor that you won't find anyplace else on the mainland.

Hong Kong is as cosmopolitan as China gets. Its urban islands boast a plethora of international restaurants, posh shopping malls, and five-star hotels amidst a dizzying array of skyscrapers and neon lights. It's the place mainland China expats run to when they need dependable health care, when they want to shop for something they can't find on the mainland, or when they need a break from the "real China." It's not all glass and glitz, however. A trek out to one of the outlying islands will put you on sandy beaches and forested hiking trails for a much-needed infusion of the natural world.

Macau, on the other hand, is limited by its size in what it has to offer.

THE BIG THREE: ECONOMIC REGIONS

Within China there are three key city clusters that together are responsible for the majority of the nation's GDP.

The Yangtze River Delta: central eastern cities located on the Yangtze or near where the river meets the East China Sea, including Shanghai, Nanjing, Suzhou, Hangzhou, and Ningbo, among others.

The Pearl River Delta: southern cities located on or near where the Pearl River meets the South China Sea, including Guangzhou, Dongguan, Shenzhen, Zhuhai, Macau, and Hong Kong, among others.

The Bohai Bay Economic Rim: northern cities located on or near the Bohai Sea, including Beijing, Tianjin, Dalian, Yantai, and Qingdao, among others.

Located opposite the Pearl River Estuary from Hong Kong, the peninsula and islands that make up Macau are tiny, home to less than half a million people all packed into eight square miles. Most are drawn to Macau for its historic old Portuguese charms or its sparkly new casinos—it's the only Chinese city where gambling is legal.

While both Hong Kong and Macau come with a lot of perks, they also come with a hefty price tag. Their real estate and cost of living are among the most expensive in the world. But if you've got a lot of money to spend, this is as good a place as any to spend it. Both Hong Kong and Macau consistently make it into the top five best places for expats to live in Asia.

The South

The best word to describe southern China, both literally and figuratively, is steamy, a land of summer typhoons and successful tycoons. It's home to Hainan Island, where the tropical sun and surf have garnered it the nickname the Hawaii of the Orient. Nearby Guangdong Province holds the economic powerhouse of the Pearl River Delta cities, including three top destination cities for expats: Guangzhou, Shenzhen, and Zhuhai. Up the coastline in Fujian Province, Xiamen Island has been captivating foreigners with its charm for centuries.

Guangzhou City, also known as Canton, has served as a major port since the days Arab traders exchanged their Muslim religious influence for a bit of silk and tea during the Tang dynasty. British merchants replaced the Arabs in the 19th century, and modern-day Guangzhou reflects these many years

© KEVIN SELDOMRIDGE

washing clothes the traditional way in southern China

of foreign influence. The Cantonese have a reputation for strong entrepreneurial spirit, cosmopolitanism, and above all, a taste for very strange foods.

The city of Shenzhen is the gateway between Hong Kong and the mainland, and it's strictly business. As the PRC's first experiment with foreign business and investment, Shenzhen is a new and prospering boomtown, narrowly beating out Shanghai for the position of having the wealthiest residents. Directly across the Pearl River is the city of Zhuhai, which is following in Shenzhen's footsteps. Zhuhai is the gateway to Macau, and its status as another of the first Special Economic Zones has created a prosperous city where there was none just 20 years ago. Both Shenzhen and Zhuhai boast clean air and pleasant living environments with easy access to the perks of nearby Hong Kong and Macau.

Up the coast and beyond the mountains of Fujian Province, the city of Xiamen covers two islands and a bit of the mainland. Its seaside gardens and meandering lanes of old Mediterranean-style villas reflect Xiamen's history as a colonial port city, while its thriving new upscale commercial areas and pristine beaches provide loads of modern-day pleasures.

The East

East China consists of the two provinces surrounding Shanghai, Jiangsu and Zhejiang, which all together make up the Yangtze River Delta economic cluster. This is one of the wealthiest areas in China, where even the farmers live in towering four-story homes.

As the saying goes, "In heaven there is paradise. On earth there are Suzhou and Hangzhou." For centuries these two cities in eastern China have had a reputation for their physical beauty, Suzhou for its ancient gardens and Hangzhou for its famous West Lake. The effect of having such

PRIME LIVING LOCATIONS

a relaxing natural environment has given Hangzhou residents a laid-back demeanor, unlike their workaholic Shanghai neighbors. Both Hangzhou and Suzhou have a thriving tourist industry, with highly developed amenities and businesses that cater to foreigners.

Farther north, Nanjing holds strong historic significance as the site of the Kuomintang headquarters and the Japanese massacre. This ancient city is once again starting to come into its own, adding amenities like a new subway system and international luxury hotels. Some say it's like Shanghai was before the development of Pudong—on the brink of great things but still a sleepy city.

Ningbo, on the coast south of Shanghai, is smaller and sleepier still, mostly known as an important trade port city as well as the jumping-off point to beautiful Putuoshan Island. Booming business in Ningbo's commercial hub has brought a growing community of foreigners within its borders.

In eastern China you can have the best of both expat worlds—the feel of a small town, including a cheaper cost of living, with easy access to Shanghai's boundless cosmopolitan amenities.

The North

The northern region surrounds Beijing and follows the coastline from Shandong Province, through the Bohai Bay Economic Rim, up to the cold borders with North Korea and Russian Siberia. In the north opportunities abound for getting out into nature, from digging your toes into the sand to digging your ski poles into fresh mountain snow. Hiking takes a spiritual twist with a climb up Mount Tai, a mandatory pilgrimage for devout Taoists. And the hilly landscape of Hebei, crisscrossed by the Great Wall and dotted with historic temples, is the play land of city-weary Beijing residents.

Bordering Beijing, Tianjin Municipality is one of the four cities that stand independent from a province, along with Shanghai, Beijing, and Chongqing. Tianjin's reputation is often linked with nearby Beijing, though there is plenty here for it to rest on its own laurels. Tianjin is one of the most prominent and influential industrial and port cities in China. Its history as a concessionary port is reflected in its varied architecture today.

Heading northeast from Tianjin, the region once grandly referred to as Manchuria is now known as "The Rustbelt," with its closed factories and unemployed workers. The Chinese government is determined to redevelop the area, however, and Liaoning's provincial capital, Shenyang, is the epitome of these efforts. This historic city has come into its own as a prime expat destination within the last couple of years. In contrast, the charming port city of Dalian on the tip of Liaoning Province's southern peninsula has long been established as a flourishing seaside resort, having escaped the industrial decline and dismal reputation of its neighbors.

The north's other famous coastal city, Qingdao, is Shandong Province's pride and glory. This place savors a reputation for incredible seafood and pristine beaches. Home to China's most famous beer and historic old Bavarian villas, Qingdao is full of surprising delights.

Inland China

Inland China, covering the bulk of the nation's geography, is home to colorful minority villages and the ancient Silk Road, the world's highest peaks and one of its lowest points, mysterious Tibet and gorgeous natural scenery, and the mighty Yangtze River that divides the Middle Kingdom into north and south. There is a richness here that has always brought tourists by the droves, and yet the lack of resources for foreign residents has kept all but a small percentage from settling here. There are scores of inland cities where you'll find only a handful of expats teaching English or studying Chinese, but only three cities have a strong enough mix of rich experience and international amenities to be considered prime destinations: Wuhan in Hunan Province, Chengdu in Sichuan Province, and Xi'an in Shaanxi Province (though Chongqing Municipality is an up-and-coming fourth).

The cloudy city of Chengdu is known for its spicy Sichuan cuisine, its portly pandas, and its time-honored teahouses. It's a growing city that is quickly climbing its way up the scale of international importance. In the past visitors simply passed through colorful Chengdu on their way to

© BARBARA STROTHER

petting a kitten at a remote Buddhist temple

WHERE TO LIVE IF...

Still not sure which place is best for you? Here are a few priorities you may want to consider.

If you...	Choose...
... want to learn Mandarin	... a smaller city with few foreigners, which will force you use the language; areas that speak Mandarin without strong Mandarin accents, such as the Northeast; avoid areas with prevalent dialects
... want to get by without learning Chinese	... a big city with a large English-speaking population; Hong Kong is the best choice, followed by Shanghai and Beijing
... may want to make a career move	... one of the key business cities, with Shanghai and Hong Kong topping the list
... want to save money or live on a shoestring budget	... a smaller city, an area with less foreign influence, or an inland location; consider Ningbo, Xi'an or Xiamen
... want to have an active nightlife/social life	... Shanghai, Beijing, or Hong Kong; avoid the smaller cities
... want to travel cheaply and see a lot of China	... a central city that makes for easy train departures in all directions; try Wuhan
... want to travel to other countries in Asia	... a northern port town for ferries and cheap flights to Japan and Korea, or a southern Pearl River Delta city for inexpensive flights around Southeast Asia
... want to interact with minority cultures	... Xi'an for the Muslim minorities, Chengdu for Tibetans, or any number of small cities in minority regions, though many are restricted for foreigners
... despise hot, muggy summers	... the northeast or high elevations; avoid the Yangtze River cities (the hottest locations in China) and the south
... despise long, frigid winters	... a southern city that boasts spring weather year-round; avoid the west and the north (except for the coastal cities with mild climates)
... need access to high-quality western medical care	... Hong Kong, which is by far the best, though Beijing and Shanghai also have western hospitals
... have health issues that would be exacerbated by heavy pollution	... Xiamen, Dalian, Zhuhai or one of the other cities that have made considerable progress limiting pollution; avoid industrial cities, especially in the north and inland

Tibet and other exotic locales nearby, but nowadays foreigners are discovering that Chengdu is not such a bad place to set down some roots.

Wuhan and Chongqing, the front and back gates to the popular Three Gorges on the Yangtze River, are known as two of China's furnaces, with blazing hot summers. Wuhan, nick-named China's Chicago, is a sprawling commercial city and key transportation hub between the inland and the prosperous east, with a colorful history of foreign missionary activity and political uprising.

The last of the prime inland locales is the most world famous: Xi'an, home to the famous Terra-Cotta Warriors. Xi'an has an amazing history that dates back 5,000 years. It was China's pride and glory when it served as the well-traveled gate of the Silk Road. Xi'an still reflects those strong Turkic influences today, with its famous mosque and large Muslim population.

HOW BIG IS THAT APARTMENT?

In the following chapters, most measurements for apartment sizes are given in square meters. The conversion between square meters and square feet is 1 square meter = 10.76 square feet. So, 100 square meters would be equal to 1,076 square feet, 200 square meters would be 2,152 square feet, and so on.

BEIJING 北京

For centuries, Beijing has served as the political heart of the Middle Kingdom. Foreign invaders, Chinese emperors, and Communist hard-liners have
all bitterly fought for control of this city, understanding that to rule China,
you must begin in Beijing. From Kublai Khan with his Mongol hordes to the
marauding Manchu invaders, Beijing has served as the base for dynastic rule
and foreign invasion. It was here that Mao Zedong established the People's
Republic of China in 1949 after defeating Chiang Kai-Shek's Nationalist
army. With the exception of the 1989 crackdown of student protesters in
Tiananmen Square and the sporadic waves of dissident jailings, Beijing has
mostly been a peaceful place. For years now, Beijing has been the center of
China's political system. The cluster of foreign embassies is located in Beijing,
and the city hosts a significant number of foreign journalists.

The Beijing Municipality is host to China's two most famous places:
Tiananmen Square at the center of the city and the Great Wall an hour's

drive north of town. When your Chinese friends take you to Tiananmen, they'll proudly point out that it's the world's largest public square, and they might insist that you view the embalmed body of their hero Mao enshrined in a mausoleum at the center of the square. Yet most westerners think of Tiananmen as the site of the bloody crackdown on the pro-democracy student movement in 1989. And Mao? Our textbooks paint him as the communist strongman who took away freedom, closed the churches, and kicked out the foreigners.

Mao watches over the center of the city where Tiananmen Square and the Forbidden City meet.

Mao may still be Beijing's most famous resident, but the city is also home to about 13 million other residents. Han Chinese make up 95 percent; the other 5 percent come from China's numerous minority groups and foreigners. It's been estimated that about 50,000 foreigners call Beijing home; most hail from other Asian countries.

Beijing has seen a boom in the businesses that cater to these expats, such as international restaurants, coffee shops (there are now more than 50 Starbucks in the city), and especially upscale western-style housing. This housing boom along with the massive facelift the city is getting in preparation for the 2008 Olympics is kicking up a lot of construction dust throughout Beijing, but especially in the northern half of the city.

The foreign firms that attract the expatriates are here to get in on Beijing's now booming economy. For years, Beijing's core businesses have been government and heavy industries such as steel, machinery, and textiles. In recent years however, Beijing has shed its "industrial communist stronghold" image, emerging as an important high-tech center. The city boasts the most educated workforce in China, and contains hundreds of research institutes and universities including Beijing University and Qinghua University. Foreign tech companies such as Motorola, Siemens, and Nortel now have major operations in the city.

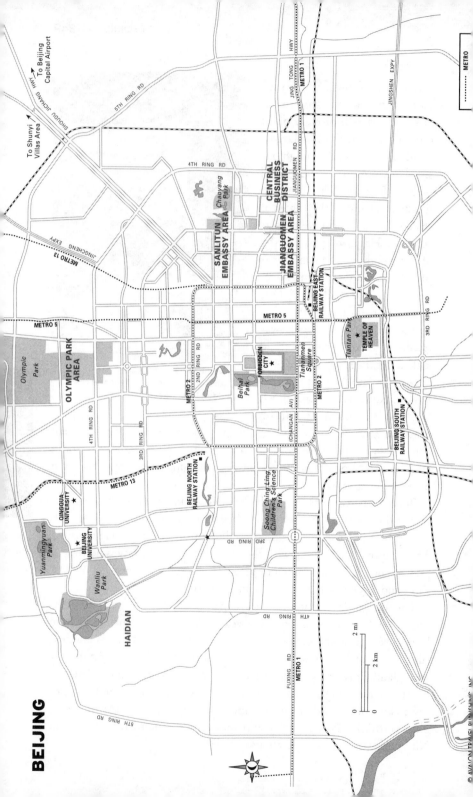

THE CHARACTER OF BEIJING

Beijingers proudly consider themselves the "true Chinese" and have been known to look down their noses at their "uncivilized" brethren from other cities and provinces. Compared to their cousins in China's other first-tier cities, Shanghai, Guangzhou, and Shenzhen, Beijingers see themselves as less materialistic, more loyal, and quite a bit more sophisticated. Beijing's hallmark cuisine, Beijing (Peking) Duck, is considered by many to be the best meal you can get in China, and perhaps even the best meal in all of Asia. Expatriates, and especially tourists, have found Beijing a wonderful place to discover the real China. With the Great Wall and the Forbidden City, how can you go wrong?

For all its culture and history, the character of Beijing is also heavily influenced by its political role as the nation's capital. It was here in Tiananmen Square where the Cultural Revolution was kicked off as thousands of young Red Guards frenetically waved Mao's little red books and vowed to stamp out culture wherever it could be found in the Middle Kingdom. Of course the results were disastrous, and China's creative class has struggled to find safe middle ground somewhere between artistic freedom and communist censorship.

Despite its reputation as a culturally and historically rich place, quite a few outsiders regard Beijing as a congested city that is choked by industrial pollution and the red tape of the city's army of bureaucrats. And like a typical tourist town, Beijing's dirty little secret is its bustling scam industry that preys on tourists. (Maybe that's why the Mongols left). You'll have an awesome time in Beijing for sure, but don't kid yourself: It's not a question of *if* you'll get ripped off, but *when*.

The Lay of the Land

The Beijing Municipality is slightly smaller than the state of New Jersey (but with quite a few more charms). It is hilly in the north and flat in the south. About 13 million people live in the metropolitan area with about 9 million in the urban core.

The Forbidden City and Tiananmen Square serve as the geographic center of the city and other important government structures are aligned directly to the north and south. The city center is circled by a series of seven concentric ring roads (although you only ever see the second, third, and fourth ring roads). Wide north–south boulevards connect with similar east–west roads, creating a grid street pattern. As long as you stay on these main roads, you'll navigate the city like an old pro in no time. Wandering off these main arteries into Beijing's infamously crooked *hutong* alleys is a sure-fire way to get lost, but also a great way to see how the locals live.

Northwest of the city center you'll find the Haidan District, which is home to the Summer Palace, numerous universities, and the Beijing Zoo. Directly to the east of downtown is the Chaoyang District. Here you'll find Sanlitun and Jiangguomen, two neighborhoods with lots of embassies and large expat populations. The Beijing Capital Airport is about a 30-minute drive to the northeast of downtown. There are numerous new expat enclaves that have been developed along this route. Quite a few of them have upscale villa-style housing.

Surprisingly the Central Business District is not located in the center of town, but to the east of Tiananmen Square between the third and fourth ring roads. The area has recently undergone major redevelopment to make it an attractive place for office buildings. Plenty of high-end housing is also being developed here to serve the businesspeople who work nearby.

CLIMATE

You'll be pleased that Beijing's weather follows the four distinct seasons, but sadly three of the seasons tend to be inhospitable. Winter (December through March) can be harsh with daytime temperatures around 30°F, and plenty of air pollution from a few remaining coal-fired electric plants and heaters. Since joining the WTO and winning the bid to host the Olympics

Beijing's bone-chilling winter weather will keep you bundled up all season.

© BARBARA STROTHER

the government is feeling pressure to clean up the environment, but with all the industrial growth and the explosion of privately owned automobiles, it's anybody's guess whether Beijing will ever be a "green" city.

In springtime (April and May) the weather is more bearable with temperatures around 50°F, but with the wicked sandstorms blowing in from the nearby Gobi Desert, your plans for enjoying Beijing's many outdoor parks and shopping streets will be ruined.

By the time summer arrives (June through August), the annoying sands will have been replaced by scorching sun, 90°F temperatures, and the dripping humidity (remember to bring plenty of deodorant). Beijing summers are enough to drive you indoors, where your only comfort will be the humming window-unit air conditioner and a cold bottle of Qingdao.

So you are left with the brief fall season (September through November) to enjoy clear skies and comfortable 70°F weather. The city will still be full of tourists from around the world (it always is in the warm months), so don't expect to have the place to yourself.

LANGUAGE

The standard Mandarin language, also called Putonghua, meaning "common speech," is based on the Beijing dialect. However, Beijingers famously add a nasally *er* sound to the end of many words. Even the greenest *laowai* should be able to pick out the Beijing accent after just a few days.

CULTURE

Beijingers boast that their city represents the culture of all of China. Considering Beijing's ancient cultural heritage and its contemporary arts scene, this reputation as cultural center may be well deserved. Most Chinese cities have some ancient sites that the locals are proud of, but few can match those found in Beijing. At the geographic and spiritual center of town, you'll find Tiananmen Square and the Forbidden City, the home of the emperors. The Summer Palace is found to the northeast of the city center. And who can match the Great Wall, which is just an hour's drive north of town? You can also visit the ancient Ming Tombs along the way.

Beijing is famous for its world-renowned opera, folk dancing, and calligraphy. You can find acrobat shows all over China, but none as good as the breathtaking Beijing acrobat show. Heck, even the little kids enjoy this one. Much of China's famous literature also came out of Beijing, including works by Lao She (*Rickshaw Boy*), Lu Xun, and the feminist Zhang Jie (*Love Must Not Be Forgotten*).

The contemporary arts scene in Beijing is also pretty vibrant. China's leading rock musicians are from Beijing, including the rock siren Cui Jian; the metal band Tang Dynasty; and the punk band Underground Baby. Quite a few of the younger generation seem to be casting off the Confucian ideals of modesty and piety and embracing western pop culture

OUR FAVORITE RIP-OFFS

In China, as anywhere in the world, you do well to trust the kindness of strangers. But, as everyone who's ever worked in the hospitality industry knows, tourists often have a fat wad of cash that makes them easy targets for rip-off artists. Listed below are some of our favorite rip-offs; sadly, many of them were learned firsthand. What they all have in common is that there was no agreement up front about price and these rip-offs occur in areas frequented by tourists. If the rip-off is for a lot of money you might consider contacting the police, otherwise just grin, bear it, and learn from the situation.

The False Bottom: The top 20 percent of your tea canister is tea, the bottom 80 percent is newspapers. The beauty of this scam is that it might take months before it's discovered.

Rotten Food: Food vendors, like the guys with the ice-cream stalls, don't throw out the rotten food, presumably so they can get a refund from their supplier, but when an unsuspecting out-of-towner walks up, why not just sell it to him?

Not My Kung Pao: If a waiter screws up an order, the locals will reject the food, putting the waiter in a bad situation with the restaurant boss. If foreigners are dining in the same restaurant they might just serve it to you, and even though you didn't order it, you'll be charged for it.

Meter's Broken: Your taxi driver claims the meter is broken and quotes a flat price for the journey that is probably way higher than you should be paying.

Each Passenger Pays: If you fall for the "meter's broken" line, and agree to a flat fee for the taxi ride, when you get to your destination, the cabbie demands that each passenger pay the agreed-upon amount.

Kickback Cabbie: You tell your cab driver, "Take me to Ba Da Ling Great Wall." He drops you off at a big gate with Ba Da Ling written above it. You pay the $5 to get in, but then realize you aren't at the Great Wall, you're at the Fake Wall. Before you realize you've been ripped off, your cabbie has pocketed his kickback, and lies to you, "I didn't know, I've never been here before."

Post-Qing Dynasty Antiques: In the dark alleys of Beijing, people will whisper to you, "Hey mister, buy Ming dynasty vase?" The thin film of dirt covering the vase makes it look authentic enough, but when you show it to a real expert, he'll tell you what you've purchased is a "post-Qing dynasty" vase. Since the Qing was the last dynasty, any vase made today would meet that description!

instead—that is, if Beijing's nightclub scene is any indication. The city is now a major stopover for DJs from around the world who play packed clubs every night. There is a wide variety of clubs with all sorts of themes including blues, techno, dance, Latin, '70s, and plenty of ethnic-themed places. The nightly variety show at the Afunti restaurant, for instance, is

Jiao Not Yuan: The paper notes for jiao (dimes) look quite similar to the yuan (dollar) notes, and when you're given change, you might be give jiao when you are owed yuan.

Tea Ceremony: This one's a Beijing specialty. A friendly college student (often a cute flirty girl) offers to show you the city sites, and your tour ends up at a "tea ceremony" shop. After the tea ceremony you are encouraged to purchase some exorbitantly priced tea. Five dollars' worth of tea ends up costing $100, and then they give you a $200–300 bill for the lame ceremony.

One-Day Watch: All over town, you can buy the souvenir watch with Mao waving to the masses. It's called a one-day watch, because that's how long it works.

Fake Waiter: A friendly man helps the waitress take your order at a restaurant. She thinks he's with you, and you think he's the restaurant manager. He'll present you a bill at the end of the meal and after you pay him, he disappears. Then the waitress appears, demanding payment.

Karaoke Kickback: Some cute, flirty college girls take you to a karaoke bar. The place is a dive so you don't worry that the menu doesn't have prices. After a few songs and a lot of drinks, the girls vanish and a tough guy shows up with your extremely high bill.

© BARBARA STROTHER

led by Muslim (gasp!) performers from Xinjiang who get the crowd worked up into a howling frenzy every night.

For those with more highbrow tastes, the city boasts about a dozen concert halls and over 30 theaters. There are also quite a few sport sites hosting a variety of professional and international competitions. You should find plenty to do every day and night in Beijing, if you have the energy.

Where to Live

Expatriates in Beijing have historically lived near the embassies just east of Tiananmen, especially in the Sanlitun and Jianguomen neighborhoods. Students and scholars typically live on or near campus near the universities in the Haidian District to the northwest of Tiananmen. The Shunyi District near the airport has recently experienced much suburban development, including numerous villa neighborhoods. Shunyi is home to quite a few expats who work for multinational firms and their families. Other expats choose to live along Changan Avenue, especially in the high-end Central Business District.

HOW ABOUT A *HUTONG?*

Hutongs, literally "alleyways," are the ancient crowded little courtyard neighborhoods only accessible by maddeningly crooked alleys too narrow for cars. Beijingers proudly boast that the *hutong* is a unique symbol of Beijing. Though sometimes dirty and decrepit, some *hutongs* do have their charms, and for expats who want to experience the real China, the *hutong* may be just the thing.

Living in a *hutong* is all about communal living. Children play together in the narrow alleys while adults gossip and sip tea at the neighborhood tea shop. The tight quarters make everyone get to know each other, but it can also be a drag, especially if your *hutong* has communal bathrooms.

Most of the *hutongs* rented by foreigners in Beijing are in the northwest near Houhai Lake or in Haidian although the Ju'er *hutong* in central Beijing has emerged as a major expat ghetto. The 60 or so foreign families in this *hutong* make up almost half of its residents.

Hutongs are called courtyard houses because you'll get a nice private outdoor courtyard as part of your house. But you also get shoddy construction, the sounds and smells of the city, and an exorbitant price to boot if you're a foreigner. A 100-square-meter home rents for about $4,000 while a sprawling 800-square-meter place can cost up to $10,000. But for those expats with new urbanist leanings, the *hutong* might be just right.

© BARBARA STROTHER

If you lived here, you'd be home by now—avoid the traffic rush, live by your workplace.

SANLITUN EMBASSY AREA

The Sanlitun neighborhood is about three miles northeast of Tiananmen Square in the Chaoyang District. It is a densely populated, exciting urban area bustling with expatriates. About 15 foreign embassies are located here including those of Australia, Canada, France, Germany, Italy, and Singapore. Quite a few of the embassy staff members choose to live in Sanlitun, especially those without children. They are drawn to all of the cool hangout spots, and would rather not join in Beijing's difficult commute. Consequently Sanlitun is host to quite a few foreign businesses that cater to the needs and tastes of this expat enclave.

Besides the embassies, Sanlitun is most famous for its restaurant and bar scene. Sanlitun Road, and the block-away Sanlitun South Road, are essentially "pub streets," with over 80 watering holes with a few restaurants and shops thrown in. There's no other place like this in Beijing. In 2005 the government widened the streets and improved the infrastructure, perhaps to keep its foreign guests as comfortable as possible as they slog down Qingdoa beer and Great Wall wine. The pub street has every variety of bar imaginable including sports bars, groovy lounges, loud techno clubs, and even a gay and lesbian place.

For entertainment options in Sanlitun that don't require heavy drinking, you can visit your furry friends at the Blue Zoo, take in a show at the Universal Theatre, or catch a game at the Worker's Stadium. If all else fails, there's always shopping. You can try the Sanlitun Clothing Market for some cheap knockoffs, or the upscale Lufthansa Center.

Sanlitun can be an exiting place to live, especially for people who either want to build their diplomatic network, or for those who are out to have a good time. The location is convenient to the city center, isn't too far from the airport if you need a quick getaway, and there are two metro stops nearby.

Most foreigners in Sanlitun live in apartments and there is a wide range of properties available. On the low end, you can rent an 85-square-meter one-bedroom apartment for as little as $750 per month at a place like the Kang Bao Garden near the Worker's Stadium. A typical two-bedroom apartment has about 150 square meters and rents for around $2,000 per month. On the high end, you can rent a 4–5 bedroom apartment with over 300 square meters for as much as $6,000 per month at a place like the Guangcai International Mansion near Worker's Stadium.

Serviced apartments are available at the Asia Hotel, City Hotel Beijing, and others. At the aptly named Embassy House, for instance, you can rent a two-bedroom serviced penthouse with just over 200 square meters for $5,500 per month. The larger four-bedroom 370-square-meter penthouse will run you $15,000 per month.

Because the area was developed before the villa era in Chinese housing, your options for villas in Sanlitun are limited. The East Lake Villas on Donshimenwai Street offer "Suzhou Garden Style" villas with 3–6 bedrooms. A three-bedroom villa with 230 square meters costs $7,000 per month; the luxury model with six bedrooms and 385 square meters costs $14,000 per month.

Sanlitun rents are high because most of these properties are built according to western standards, and being the embassy district, landlords know the individual expats are paying for rent with their employer's money, so there is no downward pressure on rents. If you have good connections you might be able to rent a modest apartment from a local for less than half the rates quoted above. If you do, you'll probably be personally responsible to set up all of the utilities, which can be a bureaucratic nightmare especially if your Mandarin isn't too hot.

JIANGUOMEN EMBASSY AREA

The Jianguomen neighborhood is Beijing's second embassy neighborhood and is located just south of Sanlitun in the Chaoyang District.

Changan Avenue, the major east–west boulevard that runs along the south of Tiananmen Square, becomes Jianguomen Road about three miles east of the Square. The neighborhood is densely populated and definitely has the urban feel. Jianguomen is also one of the city's oldest areas. In fact, Ritan Park, a peaceful place to relax or fly kites, was built in the 16th century as a temple to the sun god.

In Jianguomen you'll find embassies of the United States, Britain, Ireland, New Zealand, India, Vietnam, Mongolia, and others. Like Sanlitun, Jinguomen has quite a few businesses that cater to the large number of foreigners who live and work here. The China World Trade Center is here, as is the overpriced Friendship store. Upscale shopping can be found at and near the Oriental Plaza. Jianguomen is also host to numerous foreign businesses, especially service firms in the finance and IT sectors. Jianguomen is also well connected to the transportation system. Metro lines 1 and 2 have stations in the neighborhood, and the Beijing train station is just a few blocks away. The British international school in Sanlitun is the nearest to Jianguomen.

Many of the expatriates in Jianguomen rent apartments in one of the fancy skyscrapers. These towers function as mini-cities because they have so many amenities. In addition to the comfortable luxury apartments, people find the towers an attractive place to live because of the restaurants, imported-foods stores, salons, gyms, swimming pools, and indoor playgrounds for the little ones. Of course all of this doesn't come cheap.

A typical one-bedroom apartment at a place like the Henderson Center costs about $1,000 per month and has about 90 square meters. On the high side, a three-bedroom apartment at a place like Fairview Garden is almost 200 square meters and costs more than $2,000 per month.

Quite a few serviced apartments are also available in some of the hotels and office buildings. They tend to rent for about double the price of a normal apartment. The Asia Pacific Building, for example, rents office space and fully-serviced residential apartments. A three-bedroom place here rents for a little over $5,000 per month.

SHUNYI DISTRICT

The Shunyi District is out on the sixth ring road northeast of the city center and directly north of the Chaoyang District. The numerous farms in the area have earned Shunyi the nickname of "granary of the capital." In particular, Shunyi farmers are famous for their expertise in raising pigs and non-native vegetables, which are processed here and shipped out to markets across the country.

PRIME LIVING LOCATIONS

Because of Shunyi's proximity to the Beijing airport, and the availability of undeveloped land, the area has emerged as a major industrial area in the last few years. The new Yang Town area has been designated as a special technology zone by the government. Quite a few high-tech firms have chosen to locate here including those in the aviation, automotive, optical, electronic, and bio-pharmaceutical sectors. Some of the largest firms include Hyundai, Jeep, and Johnson Controls. These firms and others like them have attracted a large number of expatriate workers and their families to the area.

So many villa complexes have been built here that some have begun to call Shunyi "Levittown" in a nod back to the 1950s planned suburbs. And the resemblance is striking. Inside the gates of the walled compounds children ride their bikes on the sidewalks, kick soccer balls on manicured lawns, and dogs are walked every evening. It's enough to make you forget you're living in China.

There are quite a few recreation options in Shunyi (that is, if you can afford them). Two luxury golf courses do a brisk business with the expats, as does the horse racetrack. Those looking for a more adventuresome time will appreciate the two skiing centers and the two theme parks.

Shunyi is also the site of the 2008 Olympics swimming, diving, and equestrian events. New facilities for these are being constructed and numerous other major infrastructure projects are underway. Shunyi is making a major transformation from sleepy farmland to cutting-edge high-tech zone, and if you can handle the construction dust, you might find it a pleasant place to live.

With its convenient international schools and a number of foreign-based shopping outlets, Shunyi has proven to be popular among expatriate families with children. The walled compounds create a sense of security but can also isolate you from the real China. Unlike the urban areas, Shunyi doesn't have too many hangout spots. And since Shunyi is a sprawling suburb, you'll probably need to take taxis everywhere you go, which means you'll miss out on a lot of street life that you'd otherwise experience if you were biking or walking a lot.

The area near the airport where the southwestern tip of Shunyi District meets Chaoyang District is sometimes called the "Central Villa District." Auspiciously named walled complexes like Dragon Villa, Merlin Champagne, and Yosemite are located up and down Jingshan Road. The complexes consist of upscale detached villas (the nicest in China), and some also have townhouses and apartments. Each complex boasts its own amenities such as a swimming pool, tennis courts, imported-foods store, café, billiard rooms, playgrounds, and more. The Beijing Riviera even has its own skate park. All residents of the complex can enjoy all of the amenities equally regardless of whether they rent the smallest apartment or the most luxurious villa.

Housing prices in Shunyi are not a bargain. The lowest rents for smaller two- or three-bedroom apartments start around $1,500 per month, if you can find one. A more typical rent would be a bit higher. Serviced apartments start around $2,000 per month for a small place. Townhomes, which are basically duplexes with small yards, rent for around $2,000–4,000 per month for a three- to five-bedroom place. Villas, which are Shunyi's specialty, start out no lower than $3,000 and can be higher than $10,000 per month. A five-bedroom villa at Yosemite has about 400 square meters and rents for around $5,500 per month, which is typical for villas in this area.

CHANGAN AVENUE AND CENTRAL BUSINESS DISTRICT

Changan Avenue is the main east–west boulevard that runs along the south side of Tiananmen. Major local and international businesses can be found in the office buildings up and down Changan Avenue, which, incidentally, changes names many times. About five miles to the east of Tiananmen, Changan Avenue connects to an area recently designated the Central Business District (CBD). In recent years this new CBD has attracted quite a few foreign firms and expatriates who work and live in the area.

If you enjoy the excitement of life in the big city then Changan Avenue may be just right for you. In the daytime the area is abuzz with the workings of commerce as commuters, workers, businesspeople, and bureaucrats do their daily thing. At night shoppers take over, especially in the Wangfujing and Xidan shopping areas.

Beijing's coolest historical sites are in this area including Tiananmen, the Forbidden City, and the Liulichang arts-and-crafts street. And since the main train station is here, you are guaranteed a steady stream of tourists pouring into your neighborhood 365 days a year. While it might be amazing to live in such a significant historical place, after a while it might get a little tiring living in a perpetual tourist site. Some would say it's a nice place to visit, but you wouldn't want to live there. If you get to the point where you need to escape the daily grind of urban life, you'll appreciate the large parks south of Changan Avenue including the Temple of Heaven Park

© BARBARA STROTHER

The closer you live to the tourist sights, the more you'll have to deal with the throngs of tourists.

and the Beijing Amusement Park. The only international school in the area is the Beijing City International School.

There are now plenty of new high-quality high-rise apartment buildings in the CBD and up and down Changan Avenue. In the areas south of Changan you're more likely to find the so-called "Chinese apartments," in other words, the real China. The areas south of Changan Avenue have a reputation as being some of Beijing's working-class neighborhoods.

Along Changan Avenue, rents for small apartments in the fancy high-rises start as low as $500 per month for a small one-bedroom place, but a normal two- or three-bedroom apartment typically rents for around $1,300 per month. Serviced apartments are available in some of the hotels and in some of the apartment buildings. For example, a three-bedroom serviced apartment with 230 square meters rents for $3,800.

Typical housing in the CBD area is upscale, high-rise apartment buildings, so it tends to be a high-rent district. There are a few tiny apartments that rent for less than $1,000 per month, but most apartments rent from $1,500 up to $9,000 per month. At the Central Park apartments, a typical complex, a small one-bedroom place with only 85 square meters rents for over $1,300 per month. A similar two-bedroom place costs around $1,500 per month. Serviced apartments in the CBD are a few hundred dollars more per month.

Neighborhoods around Changan Avenue and the CBD are hundreds of years old, densely populated, and already "built out." Consequently there is no room for villa-style housing. So if you require a villa, you'll have to flee to the suburbs.

HAIDIAN UNIVERSITY DISTRICT

The Haidian District, northeast of the city center, is the intellectual capital of Beijing. Haidian District is home to 68 universities including

Beijing University (known as Bei Da) and Qinghua University, the top two schools in China. In addition to the universities, Haidian earned its brainy reputation as a result of the cluster of technology companies in the area. Back in the 1980s the Zhongguancun high-tech zone was established, encompassing most of the Haidian district. The zone designation created numerous incentives for high-tech businesses to locate in the area. Since then, thousands of companies now call Haidian home, including quite a few foreign firms like Cisco, Ericsson, HP, IBM, Intel, Lucent, Microsoft, Motorola, and Sony. It's a virtual who's who of high-tech business. Today Zhongguancun is known as China's Silicon Valley.

For fun in Haidian, most expats tend to hang out in the bohemian restaurant and bar scene that has developed just outside of the campuses. Young hipsters especially appreciate the trendy Wudaokou neighborhood near the Beijing Language and Culture University. Haidian also boasts some of the best outdoor parks in Beijing. If you're tired of Beijing's urban grind maybe you could use a daytrip to Fragrant Hills Park, the Purple Bamboo Forest, or the Botanical Garden. You might also enjoy visits to the zoo, the National Library, and the Beijing Exhibition Center, all located nearby.

Most of the foreigners who move to Beijing to teach or study end up living somewhere in Haidian, most likely on campus. Foreign students are offered dorms that are usually every bit as comfortable as dorm rooms in the United States, and profs and teachers can expect to be put up in a well-equipped campus apartment. Those who work in the private sector typically choose to rent a nearby apartment. Parents in this area would probably send their kids to the Beijing Zhongguancun International School.

Apartments in Haidian are a bargain compared to the other expat neighborhoods. For example, at the Fei Chang Sushe, a fancy high-rise building, you can rent a new 60-square-meter studio apartment for around $500 per month. A larger place, such as a four-bedroom 380-square-meter flat at the Dong Sheng Yuan, will only run you $2,000 per month.

Serviced apartments cost a few bucks more than regular apartments, but they are not as common in Haidian. Maybe students, professors, and high-tech workers prefer to pick up after themselves.

There is very little villa housing in Haidian, but it has been reported that there are close to 200 new villa construction projects underway, so we can assume that at least of a few of these swanky new homes will be near Haidian.

Daily Life

EXPAT SOCIAL SCENE

Expats come to Beijing for a variety of reasons. Most of the foreign diplomat core is plopped down here. Beijing's large cluster of universities has attracted quite a few foreigners as well; some estimate there are over 30,000 foreign students in Beijing. Unlike the good old days, the foreign professors aren't just ESL teachers, and the foreign students aren't coming just for Mandarin and TCM (traditional Chinese medicine). The new economic development zones have also successfully attracted numerous foreign firms to Beijing with their workers in tow especially around Shunyi and Haidian.

Twenty years ago, just about every foreigner from the West living in Beijing knew each other. Today a large expatriate community has emerged and is making an impression on the Beijing social scene. The expatriate crowd is now served by a wide variety of western-style housing, schools, shopping, restaurants, bars, nightclubs, and even the type of club where people meet because of some common interest (besides drinking).

Beijing has over 100 clubs run by expats. Quite a few of the clubs are established based on the home country of the members, including Canadian, Dutch, Italian, Polish, and even the Black Beijing club whose members are African-Americans. Some expats with intellectual leanings have formed a writer's club, a philosophy club, and a chess club. Quite a few of the clubs are alumni organizations, mostly associated with major U.S. universities. Rotary and Toastmasters have branches as well as the mysteriously exclusive Capital Club that only admits senior foreign biz types.

Weekend warriors will want to join one of the expat sports clubs—there are plenty to choose from including rugby, soccer, ultimate Frisbee, hockey, climbing, and the new national sport of China, basketball. There are also a number of children's leagues that are organized, such as those at the Lido Country Club.

RESOURCES

Beijing now has significant online and print media that targets the English-speaking crowd. English-language newspapers include the *People's Daily* and the *Washington Post: China Version*. Politically minded types will appreciate the *Beijing Review* that is published weekly in Chinese, English, and four other languages. For the lowdown on economic, industrial, and business news, check out *Business Beijing* and *Beijing This Month,* both published monthly in English. *That's Beijing* and *City Weekend* are weekly entertainment magazines that offer cynical but helpful reviews of local happenings, restaurants, and bars. You can learn a lot about the city just by reading the classifieds. These can be picked up for free anywhere expats tend to congregate. These magazines also have companion websites, which can provide invaluable information about Beijing before you move there.

HEALTH CARE

The health care system in Beijing is considered the best the mainland has to offer. The care is quite affordable, and quite a few of the doctors can speak English and have been trained according to the high standards of western hospitals. The local hospitals that are considered the best are the Sino-Japanese Friendship Hospital and Peking Union Medical Hospital, which was originally built in 1917 by American philanthropists, namely the Rockefeller Foundation. Each has separate VIP wards for foreigners. Both of these hospitals accept medical insurance from the United States. There's also the Beijing Massage Hospital. Even if you're not sick, you might want to invent some ailment so you can get a good massage!

If you demand health care that's the same quality as you'd expect in the United States, then the United Family Hospital is for you. It is Beijing's only private hospital run by foreigners and staffed by international physicians, dentists, and surgeons. The hospital has childbirth facilities, an intensive care unit, and an emergency room. The hospital is on Jiangtai Road in the Chaoyang District.

In addition to the hospitals, you can also find top-notch medical care at the Beijing United Family Clinic near the airport and at the Beijing International SOS Clinic in Sanlitun. You can also find international quality medical clinics at two hotels (Beijing Vista Clinic in the Kerry Centre

HORSE KILL CHICKEN: THE ART OF MASSAGE

The Chinese words for massage sound just like "horse kill chicken." At the Beijing Massage Hospital you can get an excellent, and cheap, "horse kill chicken." In fact, in every Chinese city you'll find massage salons, including some that specialize in blind masseurs. Most charge less than $10 for an hour-long treat. Or even cheaper, barbershops and salons often throw in a head, back, and arm massage as part of the haircut. Beware, however, if they offer to massage you in the back room late at night because that's where hairstylists become prostitutes.

and Hong Kong International Medical Clinic in the Swissotel) and one at a shopping center (International Medical Centre at the Lufthansa Center). If traditional Chinese medicine is your thing, you can try the Pingxintang TCM Clinic in Wangfujing, or the Yanhuang TCM Clinic at the former U.S. Embassy building on Qianmen Road.

SCHOOLS

The British School of Beijing in Sanlitun is the main international school operating in the embassy neighborhood. The bulk of the international schools in Beijing are located around the third ring road where the Chaoyang and Shunyi Districts come together. These schools include the Australian International School Beijing and the Beijing BISS International School. About ten schools recently moved their campuses from downtown out to newer "greener pasture" facilities in Shunyi. These schools include the International School of Beijing (a large school with almost 2,000 students) and the Western Academy of Beijing. For younger children Shunyi has the International Montessori School of Beijing, the Kinstar Bilingual School, and the propitiously-named Century Baby Bilingual Artistic Kindergarten.

Besides the local public schools, the new Beijing City International School, located in the CBD, is the only international school convenient for those who wish to live along Changan Avenue or in the CBD. BCIS is also one of the few international schools allowed to accept nationals, so expat kids attending this school will be able to integrate more into the local culture.

There are also certain local schools that offer international-standard

Students show off their kung-fu skills at an international school.

© KEVIN SELDOMRIDGE

education. These include the Ritan Middle and High School and the Beijing #55 Middle and High School, both of which are in Chaoyang near the other international schools.

Beijing Zhongguancun International School in Haidian was started by nationals and has strong links to Haidian's universities. The school uses a U.S.-based curriculum and is one of the few international boarding schools in China.

SHOPPING

For many years, visitors to Beijing have shopped for the city's four famous handicrafts: cloisonné, ivory, jade, and lacquerware. Today, it's a different story. This once-proud bastion of hardscrabble communism has emerged as a shining mecca of consumerism. You can now buy just about anything in Beijing. Formerly scarce items as mundane as a stick of deodorant or as fancy as a new Bentley are readily available—that is, if you know where to look, and if you've got the dough.

Shopping Areas

Wangfujing Street is one of Beijing's busiest shopping areas. It runs north–south and is located two large blocks east of Tiananmen Square. Here you'll find the Beijing Department Store, the mammoth Xinhua Bookstore, the Foreign Language Bookstore, and a wide variety of shops selling everything you might need (and plenty of things you don't need). It is a pedestrian street, so you'll find it an excellent place for window shopping and people watching. There are also plenty of ethnic restaurants in this area selling food from faraway places like Xinjiang.

Wangfujing caters to internationals and internationally minded locals, while Xidan is the trendy shopping area favored by locals. Xidan is two major blocks west of Tiananmen Square running north and south along Xidan Road. The main shopping mall is the higher-end Xidan Shopping Center with lots of electronics, jewelry, and clothing stores. For real upscale shopping similar to what you'd find in high-end department stores back in the States try the glamorous Lufthansa Center just north of the Sanlitun embassy neighborhood.

If you aren't into shopping for the sport of it, then you'll be pleased that there are now numerous mega-marts in Beijing stocking food, clothing, housewares, and just about everything else you need for daily life. Wherever you end up living, you should be close to a Carrefour because there are now five in the city. In the Haidian District northeast of downtown there is a Wal-Mart, and there's a Sam's Club in the Shijingshan District. Of course there are local grocery stores and general merchandise stores in every neighborhood, but the foreign mega-marts are your best bet for those hard-to-find items that expats can't live without like cheese, root beer, or Legos for the kiddies. If you have a fetish for assembling your own furniture, there's an IKEA store in Xicheng District.

AN INTERVIEW WITH RACHEL DEWOSKIN, AUTHOR OF *FOREIGN BABES IN BEIJING*

In 1994, Rachel DeWoskin moved to Beijing to take a position in a public relations firm and ended up becoming an overnight sensation as a Chinese soap opera star. An estimated 600 million Chinese viewers watched as her character, Jiexi, seduced a married Chinese man and stole him away to the United States. She tells of her experiences both on and off screen in her hugely popular book, *Foreign Babes in Beijing* (W.W. Norton & Co., 2005), which has been translated into five languages and is being made into a Paramount movie slated for release in 2007. Although she currently resides in New York City, she returns to China several times a year and plans to live there again someday.

Why did you decide to go to China?
I moved to Beijing because, after 17 years of American childhood and student-dom, I wanted to go somewhere no one else I knew was going. I wanted excitement and a jolt of culture shock, and I chose China because it was both unfamiliar and familiar. My father is a sinologist, and I spent my childhood summers riding overnight trains across internal China, peering up at giant Buddhas, climbing staircases to temples, and sleeping in the guesthouse beds of revolutionary heroes. As a kid, my first impressions were of food and words: banquets where my brothers and I ate sea slugs, "horse whip" soup, and turtle and learned to sing "Are You Sleeping" in Chinese. The words in Chinese are, "Two tigers, two tigers, run very fast, run very fast. One has no eyes, one has no tail. How weird! How weird!" Those lyrics are the first Chinese I ever learned.

Why did you stay in China as long as you did?
I loved it. The more I stayed, the less I knew, and the more I wanted to know. My impressions of China changed the way anything changes when it starts out strange and then becomes familiar. At first, Beijing seemed to me a set on which other people acted out lives I could never know anything about. And then later, it seemed like home.

What advice would you give to someone who wants to get into acting in China?
My role came by way of a fairly typical combination of randomness and *guanxi*. If you want work in TV, just be sure to read the script before you sign the contract.

Markets

Ready to brag to your pals back home about the sweet prices you're paying for cool stuff? If so, then you'll need to hit the street markets. Leave your credit cards behind, bring plenty of cash, and dust off your bargaining skills.

Near the U.S. Embassy you'll find Silk Alley, a great place to go for cheap clothing, luggage, toys and lots more. The labels might not be real, but

What were greatest rewards and frustrations of your time in China?
The greatest reward was the constant feeling of being alive, of having to work at daily interactions and conversations. The greatest frustration? The constant feeling of being alive, of having to work at daily interactions and conversations.

What do you think are the most difficult challenges faced by expats in China?
Being an expat in China is a mostly glorious and addictive business. Learning Chinese and speaking it with confidence is a challenge, but mainly, expats in China consider the delight of full-time life there to be one of the world's well-kept secrets.

What are the benefits of living in China as a foreigner today?
Access to endlessly interesting material, fabulous food, 1.6 billion potential friends. If you have a chance to go, you should absolutely go. And stay as long as you can.

© BARBARA STROTHER

© BARBARA STROTHER

Need a pair of watchdogs?

the good deals are. Another favorite is the Pearl Market on Hongqiao Street near the northern gate of the Temple of Heaven. You'll find lots more than pearls here. This market is especially popular during Beijing's numerous bad-weather days, because much of the market is indoors.

Two other markets worth checking out are the Lido Market just north of the Lido Hotel, and the Yabalu Russian Market just west of Ritan Park. The Yabalu functions somewhat like a wholesale market for goods to be exported to Russia with love. Whichever markets you end up shopping at, understand that the street markets operate on the fringes of the law. Don't expect much customer service after the sale, do expect counterfeit merchandise, and don't be surprised when your favorite market vanishes overnight, the sad victim of a disgruntled bureaucrat's wrath.

Getting Around

Beijing is relatively flat, which makes it an ideal place to own a bicycle. For short trips most Beijingers pedal to their destination. Avoid the temptation to buy a fancy bike like those in the movie *Beijing Bicycle,* because Beijing's street toughs are well-armed with bolt-cutters, and your bike won't last very long (just like in the movie). For cross-town trips, you'll appreciate Beijing's well-developed network of taxis, subway lines, and public buses.

BY TAXI

The easiest way to get around Beijing is to simply hail a taxi. You can also hire a car and driver or hire a single taxi for the whole day. While this method suits the lazy man, traveling by car might not be the speediest way to get around, especially during rush hour. Drivers pay little heed to road rules, and with the emerging middle class now hitting the road, Beijing's gridlock makes Los Angeles traffic seem like a Sunday drive in the country.

Ironically, when the traffic is heaviest it can take less time to ride a bicycle than to ride in a vehicle, even to somewhat distant destinations.

Taxi rates are still pretty reasonable, but they vary based on the size of the car. Smaller taxis currently have a 10元 minimum and charge 1.6元 per kilometer. Large cabs have a 12元 and charge 2元 per kilometer.

BY METRO

Beijing's metro system, although its trains are somewhat tired, will efficiently move you around town for just a few kuai. Line 1 runs from the west side of the city through Tiananmen Square and on to the east. Line 1 runs along Changan Avenue and is also convenient to the Jianguomen and Sanlitun areas. Line 2 is a circular route following the path of the 2nd ring road. The newly opened Line 13 runs to the northern suburbs, including the university district and loops back to Line 2. Quite a few new lines, including the Airport Line and an Olympic Line, are under construction and should be completed before the 2008 Olympics.

BY BUS

A complex network of bus routes can take you virtually anywhere in Beijing (or further into every corner of China if you can handle the ride). The busiest routes typically have clean air-conditioned buses but there are still quite a few junkers on the road. To figure out a route, purchase one of the local maps or have a local friend help you. Most local bus routes only cost 1–4元 depending on distance and whether or not it is air conditioned. The days of live chickens and ducks on public buses seem to have come to an end, but you'll still have to deal with the sardine-packed passenger system at rush hour. If you like mosh pits, then you may enjoy riding the bus during rush hour. You don't have to worry about your personal safety or getting groped, but you should definitely keep a hand on your wallet or purse.

SHANGHAI 上海

Paris of the East. Pearl of the Orient. The Whore of Asia. Whatever nickname you prefer, one thing's for sure: Shanghai is the China of the future. Whether ruled by cutthroat gangsters, foreign merchants, or communist rebels, Shanghai has always been on the cutting edge of what's new and what's hot in China. While the rest of China struggles to find the right blend of tradition and modernity, Shanghai continues marching onward as the nation's leader in business, economics, and pop culture.

Shanghai ranks at the top of just about every list that compares Chinese cities including quality of life, average income, housing quality, lowest crime rate, best infrastructure, abundant recreation, numerous business opportunities, and on and on. This city has the world's busiest port. Its Pudong maglev is the world's fastest train. Its futuristic skyline is unparalleled by any other world city, and by 2007 it will have the world's tallest building.

Shanghai is the largest city in China, with a population greater than

17 million. Most are locals, but the city's bustling economy continues to attract large numbers of Chinese from other provinces (many of whom are unregistered migrants) and a very large foreign population. In an apparent bid to maintain its position as the most cosmopolitan city in China, the local government's goal is to increase the number of foreigners living in the city to up to 5 percent of its total population. Shanghai residents tend to be stylishly dressed, well spoken, and well mannered. From the view of other Chinese people, the Shanghainese have a reputation of being stylish yet pretentious, talented but arrogant, industrious, and perhaps a little too greedy.

Since Shanghai serves as China's financial and commercial center, we might also call the city the New York or London of the East. The powerful Shanghai gangsters of old have been replaced by equally influential bankers, financiers, and investors from across China and abroad. The Shanghai Stock Exchange is the busiest exchange in mainland China, and the city is host to more than 4,000 foreign firms (about 15 percent of all foreign firms in China). Including nearby Jiangsu and Zhejiang Provinces, the Yangtze River Delta comprises a third of China's import/export activity.

Shanghai's economic growth is most evident in its building boom—they say one half of the world's construction cranes are in this city alone. Nowhere in the world will you find a more impressive architectural collection of buildings than in the Pudong New Area, a showcase for the who's who of the world's best architects. Unfortunately the boom is not without its downsides. Even with all the construction, there is still a housing shortage, and the cost of living is the highest in the mainland. Expats who agree to work for a salary comparable to what the locals earn will also have to live as the locals. If, however, your pay is based on an international standard, and your employer provides your housing, you may find yourself deciding like so many expats who've come before you that Shanghai might be a nice place to spend the rest of your working years.

HISTORY

Compared to the rest of the Middle Kingdom, Shanghai is a very young city. For centuries it was just a modest fishing village (Shanghai literally means "on the sea"). In the 16th century it became a proper city when a city wall was erected to keep out the Japanese pirates. The British took control of much of the area as a concession for winning the Opium War of 1842. They were followed by French, Americans, Russians, Japanese,

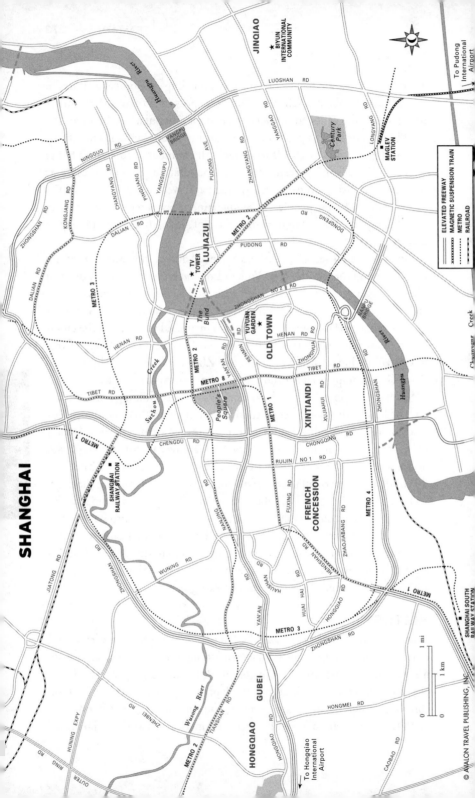

SHANGHAI ON THE BIG SCREEN

Shanghai Express: This 1930s movie is set during the civil war that overthrew the last emperor. Marlene Dietrich stars as Shanghai Lily, who rides a train to Shanghai. Shanghainese were outraged with the film's portrayal of them as bandits, and they threatened to jail the director if he ever set foot in Shanghai.

Shanghai Ghetto: The sad tale of Jewish refugees who fled Nazi Europe in World War II and settled in Shanghai.

Shanghai Surprise: This super-cheesy movie starring Sean Penn as a tie salesman and Madonna as a (gasp!) missionary got horrible reviews, but it is actually a fun, lighthearted movie that's enjoyable as long as your expectations aren't too high.

Shanghai Triad: This movie shows a 1930s Shanghai ruled by gangsters.

Temptress Moon: When the head of a wealthy Chinese family dies, his daughter tries to manage the household but gets entangled in opium and a love triangle. Set in Shanghai in the 1920s, the movie portrays the struggle between westerners, gangsters, and the Japanese for control of the city.

and others who established their own settlements. For the next hundred years, the foreign concessions covered most of the city and had their own municipal governments and even their own police forces. The International Settlement was north of the Huangpu River in what is now the Hongkou District. The French Concession is southwest of downtown and still shows strong evidence of its colonial roots.

By the 1850s Shanghai had developed into a major international trade port, especially for the bustling opium and tea trade. The foreign powers had little interest in development of a harmonious society, and for the next hundred years, the city was characterized by lawlessness, gambling, prostitution, and opium addiction.

The party ended in 1949, when communist forces took control of the city. Although Mao sent the foreigners packing, Shanghai has never shaken its reputation as a place where money is more important than following the rules, and where no pursuit is nobler than having a good time. As a result of the economic reforms of the 1980s, the city began to re-attract large numbers of foreign firms. In the resulting economic miracle, Shanghai has reclaimed the prosperity and glamour of its youth. The cost of progress, however, is pollution, congestion, destruction of historic neighborhoods, and the struggle to provide affordable housing for its 14 million legal residents and its

3 million unregistered workers who have flocked to Shanghai to pursue their own dreams of riches and prosperity.

The Lay of the Land

The muddy waters of the Huangpu River divide Shanghai into two parts. The older part of town is known as Puxi, which literally means "west of the Pu River." On the other side of the river, you'll find Pudong ("east of the Pu River"), which in the past fifteen years has undergone a miracle transformation from rice paddies to ultra-modern development. Most historical sites of interest to tourists are in Puxi, while Pudong is the site of the city's financial district and an export processing zone that has attracted a large number of multinational firms.

On the Puxi side of the river is the Bund, a wide pedestrian riverwalk where tourists and lovers take in the breathtaking views of Pudong's skyline across the river. The backdrop of the Bund is a collection of fabulous colonial-era buildings highlighted by the elegant Peace Hotel, a previous haunt for Shanghai's high-roller crime bosses, politicians, and foreign dignitaries. The Las Vegas–style neon lights of Nanjing Road, China's busy pedestrian shopping street, will guide you from the Bund to People's Square. This large city park was originally the site of the Shanghai horse racetrack, but today houses three museums and a theater and also serves as the city's transportation hub and cultural center.

The major north–south roads in Puxi are named after China's provinces, and the east–west roads are named after the major cities. Just a few blocks south of People's Square is the site of the old walled Chinese city currently known as Old Town, or the Yuyuan neighborhood, named after its famous gardens and bazaar. A few long blocks to the west of Old Town and People's Square is the upscale French Concession, home of most of the foreign consulates. The Hongqiao/Gubei District is farther out to the west, and is home to a large enclave of expatriates near the Hongqiao airport.

Across the river in Pudong is the Lujiazui Financial District, home to the Shanghai Stock Exchange, numerous banks, and two of the world's most impressive skyscrapers, the Oriental Pearl Tower and the Jin Mao building. About a ten-minute cab ride to the southeast is the Jinqiao District, home to numerous foreign firms and the bustling Biyun International neighborhood, where it feels like the foreigners outnumber the locals. Shanghai's new Pudong airport is located about 50 kilometers from Lujiazui to the southeast.

CLIMATE

The best season in Shanghai is springtime (March through May) with its pleasant temperatures around 65°F and the city's famous flowering trees that create "petal storms" all around town when the breeze blows. Summertime lasts from June through August. The days are long; the temperatures are hot (frequently above 90°F). Shanghai averages about six inches of rain each month in the summer, so things might cool down a bit, but mother nature quickly takes her revenge a couple hours later with her exhausting tropical humidity—don't even bother trying to hang up your laundry; it won't dry.

It finally cools down a bit in the fall season, which runs from September through November. Average fall temperatures are around 65°F. Shanghai winters last from December to February, and with daytime temperatures as low as 30°F, it can get a little cool, but it almost never snows. You won't have too many blue-sky days in the winter thanks to the pollution.

LANGUAGE

People who grew up in the city will speak the local Shanghainese dialect, which some say sounds like Japanese. The Mandarin spoken here, the official language of schools, government, and business, has no difficult accent, unlike the heavily accented Mandarin spoken in Beijing and so many other regions of China. Fortunately for expats, there are enough

© BARBARA STROTHER

Shanghai summers bring frequent and sudden rains.

locals who speak English that you can get by in Shanghai without knowing Mandarin or the Shanghai dialect, but we wouldn't recommend it.

CULTURE

Compared to most Chinese cities, Shanghai has relatively few historically significant cultural sites due to its short history. Shanghai's true cultural identity is best represented by the city's pop culture scene. Since the 1920s, when Hollywood brought its trade to China, Shanghai has served as the center of China's film industry. For ten years now the city has regularly

© BARBARA STROTHER

English services at the Hengshan church

hosted major international film festivals. The city itself has starred in dozens of movies including recent flicks *Temptress Moon, Shanghai Triad,* and *Godzilla: Final Wars* (where the Oriental Pearl Tower is destroyed). Despite the ubiquitous DVD bootleggers on every corner, Shanghai's movie houses

ESSENTIAL SHANGHAI BOOKS

In Search of Old Shanghai (1982) by Ling Pan is considered the authoritative history of Shanghai. Sadly it is out of print but worth reading if you can find a secondhand copy.

Life and Death in Shanghai (1988) details Nien Cheng's suffering during the Cultural Revolution of 1966-1976.

New Shanghai: The Rocky Rebirth of China's Legendary City (2000) by Pamela Yatsko describes Shanghai's return to its position as the most dynamic city in Asia.

Shanghai Diary: A Young Girl's Journey from Hitler's Hate to War-Torn China (2004) is Ursula Bacon's story of moving from Europe to the Shanghai Jewish Ghetto as an 11-year-old girl.

The Shanghai Green Gang: Politics and Organized Crime, 1919-1937 (1996) is a scholarly book by Brian G. Martin detailing the exploits of Shanghai's most notorious gang led by Pudong native Du Yuesheng, the godfather of sin city.

Shanghai Messenger (2005) by Andrea Cheng is a fifth grade-level kid's book that tells the wonderful story of an American-Chinese girl who connects with Chinese heritage while visiting Shanghai.

seem to do a brisk business showing the latest films. The art deco Cathay Theater on Huaihai Road has been showing Hollywood flicks since the 1930s, when Americans were its main customers.

The Paris of the East nickname aptly describes Shanghai's role as fashion capital of China and its "eat, drink, and be merry" attitude. The city has authentic ethnic restaurants featuring the cuisine of at least 50 different countries, including Brazil, France, Ireland, Mexico, and Turkey (with belly dancers), to name just a few. The French Concession, where most of the consulates are located, has always been the home of the international restaurants, clubs, and the like, but in recent years these places have cropped up in all corners of the city.

Where to Live

Where you live in Shanghai will most likely depend on where your job is located. Because the city sprawls out like the Los Angeles metro area, where a commute from one side to the other takes up to two hours, you'll want to live near where you work. Students and teachers at Chinese universities have little say in choosing where to live because the school usually provides on-campus housing.

Diplomats and their families tend to live in apartments in the French Concession where the 30-plus consulates are located including American, Australian, British, and Canadian. Expatriates who work for foreign firms are most likely to live and work in Hongqiao west of the city center or across the river in Pudong. Hongqiao is home to foreign firms and expatriate workers from Asia, Europe, and North America, while the Pudong foreign firms and expatriates are more likely to be from the United States and Europe. Most of the diplomat corps lives in or near the French Concession, and those working in finance will probably work in Lujiazui. Families tend to prefer Hongqiao and Jinqiao, where there's lots of green space and plenty of excellent schools, while singles prefer downtown with its vibrant energy, numerous cultural activities, and exciting nightlife.

DOWNTOWN SHANGHAI

Within Puxi, the Bund marks the eastern edge of downtown and the Suzhou Creek is considered the northern edge. The southern and western edges are somewhat arbitrary, but for clarity we'll exclude from downtown the Old Town neighborhood because few foreigners live there, and we'll cover the French Concession as a separate section.

PRIME LIVING LOCATIONS

Downtown Shanghai is characterized by small densely built city blocks with plenty of tall skyscrapers and highly congested city streets, a Chinese version of Manhattan. Living in downtown can be an exciting experience, with its appealing museums, concert halls, shopping, restaurants, and night-life. It's relatively easy to get around, on foot, by local bus, or metro. The drawbacks of living in downtown are the congestion and the pollution.

Virtually all of the downtown housing is in apartments. The demand has been very high in recent years, driving up prices, but the real estate bust of early 2006 should apply downward pressure on prices. Rents for a typical two-bedroom apartment in downtown start around $1,000 per month. Apartments in the high-rises overlooking People's Square rent for around $2,500 for a 150-square-meter two-bedroom place, up to $10,000 for a 350-square-meter five-bedroom penthouse. Serviced apartments are available at the numerous upscale hotels, such as at the Portman Ritz-Carlton, which has long been an important hub of expat activity with its imported-foods store and entertainment facilities. At the Portman, also called the Shanghai Center, rents for three-bedroom serviced apartments with 270 square meters start at $5,000 per month.

There are no international schools in downtown Shanghai, so the few foreign children unfortunate enough to live here must endure long daily commutes to their schools in the suburbs. The nearest international school is the Shanghai Community International School in Changning due west of downtown.

FRENCH CONCESSION

Back in pre-communist days, most foreigners lived and worked just north of downtown in an area known as the International Settlement, but the ever-aloof French built their own settlement to the west of the Chinese city, just southwest of the present-day People's Square. While the International Settlement has been replaced with newer construction, much of the French Concession still retains its original colonial charms. Today the French Concession is characterized by its historic western architecture, its upscale shopping, and its 30-something foreign consulates. You can easily walk around the tree-lined streets and take in the historical sites including art deco buildings from the 1930s, Sun Yatsen's former residence, and the site of Mao's first congress of the Chinese Communist Party.

The area is a must-see for tourists, but is also quite popular among the expat community because of the numerous international restaurants, the Hengshan church, and the excellent shopping. The restaurant

© BARBARA STROTHER

European architecture in the French Concession

selection includes Mexican, Brazilian, Italian, Turkish, Thai, and so on. Shanghai's three bar streets, Moaming, Hengshan, and Xintiandi, are all in this neighborhood. There's plenty of upscale shopping on Huaihai Road and Maoming Road. There are no international schools in the French Concession, but the area is convenient to Hongqiao where there are a number of schools.

Housing in the French Concession mostly consists of apartments, but if you've got the dough and the connections, you can rent one of the older historic villas. On the other hand, a modern villa, such as at the Joffre Gardens, rents for $10,000 per month for four bedrooms and 300 square meters. Rents for small 100-square-meter two-bedroom apartments in this area start out around $1,500 per month and top out as high as $10,000 for a large four-bedroom penthouse in one of the high-rises.

HONGQIAO AND GUBEI

The Hongqiao area is located about ten miles from downtown in the western suburbs. The area is relatively flat, but is not pedestrian friendly due to the long city blocks and its wide boulevards. Hongqiao was originally developed in the 1970s as a foreign trade zone complete with an international airport that anchored Hongqiao's bustling logistics business. Hongqiao has played second fiddle to Pudong over the past twenty years, but a mishmash of foreign firms, in a variety of industries but especially in manufacturing and logistics, have still chosen to locate here. Around these core industries, a massive service sector has arisen including office buildings, hotels, and exhibition centers. There are plenty of excellent options for schooling in Hongqiao as the area is home to Shanghai's largest and most established international schools. Otherwise, Hongqiao boasts few amenities that are of interest to families except the aging Shanghai Zoo. In fact, one of the neighborhoods is colloquially known as "Taitai Cheng," meaning Mistressville,

PRIME LIVING LOCATIONS

because wealthy men have rented out many of the apartments to house their illicit lovers. The Gubei neighborhood in the center of Hongqiao is getting a reputation as Shanghai's "Indiatown" because there are so many expats from India in this area, but most of Hongqiao's expats appear to be from other parts of Asia.

Hongqiao has every sort of housing including villas, serviced apartments, and apartments. There are around 30 villa complexes in and near Hong-qiao. On the low end, you can rent a smaller three-bedroom villa with about 250 square meters for around $2,000 per month. On the high end, a five-bedroom, 650-square-meter villa at Le Chateau rents for $15,000 per month. Numerous apartment rentals are available in Hongqiao, mostly in high-rise towers. Rents start out around $800 for a small 90-square-meter one bedroom and quickly climb as high as $6,000 for larger, fancier places, such as at the Shanghai Racquet Club complex, where 365-square-meter four-bedroom apartments start around $5,000.

LUJIAZUI FINANCIAL DISTRICT

Lujiazui is China's Wall Street district. The Shanghai Stock Exchange is lo-cated here as are the headquarters for many of China's largest banks. Luja-zui is located in Pudong directly across the river from the Bund. While the Bund is China's strongest reminder of its colonial period, the Lujiazui skyline proudly symbolizes China's future. From the space-age Oriental Pearl Tower to the country's tallest building, the Jin Mao Tower, there's no greater dis-play of architecture anywhere in the world. By 2007 the 101-story Shanghai World Financial Center skyscraper, the tallest building in the world, will be completed. As you wander around Lujiazui you can still find an occasional traditional *shikoumen* home with its trademark stone entryway, but most have been razed to make way for the steel-and-glass skyscrapers.

On the ground in the shadow of the skyscrapers, Lujiazui's sidewalks are busy with crowds of tourists, shoppers, and the suits who work in the office towers. Although it's crowded, it's quite easy to get around on foot or bike. Century Avenue starts at the Oriental Pearl Tower and runs south-east, where it ends at the giant steel sundial near the entrance of Century Park. With its massive pedestrian plazas, time-themed sculptures, and rows and rows of trees, some have suggested the avenue is the Chinese version of the Champs Elysées.

You can efficiently move around Lujiazui on the metro or the bus, and you can easily travel between Lujiazui and Puxi on the passenger ferries, subway, or via the psychedelic passenger tunnel. The roads can get quite congested so taxis aren't always the best way to get around especially during the rush hour gridlock or when it rains.

Besides high-finance companies, Lujiazui also houses a number of upscale hotels and a few massive shopping centers including Babaiban, Shanghai Times Square, and the Superbrand Mall. Unlike the crowded Bund across the river, the Pudong riverwalk is more suited for jogging or cycling. For other fun outings, Lujiazui also hosts the new Shanghai Ocean Aquarium, the Lujiazui Golf Club, and the Science and Technology Museum. Besides a few small kindergartens, there are no international schools in Lujiazui.

There's no room for villa housing in Lujiazui, so everyone lives in apartments. During the 1990s building boom, more apartments were built in Lujiazui than were purchased, resulting in quite a few "lights out" buildings that sat vacant. Shanghai's real estate market had been quite hot until the crash of early 2006, and in Lujiazui there seems to be more housing than jobs, which has perhaps kept the rents low. A modest two-bedroom 100-square-meter apartment can still be rented for just $600 per month. Of course serviced luxury apartments are also available. The swanky Ascott hotel has fully serviced apartments that start around $2,000 for a small 85-square-foot one bedroom, on up into the $6,000 range for a spacious 245-square-foot four bedroom.

JINQIAO BIYUN INTERNATIONAL COMMUNITY

Jinqiao, a suburb in central Pudong, was established as an Export Processing Zone in the 1990s and has been rapidly developing ever since. A few farms still remain on the fringe but they continue to give way to the rapid development of industrial sites and high-priced housing. The area is relatively flat and easily bikable, but as with most Chinese suburbs, distance to the central amenities makes residents dependent on cars, either their own or taxis.

The eastern end of Jinqiao is industrial, home to companies specializing in electronics, automotive, appliances, and bio-tech. Some of the larger foreign firms include General Motors, Kodak, Whirlpool, and Corning. Just to the south of Jinqiao is the Zhangjiang High-Tech Park, which has recently attracted a number of foreign firms including Dupont, Honeywell, and Roche.

The western half of Jinqiao consists mostly of housing, shopping, and schools. This area is known as the Biyun International District, and there is no greater concentration of westerners in China than at Biyun. With two large international schools within walking distance, you're more likely to

© BARBARA STROTHER

Have a cold drink and watch the weekend rugby matches in Biyun.

see blond kids than Chinese children. Quite a few of the businesses cater to expats also. Carrefour is the retail center of Jinqiao, and next door you'll find a variety of international restaurants and shops. A great way to spend a Sunday afternoon is watching a local soccer match from the Blue Frog restaurant terrace while enjoying the best burger in China. Other amenities of interest to expats include two top-tier golf courses (Thomson and the Shanghai Links); the new Abundant Grace Protestant church and the Jesus Sacred Heart Catholic church, both with English language services; and the China Europe International Business School, which has been ranked the number-one MBA program in Asia.

Housing in Jinqiao is among the best quality you'll find in China, and it has the prices to prove it. There are more than a dozen villa complexes here, starting around $3,000 per month (for a three-bedroom 200-square-meter place at Luoshan Oasis) and go as high as $15,000 per month for a four-bedroom, 500-square-meter place at the Regency Park. Thomson and Shanghai Links both have villas right on their golf courses. There are dozens of high-rise apartment complexes in and around Jinqiao with rents as low as $500 for a small 85-square-meter one-bedroom apartment, on up to $7,000 per month for a five-bedroom 450-square-meter place at Green Court in the heart of the Biyun neighborhood. The smaller cheaper places will be a few blocks away from Biyun Road, and you'll have to contact a local real estate agent to find them.

Daily Life

EXPAT SOCIAL SCENE

The earliest expats in Shanghai were teachers and students and they typically lived at the various university campuses across the city. Today official figures put the number of international students around 20,000 with about 5,000 of them at the prestigious Fudan University. A large number of the students and scholars are from the developing world including Africa and the Middle East. Local officials estimate the number of international students will exceed 50,000 by the year 2010.

Shanghai's social scene is legendary. The city's image as a place where the in-crowd stays out late drinking, dancing, and flirting is somewhat realistic. You can find bars and nightclubs throughout the city (even gay bars), but especially around the French Concession. Maoming Road and the Xintiandi area are both hopping spots just south of Huahai Road. The recently gentrified Xintiandi area has quite a few upscale restaurants, bars, and coffee shops. You can find it just a few long blocks west of Old Town. If you want to enjoy a quiet evening out, consider the Peace Hotel's Old Jazz Bar, where some of the band's members have been performing since before the country went communist.

sidewalk dining in Xintiandi

True to its cosmopolitan reputation, Shanghai has well over 100 expatriate clubs, some based on nationality, including clubs run by Belgians, Brits, Canucks, Italians, and the list goes on and on. There are also quite a few alumni clubs, and all sorts of groups for the artistically minded including writing, books, music, painting, and dance (salsa, anyone?). If sports are your thing, Shanghai's expats meet to participate in every imaginable sport including cycling, fencing, golf, rugby, running, squash, Ultimate Frisbee, and dozens of others. There are a few charitable organizations that you can get involved with that support orphanages,

© BARBARA STROTHER

PRIME LIVING LOCATIONS

provide wheelchairs, or perform other good works. And still other clubs are organized according to the needs of families such as moms' groups that set up play dates for the little ones.

RESOURCES

For English-language newspapers you can read the *Shanghai Daily* or the weekly *Shanghai Star.* Monthly magazines include *Shanghai Talk* and *That's Shanghai,* which both provide up-to-date info on local sights and events. *That's* is a must-read for all expats. The advertisements are a great way to find the local businesses that cater to the expat community and its classified ads can help you find just about anything including real estate, jobs, language partners, or even a sweetheart. The *City Weekend* is similar to *That's* but is issued every two weeks. Other English magazines include *BizShanghai* and *Home & Office,* which covers real estate. Many of these magazines have companion websites that can be useful, especially if you are trying to learn about the city from abroad.

HEALTH CARE

If you work for a local employer your health care will be provided by the local system. With the exception of major surgeries, quite a few expats now choose to have their medical needs served at the local hospitals and clinics rather than flying to Hong Kong or back to their home country. In recent years the local hospitals have begun to win the trust of the expatriate community. Three hospitals, all in Puxi, have special foreigner clinics: the Huashan Hospital, Huadong Hospital, and the First People's Hospital near the Bund. The Ruidong Hospital in the Jinqiao area of Pudong also serves foreigners.

If you work for an international company you'll probably be covered by the Worldlink system or a similar provider that follows international standards. There are Worldlink health and dental clinics in Puxi in Hongqiao, and at the Portman Hotel. In Pudong there's a Worldlink clinic in Jinqiao, and an SOS International clinic at Lujiazui.

SCHOOLS

The Hongqiao area is home to Shanghai's largest and most established international schools. The Shanghai American School has large elementary, middle, and high schools; technology labs; and impressive sports facilities including an aquatic center. The Yew Chung Shanghai International School, which follows a British curriculum, has a campus in Hongqiao and a boarding school in Gubei.

There are a number of international schools in and around Jinqiao. In the heart of Biyun, the Concordia International School is a top-notch college prep school with an American curriculum and a Christian emphasis. Next door is the Pinghe Bilingual School, a boarding school where most of the students come from the wealthiest families in China. A number of the students are foreigners (about 5 percent are westerners) whose parents want their children to learn Chinese. The Dulwich British School is just a few blocks away. A half-hour's drive to the east is the Shanghai American School with its sprawling 23-acre seaside campus located adjacent to the Shanghai Links golf course.

SHOPPING

Nanjing Road, Shanghai's most famous shopping street, consists of large Chinese and international department stores, specialty stores, and restaurants. It's a wide pedestrian street filled with thousands of Chinese shoppers and quite a few foreigners, especially tourists. Its futuristic neon lights and the modern architecture are straight out of *Blade Runner.* For clothing, the Silk King here is an obligatory stop on the foreign dignitary circuit. (After you've picked out your fabric and while you're waiting for them to finish sewing your *qipao,* check out the dozens of pictures of heads of state who have shopped here before.)

For upscale name-brand shopping, try Huaihai Road and Maoming Road in the French Concession. Hop on one of the double-decker buses to check out the area before you empty your wallet at some of the priciest, trendiest shops this side of Paris. In Pudong there are quite a few high-end department stores in the Lujiazui area including the venerable ten-story Next Age department store, which some claim is the largest store in the world. There are also close to a hundred big-box retailers in Shanghai including quite a few foreign-owned stores such as Carrefour, Wal-Mart, Metro, and OBI.

© BARBARA STROTHER

Shoppers on Huaihai Road stop to watch a marketing promotion.

MARKETS

The Xiangyang market is perhaps the best-known market in all of China. Originally it was a narrow alley where vendors sold thousands of pairs of Nike sneakers, Gucci heels, and North Face gear that made its way out of the back door of the factory or was just plain counterfeit. The market had expanded to carry more goods especially pirated DVDs and fake Rolexes.

BLUE FROG IN RED CHINA
AN INTERVIEW WITH RESTAURATEUR BOB BOYCE

After a steady diet of rice and noodles, expatriates from the West tend to develop cravings for western food. Sometimes a Big Mac with a red-bean milkshake and a taro pie just doesn't cut it. That's where Bob Boyce comes in. A long-time resident of China, this Montana native has built a successful restaurant business that is satisfying expat palettes across the Middle Kingdom while also introducing locals to the "best of the west" cuisine.

Tell us about your business.
I run a company based in Shanghai that includes restaurants, bars, and catering. Blue Frog, which opened in 1999, was one of the first independent restaurants in Shanghai to serve classic western food in a comfortable, contemporary atmosphere, with warm service, all at a reasonable price. It's since become a Shanghai institution, with five locations throughout the city and a Macau location opening in 2007. KABB in Xintiandi is a more sophisticated bar and grill serving luxe comfort food with a great approachable wine list. It's also something of a "see and be seen" place here in Shanghai. We also have a catering arm that does a full range of events, from large corporate functions to small house parties.

How'd you end up in the restaurant business in China?
My first job in China was with a relocation company, which stationed me in Guangzhou and Shanghai. Along the way I noticed that in these important international cities typical western food was scarce. I thought the expat community would embrace a casual restaurant with great quality, a consistent product, a reasonable price, and the friendly service you'd expect back in the States. At heart,

Bob Boyce

Sadly the government has ordered the market closed in the summer of 2006, but look for it to reopen somewhere nearby. The "Respect Intellectual Property Rights" sign at the entrance was always good for a few laughs because if you removed all the counterfeit goods from the market, you'd be left nothing but a few silk scarves.

For antique shopping in Shanghai there are two markets in the city

all my restaurants are about being able to unwind in a relaxed setting with great food and drinks.

What are some of the most difficult challenges of running a business in China today?
There is an acute skilled labor shortage. Finding staff with depth of experience is difficult, and will continue to be difficult for many years to come. We have approached this challenge by instituting a training program to develop entry-level staff into managers, but obviously, this is a longer-term solution.

What first brought you to China, and what were your initial impressions?
I first came to Beijing in 1994 to study Chinese. Even back then, China seemed like a place with huge potential for adventure and opportunity. The sheer volume of people was a sharp contrast to my home in Montana. The diversity within that volume was another initial impression – people may have all looked like Han Chinese, but once you scratched the surface, there were so many differences. I saw people with everything, and people with nothing. I was amazed at the sharp contrasts. You could spend a dollar, have a great meal, and be full – or walk across the street, spend $200, and also have a great (but very different) meal. That is actually something that is still happening today.

How have those first impressions changed over time?
It's not that my first impressions have changed so much as China has evolved. When I first arrived, there really was no middle class – just the very poor and the very rich. Now there is an increasingly affluent middle class, and there are also opportunities for everyone, no matter what their backgrounds. We have these *ayis* in our organization who can't read or write and come from extremely poor backgrounds, but they are now able to send their children to school. Their kids are fearless; they look me, a foreigner, in the eye and shake my hand, and they have the same chance of achieving their dreams as anyone else. That's a huge change.

What are the best things about living in China as a foreigner today?
The vibe of the place. Everything is on the go, and in a constant state of change. Also, the people can be amazingly hospitable and welcoming. I've stayed here all these years because I love the energy of Shanghai, the people, making sense of everything. It's amazing, and I love the opportunities available. Frankly, I don't know why anyone would be anywhere else!

center and a cluster of furniture shops in the western suburbs. The Fuyou Antiques Market is a huge four-story building in Old Town a few blocks west of the Yuyuan bazaar. The Dongtai Road Market just south of Huahai Park consists of a couple of narrow streets filled with shops overflowing with yesterday's treasures (and plenty of fakes that look a lot like yesterday's treasures). For antique furniture, you should try the Hongqiao suburbs where there's a cluster of a dozen or so large warehouses packed with antique furniture for sale. Most of the shops, like Hu and Hu (a favorite among expats) will refinish the piece according to the look you want. And compared to the flimsy furniture sold at the local furniture stores, or even at IKEA (near the Shanghai Stadium), the cost of antique furniture is really quite reasonable, but keep in mind you'll have to pay to ship it back home at the end of your stay in China.

Throughout Shanghai there are numerous other markets that never make it into the English-language guidebooks. Most neighborhoods have vegetable markets, toy and electronics markets, and "flower and bird" markets that carry all kinds of pets and bonsai trees. Just ask your Chinese friends where they shop and you're likely to find some good markets.

Getting Around

Except for the older parts of the city, Shanghai is not a very pedestrian-friendly place. The new areas and suburbs consist of large sprawling blocks that cause a lot of people to park their bikes and take taxis instead. If you really want to get around on the cheap, Shanghai has hundreds of buses that'll take you anywhere in the city—if you can figure out the routes, have a lot of time on your hands, and you don't mind the throngs of other riders. To cross from Puxi to Pudong and back, you can take a passenger ferry, even bringing your bicycle or motorcycle with you.

BY METRO

From its hub at the main railway station just north of downtown, the number 1 metro line extends farther north past Shanghai Circus World, and extends south through People's Square, then jogs southwest where it terminates at the south railway station. The number 2 metro line starts in the far western suburbs, connects to the Hongqiao airport west of town, then runs due east through People's Square, then under the Huangpu River into Pudong's financial district, then terminates at the maglev terminal to the southeast. The number 2 line is convenient for people living

the Shanghai metro on a rare off-day

in Hongqiao, Gubei, downtown, and Lujiazui. The number 3 line is an elevated light rail train that starts at the south railway station then makes a half loop around the western side of the city before connecting with the main railway station in the north side of the city. Line 4, which runs a loop around the city and goes under the Huangpu River in two spots, was opened in 2006 after numerous problems with flooding and the accidental collapse of a six-story building.

The metro is still in the first few years of an ambitious 40-year plan build a spider's web of 11 metro lines to connect every district of Shanghai including the far suburbs. The maglev train takes about 20 minutes from the terminal to the airport and at 270 miles per hour, about a third the speed of sound, it puts quite a few roller-coasters to shame.

HONG KONG AND MACAU

There's a certain excitement and exhilaration to Hong Kong and Macau, two areas located just east and west (respectively) of the Pearl River Delta off the southern coast of mainland China. These two have always been, and continue to be, popular spots for foreigners to live, work, and play—and for good reason. Time spent living in one of these locales will be a once-in-a-lifetime experience.

Hong Kong and Macau share many geographic, historical, and political similarities. Both comprise a peninsula and islands located just off the southern coast of mainland China; Hong Kong is on the east side of the mouth of the Pearl River and tiny Macau is on the west. Both were settled and governed by foreigners and have retained their international flavor through the years that the mainland was "communized" and closed to outsiders. Both are now technically part of the People's Republic of China but are classified as a Special Administration Region (SAR). Being an SAR guarantees a large measure of autonomy to maintain their

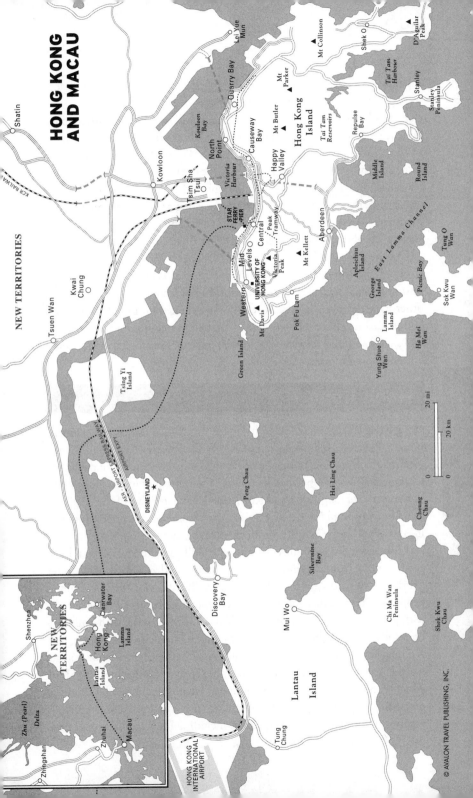

capitalist economy and local rule, an arrangement made under Deng Xiaoping's principle of "one country, two systems."

Expats headed to either of these locations will have a much different experience than those headed to the mainland. You won't feel the heavy hand of the central government in these places. Without the mainland's strict rules governing religion and free speech (or the lack of it), Hong Kong and Macau are much closer to western nations in their culture and outlook. In fact, people that hold passports from Hong Kong or Macau but are living in mainland China are often treated as foreigners and given special privileges, such as the ability to send their children to international schools.

Despite their similarities, each of these spots has its unique flair. Hong Kong's fame comes from its role as a fast-paced center for international business, finance, and some of the world's best shopping. Macau, on the other hand, enjoys a laid-back reputation founded on its colonial charm and its casinos. It's much less sophisticated than its sibling across the sea and slightly cheaper as well—though if you're looking for a bargain, you're better off on the mainland.

Hong Kong 香港

Hong Kong is a city unlike any other in the world. A city where ancient meets modern; where secular meets sacred; where East meets West. Buddhist and Christian faithful hike to the top of Hong Kong's modest mountains, while Chinese and western businessmen make their fortunes in the glimmering skyscrapers of Hong Kong and Kowloon. The neon lights of the neighborhood known simply as Central guide you to some of the hippest nightlife in Asia, while in the New Territories and in the surrounding waters farmers and fishermen ply their ancient trade with skills passed down over a dozen generations. Colonial architecture, street names, and vehicles driving on the left side of the road show the influence of the British, yet six million Chinese people remind you that you are in the Orient. Whether its Chinese temples with joss sticks burning or the Hang Sang Stock Exchange with multimillion-dollar deals cooking, Hong Kong is an exciting, fast-paced place.

Hong Kong hasn't always been this way. When the British took control in 1841 as a concession granted from the Treaty of Nanking, the Hong Kong islands were little more than muddy islands deforested by firewood pickers. Today, the islands are green and lush, the results of the British vigorous reforestation of Hong Kong, including the introduction of hundreds of new species of foliage.

Many people have an image of Hong Kong as a single island covered with concrete and skyscrapers. In reality, only about a fifth of Hong Kong's islands (and the Kowloon Peninsula) are urbanized. The remaining area includes plenty of farmland, mountain parks, and beaches. The deep waters surrounding Hong Kong and its location near the South China Sea and the mouth of the Pearl River have made it a naturally strategic hub of ocean shipping for hundreds of years. Its name literally means "fragrant harbor," a reference to the sandalwood incense production smelled by sailors miles out at sea.

Over the past 150 years Hong Kong's laissez-faire economic system has been a magnet for international investment. Hong Kong is a literal textbook example of free market capitalism at its best. Its combination of low taxes, limited regulations, and an industrious labor force have turned this once-sleepy archipelago into one of the world's foremost economic powerhouses.

The Hong Kong story does have a dark side also. Hong Kong's idyllic tropical-island location also means it suffers from regular typhoons. The population density also puts Hong Kong residents at risk of diseases such as SARS and the bird flu. The laissez-faire government situation, although it has benefited business, has also proven fertile ground for organized crime. The notorious gangs, known as Triads, are major players in black markets around the world. Their specialty? You name it—extortion, smuggling, drugs, pornography, counterfeiting, and piracy (both the waterborne type and the distribution of copied intellectual property, especially DVDs and software).

Hong Kong has never been rich in natural resources, and its economy has always been built on trade. The engines driving Hong Kong's economy today are in finance, banking, insurance, telecommunications, tourism, entertainment, and shipping. The sweatshops of old have been moved across the border into Shenzhen, and today giant cranes hoisting hundreds of containers into oceangoing ships have replaced the sweaty coolies and the picturesque junks in the harbor.

Close to seven million people call Hong Kong home, including nearly 500,000 expatriates, many of whom are of Chinese descent—having left during darker times, they are returning now that Hong Kong's standard of living is virtually the same as elsewhere in the world. Americans and Canadians now outnumber the once-dominant Brits. There are also large communities of Thais, Indians, Pakistanis, Japanese, and a plethora of Filipinos, many working as domestic helpers.

In 1997 the British turned control of Hong Kong over to the People's Republic of China. PLA troops quietly crossed the bridges in trucks and assumed the defense posts previously held by the British military. Unlike the mainland, the PLA here does not make itself very visible. The Hong Kong Police Force, on the other hand, maintains the peace. In 1997, ownership of Hong Kong reverted from the British back to Beijing, but the Hong Kong Special Administrative Region (SAR) still has its own local government that manages most governmental affairs, retaining its own currency and laws.

THE LAY OF THE LAND

The Hong Kong Special Administrative Region consists of Hong Kong Island, Lantau Island, the Kowloon Peninsula protruding from mainland China, and more than 200 smaller islands. Hong Kong Island is the original British territory and remains the center of government and business activity for the region. The Kowloon urban area is across Victoria Harbour from downtown Hong Kong. Much of the remainder of the peninsula is known as the New Territories, which make up more than 90 percent of the SAR. There are quite a few small towns, farms, fisheries, beaches, and mountain parks in the New Territories. Lantau Island to the west of Hong Kong Island is a beautiful mountainous area. More than half of Lantau is set aside as parkland and a network of hiking trails crisscrosses the mountain linking

© KEVIN SELDOMRIDGE

It's crowded on land and sea in Hong Kong.

its Buddhist and Trappist holy sites. The northern shore of Lantau is the site of the new international airport and its farmlands are rapidly giving way to development. A long bridge connects Lantau to Kowloon.

Climate

Hong Kong's climate is subtropical and similar to that of Hawaii, which shares the same latitude. The fall season, September–October, is the most pleasant. The days are warm enough for fun days at the beach, and the ocean breezes make for cool relaxing evenings. You'll never see snow in winter, though you might encounter some ice if you hike the mountain peaks on the chilliest of days. The misty months of March and April bring warmer temperatures around 70°F. The hottest months are May through August, with temperatures above 90°F, and with frequent rain pushing the humidity close to 100 percent.

Language

In Hong Kong quite a few locals speak English, so it's possible to get by with English alone. If you want to learn Cantonese or Mandarin, you'd probably be better off living somewhere in the mainland, where you'll be forced to use Chinese to communicate. If you plan to make Hong Kong your home, you should study Cantonese because it's spoken throughout the region, but Mandarin is also becoming more common since the SAR reverted back to the PRC. Street signs are written in both traditional Chinese characters and in English.

Culture

Compared to the mainland, where organized religion almost vanished under communism, religion has thrived in Hong Kong. There are hundreds of temples, shrines, and monasteries throughout the SAR. From tiny street-corner shrines to the ancient Man Mo Temple on Ladder Street in Hong Kong, you'll find the faithful just about everywhere burning incense and offering up prayers. There are quite a few Christian churches also covering quite a few denominations from Catholic to Pentecostal, and unlike the mainland foreigners aren't prohibited from worshipping with locals.

The pop culture of Hong Kong yields a powerful influence in China, but also throughout Asia and even the West. Hong Kong exports its pop culture, from fashion rock bands celebrated throughout the mainland to movie stars like Jackie Chan and Bruce Lee (even though he was born in San Francisco).

checking the names at a local ancestral shrine

WHERE TO LIVE

Unlike most living locations covered in this book, where expatriates tend to live in just a few key areas in each city, you'll find expatriates living in just about every corner of Hong Kong. When deciding where to live you'll have five major regions to choose from in the Hong Kong SAR: the north side of Hong Kong Island, the south side of Hong Kong Island, Kowloon, Lantau Island, or the New Territories.

In cost-of-living studies, Hong Kong often makes the top 10 most expensive cities, more expensive than New York and Los Angeles but just less than London. Housing will be your most expensive budget item, with rents for two-bedroom apartments starting out at HK$20,000 (US$2,580) per month, if you can find one that cheap. And because of Hong Kong's notoriously high prices, quite a few locals are unable to purchase their own homes. To provide some relief the government has built massive public-housing projects, resulting in nearly 50 percent of the residents living in public housing. (Public housing is allocated to the elderly and needy first. Since there is a lengthy waiting list and you must be a Hong Kong resident to apply, it is unlikely that many expatriates live in government housing.)

North Hong Kong Island

With its bustling city streets and massive skyscrapers all lit up with neon Chinese characters, the northern side of Hong Kong island is the Hong Kong you've seen in the movies. You can find expats living in just about every neighborhood in northern Hong Kong, but the Central and Western District in the northwest is the premier location for expatriate living. Central is the financial and commercial hub of Hong Kong, and since so many expats work in finance, they're able to live near their place of work.

The cost of living is exorbitant and the area is crowded, but there are a number of amenities that might make living in Central worth it. Public transportation, especially the MTR, makes getting around easy. It's also home to one of the coolest ways of getting around: Thousands of people use a system of public escalators and moving sidewalks every day to traverse Central's steep hills. Some escalators only run one direction and are switched from downhill in the morning to uphill in the afternoon and evening to accommodate the commuters. The restaurants, nightlife, and shopping are also legendary here. The zoo is in this area, and there are a number of parks including the Victoria Peak Garden at the top of the peak tramway. There are also plenty of churches, shopping centers, food markets, and hospitals. However, there are not many English-language international schools in this heart of urban Hong Kong.

Housing in northern Hong Kong is some of the most expensive in all of Asia, and perhaps in the entire world. The prime living location is the Mid-Levels in Central where a tiny one-bedroom flat (500 sq. ft.) rents for about HK$15,000 (US$1,900), a typical two-bedroom flat (800 sq. ft.) rents for HK$20,000 (US$2,500), and you'll have a hard time finding anything with more than two bedrooms. A serviced apartment in northern Hong Kong only costs a few thousand more, unless it's at one of the swankier hotels.

Just up the mountain at Victoria Peak, you'll find the expensive homes of the rich and famous where rents can top HK$300,000 (US$40,000) per month. (If you have to ask, you can't afford it.) You'll also find expat communities in Happy Valley and North Point where the rents are more or less than what you'd pay in Central.

Some of the world's most expensive real estate is here in Central.

Lower rents can be found in other parts of northern Hong Kong Island, such as in Kennedy Town to the west, but you'll probably be the only foreigner in your neighborhood. Tiny 200-square-foot flats can be had for about HK$6,000 (US$775). Check the local classifieds for these bargains.

South Hong Kong Island

The southern half of Hong Kong Island is less developed than the urban north and is primarily known for its fishing villages and sandy beaches. While expatriate singles and couples prefer the hustle and bustle of northern Hong Kong, expatriate families tend to prefer the quieter natural environment of the south. The Southside boasts a long coastline with numerous beaches, bays, and inlets, but also has the usual smattering of temples, parks, and shops. The giant Ocean Park with its pair of celebrity pandas also draws plenty of visitors. There are quite a few quaint villages along the coast, but the main towns are Pok Fu Lam, Aberdeen, Repulse Bay, and Stanley. As for getting around, buses serve this area, but because of the terrain, they are not very speedy.

The Pok Fu Lam area on the western coast of Hong Kong Island, with its slow pace and the tranquil confluence of mountains, beaches, and parks, is a fave of expat families. Many of the expats here work at the University of Hong Kong or at one of the many IT firms nearby, especially at the Cyberport campus. The Queen Mary Hospital is also in Pok Fu Lam, one of the most established hospitals in Hong Kong. International schools include the Kellet School and the West Island School, both British. Most of the housing in Pok Fu Lam is in high-rise buildings. A 450-square-foot one-bedroom apartment rents for around HK$10,000 (US$1,300), but since this area is favored by families, you won't find many small apartments. You can expect to pay HK$25,000 (US$3,300) for an 850-square-foot two-bedroom flat. Larger, three-bedroom flats with 2,000 square feet are available, but the rents can be more than HK$50,000 (US$6,500).

Aberdeen, Repulse Bay, and Stanley are other southern towns favored by expatriates from the United States and Europe. A number of country clubs are here including the American Club, the Hong Kong Country Club, and the Royal Hong Kong Golf Club. For mariners, there's the Aberdeen Marina Club and the Aberdeen Boat Club. For international schools, there's the Canadian International School in Aberdeen, the British South Island School, and the Hong Kong International School located in Repulse Bay, which is considered one of the premier schools in Asia. Housing costs in the Southside, although by no means a bargain, can be more affordable than other parts of Hong Kong, and you have a variety of housing options to choose from including high-rise flats, low-rise flats, luxury villas, and even boats (there's a whole community of people, including a few expats, living on boats in the harbor at Aberdeen). Small 800-square-foot one-bedroom flats can be rented for HK$10,000 (US$1,300). Luxury villas are also available, but you'll pay dearly for these.

Kowloon and the New Territories

The Kowloon Peninsula is directly north of Hong Kong Island across Victoria Harbour. The British took possession of Kowloon as a concession of the Tianjin Treaty of 1858. Today Kowloon is a densely populated modern urban area just like Hong Kong across the harbor. The Tsim Sha Tsui region at the tip of the peninsula is the heart and soul of Kowloon. Business gets done at the East Corporate Area, home to more than a few of the world's largest corporations, and there are shopping opportunities at public markets, mega-stores, and everything in between. The Hong Kong Polytechnic University is here as well as a number of museums, a coliseum, and public parks. Tsim Sha Tsui has numerous restaurants and a nightclub and bar street on Knutsford Terrace. The northern part of Kowloon is less steel and concrete and somewhat more traditionally Chinese. Kowloon is a favorite for Americans as evidenced by the three American schools here: the American International School, Concordia International School, and the International Christian School.

Housing costs in Kowloon are not as steep as in Hong Kong. A one-bedroom flat with 500 square feet in the heart of Tsim Sha Tsui rents for around HK$10,000 (US$1,300) per month, while a two-bedroom place with 1,100 square feet can be rented for as little as HK$15,000 (US$1,900). Because of the old airport (which is no longer used) much of the housing in Kowloon is low rise and it's possible to rent a townhouse. A newer 1,000-square-foot three-bedroom flat rents for around HK$25,000 (US$3,200) per month.

The New Territories were "new" back in 1898 when the British first leased them from the Chinese. Today the New Territories are mostly rural with a few small towns. Most expats who choose to live in the New Territories choose to do so because they either want to be immersed in the Chinese culture so they can learn the Cantonese language, or they value the country setting, or else they're just desperate to avoid Hong Kong's high rents. A number of expatriates have chosen to live in Clearwater Bay and Sai Kung. Both areas have plenty of green space, fresh air, and excellent opportunities for outdoor recreation, though there are no international schools in either of these areas. The MTR and KCR serves these areas well. Housing rates in both Clearwater Bay and Sai Kung are the most affordable in the SAR. A large 1,300-square-foot three-bedroom flat can be rented for just over HK$20,000 (US$2,600).

Lantau Island

With a beautiful natural setting, Lantau Island to the west of Hong Kong Island has excellent beaches and mountainous hiking trails. Modern development has grown in recent years. The new international airport is on Chek Lap Kok Island, Lantau's sister island to the north, and the new Hong Kong Disney is situated on Lantau's northeastern point. The luxury homes in Discovery Bay have attracted a significant expat community, many of whom work in the logistics industry. There are two British international schools on Lantau, one in Discovery Bay and the other in Mui Wo. Travel between Lantau Island and Hong Kong is easy using the MTR's Gold Line or ferries from Mui Wo. To get around Lantau, catch a taxi or ride the green and white public buses.

You can find some of the newest and cheapest housing in Lantau, and this is one of the few places where you can rent (or buy) a villa. Housing costs range from as low as HK$7,500 (US$1,000) per month for a small 300-square-foot one-bedroom flat on up to HK$50,000 (US$6,500) for a large three-bedroom 1,500-square-foot villa with garage and pool.

the Wisdom Path on Lantau Island

DAILY LIFE
Visa Requirements

Hong Kong allows tourists from many countries to come visa-free for a period of time. North Americans and most Europeans are allowed to visit for up to three months without a visa. If your nationality requires a tourist visa, you can obtain one from any Chinese consulate (check with the Hong Kong immigration department for your home country: www.immd.gov.hk). If you will be working in Hong Kong, however, you should arrive with the correct visa in hand as it can be quite difficult to change your type of visa from tourist to business once you are there.

Anyone who resides in Hong Kong for more than 180 days is required to apply for a Hong Kong identity card at the Registration of Persons Office. To work in Hong Kong you'll need to secure an employment visa from the Chinese embassy or consulate in your home country, or by applying directly to the Hong Kong Immigration Department. If you find you really love this place, then after legally residing in Hong Kong for seven years, you are eligible for permanent residency. Dependents are not allowed to work on their spouse's visa and must apply for their own, but they still need to be sponsored by an employer first.

Finance
MONEY

Hong Kong has its own currency, called the Hong Kong dollar, which can be broken into 100 cents. Because the Hong Kong dollar has been pegged to the U.S. dollar, the exchange rate doesn't fluctuate much (US$1 = HK$7.75). There are numerous ATM machines in Hong Kong making it convenient for you to withdraw Hong Kong dollars, even from your bank account back home. Unlike the mainland, there are no limitations on how much currency you can bring in or out of Hong Kong. Cash transactions in PRC renminbi are becoming more common and Hong Kong banks now offer yuan accounts. You can also use major credit cards here, but some shopkeepers will tack on a service fee of 5–10 percent. Quite a few locals use the Octopus smart card for purchases. Originally designed for use on the public transportation system, some restaurants and shops now accept payment with the Octopus card.

TAXES

There are no sales or capital gains taxes in Hong Kong. You will, however, have to pay a 16 percent personal tax on your earned income (businesses

MOVING IN

When it's time to move in, you'll need to have the utilities connected and you should change your locks and consider getting a steel safety door installed if your place doesn't already come with it. Hong Kong is not a violent place, but burglary has always been a problem here. To hook up your utilities, you'll first need to pay deposits of HK$400–600 (around US$100) for all utilities including water (and sewage), electricity, natural gas, telephone, cable TV, and broadband (if you choose). Utility bills will be mailed to you and most can be paid through automatic bank draft, at an ATM machine, using a payment processing service on the Internet, by mail, or in person. Typical monthly expenses are HK$50 (US$6.50) for water (although it will be billed every four months), HK$250 (US$32) for electricity, HK$300 (US$40) for natural gas, HK$100 (US$13) for telephone and at least HK$250 (US$32) for broadband.

pay 17.5 percent tax on profits). Personal income tax does not apply to income from investments, rentals, interest on your bank account, and the like. Although the tax rates are comparatively low, at the end of your first year in Hong Kong the Inland Revenue Department will mail you a bill for the tax on your first year's earnings, and a bill estimating the tax on your second year's anticipated earnings. You'll have to pay both bills right away. Your tax bill can be reduced with deductions similar to those in the U.S. system (mortgage interest, health care, senior care, and education are all tax deductible). Taxes can be paid monthly if you want to avoid the lump sum at the end of the year. Most people choose to pay every six months. The friendly folks at the Inland Revenue Department wouldn't want you to slip out of town forgetting to pay your tax bill. Unless you have one of the overly generous expat employment compensation packages where your employer pays your taxes for you, you'll have to pay taxes yourself.

RETIREMENT

Just about everyone working in Hong Kong participates in the Mandatory Provident Fund (MPF) established by the government. In the MFP program, employers and employees both contribute funds (about 5 percent of the employee's salary) into a savings account designated for retirement. Numerous local banks participate in the MFP programs. You can collect the money when you retire or leave Hong Kong. If you already have a retirement plan through your company, such as a 401k, you can avoid participating in the MFP.

Expat Social Scene

The expat community in Hong Kong has formed social clubs for just about every interest such as cricket, squash, and softball, and quite a few clubs for outdoor recreation including hiking, windsurfing, boating, diving, and the like. Hong Kong's numerous churches and the international schools also provide opportunities for expats to connect to the foreign community.

For nightlife, Lan Kwai Fong is one of the most happening areas. Located in Central, this area's abundant restaurants and bars attract large numbers of expats every night. Just to the south is the Soho area, another popular hangout spot with its diverse international restaurants, numerous watering holes, and street stalls offering low prices on everything from vegetables to antiques. Other popular nightspots where you can get your groove on include Soho East, Tsim Sha Tsui, and Wan Chai.

Resources

Hong Kong has a number of high-quality English-language newspapers and magazines. The two local newspapers are the *South China Morning Post* and the *Hong Kong Standard,* but you can also get the *Asian Wall Street Journal,* the *International Herald Tribune,* and even *USA Today.* Hong Kong is also the base for the *Far East Economic Review* and the *Financial Times. BC Magazine* is a general-interest magazine that covers current events, restaurant and club reviews, and also has a rich classifieds section where you can find everything from used cars to pets and roommates. For the politically minded, there's the *Hong Kong Voice of Democracy,* which is sure to get all the radicals jazzed up. Most of these publications have handy websites also.

Health Care

Before traveling to Hong Kong, make sure your immunizations are up to date. With its tropical climate and crowded subways, you should do your best to avoid catching a nasty case of typhoid, tuberculosis, or Hepatitis A and B. Hong Kong's doctors and dentists are trained according to western standards so you shouldn't worry about the quality of care you'll receive, but unfortunately you'll pay western prices for the care. You'll want to make sure you have ample medical insurance if you live in Hong Kong.

The emergency telephone number is 999. There are also medical hotlines (2882-4866 and 2300-6555) that can help you with just about anything related to health care including directions, fees, and so on. There are hospitals located in Kowloon, Sha Tin in the New Territories, Pok Fu Lam, and at the Mid-Levels in Central.

Schools

In mainland China, most expat families put their children in the international schools, but in Hong Kong the local schools offer a viable option. The Hong Kong school system is modeled after the British system with the first six years at primary school, followed by three years at a junior secondary school, and finally 2–4 years at a senior secondary school. The style of education is characterized by rigid discipline (including uniforms), learning through rote memorization, and challenging exams. About half the public schools teach in English, and the rest use Cantonese or a mixture of English, Cantonese, and Mandarin. Most Hong Kong schools are run by Christian organizations and are either subsidized by the government or funded through private tuition. Additionally, there are close to 50 different international schools with curricula from the United States, Britain, Canada, Australia, and other non-English speaking places. The list is a virtual United Nations, with names such as American International School, Australian International School, Canadian International School, French International School, Japanese International School, Norwegian International School, and so on. As in mainland China, most of these international schools are in the outskirts in newly developed land either in Kowloon, in South Hong Kong, or in Lantau, rather than in the heart of urban Hong Kong. The only English-language international schools in northern Hong Kong are the Sear Rogers International School (British) in the Mid-Levels, the Kiangsu and Chekiang Primary School (Anglo-Chinese) in North Point, the St. Paul's Convent (Australian) all-girls school in Causeway Bay, and the Chinese International School at Braemer Hill in northeast Hong Kong.

Shopping

Hong Kong's reputation as a shopper's paradise is well deserved. You'll find shops large and small throughout the SAR, but especially in Kowloon and northern Hong Kong. Some of the most famous upscale shopping centers include the nine-story Times Square in Causeway Bay; Pacific Place in Central; and Harbour City, one of the largest malls in Asia, in Kowloon near the cruise-ship terminal.

Your grocery bill in Hong Kong will be high if you plan to keep a western diet. A pound of beef can cost as much as $21 because it is imported. Local food, however, is affordable, especially vegetables and the abundant seafood that's so fresh it'll still be swimming when you buy it.

For street markets visit Temple Street in Kowloon where you can buy knockoff clothing and pirated goods and have an excellent local meal at one

Hong Kong's many convenient shops offer great bargains.

of the many outdoor restaurants. Across the harbor back in Hong Kong's Central neighborhood, you'll find the "Lanes," Li Yuen Streets West and East, where there are numerous street vendors.

GETTING AROUND

A vast public transportation system of taxis, subways, buses, trams, and ferries makes it easy to get around Hong Kong.

By Taxi

Taxi fares start around HK$15 (US$2) for the first two kilometers. The color of the taxi indicates its assigned zone. In urban areas the cars are red; in the New Territories they are green; and in Lantau Island taxi cabs are painted blue. A red disk visible in the passenger side of the windshield lets you know the taxi is available.

By Subway

The Mass Transit Railway (MTR) is a modern system of seven subway lines connecting the major parts of the SAR. Depending on distance, fares cost between HK$5 (US$0.65) and HK$30 (US$3.85). Seniors, children, and college students qualify for the "concessionary" fare, which is about half the full fare. Fares can be lower if you purchase a discounted tourist pass, or if you use the Octopus smart card that uses radio signals to pay the fare, so you never even have to take it out of your pocket to use it.

The MTR blue line runs along the northern edge of Hong Kong Island from Chai Wan in the east to Central in the west. The red line starts at

PRIME LIVING LOCATIONS

Central and runs up into Kowloon. The purple line also starts in Hong Kong, at North Point, then crosses Victoria Harbour and has stops in Kowloon and terminates at the famous fishing village of Sai Kung Town in the New Territories. The green line starts at a connection with the red line in the Yau Ma Tei neighborhood in Kowloon, then travels east where it connects with the purple line. The gold line runs from Hong Kong station out to Lantau Island, where it connects with the new Disneyland Resort Line. The teal line connects the Hong Kong station in Central with the new international airport. A one-way airport fare is HK$100 (US$13). If you're headed to the mainland, the Kowloon Canton East Railway will take you straight to Shenzhen.

By Bus
A complex network of buses and mini-buses connects all points far and near in the Hong Kong SAR. A letter in the route name indicates something special about the route. For instance the letter "M" used as a suffix indicates the route connects with the MTR. Bus fares range from as low as HK$2 (US$0.25) up to HK$35 (US$4.50). Fares on air-conditioned buses are slightly higher.

By Tram
There are tram routes all along the north side of Hong Kong Island. Board the street car in the back and head up to the second deck for sightseeing. For HK$2 (US$0.25), there's no better way to take in the sights. The famous Victoria tram is a funicular train that ascends to Victoria Peak where you can take in an awesome view of Victoria Harbour and the Kowloon skyline.

By Ferry
Numerous ferries cross Victoria Harbour and connect to the outlying islands. The famous green-and-white Star ferries charge only a couple dollars for a quick ten-minute harbor crossing. Ferries also connect to faraway places such as Macau and Zhuhai.

By Car
If you feel the need to have your own car, you can purchase one for about the same cost as you'd pay in the United States, but you'll pay the exorbitant "first registration" tax and numerous fees that can literally double the amount that you pay for the car. Only about 10 percent of those living in Hong Kong own their own cars.

Macau 澳门

The former Portuguese colony of Macau is the Las Vegas of the Orient. It is the only place where gambling is legal in all of China, and whether it's cards, dice, slots, ponies, F-1, or greyhounds, the Macanese know how to gamble and have a good time. Like Hong Kong, Macau is also a Special Administrative Region retaining its own currency and local rule. But unlike Hong Kong, Macau is quite small. Its land mass is only 2 percent the size of Hong Kong's and the population is only 450,000.

Over 400 years ago merchants from Portugal established a trading post on Macau. It was the first European colony in all of Asia. Catholic missionaries and military men accompanied the merchants, and the area was developed like any other European city complete with imposing forts and baroque cathedrals that still exist today.

While Macau is a bit cheaper than Hong Kong, it is still considered one of the most expensive places to live.

THE LAY OF THE LAND

Macau consists of a peninsula connected to mainland China and the two islands of Taipa and Coloâne, which are technically one island due to a

land reclamation project that links them. The Chinese city of Zhuhai is across the border to the north and Hong Kong is 70 kilometers to the east across the Pearl River Delta. Ferries to Hong Kong take about an hour, or you can take a helicopter if you're in a hurry (and money's no object).

Climate

Macau shares the same subtropical climate as Hong Kong. Summers, starting in April, are hot and humid with occasional typhoons in July and August. September through December is the most pleasant time of the year: warm, dry, and always sunny.

Macau's eclectic architectural mix

Language

Today street and place names are primarily in Portuguese, but Cantonese is the common language. In areas frequented only by locals, you might struggle if you only know English, but because Macau is an international tourism destination, English is spoken widely in and around the tourist areas.

WHERE TO LIVE

In recent years the Macau real estate market has skyrocketed, making it one of the most expensive places to live, trailing just behind Hong Kong. Real estate prices are typically advertised in dollar amounts, though those dollars are Hong Kong dollars, not U.S. And unlike the mainland, size is given in square feet, not square meters. The property market is brutally competitive in Macau, so be sure you're really ready to act when you go looking for a new home. You'll find places sold right out from under your feet if you so much as take a week to think about it.

Most of the population is concentrated within the Macau peninsula so most of the housing is located there, but newer housing has recently been built in Taipa or Coloâne, some of it built according to western tastes. New luxury developments are going into the Cotai Strip, the reclaimed land connecting Coloâne and Taipa that is slated to become Macau's version of the Las Vegas strip. There are very few villas in all of Macau, so no matter which part you choose to locate in, you will more than likely live in a high-rise apartment tower.

Macau Peninsula

Though the Macau Peninsula covers just a quarter of the SAR's total land mass, it's home to the majority of the population. The peninsula is where all the activity of the city takes place. All the major facilities and tourist venues are here, and its compact design makes it easy to walk or take a short taxi or bus ride to anywhere you want to go. It's also the most expensive of the three. At the Lake View Mansion on the Nam Van Lake, you can rent a sprawling four-bedroom luxury apartment with gorgeous views for around HK$35,000 (US$4,500). On the other end of the scale, a small studio apartment at the Lei King Kok can be rented for HK$4,000 (US$515).

Taipa

Taipa is the middle ground between the crowded yet alluring Macau Peninsula and the quiet countryside of Coloâne. If you'll be working on the

Cotai Strip, living in Taipa will be an easy commute. It's also home to The International School of Macau. The Kingsville, Macau's most luxurious apartment complex, is located here, complete with swimming pool, gym, and an easy walk to area restaurants and shops. Apartments with three or four bedrooms rent from HK$12,000 (US$1,500) to HK$25,000 (US$3,100). A typical three bedroom place has around 1,500 square feet. Ocean Garden is another popular spot; a 1,200-square-foot two-bedroom apartment with views of the hill and the sea will put you out just HK$6,000 (US$775) per month.

Coloâne

Though Coloâne is just a 15-minute drive from downtown Macau on the peninsula, it feels quite remote. Here you'll find quiet residential areas surrounded by forests, clean air, beaches, and a golf club. What you won't find here is convenient public transportation or good shopping. The Hellene Garden has 1,500-square-foot three-bedroom apartments, some with sea views, typically starting around HK$10,000 (US$1,300) up to HK$28,000 (US$3,600) for an executive unit.

DAILY LIFE

Macau can be either delightful or disappointing, depending on your expectations. If you are coming from the mainland and expecting just another Chinese city, you'll enjoy the unique cultural charms here. But if you're expecting a quaint old place brimming with history on every corner, you may be disappointed by the ways Macau is still very much a Chinese city, often dirty and in disrepair. Nevertheless, there is a growing community of expatriates in Macau who love their quirky new home.

Foreigners in Macau work in a number of fields, but the major employers are in tourism, especially the new casinos. In recent years Macau has had a shortage of workers in just about every field—health care, construction, education, you name it—and employers can't seem to hire enough people for the jobs. If, on the other hand, you're more inclined to be the boss than to have one, Macau's government has an easy "one stop" service for setting up a business that makes the process simple enough that you can get by without a lawyer.

Visas

Most nationalities can enter Macau without any visa, though how long you can stay after that depends on where you're from. Most Europeans can stay up to 90 days; North Americans, 30 days. To stay and work in Macau long term, you'll first need to land the job, and then you can apply for a work visa at any PRC embassy or consulate. Unlike the mainland, an AIDS test is not required to obtain a residence permit in Macau or Hong Kong.

Finance

Although control of Macau reverted to China in 1999, the territory retained its own municipal government and its own currency, the pataca. One hundred avos make a pataca. The pataca's exchange rate is pegged to the Hong Kong dollar at an official rate of 1:1, although you'll lose about 3 percent when changing money. Hong Kong dollars can be spent in Macau, but you should exchange or spend all your pataca before leaving Macau, because you can't spend them anywhere in Hong Kong or the mainland, except for a few generous shopkeepers in Zhuhai.

Expat Social Scene

Some say Macau's expat community is not as close-knit as you'll find on the mainland, perhaps because it is a tourist town and people tend to come and go with the tide. The luncheons and activities of the International Ladies Club of Macau is the best way to get connected if you're female, though their regular events such as cocktail parties, Easter egg hunts, and charity balls can be enjoyed by all. If you're looking for something else to do besides

Macau's economy is based on tourism and casinos.

gambling, you won't have a huge range of entertainment in this laid-back place, though you will find culturally rich museums, pleasant parks, and a number of fine beaches including a black-sand beach on Colôane where you can camp. *MacauTalk* is a bi-monthly English magazine that can keep you informed on upcoming local events such as festivals, flea markets, and art and cultural exhibits. Macau also has its own Grand Prix.

Health Care

For health care, Macau's doctors are highly qualified and the Hope Medical Clinic is a highly regarded hospital with international standards.

Schools

For schooling options in Macau, The International School of Macau follows a Canadian curriculum and is expanding to cover all grades. The School of the Nations has its roots in the Baha'i faith and is open to both Macanese and foreigners. A few international students also attend the Sheng Kung Hui primary school (a local Anglican school that teaches a U.K. curriculum) and the Sacred Heart Catholic School for girls. Kids can also get involved in several extracurricular clubs.

Shopping

Expats will be able to find most of what they want and need in Macau, and for everything else, just hop over to Hong Kong. Though Macau doesn't yet have the international hypermarkets that are all over prime cities on the mainland, you'll still find imported goods. Macau has Watson's drugstores as well as a Park'n Shop supermarket; Gourmet Fine Foods in Taipa sells goodies like cheese and cold-cuts.

GETTING AROUND

Because downtown Macau is so small you can get just about anywhere on foot, but there are plenty of buses and taxis that will get you around the whole SAR. Taxis are inexpensive—a ride from the peninsula to the tip of Coloâne Island is only about HK$75 (US$10).

THE SOUTH

Southern China is a land of boomtowns and economic growth. The Pearl River Delta (PRD), one of the three key economic regions in China, is here. It's the world's workshop; 5 percent of the world's goods are produced here. And economic reform has created a huge amount of prosperity for its residents, some of the wealthiest in the nation. Guangzhou, Shenzhen, and Zhuhai are all key cities located in the PRD and great spots for expat relocation. The other southern city that is a great place for expats but not part of the PRD is Xiamen Island in Fujian Province.

The cities of the Pearl River Delta share much in common, including the Cantonese language and cuisine as well as the ever-present influence of nearby Hong Kong. Xiamen may not feel Hong Kong's presence as much, but it does feel Taiwan's, as its proximity to Taiwan draws wealthy Taiwanese who are looking to give back to their original homeland. None of the southern cities can boast a pure Mandarin, neither in dialect nor in accent. And all are very far from Beijing, both literally as well as

© BARBARA STROTHER

figuratively, and the iron hand of the communist state sometimes just doesn't reach this far.

The Lay of the Land

The majority of prime expat locations in southern China are in Guangdong Province, lining the banks of the Pearl River as it flows into the South China Sea. Guangzhou is the northernmost of the bunch, followed by Shenzhen on the river's eastern bank and Zhuhai on its western bank. And then there's lone Xiamen, the only one of the bunch that lies far from the Pearl River, on the southeastern coast of Fujian Province.

CLIMATE

All of the Pearl River Delta cities share the same climate. Most of the year is pleasant and spring-like with ever-blooming flowers and no real winter. Summers, on the other hand, are long, sticky, muggy, hot, and humid, especially in Guangzhou, which doesn't have the ocean breeze to cool the air. Typhoons and tropical storms regularly wreak havoc on these cities. Though Xiamen also experiences an occasional typhoon, its position between the mountains and the sea gives it one of the best climates in China—a land of eternal spring.

Guangzhou 广州

Guangzhou, the capital of Guangdong Province and home to 9.4 million people, is best known in the West as Canton (though the name technically refers to its province). It occupies the strategic spot at the head of the Pearl River Delta where the east, west, and north rivers converge.

Guangzhou has been around for 2,000 years, serving as a pivotal port during the days of the Silk Road trade and again during the era of foreign concessions. Today Guangzhou is once again bustling with the activity of international trade, with 30 percent of the Fortune 500 companies having locations within its borders. It shares a spot in the top four first-tier cities of the mainland, along with Shanghai, Beijing, and Shenzhen.

Cantonese cuisine is the most famous in all of China. The locals here believe that every part of every creature whose back faces the sun is good for eating (anyone for ox genitals or duck tongues?). The little plates of snacks at Cantonese dim sum restaurants are delicious and much more palatable for those who aren't fond of exotic foods.

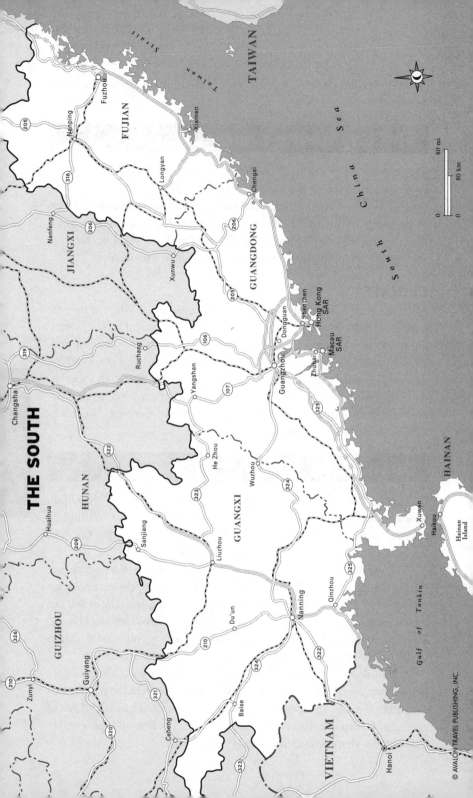

© RYAN SHAW

a Cantonese dim sum feast

Guangzhou has a reputation for being a freewheeling city, fond of quoting "the heaven is high, the emperor far away." Down here the laws are sometimes seen as merely recommendations. This place also has a reputation for thievery on its streets. Fortunately Guangzhou's crime is very rarely violent, and it still feels much safer here than any big city in America.

The downsides to life in Guangzhou include the sooty pollution and the petty criminals. This place is also infamous for the aggressive local women looking for foreign companionship.

WHERE TO LIVE

In Guangzhou housing options include standard apartments and serviced apartments, luxury villas, townhouses, and even charming old early-1900s houses in historic districts, if you're lucky enough to find one available (and have the patience to deal with the maintenance issues). The expat housing scene can be divided into four key areas: downtown Guangzhou, Tianhe, Baiyun, and Zengcheng.

Downtown

Two adjacent districts on the north bank of the Pearl River, Yuexiu and Dongshan, blend into one to create downtown Guangzhou. This area is the historic birthplace of Guangzhou with a history of over 2,000 years. It's everything you would expect of a city this big: active, busy, with

SHAMIAN ISLAND 沙面岛

Shamian Island is a historic little place that used to be the stomping grounds of European traders. This genteel spot is a nice change of pace from the downtown Guangzhou commotion across the way, making a nice place to wander among its old colonial European homes. Both Protestant and Catholic services in English are offered at the island's churches. The Qingping market here is a fascinating place, though if you can't stomach the idea of petting your food before it is slaughtered, you'll want to stay clear of the live animals section.

access to just about anything you could want (except for peace, quiet, and clean air). Downtown apartments range from places like Park View Place in Yuexiu and Eastern and Central Plazas in Dongshan, where rents start as low as $450 a month for a two bedroom with less than 100 square meters, up to super-luxury four-bedroom apartments at the Clifford Mansion that rent for $8,000 a month, with lots of options in between (though most are over $1,000 a month).

Er Sha Island, the largest island in the Pearl River, is also a part of downtown. Er Sha is a fashionable enclave for foreign staff from local consulates and businesses. The American International School Guangzhou is here, as well as a handful of western preschools. Er Sha has several housing complexes that are popular with expats, such as The Golden Arch, where five-bedroom luxury villas with up to 630 square meters have their own private swimming pools and rent in the $5,000–10,000 a month range.

Baiyun

Baiyun District covers a huge, mountainous area mostly to the north of the central city. The Nanhu (South Lake) National Tourism and Holiday Zone is here, with its heavily forested mountain park, along with the Guangzhou Nanhu International School. The biggest draw of Baiyun is its natural environment and fresh air. Just a 15-minute (on average) driving commute to the central Guangzhou districts, Baiyun provides a chance to leave the city's intense activity behind yet still easily access it when you want it.

Baiyun has plenty of villas and upscale apartment complexes to choose from. Castle Hill Luxury Homes lives up to its name with four-bedroom 412-square-meter villas renting as high as $7,500, as well as apartments renting around $1,300–1,800 for 220 square meters. Luhu Parkview's sprawling villas range from $6,800 for 330 square meters with 2–4 bedrooms, up to 900-square-meter mansions for $13,000 in a complex located within a park that includes an international golf course. If you're looking for something a little lighter on the wallet, Summer Palace rents apartments for as little as $320–620 a month for two or three bedrooms with 90–135 square meters.

Tianhe

Just east of the central downtown districts, the popular Tianhe District is a vibrant new commercial center studded with futuristic skyscrapers and glassy towers. If you're a shopaholic or a night owl, this metropolitan (and pricey) quarter is the best place to be. The eastern side of the district has a sizeable foreign community, with housing, bars, and restaurants that cater to expat wants and needs.

If you're in the market for a Tianhe apartment, you'll have tons of options (if you're in the market for a villa, better look elsewhere.) From three-bedroom serviced apartments at the Nuova Plaza ($2,000–2,500 per month) to extravagant flats renting for $4,500 at the Regal Court, you can drop a few bucks here. The Eton Eighteen and the Greenery both have apartments that start around $600 or $700 a month for a two-bedroom place with a little over 100 square meters; the Greenery also has duplexes as well as swimming, squash, and snooker.

Zengcheng

Zengcheng is technically a separate city though it falls within the municipality of Guangzhou. It comprises the easternmost region of Guangzhou, just north of Dongguan city. Zengcheng may not have as many residential complexes as the others, but what it does have is impressively large and luxurious villas, such as the gorgeous three-story American-style homes at Purple Cloud Hill with huge floor plans of 400–580 square meters. The Utahloy International School is here in Zengcheng, as well as the Economic and Technical Development Zone with its multinational corporations. Many of the ETDZ employees live in the Xintang New World Garden apartments, as well as the villas and townhouses on the expansive grounds of the five-star Phoenix City Hotel. You can expect to pay, on average, $4,000–6,000 and up for villas in Zengcheng; luxury apartments run between $1,000–3,000 a month.

Just south of Zengcheng District is Dongguan city, which has a significant Asian expat population but is still somewhat undiscovered by the western expats. If you choose Zengcheng as home, you may want to get to know what amenities Dongguan has to offer by exploring the area in your free time. If you're interested in the possibility of locating in Dongguan as an alternative to Guangzhou, and if you have an executive-level housing budget, check out the Laguna Verona, with 200 American-style villas and 400 European-style villas built around a golf course and a lake.

DAILY LIFE

If you are interested in learning Cantonese or if you already speak it, this city is obviously a great choice. But if you are hoping to pick up good Mandarin skills while in China, you'll have a harder time with it here, since Cantonese is so deeply embedded in the society. As for English, not much is spoken, although you'll see it on the road signs. It would be possible to get by here without Chinese language skills, but having at least a very basic knowledge will greatly enhance your experience.

Expat Social Scene

Guangzhou's expatriate community is enormous, bigger than Shanghai's or Beijing's, though the vast majority of foreign residents here are Asian. Most expats are in Guangzhou for business, with the usual teachers and students thrown into the mix, along with diplomatic types working at one of Guangzhou's several consulates.

Those with a spiritual bent will have their choice of English services, not just the typical Catholic and Protestant but also Mormon and Jewish. Expat sports groups gather informally for softball, soccer, basketball, rugby, bowling, and the like; others prefer to take advantage of Guangzhou's growing adventure sports like rock-climbing, caving, water-skiing, canoeing, paragliding, and hiking.

Expats will find most everything they need in Guangzhou, including tons of first-rate shopping, impressive and inexpensive restaurants of all types of cuisine, a vibrant bar scene, and both an SOS Clinic and Can-Am Clinic for western health care. The Guangzhou Women's International Club can help you get settled in and the U.S. Consulate can provide help when you need it most.

Expat resources such as the English magazine *That's Guangzhou,* with its corresponding website, and the email newsletter XianzaiGuangdong (www.xianzai.com) can direct you to local events, and the *South China Morning Post* will keep you abreast of the daily news in English.

Schools

Guangzhou has quite a few international schools for expat families. The two most popular among Americans are the centrally located American International School Guangzhou (AISG) on Er Sha Island and the Utahloy International School in the Baiyun District. AISG is the oldest international school around, and has just about filled up its new campus with over 700 students. Utahloy is about the same size though much more European in its focus. Other options include the British Guangzhou Nanhu International School in the Baiyun District, as well as the Guangzhou Grace Academy, which is perhaps the most religious school in the entire mainland. Grace Academy is located on Nanpu Island in the Panyu district, the southernmost section of the Guangzhou metropolitan area, inside an upscale housing complex called Riverside Garden.

GETTING AROUND

Getting around the central Guangzhou city is easy enough using the subway around downtown, and public buses reach every corner of the Guangzhou metro area. Expect the public transportation to be crowded, however. Even if you live too far out to take advantage of the metro and find riding buses inconvenient, taxis are always a convenient solution. If you choose to live way out in the suburbs, having a car at your disposal (preferably with driver) will make life easier, though cabs and buses service all areas.

You can leave town for other Pearl River Delta locations via a short boat or train ride from Guangzhou, and Hong Kong is less than two hours away, with a choice of eight flights, four cruises, four trains, three hovercrafts, and numerous buses to get you there. And if living in China isn't adventurous enough for you, Guangzhou is arguably the best mainland city for exploring beyond China's borders, with flights to all major Asian destinations and then some.

Shenzhen 深圳

There is a saying about Chinese cities: If you want to learn 5,000 years of history, go to Xi'an; 1,000 years, Beijing; 200 years, Shanghai; and 20 years, Shenzhen. This city was once just a fishing village with a border crossing to Hong Kong, but since it became the first Special Economic Zone (SEZ) in the 1980s, Shenzhen has taken off. It now ranks in the top four first-tier cities in China, along with Guangzhou, Shanghai, and Beijing, and has a boomtown population of 10.4 million people. It

© BARBARA STROTHER

Shenzhen has become a shopper's mecca.

also boasts the highest per capita GDP of all major mainland cities, the richest city in China.

Shenzhen has gained the position of number-one Chinese city for quality of life. It's a very international city, a shopping mecca of rich and bored Hong Kong housewives. This was the first city in China to get its pollution under control, and enjoys a reputation for having a clean and pretty seaside area. Real estate prices have skyrocketed in recent years, due mostly to the fact that they are running out of land to build on—the classic economics textbook example of supply not meeting demand.

Located on the southeastern tip of the Pearl River Estuary, Shenzhen is separated from Hong Kong by the Shenzhen River downtown and by the Hong Kong Bay in Shekou, Shenzhen's satellite city to the west and the heart of its SEZ.

WHERE TO LIVE

The prime expat housing in Shenzhen Municipality is divided into two parts; central Shenzhen city and the Nanshan District that includes the satellite city of Shekou. While central Shenzhen will give you access to all the downtown amenities as well as the border crossing to Hong Kong, expats with kids will most likely want to be in Nanshan, where all three of the key international schools for westerners are located.

Downtown Shenzhen

Central Shenzhen city is divided into two districts, Luohu and Futian. Luohu contains downtown Shenzhen proper and has the highest apartment rents of any district within Shenzhen Municipality. What you get for your money, though, is convenience and all the excitement of being in the middle of the city's hubbub. Dongmen pedestrian shopping street is here, as well as the main border crossing to Hong Kong. Though Luohu is not the most popular destination for foreigners, there definitely are some

a 24-hour coffee and tea shop for those who like to be out all hours of the night

living here. You'll find basic high-rise apartments with two or three bedrooms renting for $500–700 a month.

Futian District lies to the west of Luohu and also contains a good chunk of the central city with all its conveniences. A little farther out in Futian, the resort area around Honey Lake boasts fun spots like a water park, amusement park, and opera house, as well as a sizeable number of high-end residences that cater to expats. Futian's central apartments are a little cheaper than Luohu's, with standard two- or three-bedroom apartments renting $250–400, though there are a few places where you can rent a four- or five-bedroom flat overlooking the sea for $1,200 or so. If you'd prefer a villa, head to Honey Lake, where a five-bedroom home set in a botanical garden environment will put you out over $4,000 a month.

Nanshan District and Shekou

Nanshan District, roughly a 30-minute drive to the west of downtown Shenzhen, includes two key areas for both western and eastern expats: Shekou and the Overseas Chinese Town. Though Shekou technically refers to the central business district, the name is often used interchangeably with Nanshan district. Nanshan has tons of housing options, from convenient central apartments where you can literally run your errands, to a plethora of upscale villas, some in pleasant mountainside settings.

Shekou has traditionally been the primary hub for foreign residents. A prime location here may put you in walking distance to Sea World, where you won't find Shamu doing flips in a pool but you will find all kinds of international eateries (think Irish pub grub and Italian pizza), as well as shops with hard-to-find imported foods like Doritos and salami.

Apartments are available both in the central Shekou area as well as at high-end residential complexes farther out into the mountainside areas. Rents start around $300 for a simple place but go as high as $2,000 for more upscale spots. Nanshan's villas typically offer four- or five-bedroom layouts, most with two or three stories, and start around $3,000 a month, though some very prestigious places can go as high as $6,000–10,000 a month. A few places to consider include the seaview flats at Mont Orchid Garden, renting two or three bedrooms for around $2,000, or the similarly priced places at the quiet Guishan Villas complex, which houses the QSI International School. Jingshan Villas are also popular with foreigners since the Shekou International School is here. At the trendy and popular Coastal Rose Garden, $1,200 can rent you a three-bedroom, 130-square-meter high-rise flat with a large balcony overlooking Hong Kong beyond the sea. From here you can easily walk to the nearby Starbucks and restaurants around Shekou Square, as well as the ferry terminal.

DAILY LIFE

Shenzhen's populace are a strong mix of peoples, both from other parts of China as well as foreigners and overseas Chinese, which all use Mandarin as the common lingual denominator. You'll still hear Cantonese here, but you can expect everyone to know and speak Mandarin. English, on the other hand, is spoken here about as much as the average big Chinese city (which is to say, not much at all).

The shopping is good in Shenzhen. A smattering of international grocery stores sell the holy grails of expats—cheese, Mexican food, imported beer, and the like. Try US Grocers and Silver Palate in the same building as Park'n Shop Shekou. Of course, all the usual hypermarkets are always popular for everyday purchases, such as Carrefour, lots of Wal-Marts, Park'n Shop, Metro, Sam's Club, and Jusco. And then there's always the easy access to Hong Kong's limitless shopping options.

There's an SOS Medical Clinic in Shekou, and VIP services at the Beijing University Shenzhen Hospital and the Shenzhen People's Hospital.

The quick commute to Hong Kong makes it easy to take advantage of Hong Kong's advanced health facilities as well.

Expat Social Scene

Shenzhen has a lively expat scene and an even livelier night scene, with numerous dance clubs and western-style bars where expats and locals alike party until the sun comes up. It's very multicultural, with a good mix of people—and restaurants—from all over the globe, from a couple Brazilian barbecues and a half a dozen Starbucks to Moroccan and Indian food served in exotic settings.

If you find yourself in Shenzhen looking for a foreign friend, the sophisticated expat community here tends to gather based on common interests. Options include the Shekou International Women's Club, the Wine and Cheese Club, Toastmaster's, Shekou Hash running and drinking club, Mahjong for Ladies, and Mother with Toddlers, to name a few. The Snake Pit, in Shekou, is a legendary sports and social club that's been serving the expat community for almost 20 years. Family activities include local theme parks, water parks, safari garden, and even an indoor ski area (at the Windows of the World theme park) and horseback-riding.

Expats here can stay well informed with a daily English-language newspaper, *Shenzhen Daily*. Several websites can help you connect with others who share your interests in yoga or rugby, or to find out which restaurants are hosting Christmas parties, including www.shenzhenparty.com and www.shenzhenpeople.net, as well as the weekly email newsletter, XianzaiGuangdong (www.xianzai.com).

Schools

Shenzhen has eight international schools, though about half are for Hong Kongnese and Taiwanese families. For North Americans, the three main choices include the Shekou International School, the oldest school serving all grades with over 300 students; QIS Shekou, the fastest-growing school that also covers all grades and has over 400 students; and the newest in Nanshan, the International School of Sino-Canada, a Canadian school currently through 10th grade with 160 students.

GETTING AROUND

Getting around Shenzhen is also easy, especially since the traffic here isn't as bad as what you'll see in the congested big cities. Most expats use the cheap taxis, though the public transportation network is efficient, and bikes are convenient for those who are centrally located. Shenzhen's subway system currently has two working lines, with two lines under construction, and there are plan to extend the system considerably throughout the Shenzhen/ Shekou area. Excursions to other spots on the Pearl River can be done by boat, bus, or train. And for trips farther away, trains from Guangzhou or flights out of Hong Kong's International Airport (an easy ferry ride away) can get you to any destination you seek.

Zhuhai 珠海

They call Zhuhai the green city, and for more reasons than one. It's lush and green with forested mountains, it's environmentally green with low pollution, and it's green in light of the dollars that float around this place where the economy is blooming like its ever-present flowers. It's also green in terms of experience. Zhuhai is a new city, one of the first Special Economic Zones, which has in just 20 years put what was once a sleepy fishing village on the economic map.

Located on the southwest tip of the Pearl River Delta, Zhuhai (pop. just under one million) is consistently selected as one of the best in China for quality of life. What it lacks in ancient historical relics it makes up for in its modern urban planning: a pleasant and clean environment, wide boulevards, and a good transportation network with almost no traffic jams. Ferries connect Zhuhai to Hong Kong and the other Pearl River Delta cities, and it's just a simple walk across the border to the gambling grounds of Macau (the only place casinos are allowed in China). This lovely seaside city has a pleasant spring-like environment year-round, with sea breezes to cool down the summer heat and more than 145 islands within its boundaries. To top it off, Zhuhai is one of the cheapest cities in the Pearl River Delta, and for no better reason than that it is just less discovered by the world.

WHERE TO LIVE

Zhuhai has the cheapest housing of the prime Pearl River Delta cities. Three-bedroom apartments can run less than $200 a month, and you'll have plenty of choices in the $500–1,000 range; anything more puts you into the sweet lap of luxury. Here you'll find villas with beautiful surroundings close to beaches, or high-rise apartments with sparkling nighttime views of the city lights reflected on the sea. In Zhuhai you can expect to sit out on your balcony high above the bustling city below, propping your feet up on the intricate wrought-iron railing, sipping an ice-cold Tsingtao and gazing out at the wide blue yonder as far as the eye can see.

The three key districts for urban real estate in Zhuhai include Xiangzhou, Jida, and Gongbei. Jida and Gongbei tend to be the most expensive districts, due in part to the large number of ocean-view apartments they have along their seacoast. Zhuhai also has suburban areas with new villas and upscale apartment complexes, such as Nanping and Tangjia Districts.

Xiangzhou District

The Xiangzhou District is the central downtown area of the city, along the banks of the Pearl River Estuary. It's a convenient location for the city's amenities. In Xiangzhou you can get a high-rise three-bedroom place, with 180-degree views of the ocean from the dining room and a matching view of downtown from the living room, for just $500 a month. Several apartment complexes here that are popular with foreigners include the Haiwan Huayuan, with large four-bedroom flats boasting great views of the sea, as well as the Phoenix Garden, a large complex with a pool, shops, and restaurants.

Jida District

Jida District is a central commerce area directly south of Xiangzhou, located at the corner where the Pearl River and the South China Sea meet. Jida boasts quiet residence areas and is just a bit more expensive than Xiangzhou. Here you can find both nice, new apartments as well as sprawling five-bedroom villas, all convenient to great shopping and restaurants.

Moving west along the coast on your way to Gongbei, you'll find plenty of sea-view complexes in the area where the two districts merge. High-rise flats here rent for around $750–1,000 for two or three bedrooms; some boast two floors or on-site kids' fun rooms and fitness centers. The majority have gorgeous views of the sea.

Gongbei District

Farther down the coastline from Jida, Gongbei District is the land that borders Macau. Consider locating here if your family plans to take advantage of Macau's amenities on a regular basis, such as attending its schools or its churches, or if you are a serious gambler. Within Gongbei you'll find Zhuhai's Bar Street, including the expat-popular Cohiba bar. Most foreigners here choose central high-rise apartments with views of the mountains and the sea, though there are a few villas on offer, such as the Australian

Garden that houses the QSI International School. For $2,000 a month you can impress your friends and family in your luxury penthouse with amazing views of Macau and the great blue beyond.

Suburbs

The suburbs of Zhuhai, located west and north of the central city, are where you'll find new villa compounds and upscale apartments. The Huafa Apartments in Nanping District are a good option if you're interested in sending your kids to the innovative Yung Wing Chinese private school here. Near the entertainment hub of Tangjia, Horizon Cove is a popular spot with a lake, green hills, outdoor pool, and easy access to the area's golf courses, racetracks, and hot springs. This complex's Mediterranean-style villas rent for about $1,500–2,500; duplexes start around $750 and apartments range $250–1,000 for three bedrooms with 140 square meters. Other popular villas include the Golf Villas and Seaview Garden. Expect to pay up to $3,000 for a nice, large home with three floors.

DAILY LIFE

Zhuhai is a melting pot of Chinese that have come from all corners of the mainland in search of prime career positions in the top-rate businesses of its Special Economic Zone. Because of this, Zhuhai is uniquely more focused on speaking Mandarin as the lingua franca, unlike the typical Guangdong Province cities that are strong in Cantonese. If you want to master Mandarin but are interested in southern China, this city would be a good fit for you.

For shopping, Zhuhai has the typical international hypermarts, like Carrefour from France and Jusco from Japan, and typical Chinese department stores and malls. For medical and dental care, however, many foreigners prefer to go to the advanced facilities in nearby Macau or Hong Kong, though staff at local hospitals and clinics can handle simple medical issues just fine.

Expat Social Scene

Zhuhai is adored by its growing foreign community. In fact this city draws foreign residents working in other Pearl River Delta cities who prefer to live in Zhuhai's pleasant environment despite the commute. Due in part to the good work of the ZIA expat club as well as the expat website www.macauzhuhai.com, Zhuhai's foreign community enjoys a strong sense of connection. Like its local population, the foreign community here tends

© BARBARA STROTHER

Zhuhai's islands and beaches provide fun in the sun.

to be a melting pot of people from around the globe. Quite a few are here with their families, which adds to the sense of family-oriented community, though singles looking for action will find enough to keep them happy with Zhuhai's nightclub scene and bar street.

Expats of all ages can take pleasure in Zhuhai's aquatic sports scene, including water-skiing, boating, surfing, swimming, or working on killer tans and kingly sandcastles on its sandy beaches. Hikers will enjoy the Wanderverein Club (www.wvzh.com), which schedules expat hiking trips into the nearby hills. Golfers throughout southern China come to play at Zhuhai's courses.

Schools

Zhuhai has just one international school, QSI International School in the Gongbei District, with a program for students up to age 13. For private Chinese schools that use some English, the Yung Wing School in the suburban Nanping District does have a few foreign kids in the midst of its pretty campus, a good way to master Chinese and save money, too.

GETTING AROUND

All parts Zhuhai are easily navigable by taxi or bus, and bikes come in handy, too, for shorter distances. Ferries and helicopters crisscross the Pearl River to the other cities nearby. Two projects in the works, a bridge that will connect Zhuhai with Hong Kong and a light rail that will connect it with Guangzhou, will make it even easier to hop from one spot to another along the delta. For spots further away, domestic cities can be reached through the Zhuhai airport, and the well-connected international airports at Hong Kong and Guangzhou are also a relatively easy option.

Xiamen 厦门

Beautiful Xiamen, deep-water port and historic island playground of the rich and foreign, is considered by some to be China's cleanest and most pleasant city. Here the colonial past and modern China meet and mingle, and so do big-city business and tourist-town charms. With its agreeable climate year-round without the typical gray haze of most Chinese cities, and its fresh seafood, lovely beaches, and a nice variety of good restaurants and shopping, what's not to love?

Xiamen is well known by its old name, Amoy. This island city has been home to merchants and pirates through the ages. Its history is marked by endless port control struggles, in which the Dutch, British, French, German, Japanese, and Portuguese all played their part. Gulangyu Island, located here, is still occupied by old colonial villas that hint at its flamboyant past.

Xiamen is situated on the southeastern coast of Fujian Province in an area protected by the mountains and the sea. Taiwan is just 100 miles eastward as the seagull flies, though Taiwan-owned Quemoy Island is a mere three

GULANGYU ISLAND 鼓浪屿

Gulangyu is gloriously stuck in a bygone era, where scarlet bougainvillea climbs up colonial villas and music wafts from open windows on this little place long dubbed "piano island." Lying in the channel that separates Xiamen Island from the mainland, Gulangyu is accessed only by ferry. There are no vehicles on Gulangyu's cobblestone streets, though there are wooden handcarts used by its 20,000 residents. Many of the old colonial European homes here are in serious disrepair, which may awaken in you a remodeler's dream. While it is possible to buy one, fixing it up will prove both difficult and expensive in this place where hardware delivery trucks and concrete mixers don't fit through the narrow, hilly lanes. It is also possible to rent one of these homes (or more likely, part of one), but the quality is liable to be far below western standards.

miles from Xiamen. The people of Xiamen have a reputation for being lovers of life, not caught up in business and money like the big-city types. And Xiamen is small by Chinese standards—at 1.5 million, it's one of the smallest of China's prime expat cities. The cost of living in Xiamen is lower than most of the prime expat cities, but it's on the rise. Due to its location on the Taiwan straits, Xiamen appeals to Taiwanese investors and retirees looking for a cheap spot to spend their glory days, and the demand for real estate has driven the prices up in recent years.

© BARBARA STROTHER

Xiamen's pirates of old may be gone, but you can still find treasures in its many shops.

WHERE TO LIVE

You shouldn't have any troubles finding a nice home in a city with an auspicious name like Xiamen ("Gate of the Grand Mansion"). Though housing prices have been rising dramatically in recent years, the market is still quite inexpensive compared to the high prices of the first-tier cities. Options range from luxury mountainside flats or seaside villas renting for $3,000 a month to small and simple apartments renting as low as $100 a month.

The heart of Xiamen city lies on Xiamen Island, though the municipality also includes Gulangyu Island and a large stretch of the mainland. Most expats live in central apartments within Xiamen Island's Siming and Huli Districts.

Siming District

After administrative redistricting a few years back, Kaiyuan District was folded into Siming, covering the southern two-thirds of Xiamen Island. For practical purposes, however, the areas are still often referred to by their original names. Traditional Siming, the southern tip of the island, includes the old city, the island's best beaches, and Xiamen University.

Kaiyuan is the middle swath of the island; it's the vibrant new commercial district otherwise known as downtown and the place to be if you want an exciting nightlife, international restaurants, and easy access to great shopping venues.

The most recent housing development is along the island ring road, and this is the best place to find villas on the island. These places are farther removed from the city's activity—which can be good or bad, depending on what kind of a lifestyle you're after. At the Sunshine Coast complex, for example, you can rent a flat or a villa with great sea views and a short walk to the beach. Huge villas here rent for a little over $3,000; four- and five-bedroom apartments with great views go for around $1,000.

The predominant hotspot for expat housing in Kaiyuan is the area around Yuan Dang Lake, which is particularly popular with serviced apartments at places like the popular Marco Polo and Plaza Pacific. There's also a variety of upscale standard apartments in this vicinity, such as Hua Xin Yuan, where you can rent a large 250-square-meter apartment with a balcony as big as a second home for around $1,200.

Along the bay on Kaiyuan's western coastline is also a popular spot. Some high-rise flats here have spectacular views of the new suspension bridge and the city lit up at night, such as the Guang Ming Da Xia, which rents two-bedroom flats for less than $300 a month. The Crowne Plaza Hotel here has a few high-end serviced apartments and boasts both panoramic views of Xiamen Bay and an easy walk to the Zhongshan Road shopping area.

In addition to these two areas, you'll find standard apartments in highrises scattered throughout the district. An average three-bedroom apartment typically rents for $150–400; around $1,000 will get you into a nice five-bedroom, 250-square-meter flat with luxury furnishings and imported appliances.

Huli District

Huli district comprises the northern third of the island, separated from downtown Xiamen by a mountain. Huli is home to one of largest central business districts in the city as well as the Gaoqi International Airport. The only five-star hotel in town, the Mandarin, is here, offering both serviced apartments and villas with added perks such as bowling, indoor and outdoor pools, massage and sauna, restaurants and a coffee shop.

Villas in Huli rent for roughly $1,000–2,500 a month, such as the Jade

Lake Manor, with five bedrooms in 342 square meters renting for just under $2,000, or the International Mountain Village, where a 260-square-meter villa with a private yard and a garage rents for around $1,000. There are also plenty of standard apartments available, like those at the Long Men (Dragon Gate) World high-rise, where a top-floor three-bedroom flat rents for around $400 a month.

DAILY LIFE

The name of the local dialect is Minnan. It's quite different from Mandarin and is actually closely related to the native Taiwanese language. Most everyone here will know and speak Mandarin, however. There's not much English spoken here, so you'll most likely need to depend on Chinese friends to help out when in need.

For western medical help, the Lifeline clinic has foreign doctors and its pharmacy carries western medications, and the Zhongshan hospital also has a VIP ward for foreigners. Shopping should be easy, with the major hypermarkets such as Metro, Wal-Mart, and Trust-Mart.

Expat Social Scene

Xiamen is well loved by the people who live here. Expats come for a variety of reasons, from working with one of the large multinational companies here, such as Dell, General Electric, and Kodak, to studying at Xiamen University's Chinese-language program, reputedly one of the best in the nation.

The city's expat community is well connected. For people who are so inclined, Xiamen International Christian Fellowship is a couple-hundred strong and offers a way to meet other foreigners. Alternately, Gulangyu Island offers English services in its historic Catholic churches. Other expat groups tend to gather informally based on shared interests, like soccer or running. Singles will find plenty of life in the local night scene.

As they say, big cities are good for fun, small cities are good for families, but small Xiamen is good for families that want to have fun. When school's out, you can head to the beaches (windsurfing and parasailing available), hike along wooded paths, or splash around at the Xiamen Water World with its outdoor waterslides and pools. Or simply wander the peaceful and pretty Xiamen Botanical Gardens for some tranquil downtime.

There's an expat magazine in English, *What's On Xiamen* (with matching website), that's handy for news on events, new restaurants, theaters showing the latest blockbusters in English, or shopping finds. You can pick one up at all the popular expat spots, like the Brazilian Barbecues and The Londoner bar. Or try the Marco Polo hotel, which often serves as the center of information and activity for the expat community.

Try to get your hands on Dr. Bill Brown's book, *Amoy Magic,* printed by the Xiamen University Press, for just about everything you ever wanted to know about Xiamen but didn't know who to ask.

Schools

The Xiamen International School offers a North American education for expat kids of all ages and nationalities, with over 250 students from nearly 30 different countries. Though not located on Xiamen Island but in the Xinglin district across the causeway, XIS provides bus transportation for their students from all key areas of the city.

GETTING AROUND

Xiamen's taxis and buses are cheap, plentiful, and easy to catch; simply consult the how-to page on the *What's On Xiamen* website for handy bus routes. Getting out of town, however, is not quite as easy as getting around it. Fuzhou Province's mountainous terrain limits the possibilities with train travel, though there is now a new freeway that connects to Hong Kong and a new rail line is under construction to link up with Ningbo (and therefore

Here's one sweet way to be chauffered around the island!

Shanghai). If you plan to do your travels by plane, the international airport here flies to 90 destinations nationally and internationally, including spots in Malaysia, Indonesia, and the Philippines.

THE EAST

Eastern China is home to the Yangtze River Delta, one of China's three most important economic regions. The cities of this area in the shadows of Shanghai are one success story after another, enjoying a high level of prosperity. Several of China's prime living locations for expats are located here, including the cities of Nanjing, Suzhou, Hangzhou, and Ningbo. In each, business is booming and foreign firms are moving in by the droves, bringing their expat jobs with them.

These smaller cities in the shadows of Shanghai tend to compare themselves with their glamorous neighbor, gloating about the unique charms and perks they have that Shanghai doesn't. Marco Polo spent a considerable amount of time here and lavished his highest praises on the cities in this region. Though times have changed since Polo's day, this area still enjoys the prosperity, charm, and innovative urban administration that first caught his attention.

© RYAN SHAW

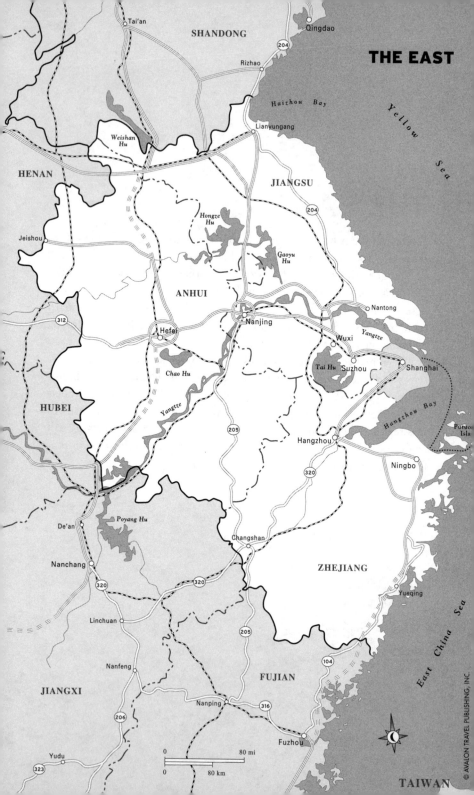

The Lay of the Land

There are just two provinces covered in this region that butts up against Shanghai and the East China Sea. Nanjing and Suzhou are both situated within Jiangsu Province, to the north. Nanjing is located in the southwestern corner of the province on the banks of the mighty Yangtze River. Suzhou lies to the southeast, just a stone's throw from Shanghai.

Zhejiang Province, south of Jiangsu, is home to two important cities for expats. Hangzhou is the provincial capital and is located in the northern tip of the province where the Qiantang River meets the Hangzhou Bay. Traveling east along the bay's shore, you eventually run into the port city of Ningbo, where the Hangzhou Bay folds into the East China Sea.

CLIMATE

Because all of the eastern cities are located within close proximity to each other, they share the same subtropical monsoon climate. They enjoy four distinct seasons, though the gray winter skies rarely bring snow. Summers are long and hot, sometimes insufferably so; July and August bring the monsoon rains.

Nanjing 南京

Throughout China's long and colorful history, Nanjing has often played a very key role. Its name literally means "southern capital," and through the years this city has been the pivotal center of six consecutive dynasties as well as the Taiping Rebellion and later the Kuomingtang. When Nanjing fell during the Sino-Japanese war, the Japanese cruelly killed, raped, maimed, and pillaged the city, an event indelibly seared into the nation's consciousness to this day.

Today Nanjing is a bustling provincial capital of 3.5 million, marked by rapid development that some compare to Shanghai's rise to prominence in the 1990s. Nanjing may never have quite the sophistication or glamour of Shanghai; on the other hand, it has kept more of its Chinese character, reflected in its ancient city wall that can still be seen in some of the oldest parts of town.

Nanjing's wooded hills turn flame red in autumn, which is the best time to wander their well-toured paths leading to historic sites and scenic viewpoints. Equally as vibrant, the cuisine is known for having a focus on color with simple seasonings. The Nanjing salted duck is its most famous specialty.

Cost of living in Nanjing is much cheaper than the larger and more glamorous cities, though as this place continues to rise in economic importance, so too will its cost of living. For now, the city can still be a bargain.

WHERE TO LIVE

Expat-quality housing can be found throughout Nanjing's seven key districts in a variety of price ranges. Downtown Nanjing's districts are divided into four quadrants (Gulou to the northwest, Xuanwu to the northeast, Baixia to the southeast, and Jianye to the southwest) that meet at Xinjiekou, Nanjing's center of finance and commerce. The remaining districts of Qixia, Jiangniang, and Yuhuatai are all located on the outskirts of the city.

Central Districts

The center of Nanjing's business and leisure is the high-rise-studded Baixia District. Baixia encompasses the city's two key shopping areas, the Confucius Temple area in its south and the head of the Xinjiekou area in its northwest. Towering upscale apartment buildings near Xinjiekou, such as the Golden Eagle International Garden, rent around $800–1,200 a month. Farther out, around Yue Ya Lake, you'll find a number of high-end residences. Luxury apartments with lake views typically start just under $1,000

the Confucius Temple area in Nanjing

a month, though small places without prime views can be had for half that. For $5,000 a month, you can get a sprawling European-style villa.

Gulou District is the oldest area of this ancient city. Here you'll find the Nanjing University with its large contingent of foreign students, as well as nearby restaurants that cater to the student lifestyle. Gulou's Hunan Road is a busy shopping street with world-renowned boutiques and department stores. Apartments in Gulou tend to be smaller and cheaper than other districts, with tiny one-bedroom flats, like those at Junlin International Mansion, renting for as little as $250 month; larger three-bedroom apartments go for around $600–800 a month.

Xuanwu District is where the central urban areas mesh with the eastern hills. This area is predominantly wooded and hilly, encompassing the Zhongshan Hill Scenic Area, with the famous mausoleum of Sun Yatsen as well as a couple of popular lakes. The luxury apartments and villas in Xuanwu cater to the international community, making this district popular with local expats. The Top Regent Garden has American-style villas as well as perks such as restaurants, massage and beauty parlor, fitness center, and an international kindergarten on the premises. Most places at Top Regent rent for $2,500–3,500, though they can go much higher depending on the size. The Royal Garden was one of the first expat-oriented villa and apartment complexes in the city; standard apartments here rent for under $1,000, but the serviced apartments run about $2,500 for a 230-square-meter three-bedroom place.

Jianye District sees a lot of tourists due to its infamous Nanjing Massacre Memorial. Nanjing's new subway stops here, an important consideration for those who want to jet around the city easily. The real estate in Jianye is similar in modesty to Gulou, though it does have a few pricey upscale apartments such as the Vanke on the banks of Mochou Lake. Five-bedroom flats at the Vanke with 248 square meters rent around $2,400, though smaller places can be had starting around $800.

Outskirts

Of all the suburban districts, Qixia is the largest, wrapping around the northeastern corner of the central city. With the river along its northern edge, this district boasts over 70 ports and harbors. It gets its name from the Qixia mountain, an area rich in scenic spots and historic sites. The Nanjing International School is here, as well as several large Chinese universities. This district is in the midst of a residential building boom that will influence the flavor of this area in the coming years, as businesses such as supermarkets and restaurants follow the growing numbers of upper-class residents here. The primary residence complex in Qixia, Royal Family, is near the international school and houses many of its teachers. Modern five-bedroom villas with 260 square meters rent for just under $3,000; large apartments range from $600–1,000.

Yuhuaitai, though on the outskirts of the city, isn't too far from Baixia's busy Confucius Temple area. Large and luxurious apartments in Yuhaitai rent around $1,500–2,000 for 3–4 bedrooms with 200–250 square meters. The Yulan Villas, located near the golf course, start around $2,200 a month but go up to an extravagant $7,000 a month for a mammoth five-bedroom home.

Jiangniang District is southeast of all the rest. There's not a whole lot to offer here right now, though this district is a key focus for future development. One option is the Green View Mandarin, with its scenic environment and amenities such as indoor and outdoor pools. Homes start at $1,500 month for a three-bedroom villa, up to $4,500 for a 350-square-meter four-bedroom house.

DAILY LIFE

Nanjing can feel like a sleepy city; but what one calls sleepy another calls laid back. Though it may be a less exciting choice as an expat destination, it is by no means a less viable option.

As for spending your cash here, Nanjing is big enough to have the key international chains. Retailers like Metro, Carrefour, Lotus, Wal-Mart, the Foreign Goods Store, as well as fast food like Pizza Hut, KFC, McDonald's, and even Starbucks, will provide most of the foods and goods that foreigners crave. International restaurants serving cuisines from around the globe are scattered throughout the city. The back markets along the busy Confucius Temple area have bargains and name-brand knockoffs unbelievably cheap. Or skip the replicas and go for the real thing in the designer boutiques, department stores, and trendy malls along Hunan Road and the Xinjiekou area.

Foreigners have several options for quality health care in Nanjing. The AEA Nanjing Clinic is located on the first floor of the Nanjing Hilton Hotel on Zhong Shan Road and offers 24-hour care to SOS members. Along with the international medical care, this multilingual clinic also has counseling services and TCM (traditional Chinese medicine) for those who are interested. There is also a VIP ward within the Jiangsu Province

© BARBARA STROTHER

the last bridge crossing the mighty Yangtze, in Nanjing

Hospital, and more than 10 other hospitals scattered around the city can provide medical services in multiple languages for foreigners.

The local Nanjing dialect is one of the few dialects with quite a bit in common with Mandarin, similar to the difference between standard American English and British English. Basic Mandarin will get you by just fine, and is highly recommended, since very little English is spoken here.

Expat Social Scene

Without the energy of Shanghai or the appealing charms of Suzhou and Hangzhou, Nanjing's expat community is somewhat less developed than other prime eastern cities, but growing.

The expat community here has a good mix of nationalities and professions, including business people, teachers, and a good-size foreign student population at Nanjing's universities. The small size of the community here means you will run into people you know.

For adults, an international soccer league, a rugby club, cricket games, as well as the Nanjing International Club, are populated by all nationalities. The nightlife of Nanjing, though not as dazzling as Shanghai or even Hangzhou, can still keep singles hopping between a few good disco clubs and karaoke bars throughout downtown. Hikers and mountain-bikers will have plenty of gorgeous green hills to keep them happy. For families, there's the indoor water park, safari park, wildlife park, fishing ponds, go-karts, or paintball, to name a few activities. Other local events and helpful living tips can be found in Nanjing's free English-language monthly, *Map Magazine*.

Schools

The primary place for expat kids is the Nanjing International School, which was originally created by parents and has since grown to 350 elementary through high school students.

GETTING AROUND

Nanjing is relatively easy to navigate by bus, taxi, bike, or its new subway system. The new metro line runs from the Olympic Stadium in the southwestern part of the city, through Xinjiekou and Gulou up to the main railway station. A second line is scheduled to be completed by 2009, connecting at Xinjiekou. Getting in and out of the city is equally straightforward, with a 3.5-hour commute to Shanghai by train or expressway and convenient overnight trains to Beijing and Xi'an. Nanjing's airport serves all key domestic destinations as well as other Asian hot spots such as Seoul and Singapore.

Suzhou 苏州

The city of Suzhou is synonymous with gardens, and we're not talking about rows of rutabagas or clumps of chrysanthemums. These are the grounds of the ancient wealthy, with paths that lead through swaying bamboo to aged pagodas, ponds graced by floating lotus leaves and darting golden koi, grotesque rock formations and quirky fir trees that twist and curve in bonsai fashion. In addition to its gardens, Suzhou is also known for the canals this 2,500-year-old city was built upon, making it the Venice of the Orient.

Modern-day Suzhou is again creating a name for itself with its urban design. This city has been recognized as a model of bringing modern growth to a city without disrupting its quaint old style. Suzhou's reputation for being a pleasant little city (pop. 1.3 million) is bringing in new foreign business and the expats are following.

WHERE TO LIVE

Though cheaper than Shanghai, Suzhou's real estate is expensive for a city of this size, reflecting the influence of having one of the world's most expensive cities so close by. Suzhou's prime expat housing is predominantly located outside of the old city center in the two districts that flank it to the west and east: the Suzhou New District and the Suzhou Industrial Park. Which of these districts you choose will largely be determined by where your job will be located.

Suzhou's famous gardens are fun for young explorers.

Suzhou New District

The Suzhou New District (SND), west of downtown, is home to over 50 multinational corporations, as well as the Etonhouse International School. The SND has plenty to choose from, from villa complexes to luxury apartments, both standard and serviced. The Regent on the Park hosts the Kinderland International Preschool on its premises, making it a great option for expat families with little *laowai*. Villas at Regent rent for $1,500–2,600. An average apartment in the New District with about 150 square meters will put you out about $600 a month; add a thousand dollars to that figure for a large three-bedroom flat at the expat enclave Garden Villa. For serviced apartments in the SND, expect to pay $300 for a very simple place up to over $1,000 for a luxurious one-bedroom flat at The Dragonfly.

Suzhou Industrial Park

The Suzhou Industrial Park (SIP), east of downtown, was developed as a joint project between the governments of China and Singapore, which is why the Suzhou Singapore International School was founded here. Thirty-five of the world's top 500 multinational firms are located within this district. Apartments in the SIP are quite plentiful; you'll have dozens of complexes to choose from in a large range from around $350 month to as high as $2,000 a month. In addition to apartments, the SIP also has several villa complexes. The Casa de Esplanade boasts that it has the only American-style houses in the city; sprawling luxury villas with 350 to 400 square meters rent for around $3,500 a month here. Less-expensive homes are available, such as those at Dushu Terrace and Han She ($1,000–2,000 for 3–5 bedrooms).

DAILY LIFE

Suzhou's proximity to Shanghai (less than an hour by train) provides an environment where expats can get a feel for a more realistically Chinese life while still having all of Shanghai's amenities at their fingertips.

Located on the Grand Canal just 80 kilometers west of Shanghai, Suzhou's softly toned local dialect is similar to Shanghai's. (In fact, Suzhou's cuisine also mimics Shanghai's, placing the same emphasis on fresh seafood and vegetables with its own distinct dishes.) But Shanghai's melting pot of residents from a variety of provinces promotes the use of Mandarin as a lingua franca, whereas in Suzhou, the use of the local dialect is more prevalent. And the use of English is much less prevalent in Suzhou than in Shanghai; you'll want to work on your Mandarin if headed here.

The vast number of tourists that pour through this city has brought the businesses that cater to them (like high-end hotels with upscale restaurants and nice health club facilities), and expats living here can also take advantage of those amenities. The shopping is decent, with a few places like Carrefour and Auchon carrying imported foods, and plenty of (mostly fake) antiques and trinkets around the tourist sites.

There are no western hospitals, though you'll find English-speakers and occasionally a foreign doctor at the local hospitals. Like everything else you can't find here, you can simply go into Shanghai to meet your medical needs.

Expat Social Scene

Suzhou's expat community is somewhat small and largely Asian. Foreign residents here tend to socialize at local restaurants and in friends' homes, and head out to Shanghai if they really want something to *do*. Family activities in Suzhou revolve around simple pleasures like bowling, hanging out at the complex pool, or an occasional day spent at the Suzhou Amusement Land and Water Park. Nearby Lake Taihu, China's third-largest lake, offers boating, swimming, fishing, and water-skiing. For information on other types of recreation, as well as English news and events, Shanghai's English media are the best resources.

Schools

Suzhou's foreign families have their choice between two international schools. The Suzhou Singapore International School has grown to over 500 students in its ten years here, with students from more than 20 countries ages three and up. The Etonhouse International School offers a curricular combination from Singapore, Australia, and Britain.

GETTING AROUND

Getting around Suzhou is easy. Bikes are a pleasant way to wander along Suzhou's old canals; if you'd prefer not to break a sweat, hop in a three-wheeled pedi-cab and let an old man do the work for you. City buses ply the common routes; taxis are as always cheap and plentiful.

Hangzhou 杭州

Hanghzou is a great place to live. Of course, we might be a little biased, since it happens to be our favorite. But it's also been ranked number-one for business by *Forbes* magazine and is one of the most popular tourist destinations in China. It's home to Zhejiang University, the largest in the nation. But Hangzhou's greatest claim to fame is the beautiful West Lake, situated right in the central city, where it has been captivating visitors since the day Marco Polo first sang its praises.

When Polo visited here in the 13th century, this city was one of the most prosperous in the world, and quite possibly the most populous as well. Modern-day Hangzhou has retained that same prosperity, due in part to

© BARBARA STROTHER

a laid-back ride around the beautiful West Lake in Hangzhou

the 20 million visitors annually that come with tourist dollars to spend. In recent years the city has revamped its ancient culture street, rebuilt its Silk Museum, redesigned the parks and paths along the lake's edge, and made admission to all tourist sites free (*very* rare in China) to guarantee a never-ending flow of happy tourists.

Hangzhou's 2.5 million residents pride themselves on being much more laid-back than nearby Shanghai, where life is all about work and money. The presence of the West Lake has made it part of the Hangzhou psyche to relax and hang out with friends at the end of the day, being peacefully rowed around the lake on a Chinese gondola while munching on dried watermelon seeds and sipping Hangzhou's world-famous Dragon Tea. Along the lake's waterside paths and parks musicians play traditional instruments and a member of the crowd may sing along, and old men practice tai chi while middle-aged women dance the jitterbug.

While the locals may not be as focused on success as Shanghaiers, they are no less successful. Hangzhou has a large and growing upper class. You'll feel their presence if you stop by one of the local malls, where suits in store windows carry thousand-dollar price tags. Unfortunately Hangzhou's real estate and cost of living have been growing along with its economy, and Hangzhou now has the fifth-highest housing costs in the mainland.

WHERE TO LIVE

Unlike most Chinese cities, the residential market in Hangzhou does not strictly follow its administrative districts. The three key housing areas include downtown Hangzhou, West Hangzhou, and along the banks of the Qiangtang River to the south of the central city.

THE MOST BEAUTIFUL WOMAN IN THE HISTORY OF CHINA

Of the four famous ancient Chinese beauties, the Zhejiang Province native Xi Shi is considered the most beautiful woman of all time. These women are admired not just for their physical appearance but for the way they used it to serve their country. Xi Shi agreed to seduce the king of Wu, distracting him with her charms and convincing him to kill his top general, which brought about his defeat in the war. Today the West Lake in Hangzhou is nicknamed after Xi Shi, claiming that both hold the position as the most beautiful in China.

Downtown Hangzhou

Hangzhou's compact central city comprises two key districts, Shangcheng and Xiacheng. Shangcheng District, situated on the lake's eastern edge, is the heart of business and tourism in the city. Xiacheng District spreads north from the northeastern corner of the lake, and is a key commercial area catering more to the wealthy local population than to loaded tourists.

If you want to live in the middle of the most happening part of Hangzhou, pick a place in Shangcheng District. Here you'll find the bar hopping and international eateries of Nanshan Street and Hubin Road, as well as the most popular stretch of West Lake's waterfront. This is a great spot for shopaholics, with fun night markets, classy department stores, small shops from the high-end to the unbelievably cheap, and a plethora of international goods of French mega-store Carrefour, all compacted within walking distance. This district is also, as could be expected, quite a bit more expensive than those that are farther from the central activity. Luxury apartments, some with lake views and many within walking distance of key spots (all are within biking distance), rent for $2,000–3,000 a month for a three-bedroom flat.

The housing in Xiacheng District is cheaper and more varied than Shangcheng while still being convenient to the downtown hot spots. Xiacheng is home to Hangzhou's newest malls, filled with boutiques of the world's most famous designer names, with price tags to match. The Wulin Road Women's Street is a female shopper's paradise; outdoor lovers can get gear and sign up for trips at the City Pack shop at Wulin Square. Plenty of western eateries and upscale hotels are scattered around the area; you won't have to go far to get your cappuccino fix. Decent-size modern apartments in this district typically rent for anywhere from $500 to $1,500 a month for two or three bedrooms with 100–200 square meters, and there are tons to choose from. For those seeking a little luxury, the White Horse apartments are near the upscale Wulin Square shopping area and Hangzhou Theater; large flats here (150 to 220 square meters) rent between $2,000 and $3,000 a month.

West Hangzhou

The area typically referred to as West Hangzhou city is technically northwest of the CBD and the lake (the northern part of Xihu District). Important spots here include the Electronics shopping street, the main campus of Zhejiang University, and the Yellow Dragon Stadium with its Trustmart mega-store and its Tourist Center. There are a few villas and townhouses

PRIME LIVING LOCATIONS

out this way, though if you're in the market for one you'll have much more to choose from along the Qiantang River. Though more convenient to the city amenities than the villas around the river, the West Hangzhou villas tend to be a little older, less likely to reflect an American home, but also a little cheaper (rents start around $1,200–2,500 a month). Apartments here are plentiful, however. Around the Yellow Dragon Stadium, rents start as low as $300 for tiny studio apartments; larger places typically run between $600–1,300, many with amenities like swimming pools, restaurants and fitness centers on the premises. A little farther north and west there are several new complexes with numerous amenities such as pools, pubs, and even preschools, such as the Century New City (three bedrooms, 150 square meters, around $1,000 per month).

Qiangtang River Region

The Qiangtang River region covers territory along the river's northern bank in both Xihu and Jianggan Districts as well as the up-and-coming Binjiang District, south of the Qiangtang River. This region is the predominant area for new housing developments. Though it's farther from the conveniences of the city, in exchange you'll get fresh air, quiet surroundings, and easy access to the Hangzhou International School in Binjiang. A 2–3 bedroom apartment with bird's-eye views of the river or the lush green hills typically rents for $800–1,500 a month with all the usual amenities.

Villas in this region are plentiful. The Notting Hill villa, typical of what's on offer in this district, boasts homes 200–350 square meters renting around $2,000–3,800 on pretty grounds with a swimming pool and restaurant. The sprawling homes at American Villas (from 300 to a whopping 500 square meters) rent for $5,000 a month; a walk through this neighborhood will make you (and Toto) completely forget that you're not in Kansas anymore.

DAILY LIFE

You'll find most products you're looking for at the big retailers like Trust-Mart and Carrefour, scattered around the city. Expats can head to the International Health Care Center and the North American International Hospital for their medical needs. For the things you can't find here, Shanghai is less than two hours away by train, bus, or private car.

The Hangzhou dialect is similar to Shanghai's, though Mandarin is widespread and typically spoken without a strong accent. Hangzhou has a fair amount of English around the city to cater to its tourists, though like most places in China, English is not widely spoken outside of the tourist venues.

Expat Social Scene

There's plenty to do in Hangzhou when the sun goes down. Hangzhou's night markets are a fun place to barter for treasures like Chinese scrolls, antique trinkets, and tons of name-brand knockoffs. The numerous clubs and pubs along Nanshan Street are popular with expats and locals alike; check out The Irish Pub if you want to hook up with the local expats. You'll find a wide variety of restaurants featuring cuisine from around the world and around

hand-drying Hangzhou's popular Dragon Well tea

© BARBARA STROTHER

the nation, especially in Hangzhou's upscale international hotels.

The Hangzhou International Business Association (HIBA) hosts regular social and business networking events, and a ladies group meets every week for lunch or an afternoon tea. Also, the Hangzhou International Church holds non-denominational English services every week.

Foreigners in Hangzhou will appreciate the resources of www.hangzhou-expat.com and local English magazine *In Touch Zhejiang,* both full of great tips, classifieds, and upcoming events for the foreign community.

Schools

The Hangzhou International School takes foreign kids of all ages for their international curriculum operating within an American system. The school has grown to over 175 students in its short four-year history.

GETTING AROUND

Getting around Hangzhou is easy, with most of the key destinations conveniently located within the compact central business district. Local bus routes are easy to get to know, and there's even a bilingual bus schedule. Taxis are cheap and plentiful (though the cabbies here will turn you down if they're looking for a higher fare). Though hills decorate the area, the city itself is quite flat, and easily navigable by bike.

Ningbo 宁波

Ningbo is a commercial city of just 1.1 million located across the Hangzhou Bay from Shanghai Municipality, at the spot where the waters of the bay mingle with the waters of the East China Sea. This ancient port town has had a long history of international trade throughout the centuries until it was eventually surpassed by neighboring Shanghai. Opened to foreign trade in the 1800s, little is left of its European concessions except a few cobblestone roads and its famous old Catholic church.

Today foreign enterprises are once again taking note of Ningbo, making business one of the main reasons why foreigners locate here. And with the new bridge to be completed by 2008 connecting Ningbo to Shanghai, this little city is in a position to profit as wealthy Shanghai's new backyard.

Ningbo's watery position, with the bay, the sea, and numerous waterways that crisscross the urban landscape, has made its cuisine famous for fish and seafood. Famous dishes include yellow croaker, swimming crab, razor clam, and oysters from the East China Sea, typically cooked in a simple way that brings out their delicate flavors. The climate is mild; the air is clean; life can be good in Ningbo.

© BARBARA STROTHER

Ships ply the East China Sea.

WHERE TO LIVE

Ningbo is divided into five key districts: Haishu, Jiangdong, Jiangbei, Beilun, and Yinzhou. Though most prime Chinese cities offer an equal amount of choices between urban and suburban living, Ningbo doesn't yet fit this mold. The suburban districts of Beilun and Yinzhou are home to a number of large foreign companies, as well as the AIAN international school in Beilun; however, the vast majority of expats choose to live in one of the three central urban districts of Haishu, Jiangdong, and Jiangbei, trading short commutes for city conveniences. These three districts are divided by the rivers that meet in the city center; Jiangdong translates as "East of the River" and Jiangbei as "North of the River," with Haishu lying south and west of the other two.

Housing costs in Ningbo are a bargain, ranging from as low as a couple hundred dollars for a small bachelor pad to under $2,000 for top of the line villas and luxury apartments. In fact, finding a very nice place to rent in the $500–700 range should be easy, and budget types can get by here on a total monthly budget of $400–600, including lodging.

Haishu District

Haishu is the political, cultural, and commercial center of the city. Tian Yi Square is here, as well as the Australian International School. Nearby are the two key residence complexes for expats, Century City and Central Garden, with hundreds of foreign families between them. Central Garden's 26-story skyscrapers and serviced apartments are popular among the young and/or single, while Century City's nine-story apartment towers offer ample space for kids to play in lush grounds and landscaped pool area. Though rents rise with the apartment's size and floor level, both complexes start around $1,000 a month for a two-bedroom flat, which is quite expensive by Ningbo's standards. Haishu also has a few villas, farther from the city center, such as those at Jinhua Yuan, which also has an on-site preschool.

Jiangbei District

Jiangbei District includes the ancient trade port area, with its version of Shanghai's Bund, the *Laowaitan,* now an entertainment area along the river. Here you'll find trendy restaurants popular with expats, with visions of its concession era past in its cobblestone streets and the old gothic church. High culture can be enjoyed at Jiangbei District's art venues and Grand Theatre.

Within Jiangbei there are both upscale apartments and modern villas where foreigners live, such as the Fangjing Garden with its picturesque

PUTUOSHAN ISLAND 普陀山岛

About 60 miles off the coast of Ningbo lies Putuoshan Island, a semi-tropical paradise that is one of China's four sacred Buddhist mountains. What you'll find on this little island, just 2 miles wide by 3.5 miles long, are numerous temples scattered throughout its lush green hills. What you won't find here is a lot of cars or commerce. A handful of mini-buses shuttle visitors from temple sites to sandy beaches during daylight hours; otherwise, most transportation is on foot.

Putuoshan Island is a tranquil place for city-worn expats to escape the urban jungle. It's the closest beach to Shanghai (whose coastline is predominantly thick mud). From Ningbo you can reach Putuoshan by a quick but often rocky two-hour express ferry where you can alternate between watching Hong Kong horror on TV monitors and watching monks in holy Buddhist garb spewing their temple lunches. A steadier option is to take the overnight ferry, sleeping in bunks in shared quarters and waking to the sight of submarines surfacing outside your porthole.

© BARBARA STROTHER

a Buddhist ceremony on the beach in Putuoshan

canals and recreation center with an outdoor pool. Older villas (built 15 years ago) that may be due for a little renovation can be rented for less than $1,000 a month at Fangjing Garden, though those that have undergone renovation will reflect it in their price. Nearby the International Village is much newer and equally popular with expats, with both apartments and villas available. Villas with 270–380 square meters start around $1,500 a month; three-bedroom apartments averaging 170 square meters rent between $600 and $1,200.

Jiangdong District

Jiangdong apartment residences tend to be just a little farther from the activity of the city center, roughly a 15-minute drive, though this area is more convenient for foreigners who will be working in the adjacent Beilun District. New apartment towers are sprouting up throughout this area, such as the Riyue Xingxheng overlooking the nearby river. Apartments in Jiangdong, though modern and comfortable, are less likely to have many expats. This will most likely change, however, in upcoming years. Jiangdong is slated for future development as they turn its old farmland into new residential complexes complete with fitness clubs and grocery stores. Already this area has the highest concentration of four- and five-star international hotel chains in the city, with more on the way.

DAILY LIFE

Of all the prime Eastern cities, Ningbo has the least amount of foreign residents and is not a tourist destination like the others. But this is exactly why some expats prefer this place to the flashier destinations like Shanghai, Hangzhou, and the rest. In Ningbo you can know and be known, rather than getting lost in the big-ness of bigger cities.

As you would expect in a place without a large number of foreigners, you won't find much English here. Luckily, Mandarin has for the most part slowly supplanted the local Ningbo dialect, making communication no more difficult than just the regular frustrations of learning standard Chinese.

Ningbo is big enough to have plenty of top international brands, like Hugo Boss and Burberry, along with the less-heeled local department stores sharing space at the trendy Tian Yi Square in the center of town. Starbucks has a couple locations in the city; big retailers like Carrefour, Auchan, and Metro are convenient places to stock up on imported goods.

Though there are no international health facilities here, four local hospitals have been designated as foreigner-friendly with English-speaking services: Ningbo No. 1 Hospital, Ningbo No. 2 Hospital, Ningbo Women and Children Hospital, and Central Hospital of Ningbo Developing Zone.

Expat Social Scene

The foreign community in Ningbo, though not that big, has a reputation for being friendly and laid back. There's a good mix within the expat community, though this city is perhaps a better spot for families than swinging singles.

Ningbo has a handful of excellent restaurants and clubs, but as some would be quick to point out, it's not Shanghai. Though if that's important to you, the bigger-than-life evening scene in Shanghai is close enough to do frequent weekends away to get your fix.

Several websites provide handy city information, such as www.hello ningbo.com, www.ningboexpat.com, and www.ningboguide.com, and the monthly English magazine *In Touch Zhejiang* supposedly covers Ningbo (though it predominantly focuses on Hangzhou). The Ningbo Expat Association meets regularly at area restaurants; the Foreign Family and Friends Association (FFA) helps the newly arrived settle in.

Schools

The primary international school in Ningbo is TAIS, The Australian International School. TAIS has programs for high school all the way down to a Chinese-only program for the under-three set, a great way to learn a second language at a great age. In suburban Beilun, you'll find Ningbo's second option, the Access International Academy Ningbo, with a global curriculum based on North American core standards.

GETTING AROUND

The city is easy to get around by foot or bike, or take a cheap and easy bus or taxi for spots farther afield. When you're ready to get out of town, Ningbo is about an hour-and-a-half drive or train ride to Hangzhou and under four hours to Shanghai, though the new bridge will cut that time in half. Ningbo's airport has flights to many domestic cities as well as a few other Asian destinations, and the nearby airports at Hangzhou and Shanghai are also an option. Better yet, Ningbo is the key launching point for ferries to Putuoshan Island, where you can spend a rejuvenating weekend rambling among its many Buddhist temples or relaxing on its subtropical beaches (some of the best beaches for hundreds of miles).

THE NORTH

Rugged and rough around the edges, northern China is industrious and well adapted to surviving in hardship. An extensive coastline gives this region several of the nation's most prominent ports and most popular seaside resorts. Their food is hearty and filling, designed to take the edge off the winter's bitter cold, and they produce the country's most famous wines and beers. In this region that surrounds Beijing, the local languages are merely slight variations of standard Mandarin, unlike other areas where local dialects are actually mutually unintelligible.

The northern port cities of Tianjin, Qingdao, and Dalian have frequently made the lists of "Most Livable Cities in China." Dalian and Qingdao boast gorgeous beaches and clean environments, while Tianjin offers big-city amenities without all the buzz of nearby Beijing. All three are a part of the Bohai Rim Economic Zone, which competes with the cities of the Yangtze River Delta and the Pearl River Delta for top economic production.

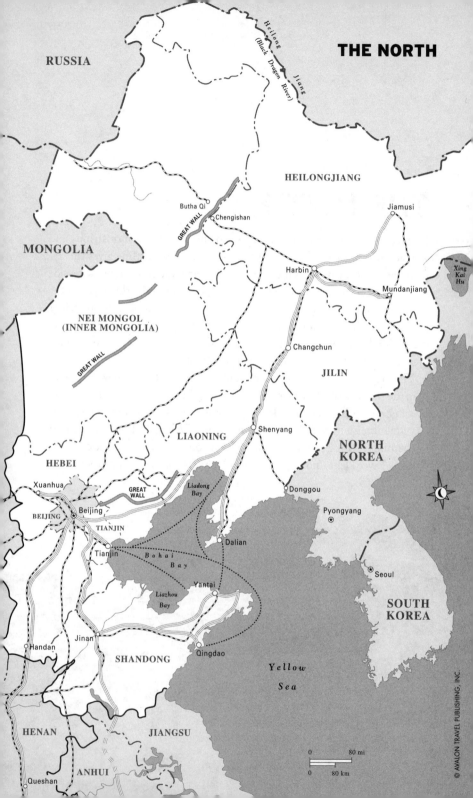

THE NORTH

RUSSIA

MONGOLIA

NEI MONGOL
(INNER MONGOLIA)

GREAT WALL

HEBEI

Xuanhua

BEIJING

Beijing

TIANJIN

Tianjin

Handan

Jinan

SHANDONG

HENAN

JIANGSU

ANHUI

Queshan

GREAT WALL

Butha Qi

Chengishan

GREAT WALL

HEILONGJIANG

Jiamusi

Harbin

Mundanjiang

Xing
Kai
Hu

Changchun

JILIN

Shenyang

LIAONING

NORTH
KOREA

Donggou

Liadong
Bay

Dalian

Pyongyang

Bohai
Bay

Yantai

Liazhou
Bay

Qingdao

Yellow
Sea

SOUTH
KOREA

Seoul

Heilong
Jiang
(Black Dragon River)

0   80 mi

0   80 km

© AVALON TRAVEL PUBLISHING, INC.

Shenyang, the only prime northern city that is not a port nor part of the Bohai Rim, is a rising star in the northeastern rust belt, a land tarnished by unemployment as the state-owned enterprises of this hearty industrial zone have been shut down for lack of profitability.

The Lay of the Land

Green hills and majestic mountains dot the terrain of northern China. Around the crescent shape of the Bohai Sea's coastline, Dalian lies at its northernmost tip, Tianjin right in its middle, and the city of Yantai lies at its southern tip, followed by Qingdao on the other side of the Shandong Peninsula. The provinces to the northeast of Beijing are collectively known as Dongbei (literally, northeast), home to both Shenyang and the tourist-popular Harbin city with its strong Russian influences.

CLIMATE
When it comes to climate, northern China can be divided into two camps. Cities that are located on the edge of the ocean, like Dalian, Qingdao, and Yantai, enjoy mild weather patterns throughout the year. But cities that are located farther away from the weather-calming effects of the Pacific Ocean endure extreme climate changes, with sizzling summers that give way to bitter cold and snowy winters.

© KEVIN SELDOMRIDGE

There's nothing like a refreshing swim in January!

Tianjin 天津

Tianjin (pop. 10 million) is the third-largest city in China and one of the four independent municipalities. A sprawling commercial city, Tianjin has been described as simultaneously "gritty" and "vibrant," the largest city nobody's heard of. Its prosperity and its reputation have always been linked with Beijing, its importance often overlooked in light of its famous neighbor. Just down the Hai River from Beijing lies Tianjin's central city; farther down the river meets the Bohai Sea at the busy port of Tanggu.

With a history similar to Shanghai's, Tianjin was once teeming with foreigners building up their colonial concessions, doing businesses in imposing banks, and worshipping in fancy cathedrals of stained glass. A walk around the city reveals ornate European villas, churches, banks, and shops playing peek-a-boo among towering modern glass skyscrapers. For a glimpse into its non-European history, Tianjin's famous antiques market is located in what was once, ironically, "Chinatown," now an area of winding *hutong* streets lined with (mostly fake) antiques.

Tianjin's Economic Development Area (TEDA) is one of the best managed in the country, which has brought in over 3,300 foreign corporations, including giants like Motorola and Nestlé. Consequently, the expat community here has plenty of international business types, as well as a good mix of the typical English teachers, foreign students, and the like.

Tianjin enjoys a climate that is temperate and seasonal. January brings below-freezing temperatures and July brings a muggy monsoon season, but spring and fall are pleasantly filled with cloudless skies. While many Chinese cities may make you exclaim, "it's nice to visit, but I wouldn't want to live here," Tianjin is just the opposite—there's not much here to keep a tourist busy for long, but it's a good place to raise a family.

WHERE TO LIVE

The first step to finding a home in Tianjin begins with determining whether you need to be in the city proper or within TEDA. TEDA is located 45 kilometers southeast of downtown Tianjin. The two areas are connected by several freeways and the subway, making it possible to commute between the two, but most people prefer to focus their attention on one or the other. To be in the heart of Tianjin is to have all the city's conveniences, history, and entertainment venues at hand. Easy access to the train station makes for quick getaways, and being closer to Beijing may prove to be convenient for those whose jobs require frequent trips to the capital. TEDA, on the other hand, is where many of the foreign businesses are located. TEDA also offers a choice of international schools and a greater variety of upscale housing complexes.

Tianjin City

Within the city of Tianjin proper, monthly apartment rentals start around $350 for a basic one bedroom up to $6,000 for an upscale and spacious place with added amenities like a health club, restaurants, and swimming pools. Serviced apartments at luxury hotels rent anywhere from $1,500 to $7,000 a month, offering the perks of hotel living (such as never having to make your bed again) without the space limitations of a hotel room. Tianjin city has fewer villas to offer than TEDA; the few here typically rent from $1,200 to $5,500. Within Tianjin city the key areas for expats include the Heping, Nankai, and Hexi Districts.

The densely populated central Heping District is Tianjin's political and economic center. Home to the antiques market and dotted with the old European architecture, Heping is a mix of the old and the new, Tianjin's history and its future. Located in Heping, the Wudadao area is a residential area of the old British and French concessions with homes from the 1920s and 1930s that were required to be built without so much as a hint of Chinese architecture. There are plenty of housing complexes scattered around this district. The Somerset Olympic Towers is popular with foreign families with its on-site preschool, bus service to the nearby international schools, an indoor pool, a gym, and a rooftop garden. Serviced apartments here range from simple one-bedroom suites to four-bedroom penthouses.

The Nankai District is Tianjin's cultural and educational center, southwest of the central city and home to two prominent universities as well as the Tianjin International School. This is the site

© BARBARA STROTHER

Tianjin's antique market is loaded with quirky finds.

of Tianjin's birthplace, as seen in its ancient city gate and drum tower, as well as its Culture Street, a new reproduction of its ancient past. Shuishang water park is also located in this district with its three lakes, arched bridges, ornate pavilions, and children's amusement center. Popular housing options for foreigners in Nankai are focused on serviced apartments. At the TEDA International Club, residents have access to the club's restaurants, nightclub, indoor ice-skating rink, bowling alley, archery, tennis courts, swimming pool, and sauna. Apartments at TEDA International run $1,100–3,080 a month for a three-bedroom place ranging from 140 square meters to 200 square meters. Other regular, non-serviced apartments in the area rent for around $500 for a two-bedroom.

Hexi District to the south was formerly a German colony and still boasts some Bavarian architecture. The You Yi Road bar area is located here, as well as Tiamjin's only five-star hotel, the Sheraton, where elegant two- to four-bedroom serviced apartments come with access to the all-day buffet, pools and sauna, disco, massage center, tennis courts, gym, business facilities, coffee garden, and Japanese restaurant. Other options include City House's cozy townhouses, the Rego Garden, and any number of towering residential skyscrapers that will give you a dizzying bird's-eye view of the city.

TEDA

The TEDA housing market is developing briskly. If you're in the market for a nice house with your own yard, you'll most likely end up in one of TEDA's villa complexes. Both the International School of Tianjin and the TEDA international school are nearby.

For those who prefer a serviced apartment, the four-star TEDA Central Hotel has deluxe apartments, with access to office space, five restaurants and bars, and recreation facilities, renting by the month for around $2,400–3,000. Villas such as those at Tian Yuan start around $2,400 rent for 210 square meters and go up to $8,000 a month for a large and luxurious 500-square-meter home. TEDA also has a wealth of classy low-rise residential apartment buildings and townhomes for lease; expect to pay more than $1,500 a month for the smaller and simpler places and $3,000–4,000 for two-storied 3–4 bedroom places. If all of this is beyond your budget, there are cheaper apartments available, those that cater more to the locals than to the wealthy foreign population that lives here. It is possible to find a nice but small two-bedroom flat in TEDA for as little as $370 a month.

DAILY LIFE

One of Tianjin's biggest appeals is that for a large city with so many western amenities, you'll get a more "Chinese" experience here than cities like Shanghai or Beijing. That's what expats love about the place—its own blend of quirkiness—and it's not uncommon to meet foreigners who've lived here, happily, for 5 or 10 years or more.

With plenty of international retailers like Carrefour and Wal-Mart, nine Starbucks locations (with more to come), and American restaurants like TGI Friday's, Tianjin's foreigners will be able to find most of the things they crave here. The local dialect is easy, being very similar to standard Mandarin (which is a good thing, since not much English is spoken here).

Tianjin also has its own SOS health clinic for foreigners, the AEA Tianjin International Clinic, located within the Sheraton Tianjin Hotel in Hexi district.

Expat Social Scene

Tianjin's foreign community feels smaller than it really is. It won't take long hanging out in expat bars before you'll start to recognize familiar faces. If you're looking to join in the expat bar scene, Cosy's is quite popular and has its own group of regulars, though Broadies, Alibaba's, and the joints along the You Yi Lu bar street all make the list. Sports lovers can be found at the Upper Deck Bar for large-screen showings of sports events. Many expats also take advantage of the weekly worship at the International Christian Fellowship.

For community events, check out the local expat magazine *Jin,* found at popular restaurants and bars or online at www.expatriate-jin.com. Additionally, the Tianjin International Community Center and the American Women's Association are two organizations that can help you get settled in to your new community here.

Schools

Tianjin has four international schools to choose from. Both the TEDA International School and the Tianjin International School (TIS) follow a North American curriculum, though TIS has a strong Christian focus. Tuition at the TEDA International School is financially subsidized by the TEDA administration but you must reside in TEDA to attend. The International School Tianjin offers an International Baccalaureate program; the Tianjing Rego International School offers the only British curriculum in the city.

PRIME LIVING LOCATIONS

GETTING AROUND

Although the city is quite spread out, it's easy enough to get around by taxi, bus, or the Tianjin subway. The metro system here is one of the oldest subway lines in the nation, though much of it has been recently rebuilt and seven more lines are planned to add to the current ones. The LRT Binhai Line conveniently connects TEDA with downtown Tianjin.

Qingdao 青岛

Ah, life in Qingdao—a laid-back time of good beaches and good beer. Though known domestically for its golden sands and deep, clear waters, its bigger claim to fame is the world-famous Tsingtao beer it brews (Tsingtao being the old way of spelling Qingdao). With over 100 years in the business, the brewery industry here has set the tone for the city. Pubs dot the landscape, and every August millions of tourists from around the world descend on Qingdao to enjoy drinking games, contests, and a rather joyful parade at the Annual Beer Festival.

It was the Germans that started all this beer business in Qingdao. When the city served as a German colony, the Germans turned a sleepy fishing village into the bustling port that Qingdao still is today. Quite a bit of the European colonial architecture remains, giving a quaint aura and small-town feel to this city of over two million.

Though its name literally translates to "Green Island," Qingdao is actually located on a peninsula that juts southward into the Yellow Sea. The quaint historic part of town lies in the west while the eastern districts are dotted with modern high-rises, upscale shopping venues, and vibrant nightlife. Farther out, suburban areas boast resort-like grounds. All along the southern coastline you'll find picturesque bays and sandy beaches. Qingdao's temperate marine climate has helped to establish it as a resort destination, with four distinct and pleasant seasons. This place well deserves its green name—it's one of China's greenest cities due to an abundance of trees and grassy areas that decorate the city. You'll also find plenty of cheap shopping and cheap food (including tons of wonderfully fresh seafood) in Qingdao.

Qingdao may not be overly cosmopolitan, and if you want a highly cultured life you should look elsewhere. But if you're into laid-back living, hanging out at the beaches and the pubs with a few good friends, Qingdao may just be the place for you.

WHERE TO LIVE

Qingdao expats can be found scattered throughout the city's seven districts, though most locate on the east side of the city along the shore in the Shinan (literally, Southwest) District, which includes the central city, or the Laoshan District, which spreads southeast along the coast. Downtown Qingdao used to be the center of town, bordering the old European neighborhood of Badaguan, but the city has purposefully been moving its central business district to the east.

Options for housing in Qingdao include numerous modern apartments and a fair number of villa complexes, all of which typically advertise whether they have a sea view and how far of a walk it is to the nearest beach. Huge luxury villas can rent upwards of $5,000 a month, though a very basic local apartment can run under $200 monthly, with lots of options in between.

KEEP YOUR EYE ON YANTAI

Located on the northeastern tip of the Shandong Peninsula, Yantai (烟台) is a prosperous little port city built up by the British in the late 1800s. Like its bigger brother Qingdao, Yantai is a charming seaside village with historic old European homes lining its coast. Though off the foreign tourist path, the Chinese love this city for its sandy beaches, fresh seafood, and bounteous orchards heavy with China's best apples and pears, as well as nearby Penglai's castle, an ivy-covered fortress where, according to local lore, the ghosts of the Eight Taoist Immortals still linger.

The small group of expats here is only a few hundred strong. Although the city is developing rapidly, it is still lacking in western conveniences such as imported foods and western medical facilities. The Yew Wah International School is in theory designed for foreign and Chinese students to study side-by-side, but in actuality few foreign kids attend, and a fair proficiency in Chinese would be required. For housing, expats have tended to stay at serviced apartments, though modern apartments can be found scattered throughout the city, and a few new villa complexes with sprawling luxury homes are going up in Yantai's outskirts.

You won't find an active nightlife here, though there are a number of good bars along the waterfront, several run by foreigners. You will, however, get a relaxed pace of life and close-knit foreign community. Not to mention the golf; half a dozen nice courses lie within an hour's drive or so. Yantai is quiet, clean, and a little bit remote, but nothing a two-hour drive to Qingdao or an hour-long flight to Beijing or Shanghai can't cure. You might just want to check it out, and bring a few friends with you... in time this little gem will be able to compete with Qingdao for expats' attention.

Real estate agents can help you locate both types of properties, or try the website www.myred star.com for oodles of classifieds for rent or sale without the use of an agent.

Shinan District

Shinan District is the tourist magnet for the city. Ensconcing downtown proper and all of the major hotels, the famous Bavarian villas of Badaguan, a number of the city's most popular beaches, the Qingdao MTI International School, and Qingdao's universities, Shinan is the place to be if you are looking for a convenient

vestiges of colonialism in Qingdao

© KEVIN SELDOMRIDGE

location. There are just a handful of villas to rent in this district, though the choices among apartments are plentiful.

The villas of Edlo Garden all face the sea, and the facilities boast numerous amenities including tennis courts, a restaurant, a supermarket, beauty salon, bank, and gift store. Huge five-bedroom homes with 370–420 square meters rent for $2,500–3,750 a month. The similarly sized and priced villas of Tianlin Garden are a short walk to the MTI International School; apartments are also available here starting at $750 for a three-bedroom flat with 160 square meters. Other sky-piercing high-rise residential buildings scattered throughout the district offer apartments at a wide range of budgets; expect to pay around $430 for a smallish two bedroom up to $2,465 or more for a sprawling five-bedroom penthouse that overlooks the sea. Beer enthusiasts might get a kick out of living at the huge Pacific Center, which offers apartments starting around $615 a month in a complex that includes a shopping center, swimming pool, tennis courts, dancing room, and the international headquarters of Tsingtao Beer.

Laoshan District

If you are in the market for a villa, you'll more than likely end up in Laoshan District. Within the district lies the Shilaoren National Tourist Resort, which includes numerous villa and luxury apartment complexes, beaches, the Qingdao International School, an amusement park, marine sightseeing district, and two golf courses. Most luxury villas have sea views, are a close walk to the shore, and have their own "garden" (lawn); both apartment and villa dwellers in these complexes share the use of indoor swimming pools, tennis courts, restaurants, or other amenities. You'll find plenty to choose from, such as the Surf Plaza, with its two-story villas and town-houses varying 260–320 square meters with rents ranging $2,000–5,700, as well as serviced apartments. The similarly priced Hui Hai Shan Zhuang has gorgeous two-story villas with large windows letting in natural light and views of the sea.

A second area within Laoshan District is the Economic and Technical Development Zone. Housing options in this area mostly consist of modern high-rise apartment complexes with mountain and sea views; rent runs about $430 for a three-bedroom with 120 square meters. These places are especially convenient for those who will be working within this zone, and most offer amenities such as swimming pools and tennis courts.

DAILY LIFE

Expats will find that Qingdao has most of what they will need to live a comfortable lifestyle.

The Qingdao Municipal Hospital, as the official medical facility for the 2008 Olympics Sailing Regatta in Qingdao, is being developed into a first class health center for foreigners as well as citizens. Another option in health care for foreigners is the Korean-run Qingdao Severance Hospital, which was created to cater to foreigners (especially Korean expats) and wealthy Chinese.

The Qingdao dialect is mostly just a slightly accented version of standard Mandarin. As a result, some find Qingdao a good place to study the language. On the other hand, not much English is spoken here outside of the establishments that cater to Qingdao's large tourist crowd.

Expat Social Scene

The Qingdao expat community is quite diverse with a large contingent of Koreans. Some come to work in one of the hundreds of foreign companies within the economic development zone; some come to teach at local schools. The foreign community here is quite active; residents boast it's the most close-knit expat community in China. For loads of options for fun things to do, pick up a copy of *Redstar* magazine or the *Qingdao Expat* to find out what's going on in the city.

Schools

There are two local international schools in Qingdao. The Qingdao MTI International School follows an American curriculum with a Christian emphasis. The Qingdao International School has a more general international curriculum.

GETTING AROUND

Qingdao is easy to navigate due to its compact location sandwiched between the mountains and the sea. Unless you choose to locate in the suburbs, getting around by foot, bike, taxi, or bus will all be cheap, easy, and quick. In suburbs some public buses and taxis are available to take you around.

Dalian 大连

Dalian is the crown jewel of the Northeast, the diamond stud in the old rust belt. It is home to 2.8 million people and the largest community of expats in the northeast. The people who live here love it, thanks to its clean streets, green parks, beautiful bays, sandy beaches, and spicy squid-on-a-stick, a delicious but rubbery treat. It's been rated the number-two most livable city in China, and the residents wonder why it didn't get a higher rating. The downside to Dalian's prosperous economic development is its rising prices. While still about 30 percent cheaper than Shanghai, the cost of living is more than what you would expect for a city of this size, though some would argue that it is well worth it.

Situated at the southern end of the Laiodong Peninsula, Dalian straddles the Bohai Bay and the Yellow Sea. Winters don't get too bad here—except for the Chicago-like winds—and summers stay mostly pleasant.

This city was once controlled by the Russians, taken over by the Japanese, returned to Russian hands, then reverted to Chinese control in the 1950s. Both foreign cultures left their mark in the architecture that lends this place its charm. Today Japanese and Koreans wield great influence in Dalian's business, with the happy result of numerous Japanese and Korean restaurants to cater to their presence here. In fact Dalian is full of great restaurants with flavors spanning China and the globe, including plenty of spots where the expats hang. The bar district along Chang Jiang Road downtown is a good place to start if you're looking to join the fun.

WHERE TO LIVE

Foreigner-friendly housing can be found scattered throughout Dalian's four key districts: Xigang, Zhongshan, Xigang Jinzhou, and Lushun.

Xigang District

Xigang District in central Dalian is the heart of the city's business and tourism. Top-notch shopping venues and acclaimed international restaurants mix with modern skyscrapers. This district is also home to the old European-style villas surprisingly built by the Japanese. Residential high-rise towers dot the urban landscape, offering modern and spacious apartments with birds-eye views to the city below and convenient access by foot around this city that is known as a great place to walk.

The University of Foreign Languages is in Xigang District, south of the city center, as are the coffee shops and pubs that cater to its students. Farther south, the Fujiazhuang resort area has several villa properties popular with foreigners. The Hai Huan Villas, located on the side of the mountain overlooking the sea, has 3–4 bedroom homes with around 200 square meters in a complex that includes a restaurant, swimming pool, tennis court, supermarket, coffee shop, beauty salon, and golf course. The gorgeous Furama Nanshan Garden Hotel has 25 spacious luxury villas that can be leased by the night, month, or year. These European-style homes start around 250 square meters for two- and three-story terraced villas that offer all the amenities of a typical five-star hotel in a lush environment with Japanese gardens and waterfalls.

Zhongshan District

Zhongshan District, in the southeastern corner of Dalian, boasts popular beaches and a myriad of tourist attractions, including an amusement park and China's largest aquarium. Within this district there are several serviced apartments that are popular with expats. The Hilton has one-to four-bedroom serviced apartments up to 300 square meters. Swissotel has 99 serviced apartments as well as three floors of offices, a short commute if you live and work here. Features include swimming pool, views of beaches and parks below, 24-hour room service, and daily breakfast buffet. Other hotels with similar serviced apartments include the Ascott Somerset Harbour Court and Shangri-La Century Tower (anyone in need of a 350-square-meter penthouse?). Incidentally, this district is also home to several hospitals with VIP wards for foreigners.

Jinzhou and Lushun Districts

Both Jinzhou and Lushun districts are places to watch for future development. There are a number of properties that are currently being built within these areas that will appeal to expats.

Jinzhou is Dalian's main economic district, and with an eager focus on foreign investment this area prides itself on being a place that is becoming foreigner oriented. Within Jinzhou, the Economic and Technological Development Zone is home to the Dalian Maple Leaf International primary school campus, making this area a convenient spot for families with young kids. And with the new villa housing options going up around the district, kids can have their own bedrooms and a yard to play in. Outdoors lovers will enjoy Daheishan Mountain, the highest peak on the peninsula and a great place to get away from the hustle and bustle of the commerce below.

Lushun District is home to great swimming, fishing, hiking, camping, boating, and island-hopping, with some 700 islands along the coast. This area is a prime spot for new villa housing as Dalian continues to grow. Nearby Jin Shi Tan (Golden Pebble) National Holiday Resort, 60 kilometers to the north of the central city, is Dalian's "back garden." Here you'll find the Maple Leaf International School Senior High Campus, golf and hunting clubs, and the Golden Pebble Beach that gives this area its name.

DAILY LIFE

The locals are used to seeing foreigners ramble along their city streets, which means they are less likely to stare and point and treat you like an odd scientific discovery. The flip side to this local exposure to foreigners is that the culture of Dalian is no longer as Chinese as it once was, having become something of a melting pot.

Dalian shares the same language base as Qingdao, a slight variation of standard Mandarin, which makes it a good option for those who want to master Chinese. On the other hand, there's not much English spoken here; Japanese is the language de jour in Dalian.

Western goods are somewhat easy to find, thanks to the city's big-box retailers, such as Carrefour, Wal-Mart, and Metro. You can even pick up imported cheese, baking ingredients, and Mexican food (all of which tend to be like the elusive holy grail in most Chinese cities) at the seafood market near the Labour Park.

VIP hospital wards that care for foreigners can be found in Zhongshan at the Dalian Friendship Hospital, the Dalian Railway Hospital, and the

© BARBARA STROTHER

Quick bowl of noodles, anyone?

First Affiliated Hospital of Dalian Medical University Part II (but let's hope you won't have to sputter out that long name in an emergency).

Expat Social Scene

Dalian's expat community, at an estimated 6,000-plus, is predominantly Japanese and secondarily Korean, with a few westerners and others thrown into the mix. Unfortunately, Dalian's biggest disadvantage is that its expat community is not very tight knit. This city suffers from a current lack of an English-language magazine that would help bring its expats together. The next best thing is Dalian's weekly email ezine, www.xianzai.com; though helpful, it's severely limited in content.

Dalian has plenty of recreation to offer the whole family: Build sandcastles at the beach, check out the 400 crocs at the Crocodile Garden, see the underwater world of Dalian's two aquariums, go hiking or fishing or island-hopping, or just relax at one of the city's many green parks. Golf heaven can be found at the Golden Pebble Golf Course, with three fairways that rank in the top 100 worldwide, all picturesquely located along the edge of dramatic seaside cliffs.

Schools

Dalian's only school for foreigners is the Dalian Maple Leaf International School, a Sino-Canadian joint venture with three impressive campuses spread around the municipality. Unlike many international schools that by

PRIME LIVING LOCATIONS

law can only admit children with foreign passports, Maple Leaf's 3,000-plus students come from all corners of China and over a dozen different nations. Students graduate with both Chinese and Canadian diplomas.

Shenyang 沈阳

Shenyang, Laioning's provincial capital with 4.5 million urban residents, is at the heart of China's efforts to revitalize the northeastern Rust Belt. Centrally located about 100 miles inland from the Bohai Sea, Shenyang's winters are long and cold, averaging a January high of just 10 degrees Fahrenheit but dropping as low as 30 below. Here the white winter snow quickly turns black from dirt and pollution. Local expats claim the best way to ward off the winter blahs is to schedule regular activities out. Luckily there are plenty of winter sports here to combat cabin fever, such as the nearby Qi Pan Shan ski resort. The fall and the spring are pleasant though, other than the occasional sandstorms, and summers are plenty hot but without the stifling humidity of most other key Chinese cities.

Shenyang's 2,300-year history as a city reached its climax as the capital of the Qing dynasty in the 1600s, leaving behind the city's most impressive attraction, the Imperial Palace. The Russians and Japanese both came

and went in various war occupations, and SOEs (state-owned enterprises) did the same, bringing industrial prosperity to the area for a short time before the poorly run companies crumbled. Now with foreign investment and government commitment to revitalization, Shenyang is finally building a position for itself that will last. Throughout the city old industrial districts are giving way to modern residential developments, upscale boutiques, and luxury hotels. Shenyang is also establishing itself as the commercial and financial center of the entire northeast, like a small-scale version of Shanghai's transformation in the 1990s. You

© BARBARA STROTHER

traditional door knockers and masks for sale at a local shop

DINING ON DOG MEAT

Dog is a signature food of the Northeast, a culinary custom imported from nearby Korea. Its popularity here is due in part to the belief that eating dog will keep you warm in the winter. You'll recognize it in your hot pot by its slightly green tint. A "three dog night" takes on a whole new meaning up here!

may just find the real China you've been looking for in this unspoiled northern city.

WHERE TO LIVE

Shenyang's cost of living is low, and it's possible to get by here on the cheap if you live like the locals. On the other hand, in recent years Shenyang has experienced the highest inflation in housing prices across the mainland. Upscale villas and luxury apartments will be cheaper than Beijing or Shanghai—but cheaper does not mean cheap.

Heping District

The downtown Heping District is convenient to all that the city has to offer. If you like the buzz of city life, the neon lights at night, the energy that comes with the nonstop activity of the big city, you'll enjoy downtown Shenyang. The U.S. Consulate is located here, as well as most of the western hotels that host the popular pubs and restaurants of the city.

Most foreigners living in central Heping rent a serviced apartment at one of the luxury hotels. The five-star Intercontinental Hotel's serviced apartments have long been a favorite with their modern western kitchens, indoor tennis courts, swimming pool, and indoor golf driving range, as well as the nearby Mulligan's Irish Bar where expats tend to congregate. For a non-hotel option, the New World Garden Villas has apartments and townhouses that rent for as little as $500 for a smaller two-bedroom apartment or around $2,800 for a spacious three-floored townhouse.

Hunnan Development Zone

On the southern edge of the city is Shenyang's hope of economic salvation, the Hunnan Development Zone, a top priority in the government's plans to bring economic growth to Shenyang. This area is where the long-term foreign residents first started to settle in Shenyang. Though on the

PRIME LIVING LOCATIONS

HAPPY IN HARBIN?

Poetically named after the Black Dragon River, Heilongjiang Province's snow-covered peaks and white glaciers resemble the northern Canadian wilderness. At the mention of this northernmost Chinese province or its famous city Harbin (哈尔滨), the first three words that come to mind are cold, cold, and cold. A winter night here sees the temperature drop to a mind- and body-numbing -20°F. In spite of its frigid climate, winter brings the greatest number of visitors to the area for Harbin's Ice Lantern Festival. If the cold doesn't take your breath away, the intricately carved and lighted towering ice sculptures will.

Harbin is also known for its strong Russian influence, and Harbin's cobblestone streets, onion domes, and ornate Russian architecture all lend a distinctly Russian elegance to the city. Here you can dine on Russian breads, vodka, and caviar in restaurants with gilded columns of a bygone era. Or wrap up tight in a Siberian fur and hit the cobbled pedestrian shopping district along Zhongyan Lu, where trendy cafés and upscale boutiques with preserved Russian facades offer a pleasant place to while away a chilly afternoon.

Harbin offers plenty of hotels, restaurants, bars, and shops that appeal to overnight visitors – but little to offer the long-term foreign resident. Without international schools or western medical facilities and little imported foods beyond that which caters to the Russian population, Harbin lacks the basic western amenities that most internationals want. Although the winters can be beautiful, the cold and the early-setting sun force many to stay isolated in their homes. The summer reveals a shabby image of the city. The countryside may be like northern Canada, but the city has been likened to Detroit – not the best option for an expat with a family, or anyone that struggles with Seasonal Affective Disorder, for that matter. However, after suffering for years from the effects of Russia's economic woes, Harbin is finally on the upswing, enjoying a relatively high standard of living with a cost of living that's just a quarter of Shanghai's or Beijing's. It may be just a few years before Harbin develops into a decent destination for thick-blooded foreigners.

Russian architecture in Harbin

© KEVIN SELDOMRIDGE

edge of the city, Hunnan feels more like a part of the town than a suburb, and commute time to downtown is only about a 15-minute drive. For serviced apartments, the Marriott offers an indoor pool, health club, and Shenyang's top Japanese restaurant conveniently located next to the Foreign Joint Venture office. Or try the Sheraton, with condominium-style apartments and multiple restaurants and bars, including Mezza, serving more than 100 different beers.

Across the street from the Marriott and Sheraton is Riverside Gardens, a large complex of villas and apartments including an imported-foods market, a health club and tennis courts, playground, and the International Club of Shenyang with its social activities. There are over 1,000 families living in Riverside Gardens; almost a third of them are from foreign countries. Apartments rent for $1,200–2,500, or double that for huge two-story flats. Furnished villa houses have 3–5 bedrooms with 200–320 square meters and rent for $3,000–4,000 a month.

Shenhe District

The Shenhe District to the east of downtown showcases Shenyang's history in its Imperial Palace and ancient culture street as well as Shenyang's modern enterprise. This is Shenyang's financial and commercial district. Here you'll find the north railway station and next to it the Gloria Plaza Hotel's serviced apartments. Other housing options in the district include the deluxe suites at the four-star Times Plaza Hotel and elegant luxury apartments at the five-star Kempinski Hotel, popular among German expatriates.

Dongling District

The southwestern Dongling District is a posh suburb, home to the rich and famous of Shenyang as well as wealthy foreign families. For those that don't mind being far from town (about a 20-minute drive just to the edge of the city), there are several high-end villa complexes available here, including the popular Civic Moon. Huge two- and three-story detached homes with large yards house families from the local consulates and foreign executives of BMW and other businesses. Civic Moon also offers apartments for those that don't need the space of a villa, as well as tennis courts, an indoor pool, two restaurants, a store, and regular shuttles to downtown. The Shenyang International School is also located within this district, making this area a prime option for foreign families with school-age children.

© BARBARA STROTHER

Preserved fruits, like salty dried plums, are a popular snack.

DAILY LIFE

Shenyang recently saw the opening of its first Subway (as in the American sandwich restaurant) and has started to build its own subway (as in the underground trains), though it won't be completed for a few more years. Like all Chinese cities, Shenyang has McDonald's, KFC, and Pizza Hut, and rumors of a Starbucks coming soon. Good international restaurants include Japanese and Korean options, as well as the typical upscale establishments at the western hotels.

Walmart, Carrefour, PriceSmart, and Metro stores are all here, as well as small grocery stores in upscale housing complexes that specialize in imported foods. Shenyang is home to a foreign medical clinic run by Global Doctors and specializing in maternity care.

The Shenyang dialect is a variation of standard Mandarin that is often used in Chinese humor to depict charming simpletons. Mandarin students should find it easy to understand (if you can ever call Mandarin easy). English is almost non-existent; make sure you've got a sturdy pocket phrasebook because you'll always want to keep it with you.

Expat Social Scene

Expats who spent time here in the past tend to refer to the city as a hardship post, but current residents say that morale is high among foreigners and that things are getting better all the time. Shenyang is finally becoming a place an expat can fall in love with and call home. And the number of expats that are calling Shenyang home is steadily growing, as they come to work at the consulates here or at one of the many foreign businesses such as GM, Boeing, and Coca-Cola.

The presence of the U.S. Consulate here means you'll have help available when you need it. The International Club at Riverside Garden is also a good place to tap into the tight-knit Shenyang expat community. And although Shenyang doesn't yet have a glossy English magazine, the Liaoning Gateway online newsletter (www.liaoning-gateway.com) will clue you in to life in Shenyang and the surrounding province.

Expats can also attend Protestant English services at the church in Xi Ta District and Catholic English mass at Shenyang's beautiful Catholic church.

Schools

Shenyang currently only has one school for foreigners. The Shenyang International School has an American-style curriculum within a Christian world view.

GETTING AROUND

Shenyang's sprawl is easily traversed by cheap taxis and public buses. If you're looking to go farther afield, express trains run from the Shenyang train stations northwest to Harbin and southeast to Beijing and beyond. Flights from Shenyang's international airport can carry you off to all corners of China as well as spots in Korea and Japan.

PRIME LIVING LOCATIONS

INLAND CHINA

The interior, the hinterlands, the middle of the Middle Kingdom: no matter what you call it, this is the *real* China. The inland region covers the greatest expanse of territory and draws the greatest number of tourists to explore its rich history, culture, and natural scenery. Even people who know very little about China are acquainted with the things that make the inland famous, such as its spicy Sichuan (Szechuan) food, its terra-cotta warriors, and its fated Three Gorges.

This region is the geographic center of the nation, but it's far from being a top economic center. Without a first-tier city or an economic region on par with the Bohai Rim or the Pearl River Delta, this area has traditionally had less reason to draw foreign businesses, though that trend is starting to change. With a determined commitment to bring this area up to speed with the development along the coast, the government is continuously advancing the infrastructure and amenities of its inland cities to make them more appealing to foreign firms.

© RYAN SHAW

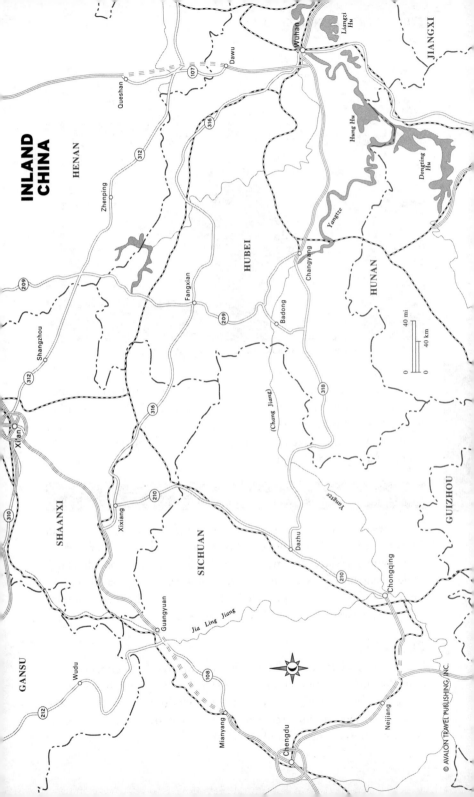

© BARBARA STROTHER

The farther inland you go, the more traditional the way of life.

The expats who've chosen to live in one of the hinterland cities are often in search of a more authentic Chinese experience. Small pockets of foreigners live and work in a vast number of places spread across this grand region, though the three cities that are the most foreigner-friendly are Wuhan, Chengdu, and Xi'an.

The Lay of the Land

The cities of Wuhan, Chongqing, and Chengdu are all situated within the Yangtze River Valley (though Chengdu actually lies a bit north of the river). Wuhan is the easternmost city, 600 miles upstream from Shanghai, while Chengdu is the westernmost, over 1,000 miles from Shanghai as the crested ibis flies. Xi'an lays a little farther north near another important Chinese waterway, the Yellow River.

CLIMATE

Due to the vast distances and the differences in terrain, the climates of the individual interior cities can vary quite a bit. The one thing they do share, though, is four strongly distinct seasons, including chilly winters with occasional snow and intensely hot summers that are all the hotter here, away from the cooling effect of the ocean.

THE MIGHTY YANGTZE

The Yangtze is China's longest river and the third largest in the world, after the Amazon and the Nile. The river made the pages of communist history for Chairman Mao's famous cross-river swims, a ploy to disprove rumors of his failing health. It's also home to the few remaining Chinese river dolphins, a unique freshwater breed that is tragically losing its battle against the big ships and the fishing nets.

When most of the world thinks of the Yangtze, the Three Gorges Dam project comes to mind. When it is completed in 2009, the new dam will be the world's largest hydroelectric project. It also will have displaced over a million residents, submerged over 1,000 archaeological sites, and tainted the splendor of the gorges, all in the name of progress.

Wuhan 武汉

Wuhan, capital of Hubei Province and home to 8.9 million people, is a combination of what were once three separate cities, Hankou, Wuchang, and Hanyang. This city's heartland position and its strong industry and commerce have garnered it the nickname of China's Chicago. It's famous for being the hottest of China's three furnaces; summers here are spent going from one air-conditioned space to another in an effort to avoid the breath-sucking intensity of the heat.

Wuhan has a colorful past. During concession-era times, Hankou was forced to open its Yangtze River port to foreigners and became a key center of missionary activity; today a handful of the old European buildings are still in use here. Wuchang, a capital city in A.D. 220, was also the spot where Sun Yatsen led the famous Wuchang Uprising that ended dynastic rule in China.

With the Yangtze River flowing through its center and more than a hundred lakes, Wuhan is a watery town famous for its fish dishes. Tourists pour through here on their way to embark on a Three Gorges river cruise. Though the city has just a handful of interesting sites, the surrounding area has quite a few popular excursions worthy of day trips or short weekend adventures.

WHERE TO LIVE

Wuhan's real estate is divided into Hankou, Wuchang, and Hanyang, the original three towns. Most newcomers to Wuhan will want to live as close to their work as possible because it can take hours to get from one corner of the city to another.

Hankou

Hankou, the northwestern piece of the Wuhan puzzle, is a fusion of the old and the new. Here you'll find the city's historic shopping streets, the best hospitals equipped to handle foreigners, and old colonial churches that are active once again. If you like being in the heart of a city's activity, convenient to its businesses, international restaurants, and trendy bars, you'll enjoy Hankou.

This district is home to many serviced apartments popular with the business crowd, such as the Swiss-Belhotel on the Park or the HK & Macao Center Business Hotel, which includes a department store on its first seven floors. The centrally located Best Western C-Bank Hotel advertises family apartments for less than $250 a month and executive apartments for a little over $300. Hankou has plenty of standard apartments as well, mostly in modern new high-rises, which typically rent for less than $300 (though a few lavish flats go as high as $2,000).

If you're looking for a quiet villa neighborhood, you'll find a variety out toward the airport and the QSI International School. Two new developments of note in Hankou include the Menghu Garden, with five-bedroom deluxe villas as well as luxury apartments, and the huge Changqing

© RYAN SHAW

Wuhan's terrain holds many lakes and rivers, including the pleasant East Lake.

Garden, with enough residences to house over 80,000 people in a variety of apartment and duplex styles. Most villas and townhomes in Hankou rent for under $1,000 a month.

Wuchang

Wuchang, on the eastern bank of the Yangtze, offers a quieter life, less active than Hankou, with plenty of green space and fresh air. It's home to the charming East Lake, the largest urban lake in China and the sister of Hangzhou's famous West Lake. Near the East Lake you'll find several key Wuhan spots, such as the East Lake Development Zone (with its many foreign businesses) and the impressive Wuhan University. Because most of the city's universities are in Wuchang, this is where foreign students and foreign teachers tend to live. The area by the lake and the universities is one of the most pleasant spots in the city, where you can enjoy walking or jogging along the lake's edge, past traditional pavilions and Chinese landscapes.

High-level luxury apartments in the central-city area of Wuchang rent for around $700–1,200 and come with amenities like indoor pools and fitness centers. Apartments by the universities or the lake can be had for under $500 a month, or considerably less if you don't mind forgoing modern amenities for simplicity. If you're in the market for a villa or townhouse, you'll find some nice places along Wuchang's lakes with rental prices below $1,500.

Hanyang

Hanyang, in the southwestern corner of the city, is the quietest of the three districts. The Economic Development Zone here is home to several multinational corporations including Coca Cola and the French joint venture, Citroën, as well as a significant French community. The South Lake International School is also here. Hanyang has quite a few villa options, starting around $750 but going as high as $4,000 for a four-bedroom luxury home. Apartment prices and availability are similar to the other districts; expect to pay just $100 for a basic place up to $500 for a decent-size three-bedroom.

DAILY LIFE

Wuhan's expats consider this place the "real China." There are not many places to hide yourself away and forget for a moment that you are living in China. Few describe Wuhan as charming, but the expat life here can be pleasant enough.

PRIME LIVING LOCATIONS

The locals speak a dialect of standard Mandarin that once competed with Beijing for the national language. If you already know some Mandarin, you shouldn't have a problem communicating here. If you don't, consider enrolling in one of the top-notch language programs at Wuhan's universities. Little English is spoken here.

For daily purchases, Wuhan's multiple international retailers include American stores Wal-Mart and PriceSmart, the German Metro, the British B&Q, and several French Carrefour stores. There are also quite a few department-store malls, though none carry the high-end international designer names.

Expat Social Scene

Foreigners move here for a variety of reasons, from teaching English to managing major corporations and everything in between. Though there is currently no English magazine, expats here will find the website www.wuhantime.com to be an invaluable source for local information. Additionally, the Wuhan Laowai group holds regular networking events, and the club W.O.M.E.N. in Wuhan meets for biweekly coffees and lunches.

One of the best places to try the inexpensive local cuisine is on Jiqing Street, where performers will sing or dance at your outdoor table for a small contribution. If you're craving a break from Chinese food, Wuhan has a decent number of international restaurants and bars, such as the expat-popular Blue Sky Coffee Bar and Giano's brick-oven pizza. For nightlife, you'll find plenty of discos, pubs, and clubs scattered around the city. At the Jianghan Lu pedestrian street, you can dine on Brazilian barbeque or Thai food in the midst of shops set in old European buildings. Hanzheng shopping street is also set in historical buildings.

Schools

Expat families have two choices for English education in Wuhan, both of which are quite small. The South Lake International School teaches an American curriculum on the campus of a local Chinese school, giving students access to amenities such as playgrounds and sports fields. The QSI International School of Wuhan offers English education for 3- to 13-year-olds in a system that focuses more on skill level than grade level.

GETTING AROUND

Due to its central location, Wuhan is an important railway junction, making it cheap and easy to hop a train headed out of town. Or venture out by overnight boat, traveling upriver to Chongqing or downriver to Nanjing or Shanghai.

Within the city, however, navigation is not so easy, since the city is absolutely huge and crossed by a complex network of waterways. You'll find the ubiquitous Chinese taxis and public buses that access every neighborhood throughout the city, albeit slowly. Wuhan's metro system is just a couple years old and currently only makes a dozen stops within Hankou along a light rail line, but several other lines are under construction that will connect the three major parts of the city. Although it isn't scheduled for completion until 2010, the new system will vastly improve the transportation situation within Wuhan. And by the way, if a taxi refuses you, don't take it personally: It's probably just not their appointed day to cross over the bridges, a system used to reduce traffic congestion.

Chengdu 成都

Chengdu, the attractive capital of spicy Sichuan Province and home to four million urban residents, is known for its icons: teahouses, hot peppers, and pandas. In Chengdu they know how to take it easy, spending lazy afternoons at tranquil riverside teahouses or long evenings eating fiery Sichuan hot pot with friends. Even the sleepy pandas of the Sichuan bamboo forests reflect this unhurried life. The Panda Research Center near Chengdu is one of the best places in the world to observe giant pandas... when they're not sleeping.

The people and the pandas may be relaxed, but the local economy is not. Chengdu serves as a key regional center for the transportation and infrastructure that has been vital in drawing a quickly growing number of foreign businesses this far west, including Intel, Siemens, and Motorola. This position as a

© STUART STROTHER

The bamboo forests of Sichuan Province are home to China's pandas, though chances of seeing a wild one are slim.

THE CHONGQING CHALLENGE

Chongqing (重庆, a.k.a. Chung-king) Municipality has an urban population of 9.2 million and a total population of more than 31 million, one of the most populated places in the world. This hilly city on the Yangtze River, long popular as the western gateway to the Three Gorges, is one of the four independent municipalities that answer directly to the central government. It's so hilly here that no one rides bicycles – as unfathomable for China as an American city without a McDonald's. With a place this big and well known, you may wonder why it's not included as a prime living location. The truth is, Chongqing is on the verge of greatness, but it's not there yet.

On the one hand, foreign businesses are moving into Chongqing, new upscale housing areas are being built, and there is a new international school. On the other hand, that international school is tiny and many of those residential areas are still in the design and construction stages. The expat community in Chongqing is quite small, and some are less than thrilled to be in this polluted metropolis nicknamed one of the furnaces of China. There are very few resources for foreigners here – no glossy English magazines, no popular expat websites announcing clubs and events.

But the central government is dedicated to turning Chongqing into a first-class city and a key commercial center. They're turning out crooked officials and polluting factories, and building infrastructure to support foreign business. They're aggressively seeking the foreign investment that will turn this town around. With all this new development in the works, Chongqing may just be on the threshold of becoming the kind of place expats would be proud to call their home away from home.

prosperous commercial center is nothing new to this ancient city. In fact, it was the first in the world to introduce paper money, to the fascination of the young Marco Polo who traveled with heavy pockets of metal coins. Today in Chengdu you can spend all your paper money on something special from Gucci or Cartier, Buick or Audi.

Impressions of Chengdu differ. On the one hand, it's very affordable and can be quite interesting; on the other hand, it's a long way from the vibrant expat life of the coastal cities. Some see the city as dusty, noisy, busy, and gloomily overcast; a place where you can taste the pollution in the air. Some see it as a place full of vitality and vigor and fascinating culture. Though there's nothing to be done about the weather, Chengdu is working on cleaning up its polluted image, thanks in part to the strong voice (and tourist dollars) of the foreigners who come through here on their way to the pristine natural environments nearby.

Chengdu is a popular resting spot for travelers on their way to the minority villages, holy mountains, and incredible scenery beyond the city. From Chengdu you can journey out to the biggest cliff-side Buddha carving in the world, or to the turquoise lakes and waterfalls of Jiuzhaigou, branded by the U.N. as one of the greatest natural legacies in the world. Chengdu is also the main gateway to Tibet; most tourists hook up with their requisite official tour group here before flying in to Lhasa.

With a 2,000-year history, Chengdu has its share of historic spots, as well as its own flavor of Chinese high culture with the Sichuan opera, a visual feast filled with humor and stage tricks. The significant Tibetan community here contributes a certain flair to the city as well, with their minority shops and colorful traditional dance shows.

WHERE TO LIVE

Foreigners heading to Chengdu will want to consider one of the three prime housing areas: the city center, south city, and the northwestern hi-tech zone. Most Chengdu expats rent apartments, though there are a growing number of villas and townhouses available.

City Center

If you like the vigor and vitality of being in the energetic core of a city, living downtown will give you easy access to all the city's shopping and entertainment venues, including the fashionable Chunqi Lu pedestrian street, the Chengdu stadium, the foreign-language bookstore, and tons of great restaurants. With all the high-end international hotels around, downtown is always jumping with the tourist crowd, which has its ups and downs. A luxury three-bedroom flat in a high-rise with spectacular city views will put you out just $600 a month.

South City

The Wuhou District, directly south of the city center, is the most popular spot for foreigners to live. This upscale area is also a busy shopping and business district and is home to one of Chengdu's two hi-tech zones. The U.S. Consulate is here, as well as the Shamrock Irish pub, one of the best places for expats to find out what's going down in the 'Du. Both Meishi International School and the QSI Chengdu School are located in this district, as well as Sichuan University.

Within the South City area, the Orchard Villas and China Garden complexes are two very popular (and very pricey, for Chengdu) options for foreigners. At Orchard Villas you'll have your choice of an apartment

($1,000–2,500), a townhouse ($3,000–4,000), or a villa (200–400 square meters, $2,500–6,500). China Gardens, which is home to the QSI International School, also has apartments (as low as $500 up to four bedrooms for $2,000), large townhouses ($3,000–6,000), and sprawling villas ($6,250–7,500). If all this is beyond your budget, try a place that doesn't cater to expats. A modern local apartment with a couple bedrooms and decent—but not sprawling—size will rent for just $200–400 a month.

Northwest City High-Tech Zone

Though the South City area has traditionally been the spot for foreigners, the trend is moving to the northwest into the High-Tech Zone of the Qingyang (green goat) and Jinniu (golden cow) Districts. This is the location of Intel's new facility, as well as Chengdu International School's beautiful new campus.

You'll find many new complexes to choose from, with more on the way. The Peninsula, which has the reputation for being one of the best in the city (with the highest rents to match), has large three- and four-bedroom apartments for $1,000–4,000 a month and huge 355-square-meter townhouses for $6,000–9,000. If you can forgo all the bells and whistles, it's still possible to find inexpensive housing in the northwestern districts. Two-bedroom flats rent for around $240 at more modest complexes.

DAILY LIFE

Expats will find most of their daily shopping needs met at all the usual hypermarkets, including Metro, Price Smart, and Carrefour. Sabrina's Country Store carries rare imported goodies like Reese's Peanut Butter Cups and Doritos (you just don't know how good these things will sound until you've gone without for a while).

The language of the locals is a Sichuan dialect. Though all official business is run in Mandarin, the heavy accent can be difficult to understand, and you may run into elderly people and villagers that don't speak Mandarin at all. On top of that, hardly anybody here speaks English. The good news is you'll be really good at charades after living in Chengdu.

For health needs, the local doctors are good, though their facilities and equipment are less so. The care here is sufficient for basic needs but expats tend to fly out to Hong Kong for more serious ailments.

Expat Social Scene

Unusual for a place so far from the populated coast, Chengdu has a burgeoning expat scene. The majority of westerners here are associated with education (English teachers, international-school teachers, and foreign exchange students), although the community of business-related expats is growing. Some foreigners choose Chengdu for its strong Tibetan influence. With a significant number of Tibetans here, it's a great place to be exposed to the culture and language without the hardship and lack of amenities you'd find in Tibet's cities.

There are a few consulates here, including one of the four American consulates in the country, as well as the China headquarters for the Peace Corps. Some of the perks of expat life in the big cities aren't yet available here, such as community groups and local English media in print or online (though Shamrock Pub's website, www.shamrockinchengdu.com lists local events).

Despite its quick growth, the expat community is still somewhat small. Foreigners heading this far out may get watched like an odd zoo animal. Add to that the dismal Chengdu skies, and you may be in for a case of the blues. We recommend taking frequent trips out of the city just to see the sun, or going for a rejuvenating soak in the hot springs north of town with its crisp mountain views. If all else fails, you can hang out with the other expats at Peter's Tex-Mex Grill and wallow in self-pity over one of their famous gooey cinnamon rolls.

If you need a break from the local mouth-blistering Sichuan cuisine, you'll have your choice of international restaurants, including Grandma's Kitchen for American home cooking and C'est la Vie for fine French cuisine. Of course, there's always Pizza Hut, KFC, Mai Dang Lao (McDonald's), and now even Subway and a couple of Starbucks.

© BARBARA STROTHER

A large community of Tibetans make their home in Chengdu.

Schools

Expat families have three international schools to choose from. The Chengdu International School (CDIS) is a Christian school with a good reputation even among its non-religious families. CDIS teaches a U.S. curriculum for preschool through high school inside a new campus in northwest Chengdu. The Chengdu QSI School, on the other hand, focuses predominantly on preschool through elementary students. Chengdu Meishi International School offers a bilingual program as part of a private Chinese boarding school that covers kindergarten through eighth grade. All three international schools are still somewhat small.

GETTING AROUND

Within Chengdu's compact city center it is easy to navigate by foot or bike, and taxis are always a cheap and easy way to get around. The public bus system is extensive and covers all areas of the city. If you can decipher the routes and you don't mind crowds, public buses are always a cheap way to get around.

As for getting out of town, in addition to the buses and trains that will take you to exotic and primitive locales, the Chengdu airport has service to all major Chinese cities as well as a few foreign ones. Should you choose to live here, you will want to get out of town regularly—just to see the sun. The combination of the climate (high humidity), geography (surrounded by mountains), and pollution result in a Chengdu sky that is almost always overcast.

Xi'an 西安

The most famous of all inland cities, Xi'an hosts more than 20 million annual tourists (97 percent domestic) traipsing through to see the famous terra-cotta warriors. Xi'an is the gateway to the ancient Silk Road, and home to a strong Muslim community. If you're into ancient history and archaeology, this is the place for you. It was the largest city in the world back in the first century, on par with Rome, Athens, and Cairo as an ancient metropolis. The number and quality of its historic sites are unrivalled in China.

But this city isn't just about its past. Xi'an is the center of China's aviation and space-flight technology and satellite monitoring. And with over 3,000 research institutions, Xi'an regularly produces significant scientific achievements. It's home to an increasing number of multinational operations, including GM, Volvo, Rolls Royce, and Siemens.

Situated within central Shaanxi Province where the Guangzhong plain meets the Qinling Mountains, nearly four million people call the city of Xi'an home. The summers here are toasty and the winters are chilly; Xi'an

© KEVIN SELDOMRIDGE

the famous terra cotta warriors, unearthed near Xi'an

gets a small amount of snow but the winter weather isn't nearly as intense as in northern locations. Xi'an also gets frequent thunderstorms and rain.

The layout of Xi'an revolves around its ancient city wall, the best preserved in China. Directions are often given based on the nearest city gate and whether inside or outside the wall. Its ancient streets are laid out on a square grid marked by the South, North, East, and West Boulevards, with the Bell Tower at the city center.

This city's cuisine has strong Muslim influences, and you'll find plenty of yummy *yang-rou* (lamb) kebab vendors on its dusty streets. One of the most famous Xi'an dishes is *yang-rou paomo,* a lamb-based soup that is poured over broken pieces of flat bread. The Muslim restaurants are festive places with Middle Eastern–style dancing and music; you'll know them by their blue lanterns hanging outside instead of the traditional red. You can also indulge at one of the city's nighttime food street markets.

Between the precipitation and pollution, you won't see many blue skies in

© BARBARA STROTHER

yummy lamb kebabs

Xi'an. But if you can put up with the environment, one of the best perks of living here is the money you can save. Xi'an is one of the cheapest of all the provincial capitals. You can get by here on as little as $250 a month. Perhaps the biggest drawbacks to life in Xi'an are the pollution and the few locals who will only see dollar signs when they look at you. Any city with this many wealthy tourists tends to inspire greedy manipulation by its less-upstanding residents.

WHERE TO LIVE

If you're looking for a place to call home in Xi'an, you'll want to be in one of three key areas: central downtown, south of downtown in the Hi-Tech Zone, or north of the city center in the Economic and Technology Development Zone.

Downtown

Downtown Xi'an is divided between two districts, Beilin and Lianhu. The vibrant Beilin District comprises the core downtown area within the city wall and some territory east and south of it. Beilin has more than its fair share of ancient sites, but it's modern as well, home to upscale malls, high-end hotels, and 17 universities. Lianhu starts inside the city's west wall and extends to the second ring road; there's much less here in terms of tourist sites or trendy spots, but it's still quite convenient to the downtown hot spots.

Beilin's housing is predominantly focused on apartment towers, such as the Wangyuan Mansion, where you can get a three-bedroom flat on one of its 23 floors for about $300 a month, just steps away from the buzz of the central city. The area just outside the east gate of the city wall has several luxury apartments; expect to pay $300–400 a month for a two- or three-bedroom unit. Beilun also has a few hotels that offer a handful of serviced apartments; check for availability at the Hyatt, Shangri-La, or the Bell Tower Hotel.

Lianhu District's apartments typically rent for $150–250 a month, though it is possible to find very modest places for less than $100 or large four-bedroom flats renting as high as a whopping $400.

South Xi'an

Moving south from downtown you'll find the Xi'an Hi-Tech Zone as well as the Qujiang Tourism and Holiday Resort Zone, which overlap with two districts, Yanta and Chang'an. This southern area will be your best location option if you plan work in the Hi-Tech zone or send your kids to its international school. The School of Chinese Studies of the Foreign Language University is also here, drawing international students. If you're in the market for a villa or a townhouse, this is the place to look, with plenty of options to choose from.

Yanta District, directly south of downtown, is predominantly where Xi'an's new Hi-Tech Zone is located. This district has been developed into a new center for the city's commerce and tourism and has the highest number of foreign firms in the city. Though you'll occasionally run across sprawling super-luxury flats that rent as high as $1,500, standard apartments in Yanta typically rent for $200–400. The Ziwei Garden is huge, attractive, and popular; recent apartment rentals ranged from around $200 for a standard three-bedroom to a penthouse with five bedrooms for less than $400, and they do have a few houses as well (around $1,200 a month). Villas in Yanta cover a range of styles and sizes renting from $1,000–2,500; within the Hi-Tech zone you can find a few townhouses and duplexes for under $1,000 a month.

Chang'an District starts below the third ring road and extends into the deep south of Xi'an's eight famous mountains. This peaceful area is seeing a lot of money pouring in from overseas businesses, so expect new development here in coming years. There are bargains to be had for the inconvenience of being farther from the city center, and apartments here typically do not exceed $250 in monthly rent. In a recent ad, $225 a month could get you a traditional brick building with two houses on two floors, one of which could be turned into a restaurant (parking lot included), at the entrance to a beautiful mountain valley on the summertime tourist route—cheap enough to make even those who don't cook dream of opening their own restaurant.

North Xi'an

Starting at the north city gate, the Weiyang District is home to the Xi'an ETDZ (Economic and Technology Development Zone). This area has a mix of fun spots, like the City Sports Games Villages and an amusement park, as well as major corporations like Siemens, Coca-Cola, and Rolls Royce. Apartments here start around $200, and you can get a large four-bedroom flat for less than $400. There are a few villa complexes here with typical rentals under $2,000, though the vast majority of villas are located in the south.

DAILY LIFE

In addition to the official Mandarin, the locals communicate in the Shaanxi dialect. Fortunately this dialect is just a slight variation from standard Mandarin, so students of Chinese will not be as troubled by communication issues here as in places with more-difficult dialects. In the areas of the city that are exposed to masses of foreign visitors, you'll find a decent amount of English for an inland city, though don't expect much English beyond the tourist sites.

As for shopping, Dong Dajie (East Avenue) has a variety of name-brand shops, and designer labels can be bought with a high price at the Century Ginwa department store. Cheap knockoffs are on offer at the various street markets around town. Imported goods are much harder to get here than in cities with more significant expat populations, though Xi'an does have the typical Watsons drugstores and hypermarts like Lotus, TrustMart, and a brand new Carrefour.

If you find yourself in a medical emergency in Xi'an, there are a couple foreign doctors in town, and the Chang'an hospital has a national reputation for having advanced facilities for a Chinese hospital.

Expat Social Scene

Xi'an's expat community isn't large, but it is growing. If you're looking for the local expats, you might find them playing snooker at Chaplin's Bar in the Bell Tower Hotel or partying on the bar street near Nan Dajie (South Avenue). The Xi'anExpat website (www.toureasy.net/expat) keeps foreigners clued into the city vibe. The Xi'an Foreign Language University has a school of Chinese studies, drawing international students. Families enjoy the Dragon Water World with its indoor waterslides, waterfalls, and fun pools, and the jungle-themed Banana Leaf Restaurant.

Some expats attend the large Catholic church in town; there are also Protestant and Mormon expat groups that meet casually. At Megafit Health Club downtown, $400 annual membership will buy you all the spinning, yoga, and wushu you could possibly need, and sometimes the classes are led by Americans.

For fine cuisine, Xi'an has Portuguese, French, Thai, and Japanese restaurants, among others. Of course, you'll also find the ubiquitous American chains of KFC, Pizza Hut, McDonald's and the like. Xi'an may not yet have a Starbucks, but the KFC-owned K Coffee offers a decent alternative.

When you need a little break from the stresses of life, you won't have to go too far out of town to find a spot to relax. Try one of the golf courses

the Hua Qing Hot Spring Palace just outside of Xi'an

in the suburbs, or slip into the misty hot waters of the Tang dynasty–style Hua Qing Hot Spring Palace, where emperors have bathed for centuries.

Schools

The Xi'an Hi-Tech International School (XHIS) is the only one in town created to meet the needs of foreign families. This school is only a few years old and still quite small, with two or three elementary grades combined into one classroom. XHIS teaches a Canadian curriculum and covers all grades.

GETTING AROUND

Getting around Xi'an is not too complicated with its extensive bus system that covers the whole city. Most public buses stop at the key city landmarks (the four gates, the bell tower, or the small or big goose pagoda), making it easy to get your bearings if you feel lost. Biking is a great way to get around the city, and taxis are cheap and plentiful. Be aware, though, that in order to keep traffic down, taxis have limitations as to when they can drive into the city center. The city has been trying for years to create a viable plan for building a subway, but the possibility of disturbing ancient relics buried beneath the city has slowed the process.

PRIME LIVING LOCATIONS

RESOURCES

Embassies and Consulates

IN THE UNITED STATES

States not mentioned in one of the consular districts below come under the jurisdiction of the embassy in Washington, DC.

THE EMBASSY OF THE PEOPLE'S REPUBLIC OF CHINA IN THE UNITED STATES
2201 Wisconsin Ave. N.W.
Washington, DC 20007
tel. 202/338-6688 or 202/588-9760
fax 202/588-9760
www.china-embassy.org

THE PRC CONSULATE IN SAN FRANCISCO
1450 Laguna St.
San Francisco, CA 94115
tel. 415/674-2900
fax 415/563-0494
www.chinaconsulatesf.org
Districts: Alaska, Nevada, Northern California, Oregon, Washington

THE PRC CONSULATE IN LOS ANGELES
443 Shatto Pl.
Los Angeles, CA 90020
tel. 213/807-8088
fax 213/380-1961
www.chinaconsulatela.org
Districts: Arizona, Hawaii, New Mexico, Southern California

THE PRC CONSULATE IN HOUSTON
3417 Montrose Blvd.
Houston, TX 77006
tel. 713/524-4311
fax 713/524-7656
www.chinahouston.org
Districts: Alabama, Arkansas, Florida, Georgia, Louisiana, Mississippi, Oklahoma, Texas

THE PRC CONSULATE IN CHICAGO
100 W. Erie St.
Chicago, IL 60610
tel. 312/803-0098
fax 312/803-0122
www.chinaconsulatechicago.org
Districts: Colorado, Illinois, Indiana, Iowa, Kansas, Michigan, Minnesota, Missouri, Wisconsin

THE PRC CONSULATE IN NEW YORK
520 12th Ave.
New York, NY 10036
tel. 212/868-7752
fax 212/502-0245
www.nyconsulate.prchina.org
Districts: Connecticut, Maine, Massachusetts, New Hampshire, New Jersey, New York, Ohio, Pennsylvania, Rhode Island, Vermont

IN CANADA
THE EMBASSY OF THE PRC IN CANADA
515 St. Patrick St.
Ottawa, Ont. K1N 5H3
tel. 613/789-9608
fax 613/789-1414
www.chinaembassycanada.org

IN GREAT BRITAIN
THE EMBASSY OF THE PRC IN THE UNITED KINGDOM
49–51 Portland Pl.
London W1B 1JL
tel. 020/7299-4049
fax 020/7436-9178
www.chinese-embassy.org.uk

IN AUSTRALIA
THE EMBASSY OF THE PRC IN AUSTRALIA
15 Coronation Dr.
Yarralumla, ACT 2600
Canberra, Australia
tel. 02/6273-4783 or 02/6273-7443
fax 02/6273-9615
http://au.china-embassy.org

IN CHINA

United States

U.S. EMBASSY
Xiu Shui Bei Jie 3
Beijing
tel. 10/6532-4153
http://beijing.usembassy-china.org.cn

U.S. CONSULATE CHENGDU
4 Lingshiguan Rd.
Chengdu
tel. 28/8558-3992 or 28/8558-9642
fax 28/8558-3520
www.usembassy-china.org.cn/chengdu

U.S. CONSULATE GUANGZHOU
1 Shamian St. South
Guangzhou
tel. 20/8121-8000
fax 20/8121-9001
www.usembassy-china.org.cn/guangzhou

U.S. CONSULATE HONG KONG
26 Garden Rd.
Central, Hong Kong
tel. 852/2523-9011
fax 852/2845-4845
http://HongKong.usconsulate.gov

U.S. CONSULATE SHANGHAI
1469 Huai Hai Zhong Lu
Shanghai
tel. 21/6433-6880
fax 21/6433-4122
www.usembassy-china.org.cn/shanghai

U.S. CONSULATE SHENYANG
52 14th Wei Rd.
Heping District, Shenyang
tel. 24/2322-0848
fax 24/2322-2374
http://shenyang.usconsulate.gov

Canada, Great Britain, and Australia

CANADIAN EMBASSY
19 Dongzhimenwai Dajie
Chao Yang District, Beijing
tel. 10/6532-3536
fax 10/6532-1684
www.beijing.gc.ca/beijing/en/index.htm

BRITISH EMBASSY
Floor 21, North Tower, Kerry Centre
1 Guanghualu
Beijing
tel. 10/8529-6600
fax 10/8529-6081
www.uk.cn/bj/index.asp

AUSTRALIAN EMBASSY
21 Dongzhimenwai Dajie
Beijing
tel. 10/5140 4111
fax 10/5140 4230
www.austemb.org.cn/indexe.htm

Planning Your Fact-Finding Trip

GUIDED TOURS

BIKE CHINA
www.bikechina.com
Bike China offers private and custom bicycle tours.

CHINA SPREE
www.chinaspree.com
This company offers set itineraries as well as custom trips throughout China.

TRAVEL CHINA GUIDE
www.travelchinaguide.com
This online travel agency offers tours plus a wealth of travel and expat information.

ACCOMMODATION OPTIONS

Short-Term Rentals

HOMTEL INTERNATIONAL
www.homtel.cn/e/eindex.asp
Private homes and rooms for rent are listed on this site.

SUBLET.NET
www.sublet.net
Private homes and rooms for rent are listed on this site.

Making the Move

LIVING IN CHINA

CHINA BLOG LIST
www.chinabloglist.org
Links to hundreds of weblogs about China.

CHINA EXPAT
www.chinaexpat.com
This site offers advice and information on China's top 50 cities.

EXPATEXCHANGE
www.expatexchange.com
This site is a general guide to expat living worldwide, including China.

LIVING ABROAD IN CHINA
info@LivingAbroadInChina.com
www.LivingAbroadInChina.com
The companion site for this book also includes updates.

INTERNATIONAL MOVING COMPANIES

CROWN RELOCATIONS
www.crownrelocations.com

INTERNATIONALMOVERS.COM
www.internationalmovers.com
This site provides quotes from multiple companies.

INTLMOVERS
www.intlmovers.com
This site also provides quotes from multiple companies.

Language and Education

MANDARIN LANGUAGE INSTRUCTION

WORLDWIDE LANGUAGE STUDY PROGRAMS
29 Harley St.
London W1G 9QR
United Kingdom
www.worldwidelanguagestudy.com/chinese.html
WLS offers short-term study programs in China and other countries.

Beijing

BEIJING FOREIGN STUDIES UNIVERSITY
2 Xisanhuan Beilu
Haidian District, Beijing
tel. 10/6891-6549
www.bfsu.edu.cn

BEIJING LANGUAGE AND CULTURE UNIVERSITY
15 Xueyuan Rd.
Haidian District, Beijing
tel. 10/8230-3923
fax 10/8230-3923
www.blcu.edu.cn

GLOBAL EXCHANGE CENTER
229 Beisihuan Zhonglu
Hai Tai Plaza, Ste. 1215
Beijing
tel. 10/6231-5029
fax 10/6231-5029
www.glexchange.net

INTERNATIONAL CULTURAL EXCHANGE CENTER (BEIJING)
Beijing University of Posts and Telecommunications
10 Xitucheng Rd.
Haidian District, Beijing
tel. 10/6228-2797
fax 10/6228-2797
www.icec.cn

Shanghai

MANDARIN TIMES
Unit 705, Apollo Building
1440 Yan An Rd.
Shanghai
tel. 21/6103-1638

fax 21/6249 5439
www.mandarintimes.com

MODERN MANDARIN
Room 510, Ruijin Business Center
96 Zhaojiabang Rd.
Shanghai
tel. 21/6437-4808
fax 21/6437-6938
www.modernmandarin.com

Other Cities
MANDARIN CHINESE LANGUAGE SCHOOL IN XIAMEN
www.studyabroadinternational.com/China/Xiamen/China_Xiamen.html
One-on-one instruction in the teacher's home.

NEW CONCEPT MANDARIN
2nd Floor, Beautiful Group Tower
74-77 Connaught Rd.
Central, Hong Kong
tel. 852/2850-4332
www.newconceptmandarin.com
This language center has options for online, classroom, and immersion learning.

ONLINE LANGUAGE TOOLS
CHINESE POD
www.chinesepod.com
At this site you can download mp3 lessons for free.

MANDARIN TOOLS
www.mandarintools.com
This site offers a downloadable dictionary and a whole lot more.

NJ STAR
www.njstar.com
At this site you can download Chinese word processing software.

UNIVERSITY INFORMATION
P.R.C. GOVERNMENT SCHOLARSHIPS
www.ebeijing.gov.cn/Study/Scholarship/default.htm
Get the lowdown on scholarships and fellowships.

Beijing
BEIJING UNIVERSITY
International Student Affairs
1st Floor, South Pavilion
Beijing
tel. 10/6275-1246
fax 10/6275-1240
www.pku.edu.cn

QINGHUA UNIVERSITY, BEIJING
Tsinghua University
Beijing
tel. 10/6278-5001
www.tsinghua.edu.cn

Shanghai
CHINA EUROPE INTERNATIONAL BUSINESS SCHOOL, SHANGHAI
699 Hongfeng Rd.
Pudong, Shanghai
tel. 21/2890-5890
fax 21/2890-5678
www.ceibs.edu

FUDAN UNIVERSITY, SHANGHAI
Foreign Students Office
Fudan University
220 Han Dan Rd.
Shanghai
tel. 21/6511-7628
fax 21/6511-7298
www.fudan.edu.cn

SHANGHAI JIAO TONG UNIVERSITY
School of International Education
1954 Hua Shan Rd.
Shanghai
tel. 21/6282-1079
fax 21/6281-7613
www.sjtu.edu.cn

Hangzhou
ZHEJIANG UNIVERSITY
Hangzhou
tel. 571/8795-1717
fax 571/87951358
www.zju.edu.cn

Health

GENERAL

ENGLISH-CHINESE MEDICAL DICTIONARY
www.esaurus.org

U.S. CENTERS FOR DISEASE CONTROL
www.cdc.gov

WORLD HEALTH ORGANIZATION
www.WHO.org

HEALTH INSURANCE

MEDAIRE
www.medaire.com
Global Doctor insurance

SOS
www.internationalsos.com

HOSPITALS AND CLINICS

THE U.S. EMBASSY LIST OF HOSPITALS IN CHINA
www.usembassy-china.org.cn/us-citizen/medical

GLOBALDOCTOR
tel. 10/8456-9191
www.eglobaldoctor.com

SOS
www.internationalsos.com

EMERGENCY PHONE NUMBERS

Emergency: tel. 999
Ambulance: tel. 120
Fire: tel. 119
Police: tel. 110

Employment

BUSINESS

CHINA JOB
www.chinajob.com
Listings of jobs in teaching and business.

JOBS IN CHINA
http://english.jobchina.net
Job postings for teaching, business, and high tech.

MONSTER
www.monster.com
This very large, U.S.-based job website lists thousands of international jobs.

ZHAOPIN
www.zhaopin.com
Hundreds of Chinese companies post their jobs on this website.

TEACHING ENGLISH

APPALACHIANS ABROAD
www.marshall.edu/gochina
English teacher placement service based at Marshall University.

ESL TEACHERS BOARD
www.ESLteachersboard.com
Schools post their teaching jobs here, and teachers upload their resumes.

PEACE CORPS
www.peacecorps.gov

TEACHING AT INTERNATIONAL SCHOOLS

THE INTERNATIONAL EDUCATOR
www.tieonline.com
The number-one international school magazine is now online.

Finance

LEGAL CONSULTING

BOSTON CONSULTING GROUP
www.bcg.com.cn
Exceptional business consulting services.

LEHMAN LEE & XU LAW FIRM
10-2 Liangmaqiao Diplomatic Compound
22 Dongfang East Rd.
Chaoyang District, Beijing
tel. 10/8532-1919
fax 10/8532-1999
www.lehmanlaw.com
Legal, tax, and business consulting.

PRICEWATERHOUSECOOPERS
26th Floor, Office Tower A
Beijing Fortune Plaza
7 Dongsanhuan Zhong Rd.
Chaoyang District, Beijing
tel. 10/6533-8888
fax 10/6533-8800
www.pwchk.com/home/eng/prctax_iit
_others.html
Tax consulting from one of the best.

INTERNATIONAL BANKS

CITIBANK
www.citigroup.com/citigroup/global/
chn.htm

CITIC SECURITIES (BROKERAGE)
www.citiccapital.com

HSBC INTERNATIONAL BANK
www.hsbc.com

STANDARD CHARTERED BANK
www.standardchartered.com.cn

Communications

MEDIA

CHINA DAILY ONLINE
www.chinadaily.com.cn

INTERNATIONAL HERALD TRIBUNE
www.iht.com

SOUTH CHINA MORNING POST
www.scmp.com

WALL STREET JOURNAL ASIA
www.awsj.com

WASHINGTON POST CHINA
www.washingtonpost.com/wp-srv/inatl/
longterm/worldref/country/china.htm

TELEPHONE

CHINA RESOURCES PEOPLES TELEPHONE COMPANY LTD (HONG KONG)
www.people.com.hk

CHINA TELECOM
www.chinatelecom.com.cn
The large state-run phone company in China.

EXPRESS MAIL SERVICES

CHINA POST
www.chinapost.gov.cn

DHL (CHINA)
www.cn.dhl.com/publish/cn/en.high.html

FEDEX (CHINA)
www.fedex.com/cn_english

UPS (CHINA)
www.ups.com/content/cn/en/index.jsx

Travel and Transportation

BY AIR
AIR CHINA
www.airchina.com.cn

CHINA EASTERN AIRLINES
www.cea.online.sh.cn or www.ce-air.com

CHINA SOUTHERN AIRLINES
www.cs-air.com

HELICOPTER ROUTES IN THE PEARL RIVER DELTA
www.helihongkong.com

Non-Affiliated Airline Reservation Sites
C TRIP
www.english.ctrip.com

ELONG TRAVEL
www.elong.net

YOEE
www.yoee.com

BY TRAIN
TRAVEL CHINA GUIDE TRAIN SCHEDULE
www.travelchinaguide.com/china-trains

BY BOAT
PEARL RIVER DELTA FERRY ROUTES
www.turbojet.com.hk

Housing Considerations

CENTURY 21 REAL ESTATE, CHINA
www.century21cn.com/en
This U.S.-based real estate company now operates in China.

EXPATRIATES.COM
www.expatriates.com
Online classifieds for housing, jobs, and more.

5I5J ("I LOVE MY HOME")
www.5i5j.com
Online Chinese real estate site with some English.

MOVE AND STAY
www.moveandstay.com
This site lists serviced apartments for executives in several Chinese cities.

SANTAFE RELOCATIONS
www.santaferelo.com
This company provides total relocation management, including all aspects of the home search.

SOU FUN REAL ESTATE
ww.soufun.com
This Chinese website has property listings for over five dozen Chinese cities, but it does not use any English.

Prime Living Locations

BEIJING

General

BEJING CITY GOVERNMENT
www.ebeijing.gov.cn

ALLO' EXPAT BEIJING
www.beijing.alloexpat.com
Online community for Beijing expats.

CHINA PULSE
www.chinapulse.com/classifieds
Online community focusing on jobs, housing, travel, etc.

Media

BEIJING REVIEW
www.bjreview.com.cn

THAT'S BEIJING
www.thatsbj.com

Housing

BEIJING REAL ESTATE
406 BaiYan Building
238 North 4th Ring Middle Rd.
Haidian District, Beijing
tel. 10/8231-8640
fax 10/8231-8740
info@beijingrealestate.com
www.beijingrealestate.com

CENTURY 21 REAL ESTATE
1725 Hanwei Plaza
7 Guanghua Rd.
Chaoyang District, Beijing
tel. 10/6561-7788
www.century21cn.com/en

Medical

BEIJING UNITED FAMILY HOSPITAL
2 Jiang Tai Lu
Chaoyang District, Beijing
tel. 10/6433-3960
emergency tel. 10/6433-2345

SOS BEIJING 24-HOUR MEDICAL HOTLINE
tel. 10/6462-9100

Organizations

AMERICAN CHAMBER OF COMMERCE
www.amcham-china.org.cn

CANADA-CHINA BUSINESS COUNCIL
www.ccbc.com.cn

CHINA-AUSTRALIA CHAMBER OF COMMERCE
www.austcham.org

DELEGATION OF GERMAN INDUSTRY AND COMMERCE
www.china.ahk.de/chamber/beijing/events

International Schools

BEIJING BISS INTERNATIONAL SCHOOL
17, Area 4, Anzhen Xi Li
Chaoyang District, Beijing
tel. 10/6443-3151
fax 10/6443-3156
www.biss.com.cn

BEIJING CHINESE SCHOOL
805 A Building
26 Chaowai St.
Chaoyang District, Beijing
tel. 10/8565-3718
fax 10/8565-3719
www.beijingchineseschool.com

BEIJING ZHONGGUANCUN INTERNATIONAL SCHOOL
6 Jinzhan Lu
Chaoyang District, Beijing
tel. 10/8434-3433
fax 10/8434-3436
www.bzis2002.com

BRITISH SCHOOL OF BEIJING
5 Xiliujie Sanlitun Rd.
Chaoyang District, Beijing
tel. 10/8532-3088
www.bsb.org.cn

ETON INTERNATIONAL SCHOOL
7th Floor, Lido Office Tower
Lido Place, Jichang Rd., Jiang Tai Rd.

Chaoyang District, Beijing
tel. 10/6430-1590
fax 10/6430-1310
www.etonkids.com/home.htm

INTERNATIONAL MONTESSORI SCHOOL OF BEIJING
China World Trade Center, North Lodge
1 Jian Guo Men Wai Ave.
Beijing
tel. 10/6505-3869
fax 10/6505-1237
www.montessoribeijing.com

THE INTERNATIONAL SCHOOL OF BEIJING
10 An Hua St.
Shunyi District, Beijing
www.isb.bj.edu.cn

WESTERN ACADEMY OF BEIJING
10 Lai Guang Ying Dong Lu
Chaoyang District, Beijing
tel. 10/8456-4155
fax 10/6432-2440
www.wab.edu

YEW CHUNG INTERNATIONAL SCHOOL OF BEIJING
Honglingjin Park
5 Houbalizhuang
Chaoyang District, Beijing
tel. 10/8583-3731
fax 10/8583-2734
www.ycef.com

Services
FOREIGN ENTERPRISE SERVICE CORPORATION
www.fescochina.com
This service can help you obtain a drivers license if you live in Beijing.

SHANGHAI

General
CITY GOVERNMENT WEBSITE
www.shanghai.gov.cn

ALLO' EXPAT SHANGHAI
www.shanghai.alloexpat.com
Online community for Shanghai expats.

EXPATS SHANGHAI
www.expatsh.com
Classified ads for housing, jobs, travel, etc.

CHINA PULSE SHANGHAI
www.chinapulse.com/classifieds
Classified ads for jobs, housing, etc.

SHANGHAI EXPAT
www.shanghaiexpat.com
Another online community catering to Shanghai expats.

LIFELINE SHANGHAI
tel. 21/6279-8990
This hotline offers community information and emotional support.

Housing
PHOENIX PROPERTY AGENCY
Unit G-H, 11th Floor, Yujia Building
1336 Huashan Rd.
Shanghai
tel. 21/6240-4052
www.shanghai-realty.net

SHANGHAI METROPOLIS REAL ESTATE AGENCY
www.metropolis-sh.com
High-end real estate agency catering to expats.

SHANGHAI PROPERTIES
www.shanghaiprops.com
No-fee rental agency by and for foreigners.

SHANGHAI REALTY
www.shanghairealty.com
No-fee rental agency.

SPACE INTERNATIONAL
Fuxing Rd., Lane 1264
Shanghai
tel. 21/5403-3338
fax 21/6467-8950
www.space.sh.cn
Real estate agency specializing in luxury properties.

Medical
SOS SHANGHAI 24-HOUR MEDICAL HOTLINE
tel. 21/6295-0099

WORLDLINK MEDICAL CENTERS
Downtown: 1376 Nanjing Xi Lu
Hongqiao: 2258 Hong Qiao Lu
Jinqiao: 51 Hongfeng Lu
24-hour Healthline: 21/6445-5999
www.worldlink-shanghai.com

Media
SHANGHAI DAILY NEWSPAPER
www.shanghaidaily.com

SHANGHAI STAR NEWSPAPER
www.shanghai-star.com.cn

THAT'S SHANGHAI MAGAZINE
http://shanghai.asiaxpat.com

Organizations
AMERICAN CHAMBER OF COMMERCE
www.amcham-china.org.cn

BRITISH CHAMBER OF COMMERCE
www.britcham.org

International Schools
BRITISH INTERNATIONAL SCHOOL SHANGHAI
600 Cambridge Forest New Town
2729 Hunan Rd.
Pudong, Shanghai
tel. 21/5812-7455
fax 21/6819-6290
www.bisshanghai.com

CONCORDIA INTERNATIONAL SCHOOL SHANGHAI
999 Ming Yue Rd., Jinqiao
Pudong, Shanghai
tel. 21/5899-0380
fax 21/5899-1685
www.ciss.com.cn

DULWICH COLLEGE INTERNATIONAL SCHOOL
222 Lan An Lu, Jinqiao
Pudong, Shanghai
tel. 21/5899-9910
fax 21/5899-9810
www.dulwichcollege.cn

SHANGHAI AMERICAN SCHOOL, PUDONG
258 Jin Feng Rd.
Zhudi Town, Shanghai
tel. 21/6221-1445
www.saschina.org

SHANGHAI PINGHE BILINGUAL SCHOOL
261 Huang Yang Rd., Jinqiao
Pudong, Shanghai
tel. 21/5031-0417
fax 21/58541617
www.shphschool.com
A top private Chinese school with a bilingual curriculum.

YEW CHUNG INTERNATIONAL SCHOOL OF SHANGHAI
11 Shui Cheng Rd.
Hongqiao, Shanghai
tel. 21/6242-3243
fax 21/6242-7331
www.ycef.com

HONG KONG AND MACAU

General
HONG KONG GOVERNMENT
www.info.gov.hk

ASIA EXPAT HONG KONG
http://hongkong.asiaxpat.com/default.asp
General city guide to Hong Kong covering real estate, jobs, lifestyle, etc.

GO HOME! EXPAT CORNER
http://hong-kong-expat-english.gohome.com.hk

MACAU GOVERNMENT
www.cityguide.gov.mo

MACAUZHUHAI: A GUIDE FOR EXPATS
www.macauzhuhai.com/macau.htm
Online guide to Macau for foreigners.

Housing
852 REAL ESTATE, HONG KONG
www.852realestate.com
No-fee real estate agency.

GLOBAL PROPERTY, HONG KONG
Suite 704, 7th Floor, Chinachem Leighton
Plaza
29 Leighton Rd.
Causeway Bay, Hong Kong
tel. 852/2808-1155
www.globalproperty.com.hk

HOUSE HUNTERS, HONG KONG
Unit B, 17th Floor, Wyndham Place
40-44 Wyndham St.
Central, Hong Kong
tel. 852/2869-1001
www.househunters.com.hk

**EAST MEETS WEST REAL ESTATE
AGENCY, MACAU**
Estrada Governador Albana de Oliveira,
No. 374 G
Nam San Garden, Block 1 RC-IRC
Taipa, Macau
tel. 853/841-217
www.emwservices.com

MOVING TO MACAU
www.movingtomacau.com
A property listing website for buying,
renting, or sharing a home.

Media
BC MAGAZINE
www.bcmagazine.net

SOUTH CHINA MORNING POST
www.scmp.com

THE STANDARD
www.thestandard.com.hk

MACAUTALK
www.ismaychina.com/macautalk.asp

Medical
BAPTIST HOSPITAL
222 Waterloo Rd.
Kowloon Tong, Kowloon, Hong Kong
tel. 852/2339-8888

HONG KONG ADVENTIST HOSPITAL
40 Stubbs Rd.
Wanchai, Hong Kong
tel. 852/2574-6211

**SOS HONG KONG 24-HOUR
MEDICAL HOTLINE**
tel. 852/2528-9900

HOPE MEDICAL CLINIC, MACAU
Fu Wah Court, 1-D
26 Ave. de Sidonio Pais, 1/F
Macau
tel. 853/589-000

Organizations
**AMERICAN CHAMBER OF
COMMERCE**
www.amcham.org.hk/home.shtml

**AUSTRALIAN CHAMBER OF
COMMERCE**
www.austcham.com.hk

**CANADIAN CHAMBER OF
COMMERCE**
www.cancham.org

**THE HONG KONG GENERAL
CHAMBER OF COMMERCE**
www.hkgcc.org.hk/business_world_h.asp

**INTERNATIONAL
LADIES CLUB OF MACAU**
tel. 853/665-2241
ilcm@hotmail.com

International Schools
**AMERICAN
INTERNATIONAL SCHOOL**
125 Waterloo Rd.
Kowloon Tong, Kowloon, Hong Kong
tel. 852/2336-3812
fax 852/2336-5276
www.ais.edu.hk

**AUSTRALIAN INTERNATIONAL
SCHOOL HONG KONG**
3A Norfolk Rd.
Kowloon Tong, Kowloon, Hong Kong
tel. 852/2304-6078
fax 852/2304-6077
www.aishk.edu.hk

BRITISH SOUTH ISLAND SCHOOL
50 Nam Fung Rd.
Aberdeen, Hong Kong
tel. 852/2555-9313
fax 852/2553-8811
www.sis.edu.hk

CANADIAN INTERNATIONAL SCHOOL
36 Nam Long Shan Rd.
Aberdeen, Hong Kong
tel. 852/2525-7088
fax 852/2525-7579
www.cdnis.edu.hk

CLEARWATER BAY SCHOOL
Lot 235, DD229
Clearwater Bay Rd.
Kowloon, Hong Kong
tel. 852/2358-3221
fax 852/2358-3246
www.cwbs.edu.hk

CONCORDIA INTERNATIONAL SCHOOL
68 Begonia Rd.
Yau Yat Chuen
Kowloon, Hong Kong
tel. 852/2789-9890
fax 852/2392-8820
www.cihs.edu.hk

DISCOVERY BAY INTERNATIONAL SCHOOL
Discovery Bay
Lantau Island, Hong Kong
tel. 852/2987-7331
fax 852/2987-7076
www.dbis.edu.hk

HONG KONG INTERNATIONAL SCHOOL
Tsin Shui Wan Au
Hong Kong
tel. 852/2812-5000
fax 852/2812-0669
www.hkis.edu.hk

INTERNATIONAL CHRISTIAN SCHOOL
45 Grampian Rd.
Kowloon City, Kowloon, Hong Kong
tel. 852/2338-9606
www.ics.edu.hk

LANTAU INTERNATIONAL SCHOOL
93 Tong Fuk Village
Lantau Island, Hong Kong
tel. 852/2980-3676
fax 852/2980-3555
www.lantau-intl-school.edu.hk

PEAK SCHOOL
20 Plunketts Rd.
The Peak, Hong Kong
tel. 852/2849-7211
fax 852/2849-7151
www.ps.edu.hk

WEST ISLAND SCHOOL
250 Victoria Rd.
Pokfulam, Hong Kong
tel. 852/2819-1962
fax 852/2816-7257
www.wis.edu.hk

YEW CHUNG INTERNATIONAL SCHOOL OF HONG KONG
10 Somerset Rd.
Kowloon Tong, Kowloon, Hong Kong
tel. 852/2338-7106
fax 852/2338-4045
www.ycef.com

INTERNATIONAL SCHOOL OF MACAO
Macau University of Science and Technology
(Block E)
Avenida Wai Long
Taipa, Macao
tel. 853/533-700
fax 853/533-702
www.tis.edu.mo

THE SCHOOL OF THE NATIONS (MACAU)
Rua de Luis G. Gomes
No. 136, Edf. Lei San, 4
Andar, Macau
tel. 853/701-759
fax 853/701-724
www.schoolofthenations.com

SHENG KUNG HUI PRIMARY SCHOOL, MACAU
Avenida Padre Tomas Pereira
Taipa, Macau
tel. 853/850-000
fax 853/850-022
www.skhps.edu.mo

THE SOUTH
Guangdong Province
Media
GUANGDONG PROVINCE NEWS
www.newsgd.com

XIANZAI GUANGDONG E-ZINE
www.xianzai.com.cn

Guangzhou
JRE REAL ESTATE, GUANGZHOU
Rm. 2108, Dongshan Plaza
69 Xianlie Zhong Lu
Guangzhou
tel. 20/2237-1226 or 20/2237-1228
www.joannarealestate.com.cn/guangzhou

CITYTALK, GUANGZHOU
www.ismaychina.com/citytalk.asp

THAT'S GUANGZHOU MAGAZINE
www.thatsgz.com

GUANGZHOU WOMEN'S INTERNATIONAL CLUB
www.gwic.org

GUANGZHOU SOS CLINIC
Guangdong Provincial Hospital of TCM, 2nd Floor
Da Tong Rd.
Er Sha Island, Guangzhou
tel. 20/8735-5040

AMERICAN INTERNATIONAL SCHOOL OF GUANGZHOU
3 Yan Yu St. South, Ersha Island
Yuexiu District, Guangzhou
tel. 20/8735-3392
fax 20/8735-3339
www.aisgz.edu.cn

GUANGZHOU GRACE ACADEMY
Riverside Garden
Guangzhou
tel. 20/8450-0180
fax 20/8450-0190
www.grace.gd.edu.cn

GUANGZHOU NANHU INTERNATIONAL SCHOOL
176 Yunxiang Rd.

Tonghe St.
Bai Yun District, Guangzhou
tel. 20/8706-0862
fax 20/8706-0330
www.gnischina.com/aboutgnis.htm

UTAHLOY INTERNATIONAL SCHOOL, GUANGZHOU
6km Sha Tai Highway
Jin Bao Gang
Tong He, Guangzhou
tel. 20/8770-3919
fax 20/8779-1696
www.utahloy.com

UTAHLOY INTERNATIONAL SCHOOL, ZENG CHENG
San Jiang Town
Zeng Cheng City
tel. 20/8291-3303
www.utahloy.com

Shenzhen
SHENZHEN PARTY
www.shenzhenparty.com
This site offers a guide to parties and events in Shenzhen.

SHENZHEN PEOPLE
www.shenzhenpeople.net
This site is a general guide to Shenzhen.

SHENZHEN WOMEN'S INTERNATIONAL CLUB
www.swiconline.com

INTERNATIONAL SCHOOL OF SINO-CANADA, SHENZHEN
166 Nanguang Rd.
Nanshan District, Shenzhen
tel. 755/2666-1000
fax 755/2645-4090
www.issc.com.cn

QSI INTERNATIONAL SCHOOL SHEKOU
8 Tai Zi Rd.
Shekou, Shenzhen
tel. 755/2667-6031
fax 755/2667-6030
www.qsi.org/SHK_HOME

SHEKOU INTERNATIONAL SCHOOL
Jing Shan Villas, Nan Hai Rd.

Shenzhen
tel. 755/2669-3669
fax 755/2667-4099
www.sis.org.cn

Zhuhai
MACAUZHUHAI:
A GUIDE FOR EXPATS
www.MacauZhuhai.com
Online guide to Zhuhai for foreigners.

WANDERVEREIN ZHUHAI
HIKING CLUB
www.wvzh.com

ZIA EXPAT CLUB, ZHUHAI
tel. 756/322-2823
zia@macauzhuhai.com

QSI INTERNATIONAL
SCHOOL OF ZHUHAI
House No. 105
2 Longxing St.
Gongbei, Zhuhai
tel. 756/815-6134
www.qsi.org/zhu_home

Xiamen
AMOY MAGIC
www.amoymagic.com
This site is a guide to Xiamen and Fujian province.

WHAT'S ON XIAMEN MAGAZINE
www.WhatsOnXiamen.com

XIAMEN INTERNATIONAL SCHOOL
Jiu Tian Hu
Xinglin, Xiamen
tel. 592/625-6581
fax 592/625-6584
www.xischina.com

THE EAST
Nanjing
JRE REAL ESTATE, NANJING
Rm. A4, 11th Floor, Golden Eagle
International Plaza
89 Hanzhong Rd.
Nanjing
tel. 25/8695-2966 or 25/8695-2988
www.joannarealestate.com.cn/nanjing

JUEE REAL ESTATE, NANJING
tel. 25/8464-2822
www.juee.com/en

MAP MAGAZINE
www.mapmagazine.com.cn

AEA NANJING HEALTH CLINIC
Hilton Hotel
319 Zhongshan East Rd.
Nanjing
tel. 25/480-2842

JIANGSU PROVINCE HOSPITAL
VIP CLINIC
300 Guangzhou Rd.
Nanjing
tel. 25/8371-8836

NANJING
INTERNATIONAL SCHOOL
Xian Lin College and University Town
Qi Xia District, Nanjing
tel. 25/8589-9111
fax 25/8589-9222
www.nanjing-school.com

Suzhou
JRE REAL ESTATE, SUZHOU
Rm. 812, Century Financial Tower No. 1
Su Hua Rd.
Suzhou Industrial Park, Suzhou
tel. 12/6761-9816 or 12/6761-9826
www.joannarealestate.com.cn/suzhou

SUZHOU ETONHOUSE
INTERNATIONAL SCHOOL
70 Jinshan Rd.
New District, Suzhou
tel. 512/6825-5666
fax 512/6825-5939
www.etonhouse-sz.com

SUZHOU SINGAPORE
INTERNATIONAL SCHOOL
208 Zhong Nan Jie
Suzhou Industrial Park, Jiangsu
tel. 512/6258-6388
fax 512/6258-0388
www.ssis-suzhou.com

Hangzhou
HANGZHOU MAOS REAL ESTATE
www.hangzhourelocation.com

HANGZHOU EXPAT
www.HangzhouExpat.com
Online expat guide to the city.

**HANGZHOU INTERNATIONAL
BUSINESS ASSOCIATION**
www.hiba.cn

IN TOUCH ZHEJIANG **MAGAZINE**
www.intouchzj.com
This magazine covers the Zhejiang province, which includes both Hangzhou and Ningbo, but the focus is primarily on Hangzhou.

**HANGZHOU
INTERNATIONAL SCHOOL**
80 Dongxin St.
Bin Jiang District, Hangzhou
tel. 571/8669-0045
fax 571/8669-0044
www.scischina.org/hangzhou

Ningbo
NINGBO EXPAT ASSOCIATION
www.NingboExpat.com

NINGBO GUIDE
http://ningboGuide.com

HELLO NINGBO CITY GUIDE
www.helloningbo.com

**ACCESS INTERNATIONAL
ACADEMY NINGBO**
1 Ai Xue Rd.
Beilun District, Ningbo
tel. 574/8686-9999
www.aian.org.cn

**AUSTRALIAN INTERNATIONAL
SCHOOL, NINGBO**
35 Da Shu Yuan Xiang
Haishu District, Ningbo
tel. 574/8730-6737
fax 574/8732-9457
www.aussieschool-china.com

THE NORTH

Tianjin
E-SMART TIANJIN
www.esmart.com.cn
Tianjin real estate and city guide.

**ROYAL-RELOCATION
CONSULTANT COMPANY**
Tower 2, 20th Floor, Suite B
15 Bin Shui Rd.
Tianjin
tel. 22/8988-1275
fax 22/2813-6943
www.royal-relocation.com

JIN **MAGAZINE**
www.expatriate-jin.com

**TIANJIN EXPATS
COMMUNITY WEBSITE**
www.tianjinexpats.net

TIANJIN INTERNATIONAL CLINIC
Sheraton Tianjin Hotel
Zijinshan Rd.
Hexi District, Tianjin
tel. 22/2352-0143

INTERNATIONAL SCHOOL TIANJIN
Weishan Rd. (Shuanggang)
Jinnan District, Tianjin
tel. 22/2859-2001
fax 22/2859-2007
www.istianjin.org

TEDA INTERNATIONAL SCHOOL
9 Xiao Yuan St.
TEDA, Tianjin
tel. 22/2859-2001
fax 22/2859-2007
www.tedainternationalschool.net

**THE TIANJIN
INTERNATIONAL SCHOOL**
1 Meiyuan Rd.
Tianjin New Technological & Industrial Garden
Nan Kai District, Tianjin
tel. 22/8371-0900
fax 22/8371-0300
www.tiseagles.com

**TIANJIN REGO
INTERNATIONAL SCHOOL**
38 Huan Dao Dong Rd.
Mei Jiang Nan Residence Zone, Tianjin
tel. 22/8816-1180
fax 22/8816-1190
www.regoschool.org

Qingdao
J&M REALTY
Qingdao World Trade Centre
Building B, Shop 204B
6 Hong Kong Middle Rd.
Qingdao
tel. 532/8388-9232
fax 532/8591-9859
www.jmrealtyco.com

JRE REAL ESTATE, QINGDAO
Rm. 1802, Merchants Bank Tower,
New World Cyberport No. 36
Hong Kong Zhong Rd.
Qingdao
tel. 32/8597-7155 or 32/8597-7156
www.joannarealestate.com.cn/Qingdao

RED STAR MAGAZINE
www.MyRedStar.com

**QINGDAO
INTERNATIONAL SCHOOL**
Middle Sector, Songling Rd.
Stone Old Man National Tourism Spot,
Qingdao
tel. 532/890-8000
fax 532/890-8950
www.qischina.org

**QINGDAO MTI
INTERNATIONAL SCHOOL**
Children's Club, 3rd Floor Children's
Activity Center
6 Dong Hai Xi Rd.
Qingdao
tel. 532/8389-5006
fax 532/8389-5012
www.qmischina.com

**YEW CHUNG INTERNATIONAL
SCHOOL, QINGDAO**
Admissions address:
Ste. 2106
36 Xianggang Zhong Lu
Qingdao
tel. 532/8909-0083
fax 532/8909-0082
www.ycis-qd.com/Qingdao

Dalian
XIANZAI DALIAN E-ZINE
www.xianzai.com.cn

**MAPLE LEAF
(INTERNATIONAL SCHOOL)**
78 Caiyun Rd.
Xigang, Dalian
tel. 411/8433-2821 or 411/790-4790
fax 411/8433-0737 or 411/790-0143
www.mapleleaf.net.cn

Shenyang
JRE SHENYANG
www.joannarealestate.com.cn/shenyang

**LIAONING GATEWAY ONLINE
NEWSLETTER**
www.liaoning-gateway.com

**GLOBAL DOCTORS SHENYANG
24-HOUR MEDICAL HOTLINE**
tel. 24/2433-0678

**SHENYANG
INTERNATIONAL SCHOOL**
12 Xiangbai Rd.
Sujiatun, Shenyang
tel. 24/8912-1177
fax 24/8981-7456
www.syistigers.com

INLAND

Wuhan
**OFFICIAL WUHAN
GOVERNMENT WEBSITE**
http://english.wh.gov.cn

WUHAN TIME EXPAT PORTAL
www.wuhantime.com
City guide to Wuhan for expats.

WOMEN IN WUHAN
womeninwuhan@hotmail.com

**WUHAN PEOPLE'S ASSOCIATION
FOR FRIENDSHIP WITH FOREIGN
COUNTRIES**
zhangtianzhi@wh.gov.cn

**SOUTH LAKE
INTERNATIONAL SCHOOL**
San Jiao Hu Xiao Xue
Wuhan Economic & Development Zone,
Wuhan

tel. 27/8423-8713
fax 27/8423-8726
www.wuhanschool.com

Chengdu
OFFICIAL CHENGDU GOVERNMENT WEBSITE
www1.chengdu.gov.cn/echengdu

SHAMROCK PUB, CHENGDU
www.ShamrockInChengdu.com

GLOBAL DOCTORS CHENGDU 24-HOUR MEDICAL HOTLINE
tel. 28/8522-6058

CHENGDU INTERNATIONAL SCHOOL
99 Shuxi Lu
Zhong Hai International Community, Chengdu
tel. 28/8759-2260
fax 28/8759-2265
www.iscchengdu.org

CHENGDU MEISHI INTERNATIONAL SCHOOL
Xinxing Rd. South, Remin Nan Rd.
Chengdu
tel. 28/8533-0968
fax 28/8533-0073
www.meishischool.com/english.htm

QSI INTERNATIONAL SCHOOL, CHENGDU
Building 17, Area A, Tongzilin Rd.
Zhonghuayuan, Chengdu
tel. 28/8519-8393
www.qsi.org/cdu

Xi'an
XI'AN EXPAT
www.toureasy.net/expat

XI'AN HI-TECH INTERNATIONAL SCHOOL (XHIS)
Chang An Technology Park
Xi'an
tel. 29/8408-1323
fax 29/8569-1659
www.jahoo-edu.com/index-1.html

Chongqing
GLOBAL DOCTORS CHONGQING 24-HOUR MEDICAL HOTLINE
tel. 23/8903-8837

YEW CHUNG INTERNATIONAL SCHOOL OF CHONGQING
M38 Orchard Manor, Renhe Town
Yubei District, Chongqing
tel. 23/6763-8482
fax 23/6763-8483
www.ycis-cq.com

Glossary

amah Cantonese for domestic helper or auntie; same as *ayi* in Mandarin

ayi domestic helper, literally "auntie"

bagua an octagonal diagram used in Daoism and feng shui, literally "eight symbols"

Chinglish awkward, often humorous, translations of Chinese into English

dao the way of nature, guiding principle for Daoists, literally "path"

dizi traditional Chinese flute

erhu traditional Chinese violin, literally "two strings"

feng shui mystical belief that architectural layout is related to *qi*, literally "wind and water"

guanxi connections through relationships, literally "closed system"

gwailo Cantonese for foreigner or foreign devil, literally "ghost person"

hutong traditional alley in Beijing (named after the *hu* people)

jiao 1/10th of a yuan, literally "horn"

junk fishing boat with square sails

kowtow to bow down, literally "to knock your head (on the ground)"

kuai slang for money, literally "a piece"

lama Buddhist holy man

laowai foreigner, literally "old outsider"

mahjong card game played with engraved tiles

nai nai grandma

pedi-cab three-wheeled bicycle taxi

pinyin Romanized system of writing Chinese words

pipa string musical instrument

PRC People's Republic of China, the mainland

Putonghua the official Mandarin language, literally "common language"

qi energy, power, or life force

qi gong exercise to channel *qi* into your life

renminbi Chinese currency, literally "the people's money"

ROC Republic of China, Taiwan

SAR Special Administrative Region (Hong Kong and Macau)

shikoumen Shanghai's old style houses, literally "stone door house"

siheyuan Beijing's courtyard homes in *hutong* neighborhoods

tai qi graceful exercise related to martial arts and harnessing the *qi* power

Uighur ethnic group from the northwest

VoIP Voice over Internet Protocol, using the Internet to make telephone calls

yin and yang opposite forces in the universe such as positive and negative, light and dark, female and male

yuan the PRC currency unit

Phrasebook

Chinese translations by Alex Chen

PRONUNCIATION

When a Chinese word is written in pinyin, the diacritic marks above the vowels tell the speaker which of the five tones to use when pronouncing the word. The first tone is called the flat tone, and it sounds a little high-pitched, like a man trying to imitate a female voice. The second tone is called rising because the pitch rises at the end of the syllable, such as when a person says "yes?" in response to a knock on the door. The third tone is the difficult tone that falls then rises, like when a person hears an unbelievable bit of gossip and responds "what?" The fourth tone is the falling tone, which sounds like you are impatient or angry. The fifth tone is a relaxed pronunciation and is mostly reserved for the last word of a sentence.

NUMBERS

ENGLISH	PINYIN	CHINESE
one	yī	一
two	èr	二
three	sān	三
four	sì	四
five	wǔ	五
six	liù	六
seven	qī	七
eight	bā	八
nine	jiǔ	九
10	shí	十
50	wǔ shí	五十
100	yì bǎi	一百
500	wú bǎi	五百
1,000	yì qiān	一千
5,000	wǔ qiān	五千
10,000	wàn	万
100,000	shí wàn	十万
500,000	wǔ shí wàn	五十万
1,000,000	yì bǎi wàn	一百万

DAYS OF THE WEEK

ENGLISH	PINYIN	CHINESE
Sunday	xīng qī tiān / xīng qī rì	星期天 / 星期日
Monday	xīng qī yī	星期一
Tuesday	xīng qī èr	星期二
Wednesday	xīng qī sān	星期三
Thursday	xīng qī sì	星期四
Friday	xīng qī wǔ	星期五
Saturday	xīng qī liù	星期六

TIME

ENGLISH	PINYIN	CHINESE
today	jīn tiān	今天
yesterday	zuó tiān	昨天
tomorrow	míng tiān	明天
the day before yesterday	qián tiān	前天
the day after tomorrow	hòu tiān	后天
this week	zhè zhōu / zhè xīng qī	这周 / 这星期
last week	shàng zhōu / shàng xīng qī	上周 / 上星期
next week	xià zhōu / xià xīng qī	下周 / 下星期
this morning	jīn tiān zǎo shàng	今天早上
this afternoon	jīn tiān xià wǔ	今天下午
this evening	jīn tiān wǎn shàng	今天晚上
tonight	jīn tiān wǎn shàng	今天晚上
last night	zuó tiān wǎn shàng	昨天晚上
one month	yí gè yuè	一个月
six months	liù gè yuè	六个月
late	wǎn	晚
early	zǎo	早
soon	bù jǔ / mǎ shàng	不久 / 马上
later on	yǐ hòu	以后
now	xiàn zài	现在
second	miǎo	秒
minute	fēn zhōng	分钟
one minute	yì fēn zhōng	一分钟
five minutes	wǔ fēn zhōng	五分钟
quarter of an hour	yí kè zhōng	一刻钟
half an hour	bàn xiǎo shí	半小时
that day	nà tiān	那天
every day	měi tiān	每天
all day	zhěng tiān	整天

USEFUL WORDS AND PHRASES

ENGLISH	PINYIN	CHINESE
Hello.	ní hǎo	你好
good morning	zǎo shàng hǎo	早上好
good afternoon	xià wǔ hǎo	下午好
good evening	wǎn shàng hǎo	晚上好
How are you?	ní hǎo ma?	你好吗?
fine	bú cuò	不错
And you?	nǐ ne?	你呢?
so-so	yì bān	一般
thank you	xiè xie	谢谢
thank you very much	duō xiè	多谢
You're welcome.	bú kè qì	不客气
It's nothing.	méi shén me	没什么

ENGLISH	PINYIN	CHINESE
yes (correct)	duì	对
no (incorrect)	cuò	错
is	shì	是
isn't	bú shì	不是
I don't know.	wǒ bù zhī dào	我不知道
please	qǐng	请
nice to meet you	hěn gāo xìng rèn shì nǐ	很高兴认识你
I'm sorry.	bù hǎo yì sī	不好意思
good-bye/see you later	zài jiàn	再见
more	gèng duō	更多
less	gèng shǎo	更少
a little	yì diǎn	一点
a lot	hěn duō	很多
big	dà	大
small	xiǎo	小
good	hǎo	好
better	gèng hǎo	更好
best	zuì hǎo	最好
bad	huài	坏
quick, fast	kuai	快
slow	màn	慢
easy	róng yì	容易
difficult	nán	难
he	tā	他
she	tā	她
it	tā	它
I don't speak Chinese well.	wǒ de zhōng wén bú tài hǎo	我的中文不太好
I don't understand.	wǒ bù míng bai	我不明白

SHOPPING

ENGLISH	PINYIN	CHINESE
I need...	wǒ yào	我要
I want...	wǒ yào	我要
How much? (quantity)	duō shǎo?	多少?
How much? (money)	duō shǎo qián?	多少钱?
May I see...	wǒ néng kàn kàn...	我能看看...
this one	zhè gè	这个
that one	nà gè	那个
expensive	guì	贵
cheap	pián yi	便宜
too much (quantity)	tài duō	太多
too much (money)	tài guì	太贵
can you go cheaper?	pián yi diǎn	便宜点

GETTING AROUND

ENGLISH	PINYIN	CHINESE
north	běi	北
south	něn	南
east	dōng	东
west	xī	西
central	zhōng	中
taxi	chū zū chē	出租车
go straight/keep going	zhí zǒu	直走
the right side	yòu biān	右边
turn right	yòu zhuǎn	右转
the left side	zuǒ biān	左边
turn left	zuǒ zhuǎn	左转
Stop!/Stop here!	tíng	停
the next street	xià tiáo jiē	下条街
Please slow down a little.	màn yì diǎn	慢一点
Hurry up a little.	kuài yì diǎn	快一点
here	zhè lǐ	这里
there	nà lǐ	那里
OK, good	xíng, hǎo	行, 好
How much do I owe you?	duō shǎo qián ?	多少钱?

HEALTH

ENGLISH	PINYIN	CHINESE
Help me please.	qǐng bāng bāng wǒ	请帮帮我
I am sick.	wǒ shēng bìng le	我生病了
pain	téng	疼
itch	yǎng	痒
lump	zhǒng zhàng / zhǒng kuài	肿胀 / 肿块
sore	suān tòng	酸痛
rash	zhěn	疹
fever	fā shāo	发烧
mucous	nián yè	粘液
discharge	pái chū	排出
pus	nóng	脓
blood	xiě	血
stomach ache	dù zi tong	肚子痛
vomiting	ǒu tù	呕吐
diarrhea	fù xiè	腹泻
constipation	biàn mì	便秘
feces/to defecate	dà biàn	大便
urine/to urinate	xiǎo biàn	小便
drugstore	yào diàn	药店
medicine	yào	药
pill, tablet	yào piàn	药片
diarrhea medicine	zhǐ xiè yào	止泻药
antacid	jiě suān yào	解酸药
cold medicine	gǎn mào yào	感冒药

ENGLISH	PINYIN	CHINESE
anti-inflammatory medicine	xiāo yán yào	消炎药
pain reliever	zhǐ tòng yào	止痛药
anti-nausea medicine	zhì ě xīn de yào	治恶心的药
antihistamine	kàng zǔ ān	抗组胺
cortisone	shèn shàng xiàn pí zhǐ sù	肾上腺皮质素
anti-fungal	shā zhēn jūn jì	杀真菌剂
analgesic cream	zhǐ tòng gāo	止痛膏
antibiotic	kàng shēng sù	抗生素
Viagra	wēi ěr gāng (kàng yáng wěi / zhì liáo bó qǐ shī tiáo)	威而刚 （抗阳痿 / 治疗勃起失调）
Prozac	bǎi yōu jiě (zhì liáo yōu yù de yào jì)	百忧解 （治疗忧郁的药剂）
birth control pills	bì yùn yào	避孕药
condom	bì yùn tào	避孕套
period	yuè jīng	月经
pad	wèi shēng jīn	卫生巾
tampon	wèi shēng mián tiáo	卫生棉条
gynecologist	fù kē zhuān jiā	妇科专家

Chinese Measurements

SHOES AND CLOTHING

Women's Clothing

U.S.:	3/4	5/6	7/8	9/10	11/12	13/14
China:	34	36	38	40	42	44

Women's Shoes

U.S.:	5	6	7	8	9	10
China:	36	37	38	39	40	41

Men's Suits/Coats

U.S.:	34	36	38	40	42	44	46	48
China:	44	46	48	50	52	54	56	58

Men's Shirts

U.S.:	14½	15	15½	16	16½	17	17½	18
China:	37	38	39	41	42	43	44	45

Men's Shoes

U.S.:	7	8	9	10	11	12	13
China:	41	42	43	44	46	47	48

Children's Clothing

U.S.:	3	4	5	6	6x
China:	98	104	110	116	122

Children's Shoes

U.S.:	8	9	10	11	12	13	1	2	3
China:	24	25	27	28	29	30	32	33	34

OTHER CHINESE MEASURES

Long distances are measured in *li;* 1 *li* equals 0.311 miles.

Acreage is measured in *mu;* 1 *mu* equals 0.1647 acres.

Small weights, such as for buying produce or dry goods, are measured in *jin;* 1 *jin* equals 1.102 pounds; *ban jin* (half a *jin*) equals 0.551 pounds.

Numbers over 1,000 are measured in *wan,* which means 10,000. For example, 40 *wan* equals 400,000.

Discounts *(da zhe)* are expressed in the percentage you pay, not the percentage the item is reduced. For example, a sale for 30 percent off will have signs displaying "70."

Suggested Reading

GENERAL

Chan, John. *China Streetsmart: What You Must Know to be Effective and Profitable in China.* Jurong: Prentice Hall, 2003. Practical advice for international business.

The China Business Handbook, 8th edition. London: Alain Charles Publishing, Ltd., 2006. Updated annually, this book will keep you up-to-date on the business trends and new regulations for foreign firms and includes a business outlook for each province.

Collis, Maurice. *Foreign Mud.* New Directions Publishing Corporation, 2002. A history of the opium trade.

Ebrey, Patricia Buckley. *Illustrated History of China.* London: Cambridge University Press, 1996. An extremely thorough and well-researched history that includes many insights not included in other similar books, such as the topic of the status of women throughout China's history.

Fishman, Ted. *China, Inc.: How the Rise of the Next Superpower Challenges America and the World* New York: Scribner Book Company, 2005. How China has risen to economic prominence over the past 30 years and what it means for America's future.

Menges, Constantine C. *China: The Gathering Threat.* Nelson Current, 2005. Nashville, TN. A worrisome look at how China's growth might negatively impact the West.

Needham, Joseph, and Robert K.G. Temple. *The Genius of China.* London: Prion, 1998. This book shows how the Chinese were often well ahead of the West on many important scientific and societal advances.

Schneiter, Fred, and Larry Feign. *Getting Along with the Chinese.* Hong Kong: Asia 2000, 2000. One of the best guides to understanding Chinese values, thinking, and customs.

Shenkar, Oded. *The Chinese Century.* Upper Saddle River: Wharton School Publishing, 2005. The 21st century belongs to China, so we're told.

Shenkar, Oded. *The Chinese Century: The Rising Chinese Economy and Its Impact on the Global Economy, the Balance of Power, and Your Job.* Upper Saddle River: Wharton School Publishing, 2004. A scholarly perspective on the China's future prospects and how it relates to western economies.

Snow, Edgar. *Red Star over China.* New York: Grove Press, 1968. A first-hand biography of Mao by a western journalist who traveled through China before the revolution.

Starr, John Bryan. *Understanding China: A Guide to China's Economy, History, and Political Culture.* New York: Hill and Wang, 1997. A broad overview and background introduction to China.

Wilkinson, Kenneth. *Chinese Language, Life & Culture.* London: Teach Yourself Books, 2002. If you only bought one general book about China, this would be a good one to start with.

FICTION

Buck, Pearl S. *The Good Earth.* New York: Pocket, 1994. A well-loved classic about a Chinese farmer and his family.

Tan, Amy. *The Joy Luck Club.* New York: Ivy Books, 1990. The tale of four Chinese mothers and their Americanized daughters.

Terada, Katsuya. *The Monkey King.* Milwaukie, OR: Dark Horse, 2005. An eccentric Hong Kong family in the 1950s.

Theroux, Paul. *Kowloon Tong.* New York: Mariner Books, 1998. A story of greed set during the handover of Hong Kong.

MEMOIR

Chang, Jung. *Wild Swans: Three Daughters of China.* New York: Touchstone, 2003. The moving memoirs of three generations of women interwoven with history of the rise of communism.

Chen, Da. *Colors of the Mountain.* New York: Anchor, 2001. The struggles of growing up in rural Fujian province as a member of the despised landlord class.

Chen, Da. *Sounds of the River.* New York: Harper Perennial, 2003. Moving from the Chinese countryside to attend college in big city Beijing.

Clissold, Tim. *Mr. China, A Memoir.* New York: Collins, 2005. The tales of a British businessman as he struggled to meet the challenges of investing in China.

DeWoskin, Rachel. *Foreign Babes in Beijing: Behind the Scenes of a New China.* New York: W. W. Norton & Company, 2005. The true account of an American woman in Beijing who finds unexpected fame as the star of a steamy soap opera.

Faison, Seth. *South of the Clouds: Exploring the Hidden Realms of China.* New York: St. Martin's Press, 2004. An intimate look at China based on 15 years as a student and a journalist in the Middle Kingdom.

Hessler, Peter. *River Town: Two Years on the Yangtze.* New York: Harper Perennial, 2002. The tales of a Peace Corps volunteer.

LANGUAGE

Ho, Yong. *Chinese-English Frequency Dictionary,* New York: Hippocrene Books, 2003. The 500 most common Chinese words.

Peng, Tan Huay, and Huoping Chen. *Fun with Chinese Characters (Vols. 1–4.)* Singapore: Federal Publications, 1988. An amusing way to see the pictographs embedded in Chinese characters and radicals.

Snow, Don. *Survival Chinese.* Shanghai: Commercial Press of China, 2002. Perfect for expats, this very practical little book on basic Chinese includes practical assignments for work with a tutor and for interacting in the local community.

CHILDREN'S BOOKS

Buck, Pearl S. *The Man Who Changed China: The Story of Sun Yat-Sen.* New York: Random House, 1953. For grades 7–9.

Haskins, James, and Dennis Hockerman. *Count Your Way Through China.* Minneapolis: Carolrhoda Books, 1988. An introduction to China through Chinese characters for numbers 1–10. Best for those under 6, though the reading level is higher.

Lee, Huy Voun. *At the Beach.* New York: Henry Holt, 1994. A story about learning Chinese characters by writing in the sand. Ages 4–10.

McMahon, Patricia. *Six Words, Many Turtles, and Three Days in Hong Kong.* Boston: Houghton Mifflin, 1997. A true account of the daily life of an eight-year-old girl who lives in Hong Kong. For elementary grades.

So, Sungwan. *C Is for China.* Parsippany: Silver Press, 1997. An alphabetical photo book about China's people and history for 4–8-year-olds.

TRAVEL GUIDES

Eyewitness Travel Guides China. London: DK Publishing, 2005.

Fallon, Steve. *Lonely Planet Hong Kong & Macau: City Guide.* Victoria: Lonely Planet Publications, 2006.

Harper, Damian, et.al. *Lonely Planet China.* Victoria: Lonely Planet Publications, 2005. Although this LP guide often gets complaints for missing or inaccurate information, it's still the most comprehensive China travel guide and a favorite among budget travelers.

Harper, Damian. *Lonely Planet Beijing.* Victoria: Lonely Planet Publications, 2005.

Harper, Damian. *National Geographic Traveler China.* Washington, DC: National Geographic, 2004. A beautifully illustrated guide with an emphasis on historical and cultural sites.

Knowles, Christopher. *Fodor's Exploring China.* New York: Fodor's Travel Publications, 2001.

Lewis, Simon, David Leffman, and Rough Guides. *The Rough Guide to China.* London: Rough Guides, 2003.

Lewis, Simon. *The Rough Guide to Beijing.* Short Gardens: Rough Guides, 2000.

Mayhew, Bradley. *Lonely Planet Shanghai.* Victoria: Lonely Planet Publications, 2004.

Morgen, Emmanuelle, and Deborah Kaufman. *Fodor's Beijing and Shanghai.* New York: Fodor's Travel Publications, 2005.

Neville-Hadley, Peter, J. D. Brown, Josh Chin, Sharon Owyang, Beth Reiber, Michelle Sans, and Graeme Smith. *Frommer's China.* Hoboken: Wiley Publishing, 2003.

Pillsbury, Adam. *The Insider's Guide to Beijing 2005–2006.* Beijing: True Run Media, 2005.

Rutherford, Scott. *Insight Guide China.* Maspeth: Langenscheidt Publishers, 2002.

Suggested Films

Beijing Bicycle. Directed by Xiaoshuai Wang. 113 min. Sony Pictures, 2002. A coming of age story of Beijing boys as they proudly express themselves through bicycle tricks.

Big Bird in China. Directed by Jon Stone. 75 min. Sony Wonder, 2004. Big Bird makes new friends and learns about China on a short trip to the Middle Kingdom.

Crouching Tiger, Hidden Dragon. Directed by Ang Lee. 120 min. Sony Pictures, 2001. The quest to retrieve a mythic sword, complete with all the glorious special effects of Chinese martial arts films.

Eat Drink Man Woman. Directed by Ang Lee. 124 min. MGM, 2002. Set in Taiwan, this movie uses amazing cooking imagery as a metaphor for the way traditional family values are giving way to modern life.

The Joy Luck Club. Directed by Wayne Wang. 139 min. Buena Vista Home Entertainment, 2002. An excellent adaptation of Amy Tan's 1990 novel by the same name.

The King of Masks. Directed by Wu Tian Ming. 101 min. Sony Pictures, 1999. A heartwarming tale of a stubborn old Sichuan street performer who desperately wants a male heir.

The Last Emperor. Directed by Bernardo Bertolucci. 218 min. Live/Artisan, 1999. A beautifully artistic film about the story of Pu Yi, the last emperor of China.

Mulan. Directed by Tony Bancroft. 88 min. Walt Disney Video, 1999. This animated Disney film tells the Chinese folk tale of a young woman who disguises herself as a man in order to join the army.

Not One Less. Directed by Yimou Zhang. 106 min. Sony Pictures, 2000. A touching story about a tiny school in the countryside.

Shanghai Knights. Directed by David Dobkin. 114 min. Walt Disney Video, 2003. In the sequel to Shanghai Noon, Chan and Wilson are at it again in this madcap comedy set in London.

Shanghai Noon. Directed by Tom Dey. 110 min. Walt Disney Video, 2000. A hilarious western starring Jacky Chan as a Chinese palace guard who travels to the United States and partners with a cowboy played by Owen Wilson.

Shaolin Soccer. Directed by Stephen Chow. 112 min. Miramax, 2004. What could be funnier than mixing soccer with kung fu?

To Live. Directed by Yimou Zhang. 132 min. MGM, 2003. Touching fictional history of one couple's life set during the years of the Cultural Revolution.

Index

Acknowledgments

We would like to thank our long-time friend and patient teacher, Gary Zhou (周泽军), for research assistance and for writing a section of the communications chapter. Many thanks to Leah Ling (凌佳薇), who provided timely and accurate research assistance. Kudos to James Bezjian for his research and writing on the sensitive subject of censorship. To Ilene Bezjian and Azusa Pacific University, we are grateful for the financial support and for providing a work environment that fosters creativity. We are especially indebted to Alex Chen (陈曦), who spent countless hours of hard work gathering and verifying information for the content of this book, including translating the entire phrasebook. For their unmatched hospitality, we are indebted to Jan and Todd Ludtke. We'd also like to thank the expatriate community in China whose stories and experiences have vastly improved our understanding of what it means to live as a foreigner in the Middle Kingdom.

www.moon.com

For helpful advice on planning a trip, visit www.moon.com for the **TRAVEL PLANNER** and get access to useful travel strategies and valuable information about great places to visit. When you travel with Moon, expect an experience that is uncommon and truly unique.

HANDBOOKS • OUTDOORS • METRO • LIVING ABRO

MAP SYMBOLS

≡≡≡ Expressway	○ City/Town	✗ Airfield	≜ Archaeological Site
≡≡ Primary Road	◉ State Capital	✈ Airport	⚲ Church
― Secondary Road			⛽ Gas Station
⋯ Unpaved Road	◉ National Capital	▲ Mountain	Mangrove
⋯ Ferry	★ Point of Interest	♠♠ Park	Reef
⋯ Railroad	▪ Other Location	⛷ Skiing Area	Swamp

CONVERSION TABLES

°C = (°F - 32) / 1.8
°F = (°C x 1.8) + 32
1 inch = 2.54 centimeters (cm)
1 foot = 0.304 meters (m)
1 yard = 0.914 meters
1 mile = 1.6093 kilometers (km)
1 km = 0.6214 miles
1 fathom = 1.8288 m
1 chain = 20.1168 m
1 furlong = 201.168 m
1 acre = 0.4047 hectares
1 sq km = 100 hectares
1 sq mile = 2.59 square km
1 ounce = 28.35 grams
1 pound = 0.4536 kilograms
1 short ton = 0.90718 metric ton
1 short ton = 2,000 pounds
1 long ton = 1.016 metric tons
1 long ton = 2,240 pounds
1 metric ton = 1,000 kilograms
1 quart = 0.94635 liters
1 US gallon = 3.7854 liters
1 Imperial gallon = 4.5459 liters
1 nautical mile = 1.852 km

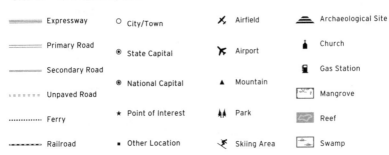

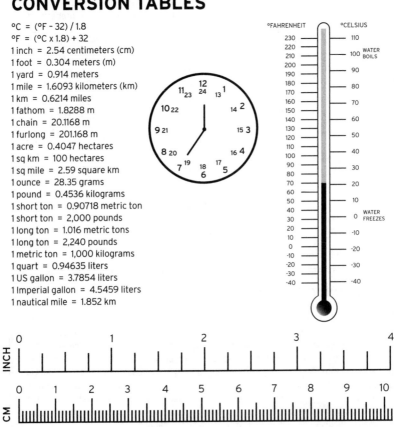

MOON
LIVING ABROAD
IN CHINA

Avalon Travel Publishing
An Imprint of Avalon Publishing
Group, Inc.

AVALON
publishing group incorporated

1400 65th Street, Suite 250
Emeryville, CA 94608, USA
www.moon.com

Editor: Grace Fujimoto
Series Manager: Erin Raber
Acquisitions Manager: Rebecca K. Browning
Copy Editor: Amy Scott
Graphics Coordinator: Domini Dragoone
Production Coordinators: Elizabeth Jang,
    Nicole Schultz
Cover & Interior Designer: Gerilyn Attebery
Map Editor: Kevin Anglin
Cartographer: Kat Bennett
Cartography Director: Mike Morgenfeld
Proofreader: Marisa Solís
Indexer: Greg Jewett

ISBN-10: 1-56691-994-0
ISBN-13: 978-1-56691-994-4
ISSN: 1932-5215

Printing History
1st Edition – September 2006
5 4 3 2 1

Text © 2006 by Stuart & Barbara Strother.
Maps © 2006 by Avalon Travel Publishing, Inc.
All rights reserved.

Some photos and illustrations are used
by permission and are the property of the
original copyright owners.

Front cover photo: Cyclists passing Tian'anmen
Gate in Tian'anmen Square, Beijing, China;
© David Noton

Title page photo: Dragon dancers;
© Barbara Strother

Back cover photo: © Barbara Strother

Printed in the United States by Malloy

KEEPING CURRENT

Although we strive to produce the most up-to-date guidebook that we possibly can, change
is unavoidable. Between the time this book goes to print and the time you read it, the
cost of goods and services may have increased, and a handful of the businesses noted
in these pages will undoubtedly move, alter their prices, or close their doors forever.
Exchange rates fluctuate – sometimes dramatically – on a daily basis. Federal and local
legal requirements and restrictions are also subject to change, so be sure to check with
the appropriate authorities before making the move. If you see anything in this book that
needs updating, clarification, or correction, please drop us a line. Send your comments via
email to feedback@moon.com, or write to the address above.